W9-CHU-013

Price Theory and Applications

Fourth Edition

Steven E. Landsburg

University of Rochester

Prepared by

William V. Weber

Eastern Illinois University

South-Western College Publishing
an International Thomson Publishing company I(T)P®

Cincinnati • Albany • Boston • Detroit • Johannesburg • London • Madrid • Melbourne • Mexico City
New York • Pacific Grove • San Francisco • Scottsdale • Singapore • Tokyo • Toronto

Publisher/Team Director: Jack W. Calhoun
Acquisitions Editor: Keri Witman
Development Editor: Susanna C. Smart
Production Editor: Peggy K. Buskey
Marketing Manager: Lisa L. Lysne

ISBN: 0-538-88680-3

3 4 5 6 7 8 GP 4 3 2 1 0 9

Printed in the United States of America

I(T)P®
International Thomson Publishing
South-Western College Publishing Company is an ITP Company.
The ITP trademark is used under license.

CONTENTS

USING THE *STUDY GUIDE*

This *Study Guide* has been prepared to accompany Steven E. Landsburg's *Price Theory and Applications*, fourth edition. When properly used in conjunction with the textbook, the *Study Guide* can be a valuable supplement in your learning of microeconomic theory. More than 800 exercises, questions, and problems with complete solutions are provided to help you in your efforts.

FEATURES

Each chapter of the *Study Guide* contains seven sections to help you with the material covered in the textbook: a list of key terms, a list of key ideas, a set of completion exercises, a graphical analysis section (when appropriate), a selection of multiple choice questions, supplemental review questions, and a set of problems for analysis. The following are some suggestions on how to successfully use each of these features of the *Study Guide*.

Key Terms. A list of the chapter's key terms, including all terms mentioned in the textbook's marginal glossary, is provided at the beginning of each chapter. Use this list to check your ability to define and explain these terms.

Key Ideas. A list of the main ideas in each section is also provided at the beginning of each chapter. Use this list when you need a quick, condensed review of the basic topics covered in the textbook.

Completion Exercises. A set of 10 fill-in-the-blank exercises is provided to check your ability to recognize and use the chapter's key terms. When you work through these exercises, choose the key term that best completes each sentence.

True-False Exercises. A set of 10 true-false exercises allows you to check your understanding of basic definitions, results, and implications of the material. When you work through these exercises, first determine if you think the statement is true or false. If you believe the statement is false, correct the statement in such a way as to make it true.

Multiple Choice Questions. A selection of 15 multiple choice questions has been included with each chapter. Even if your instructor does not choose to use multiple choice questions on exams, these questions can be worthwhile. The multiple choice questions give you a quick and easy quiz over the key definitions, results, and graphs of the chapter. By spending a relatively small amount of time on these questions, you can identify any problem areas in advance. Further, the solutions include a short explanation in addition to the letter of the correct answer, which can help you see how to approach the question when you are unsure of the answer.

Review Questions. A set of 6 review questions with complete solutions are provided with each chapter. These questions are designed to help you prepare for essay questions on an exam. Do not simply read through a review question and answer it in your head; that approach will not help you learn to write using the economist's language. Instead, you should attempt to write out in the space provided a complete paragraph responding to the review question. Check your answer against the solution to see if you've given enough detail or missed any major points.

You'll find that putting your ideas into words is easier said than done. Too often, students believe that they know the material well, only to discover on the exam that they can't put what they know down on paper. The writing skills that you need for an essay exam, like any other skills, are only developed with practice. Write out the answers to the review questions to get the practice you need.

Problems. Each chapter concludes with 4 problems that require a more advanced level of economic analysis than do the completion exercises, multiple choice questions, and review questions. Sometimes these problems will ask you to combine the material you've learned to discover new facts, other times you will be asked to do numerical exercises which use the mathematics underlying the material you've learned, and yet other times you will have to apply the material you've learned to new situations. You will not be able to simply look up the answers in the textbook; these problems will require you to think on your own as an economist.

Other Features. Two classic economic articles are reprinted in Appendices A and B of the *Study Guide*. The first is "The Use of Knowledge in Society" by F. A. Hayek, which was written in 1945. Many of Hayek's ideas are discussed in Chapter 9 of the textbook, and this article will help you understand the role of prices in communicating and synthesizing society's knowledge. The second article is "The Problem of Social Cost" by Ronald Coase, which was published in 1960. In this article, Coase shows why the Pigovian analysis of externalities is flawed and presents the theorem which now bears his name. It is highly recommended that you read this article when you study external costs and benefits in Chapter 13.

In Appendix C at the end of the *Study Guide* is FastGraph, in which selected graphs from the textbook are reprinted. FastGraph is designed to help you take notes during your instructor's lectures. Before class, remove the pages for the chapter being covered from FastGraph. During class, when your instructor refers to a specific graph from the text, you may use the appropriate page from FastGraph to follow your instructor's comments and make notes about the graph. The pages from FastGraph also contain grid lines to help you draw other graphs from your instructor's lecture.

DRAWING EFFECTIVE GRAPHS

As you already know, graphical analysis is a major part of economics. Whether you're taking lecture notes involving graphs, designing a new graph for a problem in the *Study Guide*, or drawing a graph on an exam, there are four basic rules you can follow that will make your graphs more effective.

Draw large graphs. The U.S. Postal Service has never introduced a set of stamps honoring economic graphs, and you should not be trying to design one. If you draw your graphs too small, they will be difficult to label, difficult to correct when you make an error, and impossible to read later when you're studying for an exam (or even worse, impossible for your instructor to read when your exam is being graded). Save yourself these headaches by starting with a sufficiently large set of axes—a big graph never hurts.

Use pencil when drawing graphs. You can't always draw a graph right the first time. It can be difficult to draw a curve precisely through the point you desire or to get a tangent point precisely where you want it. After you've completed a graph, you may find that it doesn't really show what you wanted it to. Be prepared to erase.

Use several colors and use them consistently. We use graphs in economics to show cause and effect, and action and reaction. These relationships are not easy to see when you are staring at a fully-completed graph. Colors can be an effective way of clarifying the causal relationships we are trying to illustrate.

In addition to a regular pencil, have two or three colored pencils ready when you take lecture notes, take an exam, or work problems. By using your colors consistently, you can keep track of the order in which things happen in the graph.

For example, suppose you have a blue pencil and a red pencil in addition to your regular pencil. Always use your regular pencil to draw the axes and the initial situation shown in the graph. Then always use your blue pencil to show the first thing that changes on your graph (e.g., for the first shift in a curve or the first area identified). Your red pencil will be reserved to show the second change in your graph. By using your colors in a consistent manner, you can easily see how the graph was designed to show economic cause and effect.

Use adequate labels on your graphs. Everything on your graph should be labeled. The last thing you want to see when you're studying the night before an exam is a mysterious curve wandering through your graphs. The curves in your graphs represent specific relationships between economic variables, and you need to know precisely what relationships are being shown. Effective use of labels will help you to keep track of what is happening in your graphs. When you use abbreviations in your labels, be sure you know what the abbreviations stand for. Also, don't hesitate to put additional explanatory notes in the margin beside and beneath your graphs.

CHAPTER 1

SUPPLY, DEMAND, AND EQUILIBRIUM

No matter how complicated economic models get, they still rest on the fundamental ideas of supply and demand. This chapter reviews the basic principles of supply and demand and shows how these ideas can be applied to analyze the effects of taxation.

KEY TERMS

- Law of demand
- Quantity demanded
- Demand
- Demand curve
- Fall in demand
- Rise in demand

- Sales tax
- Econometrics
- Law of supply
- Quantity supplied
- Supply
- Rise in supply

- Fall in supply
- Excise tax
- Equilibrium point
- Satisfied
- Economic incidence
- Legal incidence

KEY IDEAS

- **Section 1.1.** Demand is not a number but a relationship. Demand shows the relationship between price and quantity demanded, assuming other important factors (like consumer tastes, consumer income, and prices of other commodities) are held constant.

- **Section 1.2.** Supply, like demand, is also a relationship between two variables. Supply shows the relationship between price and quantity supplied, assuming other important factors (like technology, the costs of resources, and the size of the industry) are held constant.

- **Section 1.3.** When supply and demand interact, competitive forces cause the price and quantity exchanged to head towards a state of rest, known as the equilibrium point. By comparing how a sales tax and an excise tax change the equilibrium point, we discover that the two taxes have the same economic effects. Economists summarize this idea by saying that the economic incidence of a tax is independent of the legal incidence.

COMPLETION EXERCISES

1. Economists reserve the term _____ to refer to the entire price-quantity relationship that describes buyers' desires to purchase a good.

2. When referring to the specific amount that buyers have chosen to purchase at a particular price, economists use the term _____.

3. According to the _____, a rise in price will cause a fall in the quantity demanded as long as all other relevant factors are unchanged.

4. If higher incomes cause buyers to purchase more of a good regardless of the price, then there will be a _____.

5. According to the law of supply, an increase in price will cause sellers to increase their _____.

6. A technological improvement that reduces sellers' production costs would cause a _____.

7. If the price is so high that the quantity supplied is larger than the quantity demanded, then demanders are _____ but suppliers are not.

8. The legal incidence of a _____ falls entirely on demanders.

9. A per-unit tax which suppliers are required to pay when selling a good is called an _____.

10. Changing the legal incidence of a tax has no impact on its _____.

TRUE-FALSE EXERCISES

_____ 11. For a market to be in equilibrium, supply must equal demand.

_____ 12. A rise in the price of potatoes will cause a fall in the demand for potatoes.

_____ 13. A rise in the demand for floppy disks will result in a higher equilibrium price for floppy disks.

_____ 14. A fall in supply is illustrated by a downward shift in the supply curve.

_____ 15. A rise in the supply of birdseed will cause an increase in the equilibrium price of birdseed.

_____ 16. Demanders will not be satisfied when the market price is below its equilibrium level.

_____ 17. When an excise tax is imposed, the economic incidence falls entirely on suppliers.

_____ 18. If the legal incidence of an automobile tax is switched from buyers to sellers, then car buyers will be better off.

_____ 19. When a sales tax of 50¢ per pack is imposed on cigarettes, the demand curve for cigarettes shifts down by exactly 50¢ per pack.

_____ 20. When a sales tax of 50¢ per pack is imposed on cigarettes, the price buyers pay for cigarettes rises by exactly 50¢ per pack.

MULTIPLE CHOICE QUESTIONS

_____ 21. The immediate effect of a fall in the price of CD players is an increase in
A.   the demand for compact discs.
B.   the quantity demanded for compact discs.
C.   the supply of compact discs.
D.   the quantity supplied of compact discs.

_____ 22. The immediate effect of a fall in the price of compact discs is an increase in
A.   the demand for compact discs.
B.   the quantity demanded for compact discs.
C.   the supply of compact discs.
D.   the quantity supplied of compact discs.

◆◆◆ Questions 23–27 refer to the following supply-demand diagrams.

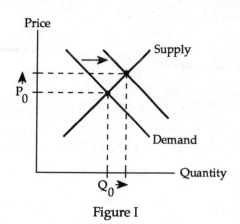

Figure I

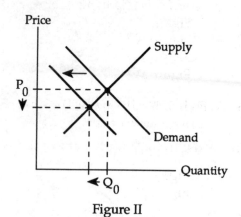

Figure II

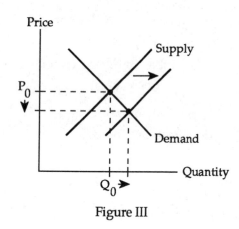

Figure III

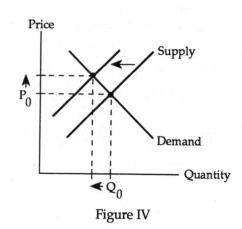

Figure IV

_____ 23. Which of the diagrams shows what happens in the market for oranges when a severe late frost in Florida damages orchards statewide?
  A. Figure I.
  B. Figure II.
  C. Figure III.
  D. Figure IV.

_____ 24. Poorer families tend to use pawn shop services more than do wealthier families. Which of the diagrams shows what happens in the market for pawn shop services when a severe recession causes a substantial reduction in households' incomes?
  A. Figure I.
  B. Figure II.
  C. Figure III.
  D. Figure IV.

_____ 25. Which of the diagrams shows what happens in the market for cotton when the prices of alternative synthetic fabrics rise?
   A.   Figure I.
   B.   Figure II.
   C.   Figure III.
   D.   Figure IV.

_____ 26. Which of the diagrams shows what happens in the market for milk when improvements in cattle feed result in higher milk yields from dairy cows?
   A.   Figure I.
   B.   Figure II.
   C.   Figure III.
   D.   Figure IV.

_____ 27. Airplane travelers take frequent taxi trips to and from airports. Which of the diagrams shows what happens in the market for trips by taxi when travelers are faced with rising airline prices?
   A.   Figure I.
   B.   Figure II.
   C.   Figure III.
   D.   Figure IV.

_____ 28. When people travel because they are faced with emergencies, the price of air travel has little effect on their decision to fly instead of using a slower form of transportation. In this situation,
   A.   the equilibrium price of air travel must be high.
   B.   the demand curve for air travel is upward sloping.
   C.   the demand curve for air travel is relatively flat.
   D.   the demand curve for air travel is relatively steep.

_____ 29. According to the law of supply, a price increase will cause
   A.   an increase in the equilibrium quantity.
   B.   a decrease in the equilibrium quantity.
   C.   an increase in the quantity supplied, provided other factors have remained unchanged.
   D.   a decrease in the quantity supplied, provided other factors have remained unchanged.

_____ 30. Suppose the price of a commodity is $20 per unit. At that price, consumers wish to purchase 4,000 units weekly and producers wish to sell 7,000 units weekly. In this situation,
   A.   unsatisfied consumers will bid up the market price.
   B.   the market price will fall because producers are not satisfied.
   C.   a rise in demand will occur to bring the market to equilibrium.
   D.   a decrease in supply is necessary for the market to reach equilibrium.

_____ 31. If the current market price is below the equilibrium price,
   A.   suppliers are satisfied but demanders are not.
   B.   demanders are satisfied but suppliers are not.
   C.   neither demanders nor suppliers are satisfied.
   D.   both demanders and suppliers are satisfied.

_____ 32. Suppose we observe that the price of cocaine has been falling, even though the
   amount of cocaine traded on the black market has also been falling. We can conclude
   that
   A.   the law of demand does not hold for cocaine.
   B.   a demand curve for cocaine doesn't exist.
   C.   the supply of cocaine must have fallen.
   D.   the demand for cocaine must have fallen.

_____ 33. A rise in the demand for bread occurring simultaneously with a fall in the supply of
   bread *must*
   A.   decrease the quantity of bread traded in the market.
   B.   increase the quantity of bread traded in the market.
   C.   increase the equilibrium price of bread.
   D.   increase the equilibrium price of bread and decrease the equilibrium quantity of
        bread.

_____ 34. Which of the following statements about sales and excise taxes is *false?*
   A.   A sales tax causes a parallel shift downward in the demand curve by precisely
        the amount of the tax.
   B.   An excise tax causes a parallel shift upward in the supply curve by precisely the
        amount of the tax.
   C.   The legal incidence of a sales tax is entirely on demanders, while the legal
        incidence of an excise tax is entirely on suppliers.
   D.   The economic incidence of a tax is evenly split between demanders and
        suppliers, no matter what the legal incidence is.

_____ 35. What do we mean when we say that the economic incidence of a tax is independent
   of its legal incidence?
   A.   The economic incidence and legal incidence of a tax are always the same.
   B.   The economic incidence of a tax will be the same no matter who bears the legal
        incidence of the tax.
   C.   Demanders and suppliers equally share the economic burden of the tax,
        regardless of the legal incidence.
   D.   Since suppliers can "pass on" a tax to demanders, the economic incidence of a
        tax will always be on demanders even when the legal incidence is on suppliers.

REVIEW QUESTIONS

36.   Distinguish between demand and quantity demanded. Distinguish between supply and quantity supplied. Why are these distinctions important?

37.   List some situations which would cause a fall in demand. List some situations which would cause a fall in supply.

38.   If there is a *rise* in supply, the new supply curve lies *below* the old supply curve. Resolve this apparent contradiction.

39. What is the equilibrium point and what is its significance?

40. When quantity supplied is smaller than quantity demanded, we say there is a shortage. When would a shortage situation be likely to occur? Why is it unlikely that such a situation would prevail in a market for very long?

41. Compare and contrast the effects of a sales tax and an excise tax.

PROBLEMS

42. The markets diagrammed below have identical supply curves but different demand
     curves.

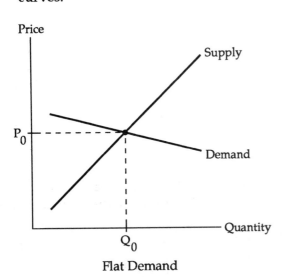

Flat Demand

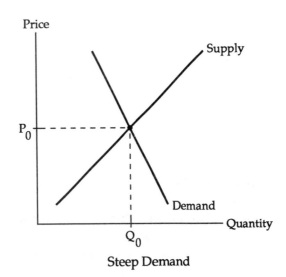

Steep Demand

i.   Suppose that an excise tax of t dollars per unit is placed on both markets. Complete
     the above diagrams to show this situation. The following should be labeled:
     a.   the new equilibrium quantity and price (Q_1, P_1),
     b.   the net price suppliers pay after the tax (P_S), and
     c.   the size of the excise tax (t).

ii. In which case (flat demand or steep demand) will the tax cause the equilibrium price
     to rise very little? In which case will the tax cause the equilibrium price to rise by nearly
     t dollars per unit?

43. i.   Let Q represent the quantity per week of a good and P represent the price measured in dollars per unit. Suppose demand is given by the formula $P = 300 - \frac{1}{3}Q$ and supply is given by the equation $P = 50 + \frac{1}{2}Q$. Find the equilibrium price and quantity.

     ii. Suppose the government imposes a sales tax of $25 per unit on this good. Find the new formula for the demand curve, the new equilibrium price and quantity, and the new post-tax price for the demanders of this good.

     iii. What fraction of the economic burden of the tax is borne by demanders? By suppliers?

44. When the government gives demanders or suppliers financial assistance to purchase or produce a good, we say the government has given a subsidy.

   i. Suppose the government gives demanders a fixed subsidy of s dollars for each unit of the good purchased. Using the diagrams below, show the effects of this subsidy on the left-hand side. The following should be labeled:
      a. the new equilibrium quantity (Q_1),
      b. the post-subsidy price paid by demanders (P_D),
      c. the post-subsidy price received by suppliers (P_S), and
      d. the size of the per-unit subsidy (s).

   ii. In the diagram on the right, repeat part i for the case where the government gives the same subsidy to suppliers for each unit of the good sold.

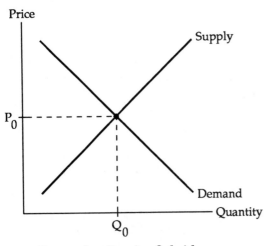

Demanders Receive Subsidy

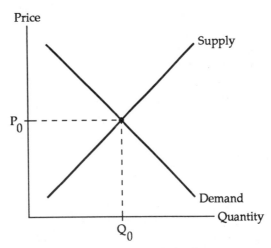

Suppliers Receive Subsidy

   iii. Using these diagrams, what can you conclude about the economic incidence of a per-unit subsidy?

45. Consider a demand curve for sexual activity among teenagers, where the "price" of a sexual encounter is interpreted as the risk of having an unwanted pregnancy.

i.   Suppose Roseanne believes that making safe, effective birth control easily available to teenagers greatly reduces their risk of having an unwanted pregnancy and decreases the total number of unwanted pregnancies. Does Roseanne believe that the demand curve is relatively flat or relatively steep? Explain.

ii. Suppose Ronald believes that making safe, effective birth control easily available to teenagers encourages greater sexual activity among teenagers and increases the total number of unwanted pregnancies. Does Ronald believe that the demand curve is relatively flat or relatively steep? Explain.

SOLUTIONS

Completion Exercises

1. demand
2. quantity demanded
3. law of demand
4. rise in demand
5. quantity supplied

6. rise in supply
7. satisfied
8. sales tax
9. excise tax
10. economic incidence

True-False Exercises

11. FALSE. For a market to be in equilibrium, quantity supplied must equal quantity demanded.
12. FALSE. A rise in the price of potatoes will cause a fall in the quantity demanded of potatoes.
13. TRUE.
14. FALSE. A fall in supply is illustrated by a leftward shift in the supply curve.
15. FALSE. A rise in the supply of birdseed will cause a decrease in the equilibrium price of birdseed.
16. TRUE.
17. FALSE. When an excise tax is imposed, the legal incidence falls entirely on suppliers.
18. FALSE. If the legal incidence of an automobile tax is switched from buyers to sellers, then car buyers will be unaffected.
19. TRUE.
20. FALSE. When a sales tax of 50¢ per pack is imposed on cigarettes, the price buyers pay for cigarettes rises by less than 50¢ per pack.

Multiple Choice Questions

21. A. No matter what the price of compact discs is, the fall in the price of CD players will cause more people to buy CD players, causing people to demand more compact discs.
22. B. According to the laws of demand and supply, a fall in price will increase the quantity demanded and decrease the quantity supplied. There is no change in either the demand or supply schedules.

23.   D. The frost will increase the cost of producing oranges, so suppliers will be able to bring fewer oranges to the market no matter what the current price. The resulting fall in supply will increase price and lower the quantity traded.

24.   A. More families will use pawn shop services during the recession. The resulting rise in demand for pawn shop services will increase both the price and the quantity traded.

25.   A. The higher prices of synthetic fabrics will cause some people to switch from synthetic fabrics to cotton. The resulting rise in demand for cotton will increase both the price and the quantity traded.

26.   C. The lower costs of producing milk will cause suppliers to provide more milk to the market no matter what the going market price is. The resulting rise in supply will lower the price and increase the quantity traded.

27.   B. Higher airline prices will lower the amount of traveling by air according to the law of demand. Regardless of the current taxi rates, travelers will require fewer trips by taxi. The resulting fall in demand will lower both the price and the quantity traded.

28.   D. In this situation, a price rise won't drive away many customers, so the demand curve must be relatively steep. (Notice we can't say anything about the price of air travel unless we know something about its supply.)

29.   C. This is simply the definition of the law of supply.

30.   B. Suppliers are unable to sell everything they wish, so they are unsatisfied and will drive down the price in order to lure buyers back to the market.

31.   A. Demanders cannot buy all that they wish at the going market price, so they are not satisfied.

32.   D. Only a fall in demand can cause both the price and the quantity traded to fall.

33.   C. The fall in supply drives down the quantity traded and drives up the price. The rise in demand drives up both the quantity traded and the price. Combining these two, we can be sure that the price will rise, but the overall effect on quantity is uncertain.

34.   D. The economic incidence, although independent of the legal incidence, need not be divided evenly between demanders and suppliers.

35.   B. It does not matter who is legally obliged to pay the tax—the final division of the burden of the tax between demanders and suppliers will not be affected by the legal incidence.

Review Questions

36. Demand and supply both refer to entire sets of price-quantity pairs showing how demanders and suppliers adjust their quantities to changes in price, assuming all other relevant factors are held constant. Quantity demanded and quantity supplied refer to the specific amounts that demanders wish to purchase and suppliers wish to sell at some particular price. Quantity demanded and quantity supplied refer to particular horizontal coordinates on the demand and supply curves. These terms allow us to distinguish between the determinants of price (demand and supply) and the effects of price (changes in quantity demanded and quantity supplied).

37. Changes in demanders' tastes or incomes could decrease demand. A decrease in the price of a substitute good (one used in place of the good in question) or an increase in the price of a complement good (one used in conjunction with the good in question) would also cause a fall in demand. A rise in the costs of resources (or other costs of production) or a decrease in the number of suppliers would decrease supply.

38. The word "rise" in the phrases "rise in supply" and "rise in demand" refers to the quantity direction in the supply and demand graphs. Because quantity is measured in the horizontal direction, the word "rise" means "rightward." If there is a rise in supply, the new supply curve lies to the right (and below) the old supply curve.

39. The equilibrium point is the point where the demand and supply curves intersect. The equilibrium point gives the only price where the amount demanders want to buy equals the amount suppliers want to sell (i.e., where quantity demanded equals quantity supplied). Since this is also the only price where both demanders and suppliers are satisfied, competitive behavior will drive the price to the equilibrium price.

40. When the going market price is below the equilibrium price, the quantity supplied will be smaller than the quantity demanded. In this situation, suppliers are satisfied but demanders are not. This situation will not last, because competition among demanders will cause the price to be bid up.

41. The legal incidence of a sales tax is entirely on demanders, so the sales tax will cause a parallel shift in demand downward by the amount of the tax. In contrast, the legal incidence of an excise tax is entirely on suppliers, so the excise tax causes a parallel shift in the supply curve downward by the amount of the tax. The sales and excise taxes are similar in that they have the same economic incidence. The quantity exchanged, the net

price paid by the demanders, and the net price received by suppliers will all be the same under sales and excise taxes of equal sizes.

Problems

42.   i.

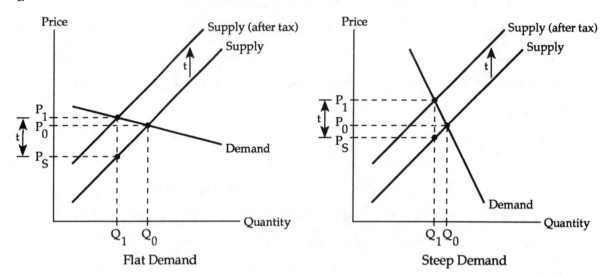

Flat Demand   Steep Demand

ii.   When demand is very flat, the equilibrium price will rise very little. In this case, the burden of the tax falls heaviest on suppliers. On the other hand, the price will rise by almost the full amount of the tax when demand is very steep, causing the burden of the excise tax to fall heaviest on demanders.

43.   i.   First equate supply and demand to find the equilibrium quantity:

$$50 + \tfrac{1}{2}Q = 300 - \tfrac{1}{3}Q \quad \Rightarrow \quad \tfrac{5}{6}Q = 250$$

$$\Rightarrow \quad Q = \tfrac{6}{5} \cdot 250 = 300 \text{ units weekly.}$$

Next substitute this into either supply or demand to get price:

$$P = 50 + \tfrac{1}{2}Q = 50 + \tfrac{1}{2} \cdot 300 = 50 + 150 = \$200 \text{ per unit}$$

or $$P = 300 - \tfrac{1}{3}Q = 300 - \tfrac{1}{3} \cdot 300 = 300 - 100 = \$200 \text{ per unit.}$$

ii.   Because the new price demanders are willing to pay must equal the old price demanders were willing to pay minus the tax of \$25 per unit, we have $P = 300 - \tfrac{1}{3}Q - 25$, which simplifies to $P = 275 - \tfrac{1}{3}Q$. Equating supply and demand now yields:

$$50 + \tfrac{1}{2}Q = 275 - \tfrac{1}{3}Q \quad \Rightarrow \quad \tfrac{5}{6}Q = 225$$

$$\Rightarrow \quad Q = \tfrac{6}{5} \cdot 225 = 270 \text{ units weekly.}$$

Again substitute this figure into either supply or demand to get price:

$$P = 50 + \tfrac{1}{2}Q = 50 + \tfrac{1}{2} \cdot 270 = 50 + 135 = \$185 \text{ per unit}$$

or $P = 275 - \frac{1}{3}Q = 275 - \frac{1}{3} \cdot 270 = 275 - 90 = \$185$ per unit.

Since the legal incidence is on demanders, the post-tax price they pay is $185 per unit + $25 per unit or $210 per unit.

iii. Demanders originally paid $200 per unit and after the tax pay $210 per unit. Demanders pay $10 per unit of the $25 per unit tax, so their share is 40% of the burden of the tax. Suppliers originally received $200 per unit and after the tax receive $185 per unit. Since the $25 per unit tax caused their price to fall by $15 per unit, the suppliers' share is 60% of the burden of the tax.

44.   i, ii.

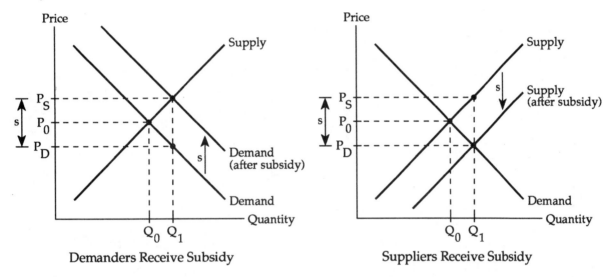

Demanders Receive Subsidy   Suppliers Receive Subsidy

iii. Just like a per-unit tax, the economic incidence of a per-unit subsidy is independent of the legal incidence.

45.   i.   Roseanne must feel that the demand curve for sexual activity is relatively steep. According to the law of demand, when you make birth control more available to teenagers and reduce their risk of an unwanted pregnancy, the quantity of sexual activity will increase. If the demand curve is steep, there won't be a substantial increase in teenagers' sexual activity. On the other hand, there will be a substantial decline in teenagers' risk of an unwanted pregnancy. The latter effect will be the dominant one, so the increased availability of birth control will reduce the total number of unwanted pregnancies.

ii.   Ronald must feel that the demand curve for sexual activity is relatively flat. If the demand curve is flat, the reduction in risk created by accessible birth control will cause a relatively large increase in the amount of sexual activity among teenagers.

Consequently, the number of unwanted pregnancies may actually increase despite the increased availability of birth control.

CHAPTER 2

PRICES, COSTS, AND THE GAINS FROM TRADE

The desire to benefit from trade underlies the supply and demand curves introduced in the previous chapter. This chapter focuses on the reasons people wish to trade. The chapter begins by discussing the meanings of prices and costs in greater detail and then shows how differences in costs create opportunities for people to gain from trade.

KEY TERMS

- Absolute price
- Relative price
- Inflation
- Cost
- Comparative advantage
- More efficient

KEY IDEAS

- **Section 2.1.** Absolute price measures the amount of currency which must be sacrificed to purchase a commodity, while relative price measures the amount of other goods which must be sacrificed to purchase a commodity. The prices studied in microeconomics are relative prices.

- **Section 2.2.** The word "cost" as used by economists means "sacrificed opportunity." If a person can do an activity at a lower cost than anyone else, that person has a comparative advantage in that activity and is more efficient than anyone else in doing that activity. Everyone is made better off when people specialize in their areas of comparative advantage and then trade to get the goods and services they desire.

COMPLETION EXERCISES

1. The amount of money that can be exchanged for a pound of bananas is called the
    _____ of bananas.

2. If you can trade two apples for three oranges, then the _____ of
    apples is 1.5 oranges per apple.

3. In microeconomics, the term "price" always refers to the _____ of
    the commodity.

4. Economists define the word _____ to mean sacrificed alternatives
    or forgone opportunities.

5. You have a _____ in typing if your cost of typing is lower than
    anyone else's cost.

6. An ongoing rise in the average level of the economy's absolute prices is called
    _____.

7. If Mexico has a lower cost of producing clothing than does the United States, then Mexico
    is _____ than the United States at producing clothing.

8. Everyone benefits when each person specializes in his area of _____
    and then engages in trade.

9. The most efficient producer of a good is the one who can produce it at the lowest
    _____.

10. If all of an economy's absolute prices would simultaneously double, its
    _____ would remain unchanged.

TRUE-FALSE EXERCISES

_____ 11. During times of inflation, the relative prices of goods and services must be rising.

_____ 12. When a microeconomist uses a supply-demand diagram, the "price" on the vertical axis should be interpreted as an absolute price.

_____ 13. If the price of wine relative to bread increases, then the price of bread relative to wine must decrease.

_____ 14. A 50% cut in all absolute prices would have no effect on relative prices.

_____ 15. The term "cost," as used by economists, refers to the amount of currency needed to purchase labor, raw materials, and other resources.

_____ 16. Specialization in the area of comparative advantage, followed by trade, makes everyone better off.

_____ 17. The most efficient producer of glass is the one who can produce glass with the fewest resources.

_____ 18. A country has a comparative advantage in wine production if its cost of producing wine is smaller than its cost of producing other goods.

_____ 19. If everyone had the same tastes, then people could not benefit from trade.

_____ 20. If a country does not have the necessary infrastructure to provide telephone services to its citizens, then it would be a waste of resources for the country to manufacture telephones.

MULTIPLE CHOICE QUESTIONS

_____ 21. Suppose the absolute price of bread is 5,000 yen per loaf and the absolute price of wine is 20,000 yen per bottle. The relative price of wine is
   A. 15,000 yen per bottle.
   B. 20,000 yen per bottle.
   C. 4 loaves per bottle.
   D. ¼ loaf per bottle.

_____ 22. Suppose there are only two goods: bread and wine. If the price of wine is 5 loaves of bread per bottle of wine, then the price of bread
   A. is ⅕ bottle per loaf.
   B. is 2½ bottles per loaf.
   C. is 5 bottles per loaf.
   D. cannot be calculated from the information provided.

_____ 23. Suppose there are only two goods: bread and wine. If the price of bread rises, then
   A. the price of wine must also rise.
   B. the price of wine must fall.
   C. the price of wine is not affected.
   D. we cannot make any prediction about changes in the price of wine.

_____ 24. When a microeconomist says the price of a commodity is $5 per unit,
   A. the dollars he is referring to represent a collection of goods in the economy.
   B. he is assuming that the price has been adjusted for inflation.
   C. he is referring to the absolute price of the commodity.
   D. he means that a person must spend $5 in currency to purchase one unit of the good.

_____ 25. If inflation caused the absolute prices of all goods to rise, then the relative price of any particular good
   A. must also have risen.
   B. must have remained unchanged.
   C. must have fallen.
   D. could have risen, fallen, or remained unchanged.

_____ 26. In Florida, an orange sells for 25¢ and a lemon sells for 10¢. In New York, 5¢ must be added to these absolute prices to cover transportation costs. Where is the relative price of oranges lower, and where is the relative price of lemons lower?
   A. The prices of oranges and lemons are lower in Florida, because buyers do not have to pay for transportation costs.
   B. The prices of oranges and lemons are lower in New York, because transportation costs always lower relative prices.
   C. Florida has the lower relative price of lemons, and New York has the lower relative price of oranges.
   D. New York has the lower relative price of lemons, and Florida has the lower relative price of oranges.

_____ 27. Will the average quality of apples sold in supermarkets be higher in Washington or in Kansas?
   A.   In Washington, because it has the comparative advantage in apple growing.
   B.   In Washington, because the costs of transporting apples to market will be lower than in Kansas.
   C.   In Kansas, because it cannot produce enough apples to meet its demand.
   D.   In Kansas, because the price of high-quality apples relative to low-quality apples will be lower than in Washington.

_____ 28. A farmer owns a plot of land which can support either corn or soybeans. Which of the following best describes the farmer's opportunity cost of growing corn on the land?
   A.   The soybeans that could have been grown on the land instead of corn.
   B.   The value of the seed, fertilizer, labor, and other resources needed to grow the corn.
   C.   The deterioration in soil quality caused by growing corn.
   D.   There is no opportunity cost because the farmer owns the land.

_____ 29. According to economists' use of the term "cost," which of the following best describes the cost of producing a commodity?
   A.   The time and raw materials used in the production of the commodity.
   B.   The alternative uses of the time and raw materials used in the production of the commodity.
   C.   The monetary value of the time and raw materials used in the production of the commodity.
   D.   All of the above represent different types of cost used by economists.

_____ 30. When are you considered to be the most efficient at producing food?
   A.   When the quantity of resources you require to produce food is smaller than the quantity you require to produce any other good.
   B.   When your cost of producing food is smaller than your cost of producing any other good.
   C.   When the quantity of resources you require to produce food is smaller than the quantity anyone else requires to produce food.
   D.   When your cost of producing food is smaller than anyone else's cost of producing food.

_____ 31. When would people find it beneficial to trade?
   A.   When they have different abilities.
   B.   When they have different tastes.
   C.   Either different abilities or different tastes would be a sufficient reason to pursue trade.
   D.   Trade is beneficial only when people have both different abilities and different tastes; just one of these reasons is not enough.

◆◆◆ Questions 32–35 refer to the following table which shows the abilities of two countries to produce food and cloth. Food and cloth are the only two commodities in the world and their production requires only labor. The amounts of labor required to produce one unit of each of these commodities in the two countries are shown in the table below.

	Country A	Country B
One Bushel of Food	6 hours	8 hours
One Bolt of Cloth	2 hours	4 hours

_____ 32. The cost of producing food in Country A is
A. 6 hours of labor.
B. 3 bushels of food per bolt of cloth.
C. 3 bolts of cloth per bushel of food.
D. ⅓ bolt of cloth per bushel of food.

_____ 33. The cost of producing cloth in Country B is
A. 2 bushels of food per bolt of cloth.
B. ½ bushel of food per bolt of cloth.
C. 2 bolts of cloth per bushel of food.
D. ½ bolt of cloth per bushel of food.

_____ 34. Which country is more efficient in the production of food, and which country is more efficient in the production of cloth?
A. Country A is the more efficient producer of both food and cloth.
B. Country B is the more efficient producer of both food and cloth.
C. Country A is the more efficient producer of food, and Country B is the more efficient producer of cloth.
D. Country B is the more efficient producer of food, and Country A is the more efficient producer of cloth.

_____ 35. When can trade benefit both Country A and Country B?
A. When Country A specializes in food production, and Country B specializes in cloth production.
B. When Country A specializes in cloth production, and Country B specializes in food production.
C. The countries cannot gain from trade, because Country A has the lower costs of production for both food and cloth.
D. The countries cannot gain from trade, because Country B has a comparative advantage in the production of both goods.

REVIEW QUESTIONS

36. Compare and contrast the absolute price and the relative price of a commodity. Which is studied in microeconomics?

37. Suppose there are only two goods: bread and wine. If the absolute prices of bread and wine both double, how are the relative prices of bread and wine affected?

38. Generally we say that the price of a commodity is measured in "dollars per unit." Explain precisely what microeconomists mean by this phrase.

39.   Travelers to Rome have remarked that they can find better quality Italian leather in New York. Use the concept of relative price to explain this phenomenon.

40.   What is cost? If you can produce a good using fewer resources than anyone else, does this imply that you can produce the good at the lowest cost?

41.   When can gains from trade be created? In other words, when can trade be beneficial to all parties involved?

PROBLEMS

42. Suppose that in Saskatchewan, an acre of land can produce either 45 bushels of wheat or 30 bushels of barley.

    i.   What is the cost of producing wheat in Saskatchewan? What is the cost of producing barley in Saskatchewan?

    ii. A classmate argues that Saskatchewan should specialize in wheat production, because the cost of growing wheat is smaller than the cost of growing barley. Do you agree? Why or why not?

    iii. Suppose Saskatchewan's only trading partner is Alberta. Under what circumstances should Saskatchewan specialize in wheat production and purchase its barley from Alberta? Explain.

43.   Suppose there are three people: an electrician, her teenage son, and their neighbor Mr. Grant. There are two jobs to do: rewiring houses and paneling rooms. The amount of time each person needs to do each of these tasks is summarized in the following table.

	Electrician	Teenage Son	Mr. Grant
Rewiring	8 hours	18 hours	12 hours
Paneling	10 hours	15 hours	12 hours

i.   Calculate the cost for each person to rewire a house.

ii.   If only Mr. Grant and the electrician specialize and trade, who will rewire houses and who will panel rooms?

iii. If only Mr. Grant and the electrician's son specialize and trade, who will rewire houses and who will panel rooms?

iv.   If all three specialize and trade, who will rewire houses and who will panel rooms? (*Hint*—There is not enough information to provide a definite answer for one of the three.)

44. Suppose there are two countries, the U.S. and Mexico. Assume that food and cloth are the only two commodities and that their production requires only labor. The amounts of labor required to produce one unit of each of these commodities in the U.S. and Mexico are shown in the following table.

	U.S.	Mexico
One Bushel of Food	2 hours	7 hours
One Bolt of Cloth	8 hours	14 hours

i. Calculate the costs of producing cloth in each of the two countries. When the U.S. and Mexico specialize and trade, which country should specialize in food production and which country should specialize in cloth production?

US cloth = 4 bushes of food per bolt of cloth

ii. Suppose that Mexico offers to give the U.S. 1 bolt of cloth in exchange for every 5 bushels of food received. (In other words, Mexico is offering to trade at a rate of 5 bushels of food per bolt of cloth.) Show that the U.S. will turn down this offer.

iii. Suppose that the U.S. makes a counteroffer to Mexico, offering 1 bushel of food in exchange for each bolt of cloth received. (So now the U.S. is offering to trade at a rate of 1 bushel per bolt.) Explain why Mexico will turn down this counteroffer.

iv. Find the rates of exchange that would be agreeable to both countries. (*Hint* — You should consider three possibilities: rates of exchange larger than the U.S.'s cost of producing cloth, rates of exchange smaller than Mexico's cost of producing cloth, and rates of exchange between their two costs.)

45.   Let P_W denote the absolute price of wine and P_B denote the absolute price of bread.

    i.   Show that the relative price of wine in terms of bread equals P_W/P_B.

    ii.   Suppose inflation causes the absolute prices to increase. Let x and y denote the percentage increases in the absolute prices of wine and bread, respectively. Use part i to show that the relative price of wine increases if $x > y$, decreases if $x < y$, and is unchanged if $x = y$.

    iii.   What conclusion about the relation between inflation and relative prices can be drawn from part ii?

SOLUTIONS

Completion Exercises

1. absolute price
2. relative price
3. relative price
4. cost
5. comparative advantage

6. inflation
7. more efficient
8. comparative advantage
9. cost
10. relative prices

True-False Exercises

11. FALSE. During times of inflation, the relative prices of goods and services <u>may rise, fall, or remain unchanged</u>.

12. FALSE. When a microeconomist uses a supply-demand diagram, the "price" on the vertical axis should be interpreted as <u>a relative</u> price.

13. TRUE.

14. TRUE.

15. FALSE. The term "cost," as used by economists, refers to <u>forgone opportunities</u>.

16. TRUE.

17. FALSE. The most efficient producer of glass is the one who can produce glass <u>at the lowest cost</u>.

18. FALSE. A country has a comparative advantage in wine production if its cost of producing wine is smaller than <u>any other country's cost of producing wine</u>.

19. FALSE. If everyone had the same tastes, then people <u>with differing abilities could still benefit from trade</u>.

20. FALSE. If a country does not have the necessary infrastructure to provide telephone services to its citizens, then it <u>would still benefit from producing and selling telephones when it has a comparative advantage in that area</u>.

Multiple Choice Questions

21. C. The 20,000 yen used to purchase a bottle of wine could have been used to purchase 4 loaves of bread. The relative price of wine is given by this amount of sacrificed bread.

22. A. Since 5 loaves of bread can be traded for 1 bottle of wine, 1 loaf of bread can be traded for ⅕ bottle of wine and *vice versa*.

23. B. For example, if the price of wine rises from 2 to 4 loaves of bread per bottle of wine, then the price of bread falls from ½ to ¼ bottle of wine per loaf.

24. A. Since "price" means the relative price, we are referring to the amounts of other goods sacrificed even when we use the term "dollars."

25. D. Rising absolute prices are consistent with rising, falling, and constant relative prices.

26. C. The relative price of oranges is 2½ lemons per orange in Florida and is 2 lemons per orange in New York, so oranges are relatively less costly in New York. The relative price of lemons is ⅖ orange per lemon in Florida and is ½ orange per lemon in New York, so lemons are relatively less costly in Florida.

27. D. The absolute price of both high-quality and low-quality apples sold in Kansas includes the cost of transportation. Because of these transportation costs, the price of high-quality apples relative to low-quality apples is lower in Kansas than in Washington. Because of the lower relative price, a Kansan who chooses to buy an apple will be more likely to purchase a high-quality apple than is a Washingtonian.

28. A. The farmer sacrifices the opportunity to grow soybeans when he chooses to grow corn on the land.

29. B. Cost always means "opportunity cost" and refers to forgone opportunities.

30. D. This is the definition of the phrase "most efficient." The costs of production (not absolute quantities of resources) are compared across individuals (not activities).

31. C. Trade can be beneficial when people have different abilities or when people have different tastes or both. Increased productivity from large-scale production can also motivate specialization and trade.

32. C. The 6 hours required to produce one bushel of food could have been used to produce 3 bolts of cloth. So 3 bolts of cloth are sacrificed for every bushel of food produced.

33. B. The 4 hours required to produce one bolt of cloth could have been used to produce ½ bushel of food.

34. D. Country A's cost of producing food is 3 bolts of cloth per bushel of food, and Country B's cost of producing food is 2 bolts per bushel. Since Country B has the lower cost, it is more efficient than Country A in food production. Country A's cost of producing cloth is ⅓ bushel per bolt, and Country B's cost of producing cloth is ½ bushel per bolt. Since Country A has the lower cost, it is more efficient than Country B in cloth production.

35.   B. Each country should specialize in producing the good for which it has a comparative advantage.

Review Questions

36.   Absolute price shows the amount of currency that must be sacrificed for a unit of a commodity, while relative price shows the amount of other goods that must be sacrificed for that unit. Microeconomics studies relative prices because these are the ones that motivate trade among individuals.

37.   Both relative prices are unchanged—the currency spent on a loaf of bread buys the same amount of wine as before the doubling of absolute prices. For instance, if bread cost $1 per loaf and wine cost $2 per bottle, then the relative price of bread is ½ bottle per loaf. If the absolute prices doubled to $2 per loaf and $4 per bottle, then ½ bottle of wine could still be traded for 1 loaf of bread, so the relative price remains unchanged.

38.   In microeconomics, price always refers to relative price—the amount of other goods sacrificed in order to obtain the commodity in question. We frequently use the term "dollar" as a shorthand to represent a basket of other goods being sacrificed to obtain the commodity.

39.   The price of high-quality Italian leather relative to low-quality Italian leather is lower in New York than in Rome because of transportation costs. (For example, suppose in Rome a high-quality leather bag costs $100 and a low-quality leather bag costs $50. The relative price of the high-quality bag in Rome is then 2 low-quality bags. Now suppose it costs $25 to export each of these bags to New York, making the high-quality bag cost $125 and the low-quality bag cost $75. Because of the transportation costs, in New York the relative price of the high-quality bag is only 1⅔ low-quality bags.) Because the price of high-quality Italian leather is lower in New York, relatively more will be bought and sold there than in Rome.

40.   A cost is a forgone opportunity or a sacrificed alternative. The absolute levels of resource use do not imply anything about cost, because in and of themselves they do not measure the sacrificed alternatives of the production undertaken. Only when the absolute levels of resource use are compared to the resources required for other production activities can anything about cost be determined.

41.   This chapter discusses three situations which can create gains from trade: differences in abilities, differences in tastes, and increased productivity from large-scale production.

First, if people have different abilities, they can specialize in their areas of comparative advantage and then trade to obtain the goods they desire. In this situation, everyone is better off because specialization caused the economy's overall production to increase, allowing everyone to consume more than if each person had relied on his own abilities. Second, if people have different tastes, mutually beneficial trades can be made where each person trades away the goods he values the least in exchange for goods he values more. Third, if large-scale production increases productivity, then the economy's overall production increases when people specialize. This increased production gives everyone higher consumption when they specialize and trade.

Problems

42. i.   If an acre of land is used to grow 45 bushels of wheat, then the opportunity to grow 30 bushels of barley has been sacrificed. Each bushel of wheat thus costs $^{30}/_{45}$, or $^2/_3$, of a bushel of barley.

Conversely, if a farmer in Saskatchewan uses an acre of land to grow 30 bushels of barley, then he has sacrificed the opportunity to grow 45 bushels of wheat. The cost of growing barley is 1½ (45 divided by 30) bushels of wheat per bushel of barley.

ii.   This logic is incorrect. The cost of growing wheat and the cost of growing barley cannot be directly compared because they are measured in different units. In fact, the two costs are just different ways of looking at the same data—one cost is simply the reciprocal of the other. To apply the principle of comparative advantage and determine if Saskatchewan should specialize in wheat production, one must compares Saskatchewan's cost of growing wheat against other provinces' costs of growing where.

iii. If Saskatchewan is to specialize in wheat production, then it must be the low-cost wheat producer. Thus, Saskatchewan should specialize in wheat production only if Alberta's cost of growing wheat is greater than Saskatchewan's cost of $^2/_3$ bushel of barley per bushel of wheat.

43. i.   Simply calculate the amount of paneling each person sacrifices to rewire a house. The costs of rewiring a house are $^4/_5$ paneled room per rewired house for the electrician, 1⅕ paneled room per rewired house for the son, and 1 paneled room per rewired house for Mr. Grant.

ii. Notice from part i that the electrician has the lowest cost of rewiring a house. Also notice that Mr. Grant has a lower cost of paneling a room than the electrician (1 rewired house per paneled room for Mr. Grant as opposed to 1¼ for the electrician). So when they specialize and trade, the electrician should rewire houses and Mr. Grant should panel rooms.

iii. From part i we know that Mr. Grant has a lower cost of rewiring a house than does the son. The son has the lowest cost of paneling a room (⅚ rewired house per paneled room for the son as opposed to 1 for Mr. Grant). So Mr. Grant should rewire houses and the son should panel rooms when they specialize and trade.

iv. The electrician should specialize in rewiring houses since she has the lowest cost of the three. The teenage son should specialize in paneling rooms since his cost to perform this task is the lowest of the three. As shown in parts ii and iii, Mr. Grant could specialize in either activity. The actual result depends on the preferences of the three people to have rewiring and paneling done and on the rate of exchange established for trading rewiring and paneling.

44. i. As always, to calculate costs we need to find the sacrificed alternatives. In the U.S., the cost of producing cloth is 4 bushels of food per bolt of cloth, and in Mexico this cost is 2 bushels per bolt. Since Mexico has the lowest cost of producing cloth, it should be the one to specialize in this activity. The U.S. should specialize in food production because its cost is ¼ bolt per bushel as compared to ½ bolt per bushel for Mexico.

ii. If the U.S. purchases cloth from Mexico under this deal, the cost of cloth will be 5 bushels of food per bolt of cloth. According to part i, however, the U.S.'s cost of producing its own cloth is only 4 bushels per bolt. The U.S. will choose the option with the lower cost and turn down Mexico's offer.

iii. If Mexico accepts the U.S.'s counteroffer, the cost of food will be 1 bolt of cloth per bushel of food. As shown in part i, however, Mexico can produce its own food at a cost of only ½ bolt per bushel. Mexico will reject the U.S.'s counteroffer because it is too costly. (Alternatively, you could argue that Mexico will not sell cloth at the price of 1 bushel per bolt because this is less than its cost to produce cloth.)

iv. Any rate of exchange between the two countries' costs of production (i.e., any rate between 2 and 4 bushels of food per bolt of cloth) will benefit both countries and be agreeable to both the U.S. and Mexico. As shown in part ii, a rate of exchange larger than 4 bushels per bolt will be rejected by the U.S., because the U.S.'s cost of producing its own cloth would be lower than the cost of buying Mexican cloth. As shown in part iii, a rate of exchange smaller than 2 bushels per bolt is unacceptable to Mexico, because Mexico's cost of producing its own food would be lower than the cost of buying U.S. food. If the rate of exchange is between 2 and 4 bushels per bolt, then both countries will benefit from trading. The U.S. can purchase Mexican cloth at a price lower than the cost of producing its own cloth, and Mexico can purchase U.S. food at a price lower than the cost of producing its own food.

45.   i.   Let the currency used be "dollars." If the absolute price of bread is P_B dollars per loaf, then 1 dollar will purchase $1/P_B$ loaves. (For example, if bread is $2 per loaf, then $1 would purchase ½ a loaf.) So each dollar spent on wine implies a sacrifice of $1/P_B$ loaves of bread. If we sacrifice P_W dollars to purchase a bottle of wine, then we are sacrificing a total of $P_W \cdot (1/P_B)$ or P_W/P_B loaves of bread to make this purchase. (For example, if wine is $10 per bottle, we are sacrificing a total of 5 loaves of bread since each dollar could have bought ½ loaf of bread.) So the relative price of wine in terms of bread equals P_W/P_B loaves per bottle.

ii.   After the inflation, the new absolute price of wine is $(1 + x)P_W$, and the new absolute price of bread is $(1 + y)P_B$. Using the formula we developed in part i, the new price of wine equals

$$\frac{(1 + x)P_W}{(1 + y)P_B} \quad \text{or} \quad \frac{1 + x}{1 + y} \cdot \frac{P_W}{P_B} .$$

There are three possible cases:

If $x > y$, then $\frac{1 + x}{1 + y} > 1$, so the price of wine has increased.

If $x < y$, then $\frac{1 + x}{1 + y} < 1$, so the price of wine has decreased.

If $x = y$, then $\frac{1 + x}{1 + y} = 1$, and so the price of wine is unchanged.

iii.   Inflation can either increase, decrease, or not affect the relative prices of commodities.

CHAPTER 3

THE BEHAVIOR OF CONSUMERS

This chapter begins a two-chapter unit investigating the factors that determine consumer demand. The first two sections of the chapter introduce the basic tools of indifference curve analysis. The chapter ends with some applications to further develop your understanding of indifference curve analysis.

KEY TERMS

- Goods
- Indifference curve
- Marginal value (of X in terms of Y)
- Convex

- Composite-good convention
- Budget line
- Optimum
- Corner solution
- Price index

- Consumer price index (CPI)
- Laspeyres price index
- Paasche price index
- Head tax
- Income tax

KEY IDEAS

- **Section 3.1.** A consumer's tastes are modeled using a set of indifference curves. Each indifference curve shows the various combinations of goods which provide the consumer with the same level of satisfaction. The marginal value of X in terms of Y is the amount of good Y that the consumer is just willing to trade for one unit of X and is equal to the absolute value of the slope of the indifference curve.

- **Section 3.2.** A budget line shows the various combinations of goods that the consumer can afford to purchase. Relative prices determine the slope of the budget line, while the consumer's income determines how far the budget line is from the origin. The consumer's optimum occurs where an indifference curve is tangent to the budget line, and thus the marginal value of a good equals the relative price of the good at the optimum.

◆ **Section 3.3.** We can make many predictions about consumer behavior by examining how the optimum changes in various situations. For example, indifference curve analysis can be used to show that there is no perfect price index to measure inflation—Laspeyres price indices make inflation seem worse for consumers than it really is, while Paasche price indices make inflation seem better for consumers than it really is. We can also use indifference curve analysis to develop a simple test to determine if people's tastes change over time. Finally, indifference curve analysis can be used to prove that an income tax lowers consumer welfare more than a head tax that raises the same revenue.

COMPLETION EXERCISES

1.   Economists model a consumer's tastes by using a family of _____.

2.   The _____ of bread in terms of wine is the amount of wine that a consumer can trade for one loaf of bread and still remain indifferent.

3.   Indifference curves are typically drawn downward sloping and
     _____.

4.   When economists use indifference curves between a commodity and "all other goods," they are using the _____.

5.   The consumer's _____ shows the possible baskets of goods that can be purchased with the consumer's income at the existing market prices.

6.   An optimum in which the consumer purchases only one of the two commodities is called a
     _____.

7.   A price index that is based on the market basket consumed in the earlier period is called a
     _____.

8.   When a _____ is used to measure inflation, price changes seem worse for the consumer than they really are.

9.   When the government levies a _____, it takes a fixed dollar amount of the worker's income regardless of the worker's total earnings.

10.   An income tax, unlike a head tax, lowers the _____ of the
      consumer's leisure time.

TRUE-FALSE EXERCISES

_____ 11.   Indifference curves from the same family cannot cross.

_____ 12.   Along a convex indifference curve, the marginal value of a good falls as the quantity
             of the good rises.

_____ 13.   A rise in income will cause an outward, parallel shift in the consumer's indifference
             curves.

_____ 14.   The slope of the budget line is determined by the consumer's income.

_____ 15.   If the marginal value of gasoline exceeds the relative price of gasoline, then reducing
             gasoline purchases will make the consumer better off.

_____ 16.   If the consumer buys sugar along with other goods at the optimum, then the
             marginal value of sugar must equal zero.

_____ 17.   Paasche price indices tend to overstate the impact of price changes on consumers.

_____ 18.   When a Laspeyres price index is used to measure price changes between 1990 and
             1998, the consumer's 1998 purchases will be used for the fixed market basket.

_____ 19.   A head tax has no affect on the worker's effective wage rate.

_____ 20.   Consumers will be indifferent between a head tax and an income tax, as long as the
             two taxes raise the same amount of revenue.

MULTIPLE CHOICE QUESTIONS

_____ 21. Which of the following is the same for all points on an indifference curve?
   A.   The level of satisfaction obtained from consumption.
   B.   The prices faced by the consumer.
   C.   The consumer's income.
   D.   All of the above.

_____ 22. Which of the following is *not* a property of the family of indifference curves representing a consumer's tastes between two goods?
   A.   Every basket of goods is on one and only one indifference curve.
   B.   No two indifference curves can cross.
   C.   The indifference curves are all downward sloping.
   D.   The indifference curves are all concave.

_____ 23. If the marginal value of bread in terms of wine is ½ bottle of wine per loaf of bread, then
   A.   consuming ½ bottle of wine makes the consumer better off than consuming 1 loaf of bread.
   B.   the consumer will remain indifferent if he trades away 1 loaf of bread in exchange for ½ bottle of wine.
   C.   wine provides half as much satisfaction to the consumer as does bread.
   D.   the consumer's optimum contains twice as much bread as wine.

_____ 24. If the consumer's marginal value is constant, then
   A.   there is no optimum purchase for the consumer.
   B.   the consumer's indifference curves must be concave instead of convex.
   C.   the consumer's indifference curves must be straight lines.
   D.   the possibility of corner solutions is eliminated.

◆◆◆ For Questions 25–27, assume that good X is on the horizontal axis and good Y is on the vertical axis in the consumer-choice diagram. P_X denotes the price of good X, P_Y is the price of good Y, and I is the consumer's income.

_____ 25. The slope of the budget line is given by
   A. $-P_X/P_Y$.
   B. $-P_Y/P_X$.
   C. I/P_X.
   D. I/P_Y.

_____ 26. Which of the following can make the budget line steeper?
   A.   A rise in the consumer's income.
   B.   A rise in the consumer's marginal value of X in terms of Y.
   C.   A rise in the price of good X.
   D.   A rise in the price of good Y.

_____ 27. Suppose the consumer is spending all of his income. If P_X/P_Y is larger than the marginal value of X in terms of Y, then the consumer
A.   will be better off if he purchases more X and less Y.
B.   will be better off if he purchases more Y and less X.
C.   will be better off if he purchases more of both goods.
D.   cannot make himself better off with any change in his purchases.

_____ 28. In the diagram on the right, at what basket is the consumer's marginal value of food in terms of clothing larger than the relative price of food in terms of clothing?
A.   Basket A.
B.   Basket B.
C.   Basket C.
D.   Both basket B and basket C.

_____ 29. If Rob's marginal value of bread is 50¢ per loaf, then
A.   Rob places a value of 50¢ on his last loaf of bread.
B.   Rob will not purchase any bread unless the price is lower than 50¢ per loaf.
C.   Rob is willing to pay an average of 50¢ per loaf for bread.
D.   Rob is willing to trade away all his bread in exchange for 50¢ per loaf.

_____ 30. Suppose food is on the horizontal axis and clothing is on the vertical axis. Consider a corner solution in which the consumer buys only clothing and no food. At this optimum, the relative price of food in terms of clothing
A.   must be less than or equal to the marginal value of food in terms of clothing.
B.   must be equal to the marginal value of food in terms of clothing.
C.   must be greater than or equal to the marginal value of food in terms of clothing.
D.   can be less than, greater than, or equal to the marginal value of food in terms of clothing.

_____ 31. Suppose a consumer's indifference curves are downward sloping, but they are concave (i.e., bowed away from the origin) instead of convex. What can be said about the consumer's optimum in this case?
A.   The consumer's optimum is always a corner solution in this situation.
B.   The consumer's optimum does not exist, because there is no tangency in this case.
C.   The consumer's optimum is at the tangency between the budget line and the indifference curve; the only difference in this case is that the indifference curve lies below the budget line.
D.   The consumer has two optima: one at the tangency and one at a corner solution.

_____ 32. Recently, the price of cheese has risen from $4 to $6 per pound and the price of fruit has fallen from $8 to $6 per pound, while Jannett's income has stayed fixed at $48 per week. After the prices changed, Jannett adjusted her buying habits and started buying 4 pounds of cheese and 4 pounds of fruit weekly. We can conclude that
A. Jannett is indifferent about the price changes.
B. Jannett is worse off after the price changes.
C. Jannett is better off after the price changes.
D. Jannett may be worse off, better off, or indifferent after the price changes.

_____ 33. Which of the following statements about price indices is *false*?
A. Price indices are based on the changes in the cost of some fixed basket of goods.
B. A Laspeyres price index is based on the basket consumed in the later period, while a Paasche price index is based on the basket consumed in the earlier period.
C. A Laspeyres price index makes price changes seem worse for consumers than they really are, while a Paasche price index makes price changes seem better for consumers than they really are.
D. The consumer price index (CPI) is a Laspeyres price index.

_____ 34. Which of the following statements about the comparison between income and head taxes is *false*?
A. Only the income tax lowers the effective wage that the consumer is paid for sacrificing leisure.
B. For both the income and head taxes, the tax bill paid is given by the vertical distance between the new and old budget lines at the post-tax optimum.
C. When the tax bill is the same under an income tax and a head tax, the consumer will be better off under the head tax.
D. When the tax bill is the same under an income and a head tax, the consumer will work more hours under the income tax.

_____ 35. In the diagram on the right, the consumer's tastes must have changed between last year and this year if
A. the consumer bought A_1 last year and buys B_1 this year.
B. the consumer bought A_1 last year and buys B_2 this year.
C. the consumer bought A_2 last year and buys B_1 this year.
D. the consumer bought A_2 last year and buys B_2 this year.

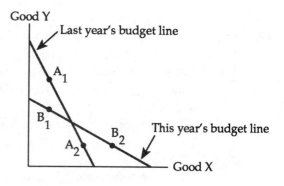

REVIEW QUESTIONS

36. Why are indifference curves downward sloping? Why are indifference curves convex?

37. What economic interpretations can be given to the slope and intercepts of the budget line? How would these values be calculated from basic price and income data?

38. Suppose there are two goods: bread and wine. Explain why the consumer can benefit from trade when his marginal value of bread in terms of wine is not equal to the relative price of bread in terms of wine.

39.   What is a corner solution? Describe two ways that a corner solution can occur.

40.   In what ways are a Laspeyres price index and a Paasche price index different? In what ways are they similar?

41.   In what ways do the effects of an income tax and a head tax differ?

PROBLEMS

42.   Last year, the price of bread was $2 per loaf and Lida spent $100 on bread. This year, the price of bread rises to $3 per loaf, while Lida's income is unchanged. To compensate her for the price change, Lida's father gives her a gift of $50. Consider an indifference curve-budget line diagram with bread on the horizontal axis and "all other goods" on the vertical axis.

i.   Does the price change make Lida's budget line flatter or steeper? Justify your choice.

ii.   After Lida receives the gift, will her new budget line lie above, lie below, or pass through her initial optimum? Justify your choice.

iii.   Complete the accompanying diagram to illustrate the situation. This year, will Lida be better or worse off than she was last year? How can you tell?

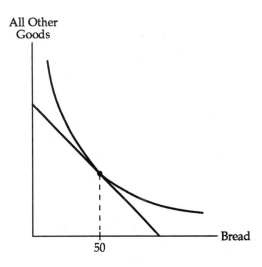

43. i.   Suppose Mohamed has $45 per week to spend on food and gasoline, where the price of food is $3 per unit and the price of gasoline is $2.25 per gallon. Sketch Mohamed's budget line on the axes on the right.

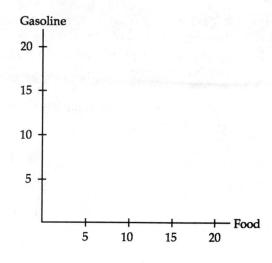

ii.   During a war, the government decides to freeze prices and ration gasoline by limiting all customers to a maximum purchase of 10 gallons per week. Barter in gasoline is strictly forbidden. Assuming that Mohamed is a law-abiding citizen and assuming that the absolute prices and Mohamed's income have not changed, on your graph from part i show how his budget line is modified by the government's rationing plan.

iii.   Provide sketches on the axes below to show that there are two possible effects that the rationing plan can have on Mohamed's optimum:
    a.   Mohamed's consumption could be unaffected by the rationing plan, and
    b.   Mohamed's level of satisfaction could be lowered by the rationing plan.

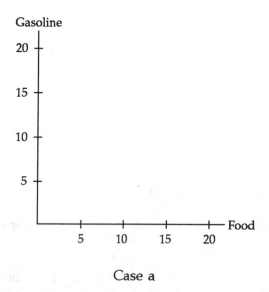

Case a

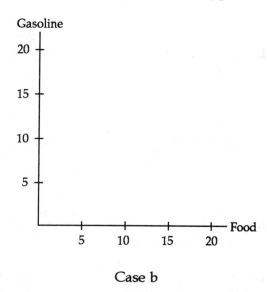

Case b

For each case, indicate whether the marginal value of food in terms of gasoline is greater than, less than, or equal to the relative price of food in terms of gasoline at the optimum under rationing.

44. Suppose the government is considering the use of two taxes: Tax A and Tax B. The diagram below illustrates the effect the two taxes have on a typical worker. The pretax optimum is at point O, the optimum under Tax A is at point A, and the optimum under Tax B is at point B.

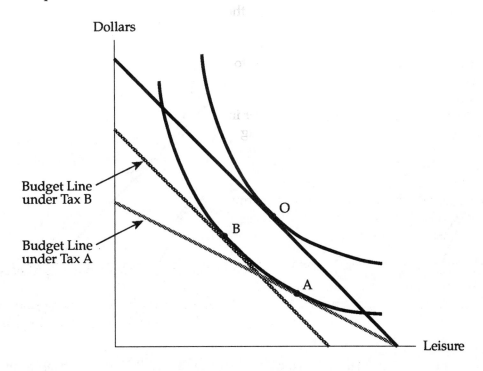

i. Is Tax A an income tax or a head tax? Is Tax B an income tax or a head tax? How can you tell?

ii. On the diagram, label the tax bills that the government collects from the worker under Tax A and under Tax B.

iii. Compare and contrast the two taxes with respect to the revenue collected by the government, the effect on the worker's welfare, and the effect on work effort. What conclusions can you reach?

45.   Suppose there are only two goods: bread and wine. Last year the consumer had an income
       of $100. This year the consumer again has an income of $100, but the absolute prices of
       bread and wine have risen. The consumer's budget lines and his optima for the two years
       are shown in the diagrams below; last year's optimum is labeled A and this year's
       optimum is labeled B.

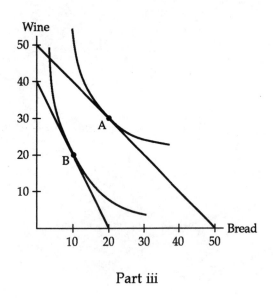

Part iii

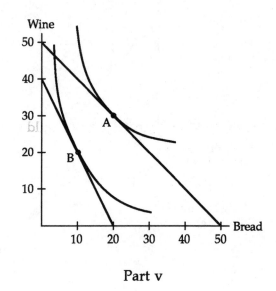

Part v

i.   Using the above information, calculate last year's and this year's absolute prices.

ii.   Show that the Laspeyres price index gives an inflation rate of 75%.

iii. Suppose the consumer is given a 75% increase in this year's income to compensate him for the price increases. Complete the left-hand diagram above to show the effect of this compensation. Did this scheme over- or undercompensate the consumer for the inflation?

iv. Prove the Paasche price index would show that last year's prices are 40% lower than this year's prices.

v. Suppose that instead of the price increase, the consumer must this year accept a 40% reduction in income from last year. Complete the right-hand diagram at the top of the previous page to show the effect of this income reduction. Is the consumer better off under the price increase or the income reduction?

vi. What general facts about the interpretations of Laspeyres and Paasche price indices can be deduced from your answers to parts iii and v?

SOLUTIONS

Completion Exercises

1. indifference curves
2. marginal value
3. convex
4. composite-good convention
5. budget line

6. corner solution
7. Laspeyres price index
8. Laspeyres price index
9. head tax
10. marginal value

True-False Exercises

11. TRUE.

12. TRUE.

13. FALSE. A rise in income will cause an outward, parallel shift in the consumer's <u>budget line</u>.

14. FALSE. The slope of the budget line is determined by <u>relative prices</u>.

15. FALSE. If the marginal value of gasoline exceeds the relative price of gasoline, then <u>increasing</u> gasoline purchases will make the consumer better off.

16. FALSE. If the consumer buys sugar along with other goods at the optimum, then the marginal value of sugar must equal <u>the relative price of sugar</u>.

17. FALSE. Paasche price indices tend to <u>understate</u> the impact of price changes on consumers.

18. FALSE. When a Laspeyres price index is used to measure price changes between 1990 and 1998, the consumer's <u>1990</u> purchases will be used for the fixed market basket.

19. TRUE.

20. FALSE. Consumers will be <u>better off under a head tax than under an income tax</u>, as long as the two taxes raise the same amount of revenue.

Multiple Choice Questions

21. A. An indifference curve shows the various baskets that the consumer finds equally desirable. An indifference curve contains no information about prices and income. Prices and income are fixed along a budget line.

22.   D. Since the consumer will place a higher value on the last unit of a good when it is relatively scarce, the marginal value is falling as we move from left to right along an indifference curve. This implies that indifference curves are convex.

23.   B. The marginal value measures the amount of wine that can replace the last loaf of bread and keep the consumer equally satisfied.

24.   C. For any given basket of goods, the marginal value is equal to the absolute value of the slope of the indifference curve at that basket. If the marginal value is constant, then the indifference curves have a constant slope and must be straight lines.

25.   A. We can rewrite the equation of the budget line as $y = -(P_X/P_Y) \cdot x + (I/P_Y)$. Applying basic algebra, we see that this equation is in slope-intercept form and the coefficient of the variable x gives us the slope.

26.   C. The slope of the budget line is given by $-P_X/P_Y$. This number becomes larger in magnitude (and so the budget line becomes steeper) if the value of the numerator P_X gets larger.

27.   B. The consumer does not have enough income to buy more of both goods. Since the amount of good Y sacrificed to obtain the last unit of X (i.e., the relative price) is larger than the additional value that the consumer receives from the last unit of X (i.e., the marginal value), the last unit of X purchased was a poor buy. The consumer will benefit from purchasing less X and more Y.

28.   B. At point B, the marginal value is larger than the relative price because the indifference curve is steeper than the budget line.

29.   A. This is simply the definition of marginal value.

30.   C. As shown by Exhibit 3-9 of the textbook, the budget line can be steeper than the indifference curve at this corner solution.

31.   A. The highest indifference curve the consumer can reach always hits the budget line at a corner when the indifference curves are concave.

32.   B. Before the price changes, 4 pounds of cheese and 4 pounds of fruit would have cost $48, the same as Jannett's income. Therefore, Jannett must be worse off, because Jannett preferred to buy a different basket of goods before the price changes.

33.   B. The Laspeyres price index looks at the cost of the market basket purchased before the price changes, while the Paasche price index looks at the cost of the market basket purchased after the price changes.

34.   D. Since the effective wage is higher under the head tax than under the income tax, the consumer will benefit from selling more leisure time under the head tax (assuming the tax bill is the same under the two taxes).

35.   C. An indifference curve tangent at A_2 and an indifference curve tangent at B_1 must cross, so they cannot belong to the same family of indifference curves.

Review Questions

36.   Indifference curves are downward sloping when we assume both commodities are goods. In this case the consumer must substitute one good for another in order to remain indifferent, so the resulting indifference curve must slope downward. Indifference curves are convex when we assume that marginal value and quantity are inversely related along an indifference curve. This assumption is reasonable because the consumer is likely to value additional units of the good very much when it is relatively scarce and very little when it is relatively abundant.

37.   The magnitude of the slope of the budget line represents the relative price of the good on the horizontal axis, and the intercepts of the budget line represent the maximal amounts of goods that can be purchased with the consumer's income. To calculate the slope of the budget line, divide the price of the good on the horizontal axis by the price of the good on the vertical axis. To calculate an intercept of the budget line, divide the consumer's income by the price of the appropriate good.

38.   If the marginal value of bread in terms of wine is larger than the relative price of bread in terms of wine, then the value of the last loaf of bread to the consumer is larger than the cost of bread in the market. Further purchases of bread would then benefit the consumer. (For example, if the marginal value is 3 bottles per loaf and the relative price is 2 bottles per loaf, then the consumer values a loaf of bread more than what it costs, and the consumer should buy more bread.) On the other hand, if the marginal value is smaller than the relative price, then the last loaf of bread consumed cost the consumer more than what he thought it was worth. So the last loaf of bread purchased was a poor buy, and the consumer would benefit from reducing his purchases of bread. (For example, if the marginal value is 1 bottle per loaf and the relative price is 2 bottles per loaf, then a loaf of bread costs more than what the consumer thinks its worth, and the consumer should

reduce his bread purchases.) Only when the marginal value is equated to the relative price is the consumer unable to benefit from further trade in the market.

39. A corner solution occurs when the consumer chooses not to purchase one of the two goods. If the indifference curves are everywhere flatter than the budget line (i.e., if the marginal value is always less than the relative price), then a corner solution will occur on the northwest corner of the budget line. The optimum occurs in the opposite corner if the indifference curves are everywhere steeper than the budget line. A second way that a corner solution can occur is if the consumer has concave indifference curves; in this case all consumer optima are corner solutions.

40. Both price indices attempt to measure a change in the cost of living based on how the cost of the market basket consumed has changed. A Laspeyres price index is based on the basket of goods consumed before the change in the cost of living, and it makes the price changes seem worse than they really are for consumers when relative prices are altered. A Paasche price index is based on the basket of goods consumed after the change in the cost of living, and it makes the price changes seem better than they really are for consumers when relative prices are altered. If the price changes do not affect relative prices, the Laspeyres and Paasche price indices will be identical.

41. Since an income tax requires the worker to pay the government a certain percentage of his wages, it will lower the effective wage rate and make the budget line showing the trade-off between leisure and dollars flatter. A head tax is paid in a single lump sum independent of the wages earned, so it does not affect the wage or the slope of the budget line. (A head tax does shift the budget line inward, however.) When the total amount paid is the same under the two taxes, the worker will provide more hours of labor and will be better off under the head tax than under the income tax.

Problems

42. i. The relative price of bread has increased, so Lida's budget line becomes steeper.
    ii. The $50 gift allows Lida to purchase the same amount of bread as last year (50 loaves) without changing the amount she spends on all other goods. Lida has just enough income to continue purchasing the same basket as she purchased last year, so her new budget line must pass through her initial optimum.

iii. Lida will be better off. Although she can continue purchasing the same basket as last year, the rise in the relative price of bread causes Lida to purchase less bread and more of all other goods. By taking advantage of this new opportunity, Lida moves to a higher indifference curve and becomes better off.

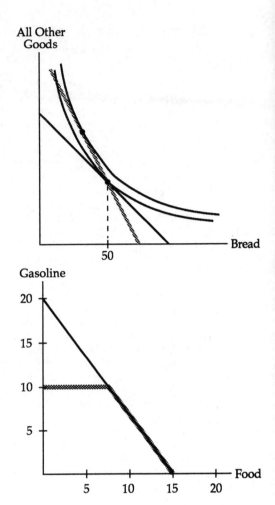

43. i, ii. The slope of the budget line remains the same after the rationing scheme because the prices have not changed. The only effect of the rationing scheme is to forbid Mohamed from consuming baskets with more than 10 gallons of gasoline. So the rationing plan has "chopped off" the budget line at this level, leaving the other possible purchases (i.e., those with less than 10 gallons of gasoline) still available.

iii. Common sense tells us that Mohamed will be unaffected by the gasoline rationing if he was already consuming less than the 10-gallon-per-week limit. On the other hand, he

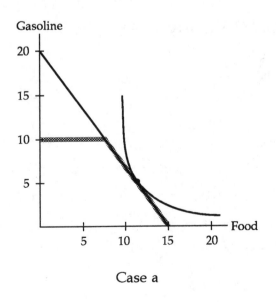

Case a

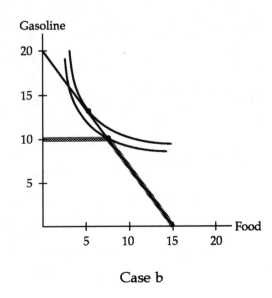

Case b

would be made worse off if he was originally consuming more than this amount. These conclusions are verified in the diagrams on the previous page. The indifference curve and the budget line are tangent in case a, so the marginal value is equal to the relative price. In case b, the indifference curve at the new optimum just nicks the corner of the budget constraint. In this situation, the indifference curve is flatter than the budget line, so the marginal value is less than or equal to the relative price. Notice the similarity between case b and a corner solution.

44.   i.   Tax A has caused the budget line to rotate, indicating that the government is taking a percentage of the worker's wage earnings, so Tax A is an income tax. Tax B has caused a parallel shift in the budget line, which shows that the worker pays the same tax no matter how much he earns, so Tax B is a head tax.

      ii. The vertical distance between the new and old budget lines at the new optimum gives the size of the tax bill paid by the worker. Notice that the pretax optimum, point O, plays no role in determining the size of the tax bill. The worker pays the government the amount RA under Tax A and the amount SB under Tax B. (Any vertical distance between the old and new budget lines would work for the head tax, since the two budget lines are parallel.)

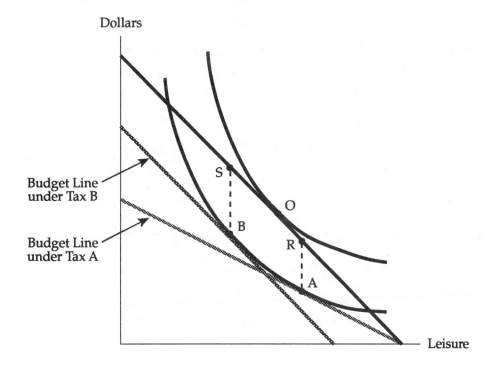

iii. The optimum points A and B are on the same indifference curve, so both taxes have the same effect on the worker's welfare. However, he works more hours and the government raises more revenue under the head tax than under the income tax. This shows that if the consumer is indifferent between a head tax and an income tax, then the head tax is the better for the government (in the sense that it raises more revenue).

45. i. Using the intercepts of the budget line, we find that last year $100 could purchase either 50 loaves of bread or 50 bottles of wine. Therefore, bread cost $2 per loaf and wine cost $2 per bottle. This year, the same $100 can purchase either 20 loaves of bread or 40 bottles of wine, so bread now costs $5 per loaf and wine costs $2.50 per bottle.

ii. For a Laspeyres price index, we need to calculate the cost of last year's basket using this year's prices. From the graph, we see that the basket purchased for $100 last year contains 20 loaves of bread and 40 bottles of wine. Since bread costs $5 per loaf and wine costs $2.50 per bottle this year, this market basket now costs $175 – a 75% increase over last year's cost.

iii. If the consumer receives a 75% increase in income to compensate him for the inflation, the new budget line will have intercepts at 35 loaves of bread and 70 bottles of wine. The new optimum must now be at a point like C. The 75% increase in income overcompensated the consumer for the 75% inflation, because it allowed him to reach a higher indifference curve than he was on last year.

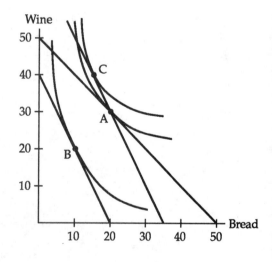

iv. For a Paasche price index, we need to calculate the cost of this year's basket using last years prices. We know from the graph that the basket purchased for $100 this year contains 10 loaves of bread and 20 bottles of wine. We know from part i that bread cost $2 per loaf and wine cost $2 per bottle last year, so this market basket cost only $60 last year. Therefore, last year's prices are 40% lower than this year's prices.

v.   If the consumer suffers a 40% cut in income instead of the inflation, then the new budget line will have intercepts at 30 loaves of bread and 30 bottles of wine. The new optimum must be at a point like D. Comparing points B and D, we see that the consumer is better off with the 40% income reduction than with the inflation.

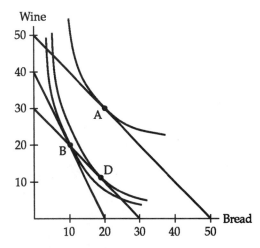

vi. Part iii shows that the Laspeyres price index makes price changes seem worse than they really are, because the consumer doesn't need a full 75% increase in income to compensate for the "75%" price increase. Part v shows that the Paasche price index makes price changes seem better than they really are, because a 40% drop in income wouldn't be as bad for the consumer as the actual price increase that makes last year's prices "40%" lower.

CHAPTER 4

CONSUMERS IN THE MARKETPLACE

This chapter establishes the foundations needed to apply indifference curve analysis to a wide variety of situations. The first two sections of the chapter examine how changes in income and changes in price affect the consumer's optimum. In the second half of the chapter, this information is applied to develop a better understanding of demand curves through the use of substitution and income effects and elasticities.

KEY TERMS

- Normal good
- Inferior good
- Engel curve
- Giffen good
- Non-Giffen good
- Substitution effect

- Income effect
- Compensated demand curve
- (Ordinary) demand curve
- Income elasticity of demand

- Price elasticity of demand
- Elastic
- Cross elasticity of demand
- Substitutes
- Complements

KEY IDEAS

- **Section 4.1.** A normal good is one for which an increase in income will increase quantity demanded at the consumer's optimum, while an inferior good is one for which an increase in income will decrease the quantity demanded. An Engel curve is used to illustrate the relationship between income and quantity demanded.

- **Section 4.2.** A demand curve can be derived using indifference curve analysis by examining how the consumer's optimum changes as the price of the good changes. This analysis shows that Giffen goods—goods that do not obey the law of demand—are a theoretical possibility.

◆ **Section 4.3.** A change in the absolute price of a commodity affects both the relative prices faced by the consumer and the consumer's purchasing power, so the quantity demanded at the optimum changes for two distinct reasons. The substitution effect shows how quantity demanded is affected by the change in relative prices, while the income effect shows how quantity demanded is affected by the consumer's altered purchasing power. A compensated demand curve is one that shows only substitution effects, while an ordinary demand curve includes both substitution and income effects.

◆ **Section 4.4.** Demand elasticities measure how sensitive quantity demanded is to changes in prices and income. Demand elasticities show the percentage change in quantity demanded that will result from a 1% increase in some other factor (such as the price of the good itself, consumer income, or the price of a related good).

COMPLETION EXERCISES

1. If higher incomes cause people to demand fewer turnips, then turnips are an

   _____.

2. The _____ will be upward-sloping for normal goods and downward-sloping for inferior goods.

3. Goods that obey the law of demand are called _____.

4. When the relative price of a good rises, the _____ always reduces the quantity demanded of the good.

5. When the price of a _____ falls, both the substitution effect and the income effect will increase the quantity demanded.

6. The _____ shows what happens to quantity demanded when a price rise reduces the consumer's purchasing power and makes him effectively poorer.

7. A _____ shows the relationship between price and quantity demanded in the hypothetical circumstance where the consumer feels no income effect.

8. The percentage change in quantity demanded resulting from a 1% increase in price is called the _____.

9. Goods that tend to be used together and have negative cross elasticities are called

_____.

10. When demand for a good is highly _____, people greatly reduce their consumption in response to a given price rise.

TRUE-FALSE EXERCISES

_____ 11. The Engel curve for a non-Giffen good must slope upwards.

_____ 12. Giffen goods have downward-sloping Engel curves and upward-sloping demand curves.

_____ 13. If the price of a good falls, then the substitution effect causes a rise in the quantity demanded.

_____ 14. If the price of a normal good rises, then both the substitution and income effects cause the quantity demanded to fall.

_____ 15. For a good to be Giffen, it must be inferior and must account for a negligible fraction of the consumer's expenditures.

_____ 16. The (ordinary) demand curve for a normal good must slope downwards.

_____ 17. Only non-Giffen goods have compensated demand curves that slope downward.

_____ 18. A good with an upward-sloping Engel curve must have a positive income elasticity of demand.

_____ 19. Goods with a large number of close substitutes tend to have highly elastic demand.

_____ 20. If two goods are substitutes, then the income elasticity of demand will be positive.

MULTIPLE CHOICE QUESTIONS

_____ 21. A pivot in the budget line, with the vertical intercept remaining fixed, will occur when
   A. the consumer's income changes.
   B. the price of the good on the horizontal axis changes.
   C. the price of the good on the vertical axis changes.
   D. the consumer's tastes change.

_____ 22. If the consumer's income and all prices simultaneously double, then the budget line will
   A. shift parallel away from the origin.
   B. shift parallel towards the origin.
   C. shift unpredictably.
   D. remain unchanged.

_____ 23. From the shape of the Engel curve in the diagram on the right, we may conclude that hamburger is
   A. a normal good.
   B. an inferior good.
   C. a normal good for low income levels and an inferior good for high income levels.
   D. an inferior good for low income levels and a normal good for high income levels.

Quantity Demanded
of Hamburger

Engel Curve
for Hamburger

Income

_____ 24. Which of the following is *not* held constant when we use indifference curve analysis to derive the demand curve for good X?
   A. The price of good X.
   B. The price of good Y.
   C. The consumer's income.
   D. The consumer's tastes.

_____ 25. When the price of a commodity changes, the resulting substitution effect
   A. always supports the law of demand.
   B. supports the law of demand only for normal goods.
   C. supports the law of demand only for inferior goods.
   D. supports the law of demand only for non-Giffen goods.

_____ 26. When the price of a commodity changes, the resulting income effect
   A. always supports the law of demand.
   B. supports the law of demand only for normal goods.
   C. supports the law of demand only for inferior goods.
   D. supports the law of demand only for non-Giffen goods.

_____ 27. The substitution and income effects for a non-Giffen inferior good
   A. both move in the same direction.
   B. move in opposite directions, with the substitution effect being the larger.
   C. move in opposite directions, with the income effect being the larger.
   D. move in opposite directions, but we cannot predict which effect will be larger.

_____ 28. Suppose the substitution and income effects both lower the quantity demanded of a good when there is a price increase. Which of the following statements is *false?*
   A. This good must be a normal good.
   B. The law of demand must hold for this good.
   C. The income elasticity of demand must be positive for this good.
   D. Demand for this good must be highly elastic.

_____ 29. Which of the following statements about the compensated demand curve is *false?*
   A. A compensated demand curve is derived assuming that the consumer is income-compensated for price changes.
   B. A compensated demand curve shows the substitution effects of price changes, but it does not include the income effects caused by price changes.
   C. Compensated demand curves are always more elastic than ordinary demand curves.
   D. Compensated demand curves always obey the law of demand.

_____ 30. When will the ordinary and compensated demand curves for a commodity be identical?
   A. When the substitution effect is zero.
   B. When the income effect is zero.
   C. When both the substitution and income effects are zero.
   D. When the substitution and income effects exactly offset each other.

_____ 31. Suppose that the Engel curve for good X shows that the consumer purchases 20 units of X when his income is $50 and that he purchases 21 units of X when his income is $55. The income elasticity of demand between the income levels $50 and $55 is calculated to be
   A. ⅕.
   B. ½.
   C. 1.
   D. 2.

_____ 32. If the income elasticity of a good is positive, we may conclude that
   A. the good is a normal good.
   B. the good is an inferior good.
   C. the Engel curve for this good must be downward sloping.
   D. the law of demand is violated for this good.

_____ 33. Suppose that the price elasticity of demand for automobiles is –2. If the price of an automobile falls from $10,000 to $9,500, we can expect the quantity demanded of automobiles to increase by
A. 2%.
B. 5%.
C. 10%.
D. 1,000 automobiles.

_____ 34. Which of the following is the most likely to be a positive number?
A. The price elasticity of demand for generic cigarettes.
B. The income elasticity of demand for generic cigarettes.
C. The cross elasticity of demand between generic cigarettes and disposable lighters.
D. The cross elasticity of demand between generic cigarettes and Marlboro cigarettes.

_____ 35. Suppose consumers demand 400 million packs of cigarettes weekly at the current price. Also suppose the price elasticity of demand for cigarettes is estimated to equal –0.5. In this situation, a 3% increase in the price of cigarettes would reduce the quantity demanded to
A. 399.5 million packs weekly.
B. 398.5 million packs weekly.
C. 394 million packs weekly.
D. 388 million packs weekly.

REVIEW QUESTIONS

36. What relationship is illustrated by an Engel curve? How is an Engel curve derived using indifference curve analysis?

37. What is meant by a normal good? When a good is normal, what conclusions can be drawn about the Engel curve, the income elasticity of demand, and the substitution and income effects?

38. Explain what the substitution and income effects of a price change represent.

39.   What is a compensated demand curve? Why do compensated demand curves always obey the law of demand?

40.   What would a price elasticity of demand equal to –3 indicate? What would an income elasticity of demand equal to –3 indicate?

41.   What are substitutes and complements? How can the cross elasticity of demand be used to identify substitutes and complements?

PROBLEMS

42.   Empirical estimates show that the income elasticity of demand for coffee equals 0.

i.   What will the Engel curve for coffee look like? Explain.

ii.   Explain why the income effect for coffee will be zero. On the axes to the right, design an indifference curve–budget line diagram showing the substitution and income effects created when the price of coffee falls.

All Other Goods

Coffee

iii.   Must the demand curve for coffee be downward sloping? How will the ordinary demand curve for coffee compare with the compensated demand curve? Explain.

43. i.   Consider the indifference curve–budget line diagram on the following page, in which
          the consumer's income is assumed to be $60 per week. Use points A, B, and C to
          derive the demand curve for good X; plot the resulting demand curve on the lower set
          of axes.

     ii.   What is the price elasticity of demand for good X? How can you tell?

     iii. What conclusion can be drawn about the substitution and income effects for good X?

     iv.   Should good X be classified as a normal good or an inferior good? Explain.

All Other Goods

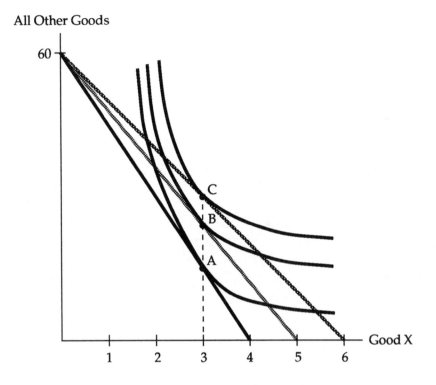

Price of Good X

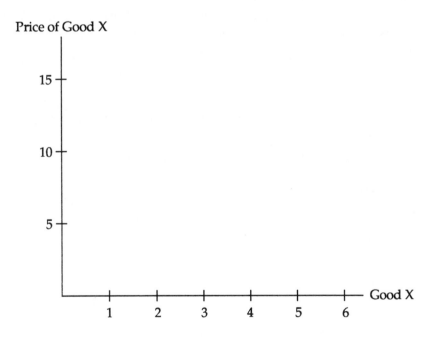

44. i.   On the diagrams below, label the substitution and income effects that would occur when the price rises from P_0 to P_1. Also determine whether each diagram shows ordinary and compensated demand for a normal good or an inferior good.

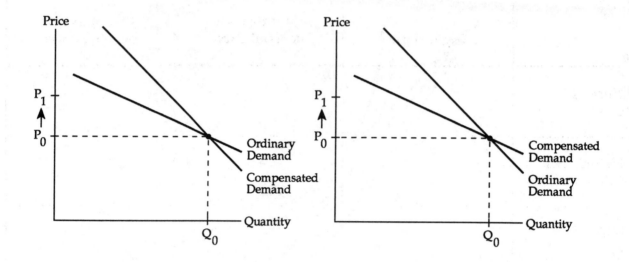

ii.   For a normal good, will the compensated demand curve be more or less elastic than the ordinary demand curve? For an inferior good, will the compensated demand curve be more or less elastic than the ordinary demand curve? Explain.

45. i. For each entry in the table below, indicate whether the graph would be upward-sloping or downward-sloping.

	Engel curve	(Ordinary) demand curve	Compensated demand curve
Normal good			
Non-Giffen inferior good			
Giffen good			

ii. For each entry in the table below, indicate whether quantity demanded would rise or fall.

	PRICE INCREASE			PRICE DECREASE		
	Substitution Effect	Income Effect	Total Effect	Substitution Effect	Income Effect	Total Effect
Normal good						
Non-Giffen inferior good						
Giffen good						

SOLUTIONS

Completion Exercises

1. inferior good
2. Engel curve
3. non-Giffen goods
4. substitution effect
5. normal good

6. income effect
7. compensated demand curve
8. price elasticity of demand
9. complements
10. elastic

True-False Exercises

11. FALSE. The Engel curve for a <u>normal</u> good must slope upwards.
12. TRUE.
13. TRUE.
14. TRUE.
15. FALSE. For a good to be Giffen, it must be inferior and must account for a <u>substantial</u> fraction of the consumer's expenditures.
16. TRUE.
17. FALSE. <u>All</u> goods have compensated demand curves that slope downward.
18. TRUE.
19. TRUE.
20. FALSE. If two goods are substitutes, then the <u>cross</u> elasticity of demand will be positive.

Multiple Choice Questions

21. B. The vertical intercept of the budget line depends only on the consumer's income and the price of the good on the vertical axis.
22. D. The relative prices have not changed, so the slope of the budget line is unchanged. The maximum amounts of the goods that the consumer can buy are also unchanged, so the budget line does not shift towards or away from the origin.
23. C. The Engel curve shown is upward sloping for low income levels, which indicates a normal good, and it is downward sloping for high income levels, which indicates an inferior good.
24. A. The demand curve for good X is derived by examining how the consumer's optimum changes as the price of good X changes while holding other factors constant.

25.   A. The convexity of indifference curves guarantees that substitution effects always move in the direction indicated by the law of demand.

26.   B. Suppose the price of a good rises. The resulting income effect will cause a fall in quantity demanded if the good is a normal good, but it will cause a rise in quantity demanded if the good is an inferior good. Only the former case works in the direction indicated by the law of demand.

27.   B. For inferior goods, the substitution effect supports the law of demand and the income effect works against the law of demand. Since the law of demand holds for non-Giffen goods, the substitution effect must be the larger of the two.

28.   D. Whether or not the good has highly elastic demand depends on the size of the price change (in percentage terms) relative to the size of the change in quantity demanded (in percentage terms).

29.   C. The compensated demand curve will be less elastic than the ordinary demand curve if the commodity in question is a normal good.

30.   B. A compensated demand curve contains only the substitution effect, while an ordinary demand curve includes both substitution and income effects. The two will be the same if and only if the income effect is zero.

31.   B. Income increased from $50 to $55, which is a 10% increase. Quantity demanded increased from 20 to 21, which is a 5% increase. The income elasticity is then $5\% \div 10\% = \frac{1}{2}$.

32.   A. A positive income elasticity indicates that income and quantity demanded move in the same directions. Goods of this type are classified as normal goods.

33.   C. A price elasticity of –2 indicates that a 1% increase in price will cause a 2% decrease in quantity demanded. The price in this case fell by 5%, so the quantity demanded must rise by $-2 \times -5\% = 10\%$.

34.   D. The price elasticity of generic cigarettes will be negative as long as the demand curve is downward sloping. Generic cigarettes are probably an inferior good, so they will have a negative income elasticity. Generic cigarettes and disposable lighters are likely to be complements, so their cross elasticity will be negative. Generic cigarettes and Marlboro cigarettes are clearly substitute goods, and substitutes have positive cross elasticities.

35.   C. Quantity demanded will change by $-0.5 \times 3\% = -1.5\%$. One and one-half percent of 400 million packs is 6 million packs, so the new quantity demanded is 394 million packs.

Review Questions

36. An Engel curve shows the relationship between income and quantity demanded, holding all other relevant factors constant. To derive an Engel curve using indifference curve analysis, we examine how the consumer's optimum changes as we make parallel shifts in the budget line. (These parallel shifts in the budget line represent changes in income.) The Engel curve is obtained by plotting the income level corresponding to each budget line against the quantity demanded of the good at the corresponding optimum.

37. A good is normal when an increase in income causes the consumer to demand more of the good. If a good is normal, then its Engel curve is upward sloping, the income elasticity of demand is positive, and the substitution and income effects work in the same direction.

38. A price change affects both the consumer's real income (meaning the consumer's level of satisfaction) and the relative prices he faces. The substitution effect shows how quantity demanded changes when relative prices change, assuming the consumer has a fixed real income. The income effect shows how quantity demanded changes when real income changes, assuming fixed relative prices.

39. A compensated demand curve is a demand curve which shows only substitution effects; any income effects have been removed. The only time ordinary demand curves violate the law of demand is when the income effect is sufficiently large and in opposition to the substitution effect. Compensated demand curves have no income effects, so this possibility cannot occur.

40. A price elasticity of –3 indicates that every 1% increase in price will cause a 3% drop in quantity demanded. An income elasticity of –3 indicates that every 1% increase in income will cause a 3% drop in quantity demanded, and so the good would be classified as an inferior good.

41. Substitutes are goods that serve roughly the same purpose and can replace one another, while complements are goods that tend to be used together. Substitutes and complements are identified by checking the sign of the cross elasticity of demand between the two goods. If this sign is positive, an increase in the price of one good will increase the quantity demanded of the other. In this case, the consumer is replacing one good with the other, and so the two goods are substitutes. If the cross elasticity is negative, an increase in the price of one good will decrease the quantity demanded of the other. In this situation, the consumer is reducing his purchases of both goods, and so the two goods are complements.

Problems

42.   i.   The zero income elasticity means that a 1% increase in income will cause a 0% change
           in quantity demanded. In other words, the quantity demanded of coffee does not
           change when income changes. The Engel curve must then be horizontal, with the
           quantity demanded remaining fixed at all income levels.

      ii. The income effect must be zero because changes in income have no effect on the
           quantity demanded of coffee. Points B and C must be vertically aligned in the
           illustration of substitution and income effects.

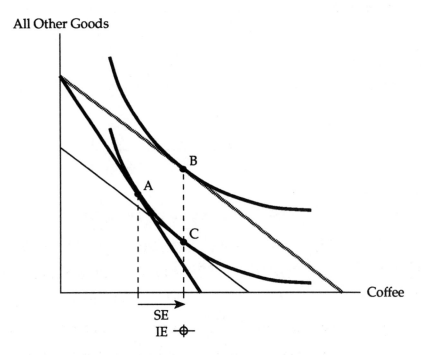

      iii. Yes, the law of demand must hold for coffee. The substitution effect, as always,
           supports the law of demand. In the case of coffee, the income effect is zero; it neither
           supports nor works against the law of demand. Therefore, the substitution effect
           guarantees that the demand curve for coffee will be downward sloping.

               The ordinary demand curve shows the sum of substitution and income effects,
           while the compensated demand curve is based solely on the substitution effect. The
           income effect is zero in this case, so the compensated and ordinary demand curves
           must be identical.

43. i.   Use the horizontal intercepts of the budget lines to determine the price of good X at
          each optimum. For example, the price of good X is $15 per unit at the optimum A,
          because the consumer

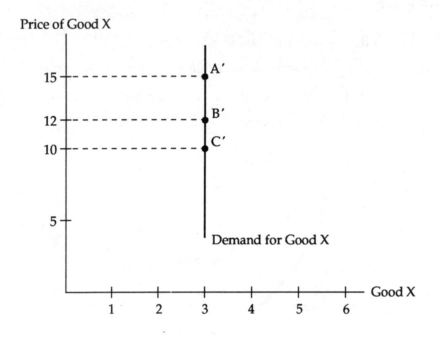

          can purchase a maximum of 4 units of X with his income of $60. Similarly, the price of
          X is $12 per unit at optimum B and is $10 per unit at optimum C. To derive the
          demand curve, these prices must be plotted against the quantity demanded at each
          optimum, which is 3 units of X in all three cases. This procedure gives us the demand
          curve shown above, where A', B', and C' correspond to the optima A, B, and C,
          respectively.

     ii. The price elasticity of demand is calculated by taking the percentage change in
          quantity demanded and dividing it by the percentage change in price. The quantity
          demanded in this case remains constant at 3 units of good X, and so the percentage
          change in quantity demanded is always zero. The price elasticity of demand for good
          X therefore equals 0.

     iii. The substitution and income effects always add up to the total change in quantity
          demanded. The change in quantity demanded is zero in this situation, so the
          substitution and income effects must exactly offset each other. The substitution and
          income effects move in opposite directions and are of the same magnitude.

iv. Good X must be an inferior good, because the income and substitution effects are moving in opposite directions.

44. i. If we follow the compensated demand curve, we get only the substitution effect. The ordinary demand curve shows the substitution and income effects combined, so the difference between the two demand curves is the income effect. This analysis is illustrated in the graphs below.

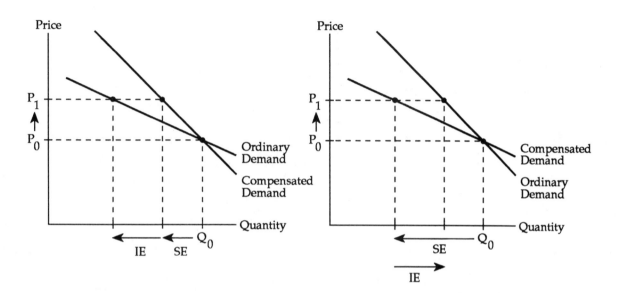

The diagram on the left must show a normal good, because the substitution and income effects are moving in the same direction. The right-hand diagram shows an inferior good, because the substitution and income effects are moving in opposite directions.

ii. The left-hand diagram shows that the compensated demand curve for a normal good will be less elastic than the ordinary demand curve. When the price rises, both the substitution and income effects cause the quantity demanded to fall. The ordinary demand curve includes both effects, while the compensated demand curve includes only the substitution effect. Therefore, we will see a smaller response in quantity demanded with the compensated demand curve, and so the compensated demand curve must be less elastic.

The right-hand diagram shows that the compensated demand curve will be more elastic than the ordinary demand curve in the case of an inferior good. When the price rises in this situation, the substitution effect causes quantity demanded to decrease, while the income effect causes quantity demanded to increase. We will observe a larger response in quantity demanded with the compensated demand curve, because it does not include the income effect that offsets part of the substitution effect. Quantity demanded is more sensitive to changes in price for the compensated demand curve, and so it must be the more elastic.

45. i.

	Engel curve	(Ordinary) demand curve	Compensated demand curve
Normal good	Upward sloping	Downward sloping	Downward sloping
Non-Giffen inferior good	Downward sloping	Downward sloping	Downward sloping
Giffen good	Downward sloping	Upward sloping	Downward sloping

ii.

	PRICE INCREASE			PRICE DECREASE		
	Substitution Effect	Income Effect	Total Effect	Substitution Effect	Income Effect	Total Effect
Normal good	Quantity falls	Quantity falls	Quantity falls	Quantity rises	Quantity rises	Quantity rises
Non-Giffen inferior good	Quantity falls	Quantity rises	Quantity falls	Quantity rises	Quantity falls	Quantity rises
Giffen good	Quantity falls	Quantity rises	Quantity rises	Quantity rises	Quantity falls	Quantity falls

CHAPTER 5

THE BEHAVIOR OF FIRMS

This chapter begins a three-chapter unit studying the supply side of the goods market. The focus for this chapter is the economic decision making of an individual firm. The first section of the chapter shows how to compare a firm's benefits and costs using the equimarginal principle, and the second section applies the equimarginal principle to analyze the firm's production and pricing decisions.

KEY TERMS

- Firm
- Marginal benefit
- Marginal cost
- Equimarginal principle

- Increasing marginal cost
- Fixed cost
- Revenue
- Marginal revenue

- Profit
- Sunk cost

KEY IDEAS

- **Section 5.1.** Marginal benefit is the additional benefit received from the last unit of some economic activity, and marginal cost is the additional cost incurred from the last unit of that activity. The equimarginal principle states that if an activity is worth pursuing at all, it should be pursued up to the point where its marginal cost equals its marginal benefit.

- **Section 5.2.** In order to maximize its profit, a firm expands its production to the level where its marginal cost equals its marginal revenue. Consequently, changes in either marginal cost or the demand for the firm's product will lead to changes in the price the firm charges and/or the quantity it produces. Changes in fixed costs, however, do not affect the price or quantity of the firm's output unless they make the firm so unprofitable that it shuts down its operations.

COMPLETION EXERCISES

1. Any person or organization that produces and supplies goods with the goal of maximizing the profit it earns is called a _____.

2. The difference between revenue and cost is called _____.

3. According to the _____, a profitable activity should be pursued up to the point where its marginal benefit equals its marginal cost.

4. In most economic models, it is assumed that firms attempt to maximize their _____.

5. The additional benefit received from an additional hour of work is called the _____ of working.

6. Insurance payments, interest payments on loan, and rental payments on a building are typical examples of a firm's _____.

7. A cost that can no longer be avoided is called a _____.

8. If growing lettuce is profitable, then a farmer should plant the amount of lettuce that makes the marginal cost of growing lettuce equal to the _____ from selling it.

9. Higher fixed costs do not get passed on to consumers in the form of higher prices; they come totally out of a firm's _____.

10. When a firm's _____ rise, it responds by producing less and/or charging a higher price.

TRUE-FALSE EXERCISES

_____ 11. The net gain from studying is maximized when the total benefit from studying equals its total cost.

_____ 12. If the marginal benefit of studying exceeds its marginal cost, then the student would benefit from increased studying.

_____ 13. If the marginal cost of raising cattle is larger than its marginal revenue, then expanding the herd would increase the rancher's profit.

_____ 14. If a coal mine is profitable, then it should be mined until its coal is completely exhausted.

_____ 15. Profit is calculated by taking price times quantity.

_____ 16. When a firm doubles its production, its fixed costs will also double.

_____ 17. If the price of hamburger meat falls, then the local grill will find it profitable to lower its price and sell more burgers.

_____ 18. When the price of paper rises, a magazine publisher earns the most profit when it chooses not to raise its price.

_____ 19. When faced with a rent increase on his office space, the local accountant should raise his price to keep his profit from falling.

_____ 20. Higher fixed costs will cause an increase in the firm's marginal costs.

MULTIPLE CHOICE QUESTIONS

_____ 21. You spent $15 on a compact disc, only to discover that you hate the music and will never play it again. You can either keep the disc or sell it for $3 to a used record store. Assuming that you have no other options, you should
   A. keep the disc because it cost far more than $3.
   B. keep the disc because its marginal cost of $15 exceeds the marginal benefit of selling it.
   C. sell the disc because its marginal cost of $15 exceeds the marginal benefit of selling it.
   D. sell the disc because the $15 you spent are sunk.

_____ 22. The government has spent $200 million to build a new hydroelectric dam. An additional $50 million in funding is needed to complete the project, but because of budget cuts the government is considering the possibility of abandoning the project. When should the government *not* complete the dam?
A. When the additional benefits from completing the dam are projected to be less than $50 million.
B. When the additional benefits from completing the dam are projected to be less than $150 million.
C. When the additional benefits from completing the dam are projected to be less than $250 million.
D. The government should complete the dam under any circumstances to avoid wasting the $200 million already spent.

_____ 23. A power company has spent $10 million to date on a nuclear power plant, which can be completed for an additional $3 million. However, a new study shows that the electricity generated by the plant will bring in only $5 million in additional revenue. The company
A. should complete the plant because the marginal cost outweighs the marginal benefit.
B. should complete the plant because the marginal benefit is larger than the marginal cost.
C. should accept the $10 million loss and not complete the plant.
D. should not complete the plant because the marginal benefit is smaller than the marginal cost.

◆◆◆ Questions 24–27 refer to the following tables which show the demand for a firm's product and the firm's total cost of production.

Demand			Total Cost	
Quantity	Price		Quantity	Dollars
0 units	$40 per unit		0 units	$ 0
1	35		1	4
2	30		2	13
3	25		3	28
4	20		4	50
5	15		5	80

_____ 24. The marginal cost of producing the third unit is
A. $28 per unit.
B. $25 per unit.
C. $15 per unit.
D. $9.33 per unit.

_____ 25. The marginal revenue received from selling the fifth unit is
A. $75 per unit.
B. $15 per unit.
C. $3 per unit.
D. –$5 per unit.

_____ 26. According to the equimarginal principle, how many units should the firm produce in order to maximize its profit?
  A. 2 units.
  B. 3 units.
  C. 4 units.
  D. 5 units.

_____ 27. The maximum amount of profit this firm can earn is
  A. $80.
  B. $75.
  C. $53.
  D. $47.

_____ 28. As more and more output is produced, a firm's marginal cost generally tends to
  A. increase.
  B. decrease.
  C. remain constant.
  D. change unpredictably.

_____ 29. If marginal revenue exceeds marginal cost, then
  A. the firm is earning a positive level of profit.
  B. the firm should shut down.
  C. the firm's profit will increase if the firm increases its output.
  D. the firm's profit will increase if the firm decreases its output.

_____ 30. Which of the following is the most likely to increase a firm's marginal cost?
  A. An increase in the wage rate.
  B. The adoption of new cost-effective technology.
  C. A fall in the demand for the firm's product.
  D. An increase in the cost of an operating permit required by the local government.

_____ 31. Suppose some of a firm's competitors go out of business, causing the demand for the firm's product to increase. The firm reacts by increasing its production because
  A. its marginal cost has increased.
  B. its marginal cost has decreased.
  C. its marginal revenue has increased.
  D. its marginal revenue has decreased.

_____ 32. Assuming it does not shut down, an increase in the firm's fixed costs will
  A. force the firm to increase the price it charges for its product.
  B. cause the firm to decrease the quantity it produces.
  C. increase the firm's marginal cost.
  D. be paid for out of the firm's profit.

_____ 33. If the demand curve for a firm's product is downward sloping, a decrease in the firm's marginal cost would cause the firm to
   A.   produce more output and charge a higher price for its product.
   B.   produce more output and charge a lower price for its product.
   C.   produce less output and charge a higher price for its product.
   D.   produce less output and charge a lower price for its product.

_____ 34. Which of the following will *not* affect a firm's production and pricing decisions?
   A.   An increase in the price of the insurance policy required by government regulations.
   B.   An increase in the price of the skilled labor it hires.
   C.   An increase in the price charged by its competitors.
   D.   An increase in the price of the raw materials it uses in its production.

_____ 35. Which of the following could cause the firm to increase both the quantity it produces and the price it charges?
   A.   An increase in the price of the insurance required by government regulations.
   B.   An increase in the price of the skilled labor it hires.
   C.   An increase in the price charged by its competitors.
   D.   An increase in the price of the raw materials it uses in its production.

REVIEW QUESTIONS

36. State the equimarginal principle. What course of action would you recommend if it were discovered that the marginal cost of an activity currently outweighs its marginal benefit?

37. What are sunk costs? Why should sunk costs have no effect on economic decision making?

38. What pattern do we generally observe in the marginal cost of production and why does it occur?

39.   According to the equimarginal principle, what could cause a profit-maximizing firm to increase its production?

40.   Why is a firm's marginal cost unaffected by an increase in fixed costs? How would an increase in fixed costs affect the firm's production and pricing decisions?

41.   What factors can change a firm's marginal cost? What factors can change a firm's marginal revenue?

PROBLEMS

42. The state passes a law requiring all accountants to take and pass an annual licensing exam at a cost of $500 per year. Andrea is an accountant affect by the new law.

   i.   Explain why Andrea will not raise her price even though she has to take the exam.

   ii. Explain why Andrea may raise her price because her competitors have to take the exam.

43. i. A firm's total cost schedule and the demand for its product are summarized in the table below. Complete the table and use the equimarginal principle to determine the level of output that maximizes the firm's profit. Also determine the price charged by the firm and its maximum profit level.

Costs			Revenues			
Quantity Produced	Total Cost	Marginal Cost	Quantity Demanded	Price	Total Revenue	Marginal Revenue
0 units	$ 0	—	0 units	$130 per unit		—
1	50		1	120		
2	102		2	110		
3	157		3	100		
4	217		4	90		
5	285		5	80		
6	365		6	70		
7	462		7	60		
8	582		8	50		

ii. Suppose the firm signs a contract with an advertising firm, agreeing to pay $100 for its efforts. Suppose the effect of the advertising is to increase the price consumers are willing to pay for the firm's product by $60 per unit at each and every quantity. Complete the table below to show the new situation that the firm faces. As in part i, determine the firm's level of output, price changed, and maximum profit.

Costs			Revenues			
Quantity Produced	Total Cost	Marginal Cost	Quantity Demanded	Price	Total Revenue	Marginal Revenue
0 units		—	0 units			—
1			1			
2			2			
3			3			
4			4			
5			5			
6			6			
7			7			
8			8			

iii. Suppose instead that the advertising is totally ineffective and does not change the demand for the firm's product. How will the level of output, price charged, and maximum profit determined in part i change under these circumstances? Explain.

44. Suppose that x books can be produced for a total cost of $x^2 + 2x$ dollars. (For example, 1 book can be produced for $1^2 + 2 \cdot 1 = 3$ dollars; 2 books can be produced for $2^2 + 2 \cdot 2 = 8$ dollars; and so forth.)

    i. Find and simplify an algebraic formula for the marginal cost of producing the xth book.

    ii. Suppose the book company has agreed to pay an author a flat fee of $500 for the right to reprint some of his material. Will this agreement increase, decrease, or not change the firm's marginal cost? Prove your answer by finding and simplifying an algebraic formula to represent this situation.

    iii. Suppose instead that the cost of producing the cover for each book has risen by $3 per cover. Will the firm's marginal cost increase, decrease, or remain unchanged in this situation? Again prove your answer by finding and simplifying an algebraic formula to represent the situation.

45.   Suppose the government is considering two different policies for increasing the nation's steel production. The first policy is to give firms in the steel industry an excise subsidy of $10 per ingot. (In other words, the government will give the firm $10 for every ingot it produces.) The second policy is to grant each firm in the steel industry an annual lump-sum subsidy of $10,000. The graphs below show the marginal cost and marginal revenue for the typical firm in the steel industry.

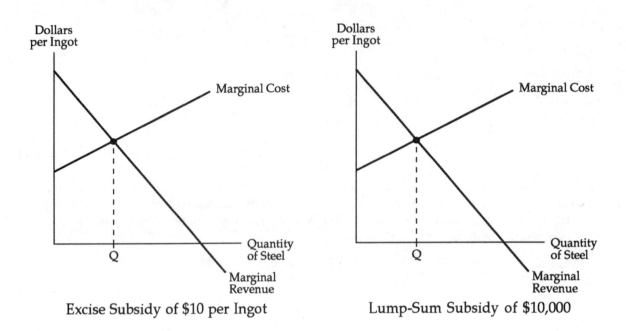

Excise Subsidy of $10 per Ingot   Lump-Sum Subsidy of $10,000

i.   Describe the effect that each policy has on marginal cost, and explain how each policy affects the firm's output. Complete the above graphs to illustrate your arguments.

ii.   If you were a government advisor, which policy would you recommend? Why?

SOLUTIONS

Completion Exercises

1. firm
2. profit
3. equimarginal principle
4. profits
5. marginal benefit

6. fixed costs
7. sunk cost
8. marginal revenue
9. profit
10. marginal costs

True-False Exercises

11. FALSE. The net gain from studying is maximized when the <u>marginal</u> benefit from studying equals its <u>marginal</u> cost.
12. TRUE.
13. FALSE. If the marginal cost of raising cattle is larger than its marginal revenue, then <u>reducing</u> the herd would increase the rancher's profit.
14. FALSE. If a coal mine is profitable, then it should be mined until <u>the marginal cost of mining coal equals the marginal revenue from selling it</u>.
15. FALSE. Profit is calculated by taking <u>revenue minus cost</u>.
16. FALSE. When a firm doubles its production, its fixed costs will <u>remain unchanged</u>.
17. TRUE.
18. FALSE. When the price of paper rises, a magazine publisher earns the most profit when it <u>raises its price and sells fewer magazines</u>.
19. FALSE. When faced with a rent increase on his office space, the local accountant should <u>keep his price unchanged in order to maximize his profit</u>.
20. FALSE. Higher fixed costs will <u>have no effect on</u> the firm's marginal costs.

Multiple Choice Questions

21. D. The $15 you spent on the disc are sunk and cannot be recovered. Taking the $3 is better than keeping the worthless disc.
22. A. The $200 million are sunk and should not affect the government's decision. The project should be scrapped only if the projected benefits are smaller than the marginal cost of $50 million.

23.   B. By completing the power plant, the power company gets a net gain of $2 million. This gain will in part offset the sunk $10 million, which is better than simply writing off this loss.

24.   C. Producing 2 units costs $13 and producing 3 units costs $28, so the third unit contributes an additional $15 in cost.

25.   D. If 4 units are sold, the firm gets $80 ($20 per unit × 4 units) in revenue. If 5 units are sold, the firm gets $75 ($15 per unit × 5 units) in revenue. The fifth unit sold lowers the firm's revenue by $5.

26.   B. At 3 units of output, both marginal revenue and marginal cost equal $15 per unit, so profit must be at a maximum according to the equimarginal principle.

27.   D. The total cost of producing 3 units of output is $28, and the total revenue received from selling 3 units is $75 ($25 per unit × 3 units), which leaves a profit of $47.

28.   A. Firms generally face increasing marginal cost because they must turn to less productive resources as they produce more and more output.

29.   C. The firm's revenue is increasing faster than its cost, so its profit is increasing and the firm should pursue further production.

30.   A. Higher labor costs would increase the cost of producing the last unit of output and hence increase the firm's marginal cost.

31.   C. Marginal revenue is derived from the demand curve for the firm's product. When increased demand causes an increase in marginal revenue, the profit-maximizing quantity moves to the right.

32.   D. Fixed costs do not affect the cost of the last unit produced, so fixed costs do not affect marginal cost. Therefore, an increase in fixed costs does not affect the quantity or price of the firm's output. An increase in fixed costs simply reduces the firm's profit.

33.   B. The intersection of marginal cost and marginal revenue will move to the right, indicating that the firm will increase the quantity it produces. The law of demand implies that the firm must lower its price in order to sell the additional output.

34.   A. The required insurance does not change as the firm's production level changes, so it is a fixed cost. Changes in fixed costs do not affect marginal cost or marginal revenue, and therefore they cannot affect the firm's production and pricing decisions.

35.   C. An increase in the price of a substitute good will increase the demand for the firm's product. The higher demand could allow the firm to charge a higher price and also could

increase marginal revenue. The intersection of marginal cost and marginal revenue would move to the right, indicating a higher output level.

Review Questions

36. The equimarginal principle states that if an activity is worth undertaking at all, then it should be pursued up to the point where its marginal cost equals its marginal benefit. If an activity's marginal cost were larger than its marginal benefit, then the cost of the last unit of an activity would be greater than the benefit it generated. Consequently, the last unit of the activity should not be undertaken in this case, and less of the activity should be pursued. (Note that this conclusion does *not* say that the activity should be totally abandoned, only that it should be cut back.)

37. Sunk costs are costs that can no longer be avoided, such as costs paid in the past. These costs cannot be recovered whether or not an activity is pursued, and so they do not influence marginal cost or marginal benefit. Fixed costs do not affect anything marginal, and so they have no effect on economic decision making.

38. The marginal cost of production tends to increase as more and more of a good is produced. This condition results from the scarcity of resources. For example, land, labor, and machinery can become less and less effective in the production process as they begin to get overused. Furthermore, the most productive resources may no longer be available as the firm continues to increase its output, forcing the firm to rely on less productive resources. Both of these factors create higher marginal cost.

39. The equimarginal principle shows that the firm's production could increase for two possible reasons: lower marginal cost and higher marginal revenue. If the marginal cost curve shifts down or the marginal revenue curve shifts up, then the intersection of the two curves moves to the right, which indicates that the firm will increase its output level.

40. Fixed costs must be paid no matter how much output the firm produces. Fixed costs are sunk the instant the firm chooses to produce its product, so any changes in fixed costs cannot affect the additional cost attributable to the last unit of production. In other words, changes in fixed costs cannot affect marginal cost. Consequently, any changes in fixed costs will not affect the firm's production and pricing decisions, unless they affect profit so adversely that the firm is forced to shut down.

41.   Any change that affects the additional cost attributable to the last unit produced—such as a change in the cost of labor, the cost of raw materials, or the available technology—will affect marginal cost. However, changes in fixed costs like insurance premiums and rental payments do not affect marginal cost. Any change that affects the demand for the firm's product—such as a change in consumers' tastes, consumers' incomes, or the price and availability of competing products—will affect marginal revenue.

Problems

42.   i.   The required exam is a new fixed cost for Andrea. Fixed costs do not affect marginal costs, and according to the equimarginal principle, only marginal costs affect economic decision making. Since her marginal costs are unchanged, Andrea cannot improve her profit by raising her price and providing fewer accounting services.

       ii.   The additional fixed cost imposed by the exam, if sufficiently large, could cause some of Andrea's competitors to end their practices. In this case, Andrea will see an increase in the demand for her accounting services. The marginal revenue of her accounting services would rise, which would cause Andrea to raise her price and provide more accounting services.

43.   i.   The firm chooses to produce 4 units of output, because this amount is where marginal cost equals marginal revenue. According to the demand schedule, the firm should charge $90 per unit for this amount of output. The firm's profit will equal its total revenue minus its total cost, which is $360 – $217 or $143.

	Costs			Revenues		
Quantity Produced	Total Cost	Marginal Cost	Quantity Demanded	Price	Total Revenue	Marginal Revenue
0 units	$ 0	—	0 units	$130 per unit	$ 0	—
1	50	$50 per unit	1	120	120	$120 per unit
2	102	52	2	110	220	100
3	157	55	3	100	300	80
4	217	60	4	90	360	60
5	285	68	5	80	400	40
6	365	80	6	70	420	20
7	462	97	7	60	420	0
8	582	120	8	50	400	–20

       ii.   Once the contract is signed, the advertising becomes a fixed cost that must be paid no matter how much output the firm produces. Consequently, all entries in the total cost column have risen by $100, but the marginal cost column is unchanged. The entries in the price column have increased by $60 per unit, indicating that consumers are now willing to pay $60 per unit more at each and every quantity because of the advertising. Notice that marginal revenue has changed because demand has changed, affecting the application of the equimarginal principle. The firm will increase its output to 6 units (where marginal cost equals the new marginal revenue), charge $130 per unit, and make a profit of $315.

Costs			Revenues			
Quantity Produced	Total Cost	Marginal Cost	Quantity Demanded	Price	Total Revenue	Marginal Revenue
0 units	$100	—	0 units	$190 per unit	$ 0	—
1	150	$50 per unit	1	180	180	$180 per unit
2	202	52	2	170	340	160
3	257	55	3	160	480	140
4	317	60	4	150	600	120
5	385	68	5	140	700	100
6	465	80	6	130	780	80
7	562	97	7	120	840	60
8	682	120	8	110	880	40

iii. If the advertising does not affect demand, then neither marginal cost nor marginal revenue will have changed from part i. Therefore, the equimarginal principle implies that the quantity and price of the firm's output will be unchanged. The fixed cost of advertising will come totally out of the firm's profit, lowering it to $43.

44. i. According to the problem, producing x books requires a total cost of $x^2 + 2x$ dollars. If we substitute $x - 1$ for x in this formula, we see that producing $x - 1$ books requires a total cost of $(x - 1)^2 + 2(x - 1) = (x^2 - 2x + 1) + (2x - 2) = x^2 - 1$ dollars.

To find marginal cost, we need to find the additional cost attributable to the xth book. If we take the total cost of producing x books and subtract the total cost of producing $x - 1$ books, we will get the cost of the xth book. Therefore, marginal cost equals $(x^2 + 2x) - (x^2 - 1) = 2x + 1$ dollars per book.

(*Note* – If we used calculus and made the units infinitesimally small, the formula for marginal cost would become $2x + 2$ dollars per book.)

ii. The payment to the author is made no matter how many books are produced, so it is a new fixed cost. Changes in fixed costs do not affect marginal cost, so marginal cost should remain unchanged.

To show this result algebraically, repeat the procedure used in part i. First notice that the total cost of producing x books is now $x^2 + 2x + 500$ dollars. Next find the total cost of producing x − 1 books by substituting x − 1 for x in this formula: $(x − 1)^2 + 2(x − 1) + 500 = (x^2 − 2x + 1) + (2x − 2) + 500 = x^2 + 499$ dollars. Finally, marginal cost will be equal to the difference between the total cost of producing x books and the total cost of producing x − 1 books: $(x^2 + 2x + 500) − (x^2 + 499) = 2x + 1$ dollars per book. We see that marginal cost is still $2x + 1$ dollars per book despite the $500 increase in fixed costs.

(*Note* − If we used calculus and made the units infinitesimally small, the formula for marginal cost would again become $2x + 2$ dollars per book.)

iii.   The more expensive cover will increase the cost of the last book produced by $3, so marginal cost will increase by $3 per book.

To prove this algebraically, we again need to repeat the procedure used in part i. First notice that the cost of producing each book has increased by $3, so x books will cost 3x dollars more to produce. The total cost of producing x books must now be $x^2 + 2x + 3x$ or $x^2 + 5x$ dollars. Next, use this formula to calculate the cost of producing x − 1 books: $(x − 1)^2 + 5(x − 1) = (x^2 − 2x + 1) + (5x − 5) = x^2 + 3x − 4$ dollars. Finally, take the difference between the total costs of producing x and x − 1 books to find marginal cost: $(x^2 + 5x) − (x^2 + 3x − 4) = 2x + 4$ dollars per book. As we predicted, marginal cost has increased by $3 per book, from $2x + 1$ to $2x + 4$ dollars per book.

(*Note* − If we used calculus and made the units infinitesimally small, the new marginal cost formula would be $2x + 5$ dollars per book.)

45.   i.   The firm will get $10 for each ingot produced from the excise subsidy. The firm's cost of producing the last ingot is lowered by $10, so marginal cost falls by precisely $10 per ingot. The reduced marginal cost will cause the firm to increase the quantity of its output as shown in the left-hand graph below.

The annual lump-sum subsidy will lower the firm's fixed costs, because the government pays the firm $10,000 no matter how much the firm produces. The cost of producing the last ingot is unchanged, and so marginal cost is also unchanged. Consequently, the application of the equimarginal principle is unaffected by the lump-sum subsidy, and the firm's output level will be unchanged as shown in the right-hand graph below. The lump-sum subsidy will simply help pay the firm's fixed costs and increase the firm's profit by $10,000.

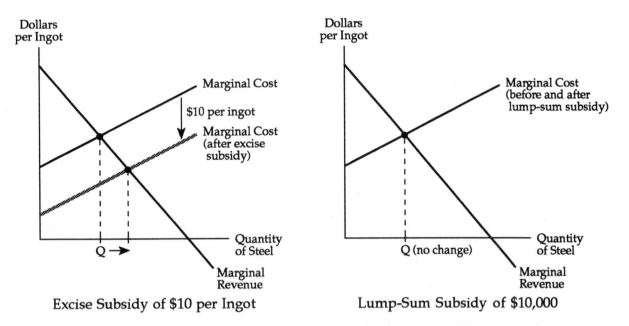

Excise Subsidy of $10 per Ingot   Lump-Sum Subsidy of $10,000

ii.   If the government's goal is to increase steel production, the excise subsidy should be chosen. As shown in part i, the excise subsidy induces existing steel producers to increase their output. The immediate effect of the lump-sum subsidy is to increase the firm's profit, not its output. The lump-sum subsidy would only stimulate steel production after a substantial period of time, as new firms are attracted to the steel industry by the higher profit created by the $10,000 subsidy.

CHAPTER 6

PRODUCTION AND COSTS

This chapter continues the study of the supply side of the goods market with a closer examination of costs. A firm's costs depend on two factors: the available technology and the prices of inputs. This chapter develops the tools economists use to describe a firm's technology and analyzes the relationship between production and cost.

KEY TERMS

- Consumption goods (or outputs)
- Factors of production (or inputs)
- Capital
- Fixed factor of production
- Variable factor of production
- Short run
- Long run
- Total product (TP)
- Short-run production function
- Marginal product of labor (MPL)
- Average product of labor (APL)
- First stage of production

- Second stage of production
- Diminishing marginal returns
- Point of diminishing marginal returns
- Rental rate (P_K)
- Wage rate (P_L)
- Fixed cost (FC)
- Variable cost (VC)
- Total cost (TC)
- Average variable cost (AVC)
- Average (or average total) cost (AC)
- Marginal cost (MC)
- Technologically inefficient
- Unit isoquant

- Isoquant
- Marginal rate of technical substitution of labor for capital ($MRTS_{LK}$)
- Production function
- Isocost
- Expansion path
- Long-run total cost (LRTC)
- Long-run average cost (LRAC)
- Long-run marginal cost (LRMC)
- Increasing returns to scale
- Constant returns to scale
- Decreasing returns to scale

KEY IDEAS

◆ **Section 6.1.** In the short run, some inputs are fixed (that is, the quantity of those inputs cannot be changed during the given time period) and some are variable (that is, the firm can change the quantities it employs). Total, average, and marginal product curves describe the relationship between the amount of a variable input employed and the resulting level of output, assuming all other inputs are fixed. Total, average, average variable, and marginal cost curves describe the relationship between output and cost in the short run and can be derived from the product curves. The U-shape of short-run average, average variable, and marginal cost curves reflects the diminishing marginal returns to the variable input which are eventually encountered.

◆ **Section 6.2.** In the long run, all inputs are variable. An isoquant shows the various combinations of labor and capital that can be used to produce a given level of output. The slope of an isoquant measures the marginal rate of technical substitution of labor for capital, which is the amount of capital that can replace a unit of labor while holding the output level fixed. An isocost shows the various combinations of labor and capital that can be employed at a given cost; the slope of the isocosts is determined by the relative price of labor in terms of capital. The expansion path is the set of tangencies between isoquants and isocosts; these points are the cost-efficient combinations of labor and capital available in the long run. At all points on the expansion path, the marginal rate of technical substitution of labor for capital equals the relative price of labor in terms of capital. Long-run total, average, and marginal cost curves describe the relationship between output and cost in the long run and can be derived from the expansion path. Assuming factor prices are fixed, the long-run average cost curves is downward-sloping when there are increasing returns to scale, horizontal when there are constant returns to scale, and upward-sloping when there are decreasing returns to scale.

◆ **Section 6.3.** The isoquant-isocost diagram can also be used to derive short-run product and cost curves, which allows us to directly compare short-run and long-run costs. This analysis shows that short-run total cost is always at least as great as long-run total cost. Consequently, every short-run total cost curve is tangent to the long-run total cost curve. The same results hold for average cost.

COMPLETION EXERCISES

1. Economists classify the _____ into three broad categories: land, labor, and capital.

2. In economic models of firm behavior, the _____ refers to a period of time sufficient for all inputs to be variable.

3. The additional output attributable to the last unit of labor employed is called the

    _____ .

4. An additional worker will increase the average product of labor when the firm is operating in the _____.

5. If labor is the only variable factor, then the firm's variable cost equals the _____ times the amount of labor used.

6. The _____ shows the set of all technologically efficient combinations of labor and capital that can produce one unit of output.

7. At all points on the expansion path, the _____ must equal the relative price of labor in terms of capital.

8. The long-run average cost curve will be horizontal if the firm's technology exhibits _____.

9. If a 5% increase in all inputs causes total output to increase by only 2%, then the firm's technology exhibits _____.

10. The points on the firm's _____ are used to derive the firm's long-run cost curves.

TRUE-FALSE EXERCISES

_____ 11. During the short run, the firm cannot change the price of its product.

_____ 12. Throughout the first stage of production, the marginal product of labor rises as more workers are used.

_____ 13. When there are diminishing marginal returns, each additional worker adds less and less additional output.

_____ 14. In the second stage of production, the crowding caused by an additional worker makes the other workers less productive.

_____ 15. Total cost equals the sum of average and marginal costs.

_____ 16. When labor is the only variable input, short-run marginal cost equals the wage rate divided by the average product of labor.

_____ 17. Along an isocost, the firm's marginal cost is constant.

_____ 18. When there are constant returns to scale, a 5% increase in labor usage leads to a 5% increase in output.

_____ 19. Under conditions of decreasing returns to scale, a firm's long-run average cost curve slopes downward.

_____ 20. Short-run average cost is always greater than or equal to long-run average cost.

MULTIPLE CHOICE QUESTIONS

_____ 21. If the firm can adjust its employment of some but not all factors of production, then
A.   the firm is in the short run.
B.   labor yields diminishing marginal returns.
C.   all factors of production are variable.
D.   the firm cannot change its level of output.

_____ 22. Which of the following would cause the total product of labor curve to shift upward?
A.   An increase in the amount of labor employed.
B.   An increase in the amount of capital employed.
C.   An increase in the wage rate.
D.   An increase in the rental rate.

_____ 23. The short-run marginal cost curve becomes upward sloping because of
A.   rising input prices.
B.   diminishing marginal returns to labor.
C.   decreasing returns to scale.
D.   a diminishing marginal rate of technical substitution of labor for capital.

_____ 24. When labor's marginal product is greater than its average product, the firm is
A.   experiencing decreasing returns to scale.
B.   beyond the point of diminishing marginal returns.
C.   in the first stage of production.
D.   in the second stage of production.

_____ 25. Assume capital is fixed and labor is variable in the short run. If the wage rate paid to labor rises, which of the following short-run cost curves will shift upward?
   A. The average cost curve.
   B. The average variable cost curve.
   C. The marginal cost curve.
   D. The marginal, average, and average variable cost curves will all shift upward.

_____ 26. Which of the following statements about the isoquant diagram is _false?_
   A. Each isoquant shows the technologically efficient combinations of labor and capital that can produce a particular level of output.
   B. The magnitude of the slope of an isoquant equals the $MRTS_{LK}$.
   C. Points that lie to the northeast of the unit isoquant are technologically inefficient ways of producing one unit of output.
   D. Isoquants are convex because of diminishing marginal returns to labor.

_____ 27. Which of the following statements about the marginal rate of technical substitution of labor for capital ($MRTS_{LK}$) is _false?_
   A. The $MRTS_{LK}$ gives the amount of capital which can be substituted for a unit of labor while keeping the output level constant.
   B. The $MRTS_{LK}$ equals the marginal product of capital divided by the marginal product of labor.
   C. The $MRTS_{LK}$ along an isoquant is decreasing as more labor and less capital is used.
   D. All points on the firm's expansion path have the same $MRTS_{LK}$.

_____ 28. Which of the following statements about the expansion path is _false?_
   A. In the long run, the firm will limit its use of labor and capital to combinations that lie on the expansion path.
   B. The expansion path shows combinations of labor and capital that minimize the cost of producing given levels of output.
   C. The expansion path shows combinations of labor and capital that maximize the output produced for given levels of total cost.
   D. The firm's long-run profit is at a maximum for all combinations of labor and capital on the expansion path.

_____ 29. A firm is currently producing 600 units of output using 150 hours of labor and 50 hours of capital. The marginal product of labor is 10 units of output per hour, and the marginal product of capital is 30 units of output per hour. If the wage rate is $5 per hour and the rental rate is $10 per hour, then
   A. the firm's use of labor and capital is cost-efficient.
   B. the firm can produce more output for the same total cost by using more labor and more capital.
   C. the firm can produce more output for the same total cost by using more labor and less capital.
   D. the firm can produce more output for the same total cost by using more capital and less labor.

_____ 30. Assume that labor is on the horizontal axis and capital is on the vertical axis in the isoquant-isocost diagram. If the wage rate paid to labor rises, then the expansion path will
    A. shift up.   C. shift unpredictably.
    B. shift down.   D. not change.

_____ 31. Assuming input prices are fixed, a downward-sloping long-run average cost curve indicates that the firm is experiencing
    A. increasing returns to scale.
    B. constant returns to scale.
    C. decreasing returns to scale.
    D. diminishing marginal returns to labor.

_____ 32. Which of the following provides an explanation of decreasing returns to scale that is acceptable to most economists?
    A. Specialization of labor.
    B. Limited factory space.
    C. Limits on entrepreneurial skills.
    D. Increasing input prices.

◆◆◆ Questions 33–35 refer to the following diagram. The wage rate is assumed to be $20 per hour, the rental rate is assumed to be $10 per hour, and capital is assumed to be fixed at 20 hours in the short run.

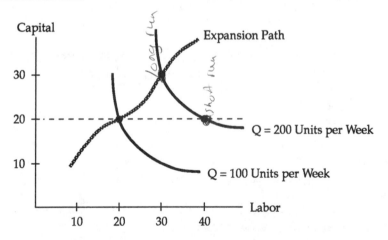

_____ 33. The short-run total cost of producing 200 units of output per week is
    A. $500.   C. $900.
    B. $600.   D. $1,000.

_____ 34. The long-run average cost of producing 200 units of output per week is
    A. $3 per unit.   C. $5 per unit.
    B. $4.50 per unit.   D. $30 per unit.

_____ 35. The short-run total cost curve must be tangent to the long-run average cost curve
    A. at 100 units of output per week.
    B. at 200 units of output per week.
    C. somewhere between 100 and 200 units of output per week.
    D. at some output level below 100 units per week.

REVIEW QUESTIONS

36.   What pattern do we generally observe in the average product of labor and why does it occur?

37.   Suppose a firm's short-run production function is described by the formula $Q = \sqrt{L}$. The firm's fixed costs are $100, and the wage rate is $5 per hour. Find and simplify algebraic formulas expressing the firm's short-run total, average, and marginal costs as functions of output.

38.   What does the slope of an isoquant represent? What does the slope of an isocost represent? When will these two values be equal for a firm?

39.   What is the significance of the points on the firm's expansion path? What equation characterizes these combinations of labor and capital?

40.   Explain why each short-run average cost curve lies above and is tangent to the long-run average cost curve.

41.   How are diminishing marginal returns to labor and decreasing returns to scale similar? How are they different?

PROBLEMS

42.   i.   The following table shows how the firm's total product varies with the amount of labor it employs. Complete the table by calculating the firm's average and marginal products of labor.

Quantity of Labor	Total Product (TP)	Average Product of Labor (APL)	Marginal Product of Labor (MPL)
1 worker	10 units of output	10 units per worker	10 units per worker
2	22		
3	36		
4	48		
5	58		
6	66		

ii.   Identify the first and second stages of production.

iii.   When does the firm reach the point of diminishing marginal returns?

43.   i.   Under a new government law, each television produced must now contain a "V-chip"
            that permits parents to block reception of certain programs. The V-chip raises firms'
            production costs by $50 per television. Will the new law affect a television
            manufacturer's short-run average cost curve? Will the new law affect the short-run
            marginal cost curve? Explain.

      ii.   Under a new government law, each television manufacturer must contribute $10,000
            per year to help fund a commission that establishes technological formats and
            standards for the television industry. Will the new law affect a television
            manufacturer's short-run average cost curve? Will the new law affect the short-run
            marginal cost curve? Explain.

44.   A firm produces 2,000 video tapes per day using 10 workers and 5 machines. A worker costs $160 per day, and a machine costs $280 per day. Either 2 additional workers or 1 additional machine would increase the firm's output to 2,200 tapes per day.

    i.   Calculate the marginal rate of technical substitution of labor for capital (i.e., the slope of the firm's isoquant).

    ii.   Calculate the relative price of labor in terms of capital (i.e., the slope of the firm's isocost).

    iii.   Financial constraints prevent the firm from spending more than $3,000 per day on its inputs. What, if anything, can the firm do to increase its output beyond 2,000 tapes per day? Explain.

45.   Suppose a firm's technology is described by the production function $Q = \sqrt{K \cdot L}$.

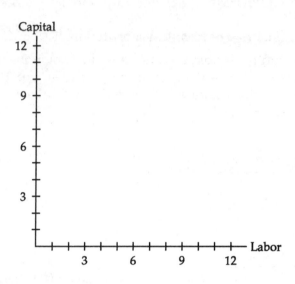

i.   On the axes above, graph the isoquant for the output levels Q = 2, 4, and 6. (*Hint:* You
        need to find combinations of L and K that will make Q equal these values in the
        formula of the production function. For example, both L = 1, K = 4 and L = 2, K = 2
        make Q = 2 in the formula, so both of these points are on the Q = 2 isoquant.)

ii.   Suppose P_L = $3 per hour and P_K = $3 per hour. On your diagram, graph the isocosts
        corresponding to total costs of $12, $24, and $36. Using the isoquants and isocosts
        you've graphed, locate three points on the expansion path. Sketch in the expansion
        path on your diagram.

iii.   Explain why this technology exhibits constant returns to scale.

iv. Using the three points you found on the expansion path, calculate the firm's long-run average cost at each of those points. Summarize your calculations in the appropriate table below and sketch the firm's long-run average cost curve on the axes provided.

v.   Suppose the firm's level of capital usage is fixed at K = 4 in the short run. On your isoquant diagram, find three points available to the firm in the short run. Calculate the firm's short-run average cost for each of these points. As in part iv, summarize your results in the appropriate table and sketch the firm's short-run average cost curve on the axes provided below.

Q	L	K	LRTC	LRAC
2				
4				
6				

Q	L	K	SRTC	SRAC
2		4		
4		4		
6		4		

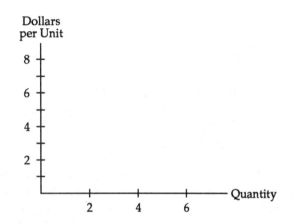

vi. Explain why the short-run and long-run average cost curves graphed in part v have such different shapes.

SOLUTIONS

Completion Exercises

1. factors of production
2. long run
3. marginal product of labor
4. first stage of production
5. wage rate

6. unit isoquant
7. marginal rate of technical substitution
8. constant returns to scale
9. decreasing returns to scale
10. expansion path

True-False Exercises

11. FALSE. During the short run, the firm cannot change its employment of fixed inputs.
12. FALSE. Throughout the first stage of production, the average product of labor rises as more workers are used.
13. TRUE.
14. TRUE.
15. FALSE. Total cost equals the sum of fixed and variable costs.
16. FALSE. When labor is the only variable input, short-run marginal cost equals the wage rate divided by the marginal product of labor.
17. FALSE. Along an isocost, the firm's total cost is constant.
18. FALSE. When there are constant returns to scale, a 5% increase in the use of all inputs leads to a 5% increase in output.
19. FALSE. Under conditions of decreasing returns to scale, a firm's long-run average cost curve slopes upward.
20. TRUE.

Multiple Choice Questions

21. A. The short run is defined as a period of time during which some inputs are fixed and some inputs are variable.
22. B. With additional capital, more output could be produced at each level of labor usage, so the total product curve would shift up.
23. B. Marginal cost is upward sloping beyond the point of diminishing marginal returns. In this situation, each hour of labor provides less and less additional output, and so each additional unit of output must require higher and higher labor costs.

24. C. When marginal product is greater than average product, an additional laborer is more productive than the average laborer because of increased opportunities for specialization.

25. D. Variable cost has increased, and so average variable coat and average cost have risen. Changes in variable cost affect the additional cost attributable to the last unit of output produced, so marginal cost rises as well.

26. D. Isoquants are convex because the $MRTS_{LK}$ is diminishing along an isoquant as more labor and less capital is used.

27. B. The $MRTS_{LK}$ is equal to the marginal product of labor divided by the marginal product of capital. If one less hour of labor is employed, MPL units of output are lost. One unit of output could be produced by 1/MPK hours of capital, and so MPL/MPK hours of capital could replace 1 hour of labor without altering the level of output.

28. D. A firm's costs and revenues must be compared to determine if profit is at a maximum. The expansion path can be used to determine a firm's long-run costs, but it contains no information about the firm's revenues.

29. D. The absolute value of the slope of the isoquant is given by MPL divided by MPK, which equals $^{10}\!/_{30}$ or $\frac{1}{3}$ hour of capital per hour of labor. The absolute value of the slope of the isocost is P_L divided by P_K, which equals $^5\!/_{10}$ or $\frac{1}{2}$ hour of capital per hour of labor. The isocost is steeper than the isoquant, so the firm's use of labor and capital lies below the expansion path. In this case, the firm needs to use more capital and less labor to keep total cost fixed and reach the expansion path.

30. A. The isocosts become steeper when the wage rate rises, and so the set of tangencies between the isoquants and isocosts will lie further up the isoquants.

31. A. When increasing returns to scale exist, a 1% increase in all inputs causes output to increase by more than 1%. In this case, output is rising by a greater percentage than the firm's total cost, which makes the long-run average cost curve downward sloping.

32. C. Decreasing returns to scale is a reasonable assumption only if some factors, such as entrepreneurial skills, are fixed even in the long run.

33. D. In the short run, the firm will use 40 hours of labor and 20 hours of capital to produce 200 units of output weekly. The firm will spend $800 on labor and $200 on capital, for a total of $1,000.

34. B. In the long run, the firm will use 30 hours of labor and 30 hours of capital to produce 200 units of output weekly. The firm will spend $600 on labor and $300 on capital, for a

total of $900. Long-run average cost must then be $900 ÷ 200 units of output = $4.50 per unit.

35.   A. Only one point on the expansion path contains the short-run level of capital. The firm will use 20 hours of labor and 20 hours of capital to produce 100 units of output weekly in both the short run and the long run. The short-run and long-run total cost of 100 units is $600.

Review Questions

36.   The average product of labor tends to be increasing for low levels of output and decreasing for higher levels of output. Recall that capital is assumed to be a fixed input in the short run. At relatively low levels of output, the firm is in the first stage of production. As more labor is used, the firm can take advantage of increased specialization of labor. Consequently, the additional worker makes the other workers more productive, and so the average product of labor is rising. At relatively high levels of output, the firm is in the second stage of production. The fixed capital is scarce relative to the available labor. An additional worker adds to crowding and thus reduces the productivity of other workers.

37.   First notice that the short-run production function implies $L = Q^2$. This formula along with the wage rate of $5 per hour allows us to calculate variable cost: $VC = P_L \cdot L = 5Q^2$. Next, we can use the formula for VC along with the fixed cost of $100 to calculate total cost and average cost: $TC = VC + FC = 5Q^2 + 100$, and $AC = {}^{TC}/_Q = (5Q^2 + 100)/Q = 5Q + {}^{100}/_Q$. Fixed costs do not affect marginal cost, so we may use either variable cost or total cost to calculate marginal cost. If we use variable cost, we get $MC = 5Q^2 - 5(Q - 1)^2 = 5Q^2 - (5Q^2 - 10Q + 5) = 10Q - 5$. (*Note* – If we used calculus and made the units infinitesimally small, the marginal cost formula would simplify to $MC = 10Q$.)

38.   The absolute value of an isoquant's slope equals the marginal rate of technical substitution of labor for capital ($MRTS_{LK}$), which shows the amount of capital which can be substituted for the last unit of labor used while still keeping the same level of output. The absolute value of the isocosts' slope is equal to the ratio of the wage and rental rates (P_L/P_K), which measures the relative price of labor in terms of capital. These two values will be equal in the long run, when the firm can vary all its factors and choose a cost-efficient combination of labor and capital from its expansion path.

39. The expansion path shows the combinations of labor and capital that are cost-efficient for the firm in the long run. If the firm wishes to produce the maximum output for a given total cost, it must choose a point on the expansion path. Furthermore, if the firm wishes to produce a particular level of output for the lowest possible total cost, it must again choose a point on the expansion path. The equation $MRTS_{LK} = P_L/P_K$ holds for all points on the expansion path.

40. When the firm makes its long-run choice from the expansion path, it is committed to that level of capital usage for the short run. As long as the firm stays on the expansion path, it will produce its chosen output level at the lowest possible average cost. If the firm makes any short-run deviation from this level of output, its average cost will be higher than the minimum possible because the fixed level of capital implies that the firm cannot remain on its expansion path. Therefore, the firm's short-run average cost will be higher than its long-run average cost for levels of output different from its long-run choice.

41. Diminishing marginal returns to labor and decreasing returns to scale both describe how output changes when the firm's use of inputs changes. Other than this similarity, the two concepts have little in common. First, the concept of diminishing marginal returns deals with output at the margin, while the concept of decreasing returns to scale deals with total and average output. When diminishing marginal returns to labor exist, the *additional* output attributable to the last hour of labor employed is falling. When decreasing returns to scale exist, a 1% increase in the use of all inputs causes *total* output to increase by less than 1%. Second, marginal returns applies in the short run while returns to scale applies in the long run. The short-run marginal cost curve becomes upward sloping because of diminishing marginal returns to labor. On the other hand, the long-run average cost curve becomes upward sloping when decreasing returns to scale exist.

Problems

42. i. Divide total product by the amount of labor to get the average product of labor. Divide the change in total product by the change in labor usage to get the marginal product of labor. These calculations are summarized in the table at the top of the following page.

    ii. In the first stage of production, average product is rising and marginal product is larger than average product. This occurs when the firm employs fewer than 4 workers.

Quantity of Labor	Total Product (TP)	Average Product of Labor (APL)	Marginal Product of Labor (MPL)
1 worker	10 units of output	10 units per worker	10 units per worker
2	22	11	12
3	36	12	14
4	48	12	12
5	58	11.6	10
6	66	11	8

In the second stage of production, average product is falling and marginal product is smaller than average product. This occurs when the firm employs more than 4 workers.

iii. The firm reaches the point of diminishing marginal returns at the third worker, when labor's marginal product begins to decline.

43. i. Both the average and marginal cost curves will shift upwards by $50 per television. The new law affects the cost of producing *each* television. Since the cost of producing the first, second, and each subsequent television has risen by $50, the average cost of producing a television has also risen by $50. Marginal cost increases because the cost of the last television produced has risen by $50.

ii. The law imposes a new fixed cost on the television manufacturer. Average cost is the sum of average fixed cost and average variable cost, so the average cost curve shifts upwards by $10,000 divided by the number of televisions produced. On the other hand, the new fixed cost does not affect the cost of the last television produced, so the marginal cost curve is unchanged.

44. i. Since 2 workers increase the firm's output by 200 tapes, the marginal product of labor is 100 tapes per worker. Since 1 machine increases the firm's output by 200 tapes, the marginal product of capital is 200 tapes per machine. The marginal rate of technical substitution equals the ratio of marginal products, so $MRTS_{LK}$ equals 100 tapes per worker divided by 200 tapes per machine, or ½ machine per worker.

ii. The relative price of labor in terms of capital equals the wage rate divided by the rental rate. Thus, the relative price is $160 per worker divided by $280 per machine, or 4/7 machine per worker.

iii. Notice that the firm's total cost is $160 × 10 workers + $280 × 5 machines, or $3,000. However, the firm is not on its expansion path because $MRTS_{LK}$ does not equal P_L/P_K. Therefore, the firm can increase its output without raising its total cost. Since $MRTS_{LK}$ is less than P_L/P_K, the firm is below its expansion path and should employ less labor and more capital.

45. i. The points (1, 4), (2, 2), and (4, 1) are on the $Q = 2$ isoquant, the points (2, 8), (4, 4), and (8, 2) are on the $Q = 4$ isoquant, and the points (4, 9), (6, 6), and (9, 4) are on the $Q = 6$ isoquant. The isoquants are shown in the top graph on the following page.

   ii. The isocosts all have a slope of –1 with vertical intercepts at 4, 8, and 12. The tangencies between the isoquants and isocosts fall at the points (2, 2), (4, 4), and (6, 6). Thus, the expansion path in this case is a 45° line from the origin, as shown at the top of the following page.

   iii. The easiest way to show that this technology exhibits constant returns to scale is to consider the points (2, 2), (4, 4), and (6, 6) on the expansion path. The amounts of labor and capital double from the first point to the second, and the isoquant map shows that the output level also doubles from $Q = 2$ to $Q = 4$. Similarly, the amounts of labor and capital increase by 50% from the second point to the third, causing the output level to increase by 50% from $Q = 4$ to $Q = 6$. By definition, this technology exhibits constant returns to scale.

   iv. The isocosts provide LRTC for each point on the expansion path. Find LRAC using the formula $LRAC = {}^{LRTC}\!/_Q$. The resulting table and graph are shown on the following page.

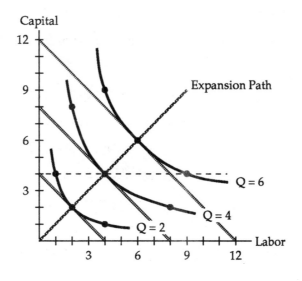

Q	L	K	LRTC	LRAC
2	2	2	12	6
4	4	4	24	6
6	6	6	36	6

Q	L	K	SRTC	SRAC
2	1	4	15	7.5
4	4	4	24	6
6	9	4	39	6.5

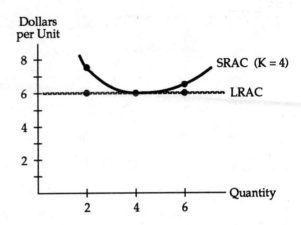

v.   Use the factor prices to calculate SRTC for each point on the horizontal line at K = 4. Find SRAC using the formula SRAC = $^{SRTC}\!/_Q$. The resulting table and graph are shown above.

vi. The shape of the short-run average cost curve is determined by marginal returns to labor. For this firm, short-run production obeys the law of diminishing marginal returns to labor, which makes the SRAC curve have its standard U-shape. On the other hand, the shape of the long-run average cost curve is determined by returns to scale. This firm's production exhibits constant returns to scale, which makes its long-run average cost curve horizontal.

CHAPTER 7

COMPETITION

This chapter concludes the three-chapter unit studying the supply side of the goods market. The chapter provides new insights into supply-demand analysis by combining the information on profit-maximization from Chapter 5 with the fundamentals of production and cost studied in Chapter 6.

KEY TERMS

- Perfectly competitive firm
- Short-run supply curve
- Long-run supply curve
- Shutdown price
- Elasticity of supply

- Competitive industry
- Factor-price effect
- Accounting profit
- Economic profit
- Zero-profit condition

- Break-even price
- Constant-cost industry
- Increasing-cost industry
- Decreasing-cost industry

KEY IDEAS

- **Section 7.1.** A competitive firm's demand and marginal revenue curves are horizontal at the market price. The competitive firm's supply curve is the portion of its marginal cost curve that lies above its average variable cost curve. The firm will shut down if the price falls below its average variable cost.

- **Section 7.2.** The short-run supply curve for a competitive industry is the horizontal sum of all the individual firms' supply curves. If the industry accounts for a substantial portion of the demand for a variable input, then the factor-price effect must also be taken into account, which makes the industry's short-run supply less elastic. Changes in marginal cost will cause a shift in the industry's short-run supply curve, but changes in fixed costs will not affect the industry's short-run supply.

◆   **Section 7.3.** The competitive firm's long-run supply curve is that portion of its long-run marginal cost curve that lies above its long-run average cost curve. The firm's long-run supply will be more elastic than its short-run supply.

◆   **Section 7.4.** In the long run, entry and exit are unrestricted in a competitive industry. A firm will enter (exit) an industry if the market price is greater than (less than) its break-even price. If all firms are identical, then all firms earn a zero profit in the long run and produce their output at the lowest possible average cost.

◆   **Section 7.5.** A constant-cost industry is one in which all firms have identical cost curves which do not change as the industry expands or contracts. Constant-cost industries typically do not require specialized skills and are too small to affect the price of any input. The long-run supply curve for a constant-cost industry is horizontal at the firms' break-even price.

◆   **Section 7.6.** An increasing-cost industry is one in which the break-even price for new entrants rises as the industry expands. An industry will be increasing-cost if some firms are more efficient than others or if the factor-price effect causes higher production costs as the industry expands. The long-run supply curve for an increasing-cost industry is upward sloping but more elastic than the short-run supply curve. A decreasing-cost industry is one in which the break-even price for new entrants falls as the industry expands. This occurs when the entry of new firms allows the industry to be more efficiently structured, causing production costs to fall. The long-run supply curve for a decreasing-cost industry is downward sloping.

◆   **Section 7.7.** The competitive model can be used to analyze taxes, rent controls, and other policies. Increases in fixed costs or marginal costs will reduce firms' profitability and raise their break-even prices, causing an upward shift in the industry's long-run supply curve.

◆   **Section 7.8.** Changes in competitive equilibrium are analyzed by identifying any shifts in short-run supply, long-run supply, and demand which have occurred. Changes in marginal costs will shift the short-run supply curves for both individual firms and the industry. Changes in profitability will affect an individual firm's break-even price and, if the change is industry-wide, will shift the long-run supply curve. Sunk costs, however, do not affect firms' entry-exit decision or the industry's long-run supply curve.

COMPLETION EXERCISES

1.   The demand and marginal revenue curves for a _____ are horizontal at the going market price.

2.   A competitive firm's _____ is that portion of its marginal cost curve that lies above its average variable cost curve.

3.   If all firms are identical, then all firms must earn zero _____ in the long run.

4.   The minimum value of a competitive firm's average variable cost equals the firm's

_____.

5.   The minimum value of a competitive firm's average cost equals the firm's

_____.

6.   If an industry represents a substantial fraction of the demand for a variable factor of production, then the _____ makes the industry supply curve less elastic than the horizontal sum of individual firms' supply curves.

7.   A firm's _____ does not reflect the opportunity costs of being in another industry and is thus larger than its economic profit.

8.   If some firms are more efficient and have lower break-even prices than others, then the industry will be classified as an _____.

9.   The long-run supply curve for a _____ is horizontal at the firms' break-even price.

10. In a _____, the entry of new firms allows the industry to be more efficiently structured and lowers firms' break-even prices.

TRUE-FALSE EXERCISES

_____ 11. The demand curve faced by a competitive firm is downward sloping and relatively elastic.

_____ 12. A competitive firm chooses its output level so that its average cost equals the market price.

_____ 13. A competitive firm will shut down in the short run if the market price falls below its average cost.

_____ 14. The factor-price effect makes short-run industry supply less elastic than it otherwise would be.

_____ 15. Changes in fixed costs have no effect on an industry's short-run supply curve.

_____ 16. A competitive industry's supply response is more elastic in the short run than in the long run.

_____ 17. When a competitive firm earns zero profit, it produces its output at the lowest possible average cost.

_____ 18. A new licensing fee would cause an upward shift in an industry's long-run supply curve.

_____ 19. For a competitive constant-cost industry, the long-run supply curve is horizontal at the firms' shutdown price.

_____ 20. If new entrants have higher break-even prices than existing firms, then the long-run supply curve will be upward sloping.

MULTIPLE CHOICE QUESTIONS

_____ 21. Which of the following statements about a competitive firm is *false*?
   A. A competitive firm can sell any quantity of output at the established market price.
   B. A competitive firm faces a downward-sloping demand curve for its product.
   C. Marginal revenue equals price for a competitive firm.
   D. A competitive firm equates price and marginal cost in order to maximize its profit.

_____ 22. A competitive firm's supply curve coincides with its
   A. marginal cost curve.
   B. marginal revenue curve.
   C. average cost curve.
   D. average variable cost curve.

_____ 23. Suppose that a competitive firm's marginal cost curve is U-shaped and crosses the marginal revenue curve at the quantities Q_1 and Q_2. The firm should
   A. produce Q_1 in order to maximize its profit.
   B. produce Q_2 in order to maximize its profit.
   C. produce Q_2 only if the losses on the first Q_1 units are outweighed by the profits earned on the units between Q_1 and Q_2.
   D. produce either Q_1 or Q_2 because both provide the firm with its maximum possible profit.

_____ 24. A competitive firm has short-run total costs of $5,000, of which $1,500 are fixed costs. The firm's total revenue is $4,000. Assuming that the firm's marginal cost does equal the market price, what action should the firm take in the short run?
- A. The firm has losses and should exit the industry in the short run.
- B. The firm should shut down its operations in the short run in order to avoid a $1,000 loss.
- C. The firm should raise its price in the short run in order to increase its total revenue.
- D. The firm should continue to operate in the short run and accept the $1,000 loss.

_____ 25. When is a competitive profit-maximizing firm in a long-run equilibrium?
- A. When the market price equals both its marginal cost and its average cost.
- B. When the market price exceeds its break-even price.
- C. When the market price is less than its average cost but greater than its average variable cost.
- D. When the market price is high enough for the firm to earn a positive economic profit.

_____ 26. When can the horizontal sum of individual firms' short-run supply curves be interpreted as the industry's short-run supply curve?
- A. When the firms are earning zero economic profits.
- B. When there is no factor-price effect.
- C. When industry expansion would drive up the prices of variable inputs.
- D. When the industry is a constant-cost industry.

_____ 27. In competitive equilibrium, the industry automatically produces at the lowest possible cost because each firm
- A. applies the equimarginal principle to minimize the total costs incurred by the industry.
- B. chooses its output level in order to minimize its cost, making average costs equal throughout the industry.
- C. attempts to maximize its profit, so all firms equate their marginal costs to the same market price.
- D. acts in order to earn the greatest possible profit, and so each firm must minimize its own total cost.

_____ 28. As the industry's output level rises during the short run, the factor-price effect
- A. increases firms' marginal costs and makes the industry's short-run supply curve less elastic.
- B. attracts new firms to the industry in the long run.
- C. causes firms to produce their output at the lowest possible average cost.
- D. occurs when the industry represents a negligible fraction of the demand for its variable inputs.

_____ 29. A competitive firm's break-even price is equal to the minimum value of its
- A. marginal cost.
- B. average cost.
- C. average variable cost.
- D. fixed and sunk costs.

_____ 30. In which of the following situations will the long-run supply curve be horizontal?
    A.   When long-run average costs in the industry increase as output is expanded.
    B.   When firms are identical and there is a factor-price effect.
    C.   When firms have different break-even prices.
    D.   When firms are identical and input prices do not change as the industry expands.

_____ 31. The long-run supply curve for a competitive increasing-cost industry is
    A.   upward sloping and more elastic than the short-run supply curve.
    B.   upward sloping and less elastic than the short-run supply curve.
    C.   horizontal.
    D.   downward sloping.

_____ 32. Which of the following could cause an industry to be a decreasing-cost industry?
    A.   The factor-price effect.
    B.   The development of subindustries in response to industry growth.
    C.   Increasing returns to scale in the firms' production processes.
    D.   Differing quality of inputs across firms.

_____ 33. Suppose a competitive industry is initially in a long-run equilibrium. If firms' fixed costs increase, then the industry's short-run supply curve will
    A.   shift to the left in the short run and shift further to the left in the long run.
    B.   shift to the left in the short run but not shift further in the long run.
    C.   remain unchanged in the short run but shift to the left in the long run.
    D.   remain unchanged in both the short run and the long run.

_____ 34. Suppose a competitive constant-cost industry is initially in a long-run equilibrium. Consider the effect of an increase in the prices that firms must pay for their variable inputs. Which of the following statements about the industry's supply adjustments is *false*?
    A.   Higher marginal costs will cause the industry's short-run supply curve to fall in the short run.
    B.   Firm will have short-run economic losses and exit the industry in the long run.
    C.   Long-run supply adjustments will have no effect on the industry's short-run supply curve.
    D.   The market price will return to its initial level in the long run.

_____ 35. Which of the following describes the economic incidence of an excise tax levied on a competitive constant-cost industry?
    A.   The economic incidence of the tax falls entirely on firms in both the short run and the long run.
    B.   The economic incidence of the tax falls entirely on consumers in both the short run and the long run.
    C.   The economic incidence of the tax is split between firms and consumers in the short run, but it falls entirely on consumers in the long run.
    D.   The economic incidence of the tax is split between firms and consumers in both the short run and the long run, but it falls heavier on consumers in the long run.

REVIEW QUESTIONS

36. How are a firm's short-run and long-run supply curves related to the firm's cost curves?

37. What is the difference between a firm's shutdown of operations and its exit from the industry? What must happen to the market price to make a competitive firm shut down its operations? What must happen to the market price to make a firm exit from the industry?

38. Why are short-run economic losses an insufficient reason for a firm to shut down?

39. Explain why the factor-price effect tends to make the industry's short-run supply curve less elastic than it otherwise would be.

40. Describe what happens to firms' break-even price as they enter a (i) constant-cost industry, (ii) increasing-cost industry, and (iii) decreasing-cost industry.

41. Indicate what factors can cause a shift in each of the following supply curves: (i) the firm's short-run supply curve, (ii) the industry's short-run supply curve, (iii) the firm's long-run supply curve, and (iv) the industry's long-run supply curve.

PROBLEMS

42.   Brooms are produced by a competitive constant-cost industry. Brenda's Brooms, like all other firms in the industry, produces 30,000 brooms per year at a long-run average cost of $10 per broom.

    i.   Suppose Brenda is faced with a rent increase of $6,000 per year, but Brenda's competitors do not have any comparable increase in their costs. Will the rent increase cause Brenda to exit the industry in the long run? Explain.

    ii.   Suppose a fire causes $6,000 worth of damage at Brenda's Brooms, while Brenda's competitors do not suffer any comparable damages. Will the fire cause Brenda to exit the industry in the long run? Explain.

43. Each pair of diagrams below shows a competitive constant-cost industry and a competitive increasing-cost industry, with each industry initially in a long-run equilibrium labeled E_0. For each of the following situations, make the appropriate shifts in the supply and/or demand curves and determine how market price and quantity will be affected in both the short run and the long run for each type of industry. Label the short-run equilibrium E_1 and the long-run equilibrium E_2.

i.   A recession causes a decrease in demand.   *Increase in Demand.*

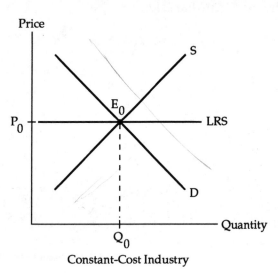

Constant-Cost Industry

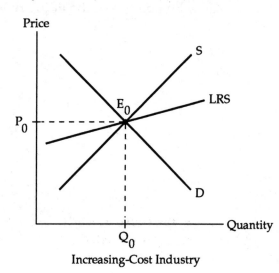

Increasing-Cost Industry

1 fun

ii.   The government imposes an annual licensing fee on all firms in the industry.

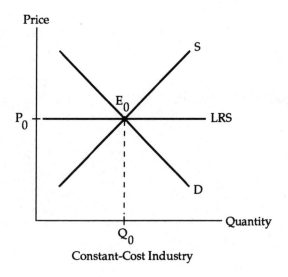

Constant-Cost Industry

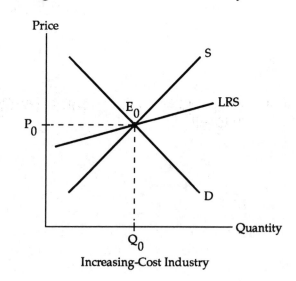

Increasing-Cost Industry

44. Recycled paper is produced and sold by a competitive constant-cost industry at a price of $100 per ton. The government is considering two policies to increase the production of recycled paper. Under the first policy, paper recycling firms would receive a subsidy of $20 per ton of recycled paper produced. Under the second policy, the government would build and operate 10 new paper recycling centers.

    i.   Describe the short-run and long-run impacts of the subsidy program on the recycled paper industry.

    ii.   Describe the short-run and long-run impacts of the government-operated firms on the recycled paper industry.

    iii.   Which policy is more effective at increasing the production of recycled paper in the long run?

45. Consider a competitive constant-cost industry in which each firm's marginal and average costs are given by the formulas $MC = 10q$ and $AC = 5q + {720}/{q}$, where q represents the quantity supplied by the firm.

   i. Determine the quantity supplied by each firm in the long run, and determine the long-run market price in this industry.

   ii. Suppose the market demand for the good produced by this industry is given by the formula $P = 360 - \frac{1}{3}Q$, where P is the market price and Q is the market quantity. Use your answer to part i to determine the equilibrium market quantity and the number of firms in the long run.

iii. Find a formula relating P and Q that represents the industry's short-run supply for the situation in part ii. (*Hint* – Combine the equations P = MC and Q = Nq, where N is the number of firms in the industry. You may ignore the possibility of firms shutting down in the short run.)

iv. Suppose market demand increases to P = 420 – ⅓Q. Use your answer to part iii to determine the market price, market quantity, and profit made by each firm in the new short-run equilibrium.

v. Continue to assume that market demand has increased to P = 420 – ⅓Q. Use your answer to part i to determine the market price, market quantity, and the number of firms in the new long-run equilibrium.

SOLUTIONS

Completion Exercises

1. (perfectly) competitive firm
2. short-run supply curve
3. economic profit
4. shutdown price
5. break-even price

6. factor-price effect
7. accounting profit
8. increasing-cost industry
9. constant-cost industry
10. decreasing-cost industry

True-False Exercises

11. FALSE. The demand curve faced by a competitive firm is <u>horizontal at the going market price</u>.

12. FALSE. A competitive firm chooses its output level so that its <u>marginal</u> cost equals the market price.

13. FALSE. A competitive firm will shut down in the short run if the market price falls below its <u>average variable cost</u>.

14. TRUE.

15. TRUE.

16. FALSE. A competitive industry's supply response is <u>less</u> elastic in the short run than in the long run.

17. TRUE.

18. TRUE.

19. FALSE. For a competitive constant-cost industry, the long-run supply curve is horizontal at the firms' <u>break-even</u> price.

20. TRUE.

Multiple Choice Questions

21. B. The demand for a competitive firm's product is horizontal at the established market price.

22. A. Any firm will choose the quantity where marginal revenue equals marginal cost in order to maximize its profit, and marginal revenue equals market price for a competitive firm. Therefore, the quantity that a competitive firms supplies at a particular price can be read off its marginal cost curve.

23. C. Marginal cost exceeds marginal revenue before Q_1, so the firm has losses on these first sales. Between Q_1 and Q_2, marginal revenue exceeds marginal cost, so the firm earns profits on these later sales. These profits must outweigh the losses on the first Q_1 units for production to be worthwhile to the firm.

24. D. The fixed costs are sunk in the short run, so only variable costs affect the firm's decision to shut down. The firm's revenue of $4,000 exceeds its variable costs of $3,500 (total costs of $5,000 minus fixed costs of $1,500), so the firm minimizes its losses by continuing to produce in the short run.

25. A. For the firm to maximize its profit, the market price must equal its marginal cost. Profit must be zero in a long-run equilibrium, so the market price must also equal the firm's average cost.

26. B. The horizontal summation of firms' short-run supply curves is the industry's short-run supply curve only if the input prices remain unchanged as the industry's output changes. The factor-price effect would raise input prices when the industry expands, making short-run industry supply less elastic than the horizontal summation.

27. C. The equimarginal principle implies that firms' marginal costs should be equalized in order for the industry to have minimum costs. Competition achieves this result in a decentralized manner through the profit-maximizing behavior of firms.

28. A. When the factor-price effect occurs, increased output by the industry creates a higher demand for variable inputs, which in turn causes the prices of those variable inputs to rise. These higher input prices raise firms' marginal costs and lower their output. The industry supplies a lower amount when the factor-price effect exists, so the supply curve is less elastic in this case.

29. B. A profit-maximizing firm breaks even when the market price equals marginal cost equals average cost. This situation can only occur at the minimum of the firm's average cost curve.

30. D. The long-run supply curve will be horizontal when the industry is a constant-cost industry.

31. A. Higher prices are required for the industry to expand in the long run because firms' entry costs will be higher, and so the long-run supply curve must be upward sloping. The industry's long-run supply curve will be more elastic than its short-run supply curve because entry and exit allow for a more flexible supply response in the long run.

32.   B. In decreasing-cost industries, the long-run average cost in the industry is falling as the industry expands. This situation can occur when the industry becomes large enough to support a subindustry that can provide some factor of production at a lower cost.

33.   C. Changes in fixed costs do not affect firms' short-run behavior, and so the industry's supply is unaffected in the short run. During the long run, losses will force some firms to exit the industry, causing the industry's short-run supply curve to shift to the left.

34.   C. Exit of firms from the industry in the long run will cause the industry's short-run supply curve to shift to the left.

35.   C. The firms' marginal and average costs will increase by the amount of the tax, so the industry's short-run and long-run supply curves will also shift up by the amount of the tax. The intersection of the demand and short-run supply curves will be higher by an amount less than the tax, so the economic incidence of the tax is split between consumers and firms in the short run. The intersection of the demand and long-run supply curves will be higher by an amount exactly equal to the tax, so the economic incidence of the tax falls entirely on consumers in the long run.

Review Questions

36.   The firm's short-run supply curve is the portion of its short-run marginal cost curve which lies above its average variable cost curve. The firm's long-run supply curve is the portion of its long-run marginal cost curve which lies above its long-run average cost curve.

37.   Shutting down occurs in the short run — the firm is not producing output, but its fixed inputs (e.g., its plant and capital) are committed to the industry. Exiting an industry occurs in the long run — the firm relocates its resources (including, for instance, its plant and capital) to different, more profitable employment. A competitive firm will shut down its operations in the short run when the market price falls below its average variable cost. It will exit the industry in the long run when the market price is less than its average cost.

38.   A firm has short-run losses if its total revenue does not exceed the sum of its fixed and variable costs. However, the fixed costs are sunk in the short run, so they are irrelevant to the firm's decision to shut down. As long as the firm's total revenue exceeds its variable costs, the firm will be able to recover at least part of its fixed costs. Consequently, production will benefit the firm even if it does not recover all of its fixed costs and suffers some economic losses.

39. When an industry accounts for a substantial proportion of the demand for some variable factor of production, higher industry output will increase demand for that factor and raise its price. The higher input price will increase firms' marginal costs, causing firms to reduce their output levels. Therefore, a given price increase will result in a smaller quantity response by the industry when the factor-price effect occurs, and so the short-run supply curve will be less elastic than it otherwise would be.

40. (i) In a constant-cost industry, all firms are identical and there are no factor-price effects. Thus, the break-even price does not change as firms enter and exit the industry. (ii) An increasing-cost industry can arise in one of two ways. First, the factor-price effect causes input prices to rise as new firms enter the industry. Second, new entrants may be less efficient than existing firms. In either case, the break-even price for new entrants increases as the industry expands. (iii) In decreasing-cost industries, industry expansion creates improvements in the industry's structure, such as the development of subindustries that can provide some inputs at lower cost. New entrants will cause a reduction in firms' break-even prices.

41. (i) The firm's short-run supply curve coincides with its short-run marginal cost curve. Therefore, any change that affects the additional cost attributable to the last unit produced in the short run—such as a change in the cost of variable inputs—will shift the firm's short-run supply curve. (ii) Changes in marginal costs will also shift the industry's short-run supply curve, because the industry's short-run supply curve is derived from the horizontal summation of the individual firms' short-run supply curves. (iii) The firm's long-run supply curve coincides with its long-run marginal cost curve. Any change that affects the additional cost attributable to the last unit produced in the long run—including changes in the costs of inputs that were fixed in the short run—will shift the firm's long-run supply curve. (iv) The industry's long-run supply curve is derived from the break-even prices of firms. Consequently, anything that changes firms' long-run average costs will affect firms' profitability and will shift the industry's long-run supply curve.

Problems

42. i.   Yes, the rent increase will cause Brenda to exit the industry in the long run. Before the rent increase, both the market price and Brenda's break-even price were $10 per broom. The rent increase adds to Brenda's total costs, raising her break-even price to $10.20

per broom. Since the market price is below her break-even price, Brenda will exit the industry.

ii.   The damages from the fire are a sunk cost that cannot be recovered. The $6,000 worth of damages do not affect Brenda's break-even price and thus do not cause her to exit the industry.

43.   i.   The decrease in demand will lower price and output in the short run. Firms will exit the industry in the long run because of negative profits, which lowers the output level even further. In the constant-cost industry, the market price will rise back up to the original level in the long run. In the increasing-cost industry, the market price does not rise back fully to the original level for the increasing-cost industry, because the remaining firms have lower break-even prices.

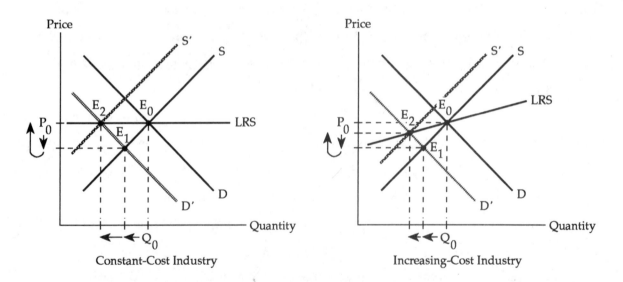

Constant-Cost Industry   Increasing-Cost Industry

ii.   The licensing fee is a new fixed cost. Changes in fixed costs do not affect firms' marginal costs, and so supply and the market equilibrium do not change in the short run. The licensing fee does raise firms' long-run average costs and their break-even prices, and so the long-run supply curve shifts up. Some firms exit the industry in the long run, causing the market price to rise and the quantity to fall. The price does not rise as much in the increasing-cost industry as in the constant-cost industry, because the firms remaining in the increasing-cost industry have lower break-even prices (net of the new licensing fee).

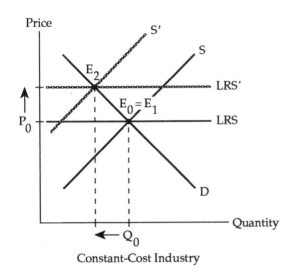

Constant-Cost Industry

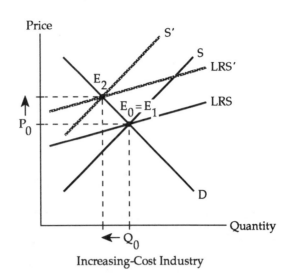

Increasing-Cost Industry

44. i.   The subsidy reduces firms' marginal costs by \$20 per ton. The short-run supply curve shifts down by \$20 per ton. The market price falls by less than \$20 per ton, so the short-run benefits of the subsidy are split between producers and consumers. Firms increase their production and earn short-run profits. Since the subsidy reduces firms' break-even price by \$20 per ton, new firms enter the industry in the long run. Production rises, the price falls to \$80 per ton, and firms again earn zero profit.

ii. The new government-operated firms cause a rightward shift in the short-run supply curve. Market price falls and production rises. Firms, however, have short-run losses since the price is lower than their \$100 per ton break-even price. In the long run, firms exit the industry until the price and output return to their original levels.

iii. The subsidy is more effective at increasing production because it attracts new entrants to the industry. On the other hand, the government-operated firms add nothing to the industry's output in the long run.

45. i.   In the long run, the firm will produce the quantity where average cost is at a minimum, which is also the only quantity where marginal cost equals average cost. This fact gives us the equation $10q = 5q + {}^{720}\!/_q$. Solve this equation for q:

$10q = 5q + {}^{720}\!/_q \ \Rightarrow\ 5q = {}^{720}\!/_q \ \Rightarrow\ 5q^2 = 720 \ \Rightarrow\ q^2 = 144 \ \Rightarrow\ q = 12$ units.

In long-run equilibrium, $P = MC = AC$, so substitute $q = 12$ into either the equation for MC or AC to get the long-run price: $P = MC = 10q = 10 \cdot 12 = 120$ dollars per unit, or $P = AC = 5q + {}^{720}\!/_q = 5 \cdot 12 + {}^{720}\!/_{12} = 60 + 60 = 120$ dollars per unit.

ii. Substitute the long-run price from part i into the formula for the demand curve to solve for the long-run equilibrium quantity: $120 = 360 - \frac{1}{3}Q \Rightarrow \frac{1}{3}Q = 240 \Rightarrow Q = 720$ units.

From part i, we know each firm produces 12 units in long-run equilibrium, so there must be $\frac{720}{12}$ or 60 firms in the industry.

iii. Firms maximize profits by producing the quantity where P = MC, so the individual firm's supply curve is given by the formula $P = 10q$. The number of firms in the short run is fixed at 60, so $q = \frac{1}{60}Q$. Substituting the latter formula into the former formula gives $P = 10 \cdot \frac{1}{60}Q$ or $P = \frac{1}{6}Q$ for the industry's short-run supply curve.

iv. Short-run supply is given by $P = \frac{1}{6}Q$ and demand is given by $P = 420 - \frac{1}{3}Q$, so simply equate these two to find the short-run equilibrium quantity: $\frac{1}{6}Q = 420 - \frac{1}{3}Q \Rightarrow \frac{1}{2}Q = 420 \Rightarrow Q = 840$ units.

Substitute this quantity into either the supply or demand formulas to solve for the short-run equilibrium price: $P = \frac{1}{6} \cdot 840 = 140$ dollars per unit, or $P = 420 - \frac{1}{3} \cdot 840 = 420 - 280 = 140$ dollars per unit.

From part ii, we know there are 60 identical firms, so each firm produces $\frac{840}{60}$ or 14 units of output in the short run. The average cost of producing 14 units can be found using the formula for average cost:

$AC = 5q + \frac{720}{q} = 5 \cdot 14 + \frac{720}{14} = 70 + 51\frac{3}{7} = 121\frac{3}{7}$ dollars per unit.

The firm on average pays $\$121\frac{3}{7}$ and receives $140 for each unit of output, for a profit of $\$18\frac{4}{7}$ per unit of output. The firm sells 14 units, so the firm's total profit is $\$18\frac{4}{7} \cdot 14$ or $260.

v. In the long run, the market price must return to firms' break-even price, which is $120 per unit as shown in part i. Substitute this price into the new demand curve to get the long-run equilibrium quantity: $120 = 420 - \frac{1}{3}Q \Rightarrow \frac{1}{3}Q = 300 \Rightarrow Q = 900$ units. As shown in part i, each firm produces 12 units in long-run equilibrium, and so there must now be $\frac{900}{12}$ or 75 firms in the industry.

CHAPTER 8

WELFARE ECONOMICS AND THE GAINS FROM TRADE

This chapter introduces an area of microeconomics called welfare economics, which studies the gains from trade created in an economy. The first part of the chapter shows how to use consumers' surplus and producers' surplus to evaluate policies using the efficiency criterion. The remainder of the chapter focuses on the Invisible Hand Theorem, which states that the gains from trade in a competitive equilibrium are as large as possible, even when all markets and the interactions among them are taken into account.

KEY TERMS

- Value
- Consumer's surplus
- Producer's surplus
- Social gain (or welfare gain)
- Normative criterion
- Efficiency criterion
- Deadweight loss
- Pareto criterion

- potential Pareto criterion
- Price ceiling
- Effective price ceiling
- Labor theory of value
- General equilibrium analysis
- Invisible Hand Theorem
- Edgeworth box
- Endowment point

- Region of mutual advantage
- Contract curve
- Competitive equilibrium
- Production possibility curve
- Open economy
- Autarkic relative price
- World relative price

KEY IDEAS

- **Section 8.1.** Consumers' surplus is the amount by which the value of consumers' purchases exceeds their expenditures. Consumers' surplus measures consumers' gains from trade and is estimated using the area beneath the demand curve down to the price paid and out to the quantity demanded. Producers' surplus is the amount by which the producers' revenues exceed their variable costs. Producers' surplus measures producers' gains from trade and is estimated using the area above the supply curve up to the price received and out to the quantity supplied.

◆ **Section 8.2.** A normative criterion is a general method for choosing among various social policies. One normative criterion that is commonly used in microeconomics is the efficiency criterion, which always recommends the policy that creates the greatest social gain. If an alternative policy creases a smaller social gain, the difference is called the deadweight loss from that policy.

◆ **Section 8.3.** Consumers' surplus, producers' surplus, and the efficiency criterion can be applied to evaluate the effects of numerous government policies. This analysis shows that sales taxes, subsidies, price ceilings, and tariffs typically reduce the social gain created by the competitive market.

◆ **Section 8.4.** General equilibrium analysis takes into account all markets simultaneously, including all the interactions among the markets. The Edgeworth box and the production possibility curve are two basic tools used to study general equilibrium. One of the most important results of general equilibrium analysis is the Invisible Hand Theorem, which states that a competitive equilibrium is Pareto optimal.

COMPLETION EXERCISES

1.   The maximum amount that a consumer is willing to pay for a good is called the

    _____ of the good to the consumer.

2.   Consumers' gains from trade are measured using _____.

3.   The area above the supply curve up to the price received and out to the quantity supplied

    is called _____.

4.   If a policy lowers the total gains from trade created in the market, the reduction in social

    gain is called a _____.

5.   According to the efficiency criterion, one policy is better than another when it creates more

    _____.

6.   According to the _____, one policy is better than another only if

    every individual agrees that it is preferable.

7. A competitive equilibrium makes social gain as large as possible; this result is known as the _____.

8. Economic modeling that accounts for all markets simultaneously as well as the interactions among them is called _____.

9. In an Edgeworth box economy, the set of all Pareto-optimal points is called the _____.

10. A _____ shows the various combinations of goods that can be produced in an economy.

TRUE-FALSE EXERCISES

_____ 11. The total value of a consumer's purchases is equal to the area under the demand curve out to the quantity demanded.

_____ 12. Consumer's surplus measures the total value that an individual receives from consuming a good.

_____ 13. Producer's surplus equals a firm's revenue minus its variable costs of production.

_____ 14. The efficiency criterion always recommends the policy that creates the most consumers' surplus.

_____ 15. The deadweight loss of a tax equals the costs incurred from collecting the tax.

_____ 16. The Pareto criterion recommends a policy change when it is unanimously preferred.

_____ 17. The value of an item is determined by the amount of labor used in its production.

_____ 18. The competitive equilibrium creates a maximal amount of social gain.

_____ 19. In an Edgeworth box economy, the competitive equilibrium lies on the contract curve and within the region of mutual advantage.

_____ 20. A country's gains from trade are largest when the autarkic and world relative prices
are equal.

MULTIPLE CHOICE QUESTIONS

_____ 21. A situation is considered "best" by the efficiency criterion when
   A.   consumers' surplus can be increased by further trading.
   B.   social gain cannot be increased.
   C.   it is impossible to make one person better off without also making someone else
        worse off.
   D.   everyone agrees that it is fair and equitable.

_____ 22. Which of the following criteria will reject a policy if and only if there exists some
alternative that would be preferred by everyone?
   A.   Majority rule.
   B.   The efficiency criterion.
   C.   The potential Pareto criterion.
   D.   The Edgeworth criterion.

_____ 23. The value of a good is determined by
   A.   the amount of labor used in the good's production.
   B.   the cost of all the resources used to produce the good.
   C.   consumers' willingness to pay for the good.
   D.   the degree to which the good is a necessity or a luxury.

_____ 24. The Invisible Hand Theorem states that
   A.   competitive behavior eliminates any shortages and surpluses.
   B.   the competitive equilibrium is Pareto optimal.
   C.   production costs are as small as possible in the competitive equilibrium.
   D.   under any reasonable normative criterion, competition provides the "best"
        possible allocation of resources.

◆◆◆ Questions 25 and 26 refer to the
accompanying diagram which shows the
effects of an excise subsidy given to firms.
The initial price and quantity are P_0 and Q_0.
After the subsidy is granted, the
equilibrium quantity is Q_1, firms receive the
price P_s, and consumers pay the price P_d.

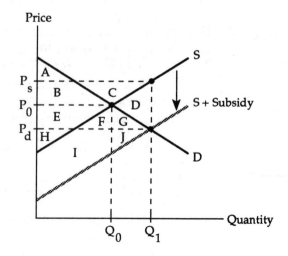

_____ 25. Before the subsidy is given to firms,
the social gain is
   A.   A + B.
   B.   A + B + E + F + G.
   C.   A + B + E + H.
   D.   E + H.

_____ 26. After the subsidy is given to firms, the social gain is
   A.   A + B + E + H.
   B.   A + B + E + H – D.
   C.   A + B + E + F + G + H + I + J.
   D.   A + B + E + F + G + H + I + J – C – D.

◆◆◆ Questions 27–29 refer to the accompanying diagram which shows the effects of a tariff. Initially, the price is P_0, domestic firms produce Q_0 units, and $Q_1 - Q_0$ units are imported from foreign firms. When the tariff is imposed, the price increases to $P_0 + t$.

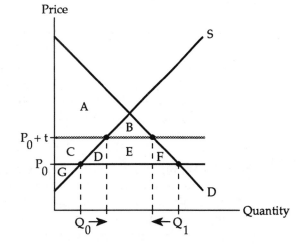

_____ 27. When the tariff is imposed, consumers' surplus falls
   A.   from A + B + C + D + E + F to A + B.
   B.   from A + B + C + D + E to A + B.
   C.   from A + C + G to A.
   D.   from A + C to A.

_____ 28. When the tariff is imposed, producers' surplus increases from G to
   A.   C + G.
   B.   C + G – B.
   C.   C + G – D – E – F.
   D.   C + D + E + F + G.

_____ 29. When the tariff is imposed, the government collects
   A.   area D + E + F in tax revenue without creating a deadweight loss.
   B.   area D + E + F in tax revenue, but a deadweight loss of B is also created.
   C.   area E in tax revenue, but a deadweight loss of B + D + F is also created.
   D.   area E in tax revenue, but a deadweight loss of D + F is also created.

_____ 30. The diamond-water paradox is resolved by noting
   A.   the competitive equilibrium is Pareto optimal.
   B.   that a low price and a high consumers' surplus can exist simultaneously.
   C.   that the labor theory of value does not hold for natural resources like diamonds and water.
   D.   goods that provide substantial consumers' surplus must also command a high market price.

_____ 31. Which of the following should be used to conduct general equilibrium analysis of an economy with production?
   A.   Supply and demand.
   B.   Consumers' and producers' surplus.
   C.   The Edgeworth box.
   D.   The production possibility curve.

_____ 32. Which points in the Edgeworth box are Pareto optimal?
A.   The points on the contract curve.
B.   Points in the region of mutual advantage.
C.   The competitive equilibrium is the only Pareto-optimal point in the Edgeworth box.
D.   All points in the Edgeworth box represent Pareto-optimal allocations of goods.

_____ 33. Which of the following statements about the competitive equilibrium in an Edgeworth box economy is *false*?
A.   The competitive equilibrium must be to the southeast of the endowment point.
B.   The competitive equilibrium must be on the contract curve.
C.   The competitive equilibrium must be in the region of mutual advantage.
D.   The competitive equilibrium must be at the tangency between two indifference curves.

_____ 34. Consider a small country that is considering the opening of international trade. If the country's autarkic relative price differs substantially from the world relative price, then
A.   the country is too small to gain from trade.
B.   the country's gains from trade will be greatest if it imposes tariffs on imported goods.
C.   the country's production is incompatible with the world competitive equilibrium.
D.   the country will realize relatively large gains from trade.

_____ 35. Consider a production possibility curve with food on the horizontal axis and cloth on the vertical axis. Which of the following statements about the production possibility curve is *false*?
A.   The production possibility curve bows outward from the origin.
B.   In the absence of trade, the slope of the production possibility curve represents the relative price of cloth in terms of food.
C.   The slope of the tangency between the production possibility curve and an indifference curve determines the autarkic relative price.
D.   Production in an open economy occurs where the slope of the production possibility curve equals the world relative price.

REVIEW QUESTIONS

36.   What is a deadweight loss? List some situations which will create deadweight loss. According to the Invisible Hand Theorem, how can deadweight loss be avoided?

37.   What is the efficiency criterion? What is the potential Pareto criterion? Explain why a market outcome that is less efficient than the competitive equilibrium will be rejected by the potential Pareto criterion.

38.   What is the diamond-water paradox? How is this paradox resolved?

39.   What is the labor theory of value? Why is it wrong?

40.   In an Edgeworth box economy, how do we illustrate (i) the contract curve, (ii) the region of mutual advantage, and (iii) a competitive equilibrium? How is the Invisible Hand Theorem illustrated in an Edgeworth box economy?

41.   What point on the production possibility curve will be produced in an economy without trade? What point will be produced in an open economy? If these two points are the same, what can be said about the gains from trade?

PROBLEMS

42. i. Suppose the government imposes a sales tax on consumers of a commodity. Complete the diagrams below to show how the elasticity of supply will affect the size of the resulting deadweight loss, all other things being equal. Assume that the initial equilibrium price and quantity are P_0 and Q_0. Include the following on the completed diagrams:

     a. an appropriate supply curve (S) for each diagram,
     b. the shift in the demand curve caused by the sales tax,
     c. the new equilibrium quantity (Q_1), price paid by demanders (P_d), and price received by suppliers (P_s), and
     d. the deadweight loss created by the sales tax.

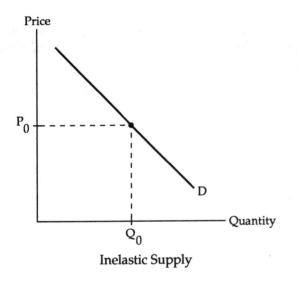

Inelastic Supply

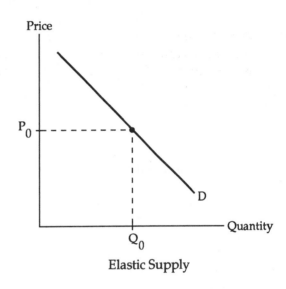

Elastic Supply

ii. Use the above result to determine if the deadweight loss will tend to be larger in the short run or in the long run. Justify your answer.

43.   The diagram below shows the general equilibrium of an open economy that has imposed a tariff. The economy produces at point A, and then trades with the rest of the world to get point B.

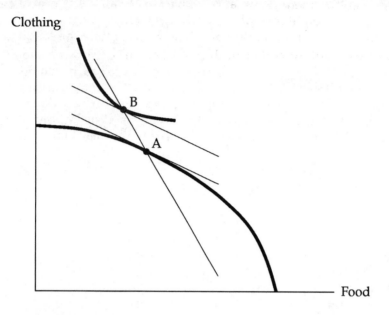

i.   Where in the diagram can you find the world relative price? Where in the diagram can you find the economy's domestic relative price?

ii.   Was the tariff placed on imported food or imported clothing? How can you tell?

iii.   Complete the diagram to show what would happen if the tariff were abolished. (You may assume that the economy is sufficiently small that the abolishment of its tariff would not affect the world relative price.) Would the economy's gains from trade increase if the tariff were abolished? If so, why would an economy choose to impose a tariff in the first place?

44.   Suppose there are 24 units of food and 18 units of clothing to distribute between Ali and Bob. At the endowment point, Ali has no food and 9 units of clothing, and her marginal value is 1½ units of clothing per unit of food. Bob has 24 units of food and 9 units of clothing at the endowment point, and his marginal value is ½ unit of clothing per unit of food.

   i.   Is this distribution of goods on the contract curve? How can you tell?

   ii. Complete the Edgeworth box diagram below to illustrate this situation. The following should be clearly labeled:
            a.   the dimensions of the Edgeworth box,
            b.   the endowment point,
            c.   the consumers' marginal values, and
            d.   the region of mutual advantage.

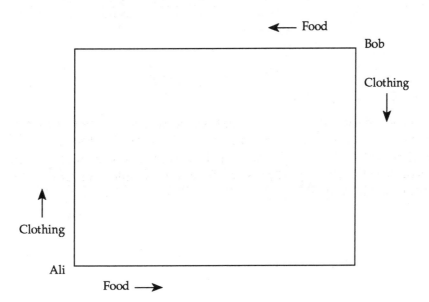

45.   Mark's monthly demand for comics is shown in the diagram below. Mark currently buys his comics from Midgard Comics, a locally run store. Midgard charges Mark the cover price of $3.00 per book, and Mark buys 8 books per month.

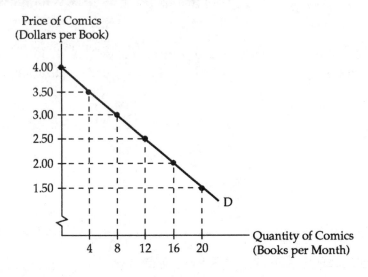

i.   Calculate the amount of consumer's surplus that Mark receives each month from his comic book purchases.

ii.   Mountain Top Comics provides a mail order comic subscription service. Mountain Top charges its customers less than the cover price—only $2.00 per book. However, Mountain Top also charges a flat monthly shipping fee of $9.50 regardless of the number of books ordered. Should Mark continue to buy books from Midgard, or should he switch to Mountain Top? Explain.

iii.   Suppose Midgard offers Mark a "best customer" discount of $0.50 per book. Should Mark now continue to buy books from Midgard, or should he switch to Mountain Top? Explain.

SOLUTIONS

Completion Exercises

1. value
2. consumers' surplus
3. producers' surplus
4. deadweight loss
5. social gain

6. Pareto criterion
7. Invisible Hand Theorem
8. general equilibrium analysis
9. contract curve
10. production possibility curve

True-False Exercises

11. TRUE.

12. FALSE. Consumer's surplus measures the <u>gains from trade</u> that an individual receives from <u>purchasing and</u> consuming a good.

13. TRUE.

14. FALSE. The efficiency criterion always recommends the policy that creates the most <u>social gain</u>.

15. FALSE. The deadweight loss of a tax equals the <u>reduction in social gain caused by</u> the tax.

16. TRUE.

17. FALSE. The value of an item is determined by the <u>consumer's willingness to pay for the good or service being offered</u>.

18. TRUE.

19. TRUE.

20. FALSE. A country's gains from trade are <u>zero</u> when the autarkic and world relative prices are equal.

Multiple Choice Questions

21. B. One situation is more efficient than another if it creates more social gain.

22. C. The potential Pareto criterion rejects any proposal that could be unanimously defeated, even by a candidate not under consideration.

23. C. The value of a good to a consumer is defined to be the maximum amount that he would pay for the good.

24.   B. Competitive equilibrium is Pareto optimal, that is, it creates a maximal amount of social gain.

25.   C. The consumers' surplus equals A + B, and the producers' surplus equals E + H.

26.   B. After the subsidy is granted, consumers' surplus rises to A + B + E + F + G, and producers' surplus rises to B + C + E + H. Financing the subsidy costs taxpayers B + C + D + E + F + G. The social gain is the sum of consumers' and producers' surpluses minus the costs to taxpayers, which equals A + B + E + H − D.

27.   A. Consumers' surplus is measured by the area beneath the demand curve down to the price paid and out to the quantity demanded.

28.   A. Producers' surplus is measured by the area above the supply curve up to the price received and out to the quantity supplied.

29.   D. The tax revenue is measured by rectangle E, which has a base equal to the number of units taxed and a width equal to the size of the per-unit tax. Before the tariff is imposed, the sum of consumers' and producers' surpluses is A + B + C + D + E + F + G. After the tariff is imposed, the sum of consumers' surplus, producers' surplus, and the gains to tax recipients is A + B + C + E + G. The difference between these two, D + F, is the deadweight loss.

30.   B. Although water creates a large consumers' surplus, it need not command a high market price like diamonds. Water's low price and high consumers' surplus can coexist, because price is determined by consumers' marginal willingness to pay.

31.   D. The production possibility curve shows the various combinations of goods which can be produced using the available resources and technology, so it is appropriate for use in analyzing the general equilibrium of an economy with production.

32.   A. If the distribution of goods occurs where two indifference curves are tangent, then there is no unanimously preferred outcome.

33.   A. The competitive equilibrium will be either to the northwest or the southeast of the endowment point, depending on how the consumers' indifference curves are crossing.

34.   D. All other things being equal, the more the autarkic relative price differs from the world relative price, the greater will be the country's gains from trade.

35.   B. The slope of the production possibility curve determines the relative price of the good on the horizontal axis—in this case, the relative price of food in terms of cloth.

Review Questions

36.   A deadweight loss is the reduction in social gain that occurs when an economic policy lowers the total gains from trade created by the market. Excise taxes and subsidies, price floors and ceilings, tariffs, and robbery can all create deadweight loss. The Invisible Hand Theorem claims that the competitive equilibrium is Pareto optimal, and so competitive markets do not create deadweight loss.

37.   The efficiency criterion ranks market outcomes on the basis of the amount of social gain created. According to the potential Pareto criterion, any proposal that could be unanimously defeated should be rejected. If a market outcome is less efficient than the competitive equilibrium, then there is a deadweight loss. Such a situation will be rejected by the potential Pareto criterion, because additional gains from trade equal to the deadweight loss can be created and distributed among the market participants, making them all better off.

38.   Classical economists were puzzled that a valuable necessity like water could have a low price while an unnecessary luxury like diamonds could command a high price. The classical economists made the error of believing that the price of a good is determined by the total value consumers receive from it. In actuality, the price of a good equals the marginal value—the additional value attributable to the last unit of the good consumed. The net total value consumers receive is measured by consumers' surplus, not price. Consequently, a good can simultaneously have a low price and high consumers' surplus (like water), or it can have both a high price and low consumers' surplus (like diamonds).

39.   According to the labor theory of value, the value of a commodity is determined by the amount of labor used in its production. This assertion is clearly false—just because a commodity was produced from a large amount of labor does not mean that consumers will be willing to pay a high price for the commodity in the market. Value is determined by demand, not by the amount or cost of the inputs.

40.   (i) The contract curve is the set of all tangencies between the indifference curves in the Edgeworth box. (ii) The region of mutual advantage is the lens-shaped area between the two indifference curves which pass through the endowment point. (iii) The consumers' budget lines coincide in the Edgeworth box and also pass through the endowment point. The competitive equilibrium is the point on the budget line where two indifference curves are tangent.

The Invisible Hand Theorem claims that the competitive equilibrium is Pareto optimal. All points on the contract curve are Pareto optimal, and so the competitive equilibrium in the Edgeworth box must lie on the contract curve.

41.   In an economy without trade, the production point is where the production possibility curve and an indifference curve are tangent. The common slope at this tangency represents the autarkic relative price. In an open economy, the production point occurs where the slope of the production possibility curve equals the world relative price, because this point makes the budget line as far from the origin as possible. If these two production points are the same, then the autarkic relative price is equal to the world relative price and there are no gains from trade.

Problems

42.   i.   The completed diagrams show that the deadweight loss becomes larger as the supply curve becomes more elastic.

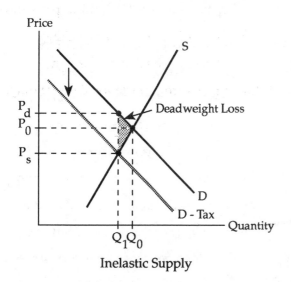

Inelastic Supply

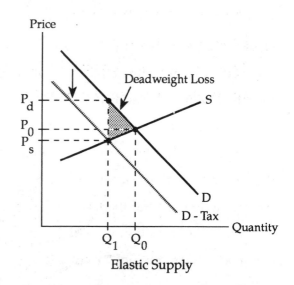

Elastic Supply

ii.   From Chapter 7, we know that the long-run supply curve is more elastic than the short-run supply curve. The deadweight loss created by a sales tax therefore tends to be larger in the long run than in the short run.

43.   i.   The economy trades with the rest of the world to get point B in exchange for point A, so the line connecting points A and B must be the economy's budget line. The slope of this budget line gives the world relative price of food in terms of clothing.

The slope of the production possibility curve gives the relative price of food in terms of clothing within the economy, and the slope of the indifference curve must equal this relative price at the optimum. Therefore, the domestic relative price is equal to the slopes of the tangent lines at points A and B.

ii. The budget line through points A and B is steeper than the tangent lines at points A and B, so the world relative price of food in terms of clothing must be larger than the domestic relative price. The tariff made the economy's food relatively less expensive and its clothing relatively more expensive than the rest of the world's food and clothing. The domestic price of clothing is higher than the world price, so the tariff must have been placed on imported clothing.

iii. The effects of abolishing the tariff are shown below. If the tariff were abolished, the economy would produce at point A' and trade to get point B'. The economy's gains from trade would certainly increase, because point B' is on a higher indifference curve than point B. However, the economy would also produce more food and less clothing (because point A' is to the southeast of point A), so the economy's clothing producers would be against removal of the tariff. In effect, the tariff on imported clothing "protects" inefficient domestic clothing producers from more efficient foreign competition. The cost of this "protection" is lower gains from trade for the economy.

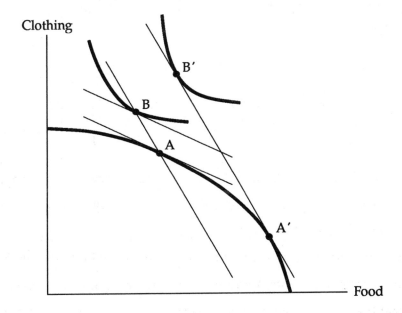

44. i. This distribution of goods is not on the contract curve, because trading can make both Ali and Bob better off. For example, consider a trade at the rate of 1 unit of clothing per unit of food. Bob's marginal value indicates that he will be indifferent if he trades away 1 unit of food in exchange for ½ unit of clothing. By receiving 1 full unit of clothing instead of only ½ unit in the trade, Bob will be made better off. According to Ali's marginal value, 1½ units of clothing is the most she would pay in exchange for 1 unit of food, so Ali will be better off if she trades away only 1 unit of clothing in exchange for 1 unit of food. Both Ali and Bob agree that a trade at the rate of 1 unit of clothing per unit of food is preferable to keeping the endowment point, so the distribution of goods at the endowment point cannot be on the contract curve. (Notice that any rate of exchange between their marginal values would be acceptable to both.)

     ii.

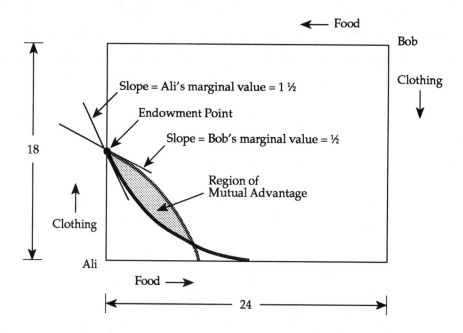

45. i. The consumer's surplus triangle has a height of $1.00 per book and a base of 8 books. The area of a triangle is given by ½ times the base times the height, so Mark recieves $4.00 in consumer's surplus (½ × 8 books × $1.00 per book).

     ii. If Mark switches to Mountain Top, he would begin to purchase 16 books per month. If there were no shipping charge, his consumer's surplus would be $16.00 (½ × 16 books × $2.00 per book). After paying the $9.50 shipping fee, Mark's net consumer's surplus is $6.50. This amount is more than Mark receives from buying books at Midgard, so Mark should switch to Mountain Top.

iii.   If Mark receives a $0.50 per book discount from Midgard, he would buy 12 books per month and receive $9.00 in consumer's surplus ($\frac{1}{2} \times 12$ books $\times$ $1.50 per book). This amount is more than the $6.50 in surplus that Mark would receive from buying books from Mountain Top, so Mark should continue to buy books from Midgard if he receives the "best customer" discount.

CHAPTER 9

KNOWLEDGE AND INFORMATION

This chapter examines the relationship between prices and information. The first half of the chapter examines efficient markets like those for financial assets, in which prices fully reflect all available information. The second half of the chapter examines situations in which the market outcome fails to be Pareto optimal because information is asymmetrically distributed.

KEY TERMS

- Rent
- Efficient market
- Social planner
- Fabian socialism

- Technical analysts
- Speculative bubble
- Signal
- Adverse selection

- Moral hazard
- Principal-agent problem
- Efficiency wage

KEY IDEAS

- **Section 9.1.** Prices determined in competitive markets synthesize the knowledge of society's members, communicate this information back to consumers and firms, and provide incentives for them to use this information and act on their own unique knowledge. A social planner could not have access to this vast amount of knowledge and therefore could not achieve the gains from trade attained in a competitive market system.

- **Section 9.2.** Efficient markets are those in which prices fully reflect all available information. Markets for financial assets are among the most efficient markets in the economy, which is substantial evidence against the claims of technical analysts.

- **Section 9.3.** When information is distributed asymmetrically, market outcomes may not be Pareto optimal. Examples of situations where asymmetric information produces suboptimal results include signaling, adverse selection, moral hazard, and principal-agent problems.

COMPLETION EXERCISES

1.   The market price fully reflects all available information in an _____.

2.   The producer's surplus earned by a factor of production is called

     _____.

3.   Proponents of _____ argued that rent on land had no economic function and could be fully taxed without any reduction in efficiency.

4.   Some financial advisors, most notably the _____, believe that the pattern of past stock prices provides useful information about their future prices.

5.   During a _____, expectations of rising stock prices cause stock prices to rise.

6.   The problem of _____ occurs when an insurance company cannot distinguish between people who are good risks and people who are poor risks.

7.   One theory argues that a college education does not increase a person's productivity— instead employers simply use the college degree as a _____ that a potential employee is more productive.

8.   When an employer cannot fully monitor an employee's work, we say there is a

     _____.

9.   People who are insured tend to take more risks than people who are uninsured, and insurance premiums must be higher to compensate the insurance company for this

     _____.

10. The theory of _____ argues that employers pay wages above the equilibrium rate to help remedy a principal-agent problem.

TRUE-FALSE EXERCISES

_____ 11. Fabian socialists argue that confiscation of rents does not affect social welfare.

_____ 12. Hayek argues that the breadth of scientific knowledge makes social planning a viable alternative to competitive markets.

_____ 13. The traditional measure of deadweight loss always provides an accurate measure of social losses.

_____ 14. In an efficient market, knowledge of past price changes provides valuable information that significantly improves predictions of future price changes.

_____ 15. Financial markets tend to be efficient.

_____ 16. If the stock market is efficient, then all available information is embedded in the current price of the stock.

_____ 17. Signals are socially costly, so signaling equilibria are suboptimal.

_____ 18. An insurance company faces an adverse selection problem when it cannot distinguish between high-risk and low-risk people.

_____ 19. The moral hazard problem occurs because people tend to take the same risks whether they are insured or uninsured.

_____ 20. Principal-agent problems occur when employers cannot receive rent from their employees' work efforts.

MULTIPLE CHOICE QUESTIONS

_____ 21. What is meant by economic rent?
   A.   Rent is the amount earned in excess of the minimum amount necessary to hire a factor of production.
   B.   Rent is another term for social gain.
   C.   Rent is any incentive that causes owners to provide a resource to those people who place the lowest marginal value on it.
   D.   Rent is a payment which creates no social gain and simply enriches the owner of a resource.

◆◆◆ Questions 22 and 23 refer to the following tables which show the marginal cost schedules for three different firms. Also assume that the three firms must produce a total of 6 units of the good if social gain is to be maximized.

Firm A			Firm B			Firm C	
Quantity	MC		Quantity	MC		Quantity	MC
1 unit	$1 per unit		1 unit	$3 per unit		1 unit	$1 per unit
2	3		2	7		2	2
3	6		3	12		3	3

_____ 22. If a competitive price system is used to allocate production of the 6 units, then the total cost will be
A. $12.   C. $17.
B. $13.   D. $18.

_____ 23. If a social planner allocates production of the 6 units by dividing it equally among the three firms, this will create a social loss of
A. $0 (i.e., there will be no social loss).
B. $3.
C. $4.
D. $5.

◆◆◆ Questions 24 and 25 refer to the graph on the right, which shows the supply and demand for military service.

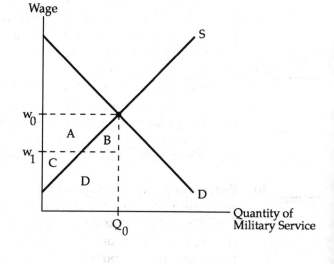

_____ 24. Suppose the government relies on a volunteer army of size Q_0 and pays soldiers the wage w_0. The social cost of this army is
A. the area A + C.
B. the area A + B + C + D.
C. the area B + D.
D. impossible to determine from the given information.

_____ 25. Suppose the government drafts Q_0 persons into the army and pays them the wage w_1. The social cost of this army is
A. the area B + D.
B. the area C + D.
C. the area B + C + D.
D. greater than the area B + D.

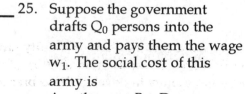

◆◆◆ Questions 26–28 refer to the graph on the right, which shows the supply and demand for a resource. The owner of the resource is receiving price P_0 and is providing the quantity Q_0.

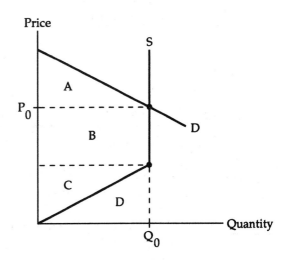

_____ 26. The revenue collected by the owner of the resource is measured by
A.   area A + B + C.
B.   area B + C + D.
C.   area B + C.
D.   area C + D.

_____ 27. The rent earned by the owner of the resource is measured by
A.   area B.
B.   area C.
C.   area D.
D.   area B + C.

_____ 28. Suppose the government confiscates the rent and pays the owner area D to supply Q_0 units of the resource. We can expect the result to be inefficient because
A.   the total value created for consumers will be smaller than area A + B + C + D.
B.   the area B will become a deadweight loss.
C.   the resulting producer's surplus will be smaller than area B + C.
D.   the social gain will fall from area A + B + C to area A + B + C − D.

_____ 29. In an efficient market,
A.   no economic rents will be created.
B.   the informational content of prices is diluted by inflation.
C.   the pattern of past prices will provide useful information about future prices that is unavailable elsewhere.
D.   the market price will fully reflect all available information.

_____ 30. People with automobile insurance drive less carefully than people without insurance, and automobile insurance premiums must be adjusted upwards to account for this fact. This situation is an example of
A.   adverse selection.
B.   a speculative bubble.
C.   moral hazard.
D.   the principal-agent problem.

_____ 31. Consumers prefer high-quality products, but they sometimes have difficulty judging the quality of a product. Consumers often use brand names as an indication of the quality of a product, and firms spend substantial money to develop these brand names. This situation is an example of
A.   signaling.
B.   adverse selection.
C.   efficient markets.
D. · rent.

_____ 32. When do insurance companies encounter the problem of adverse selection?
  A. When simply having insurance causes people to take more risks than they would otherwise.
  B. When they do not have enough information to distinguish between people who are "good risks" and those who are "bad risks."
  C. When the price of insurance premiums fully reflects all available information.
  D. When the insurance company suffers large losses because a major catastrophe has affected a large number of people simultaneously.

_____ 33. Which of the following situations results from a principal-agent problem?
  A. People leaving their doors unlocked because they are insured for loss against theft.
  B. People "dressing up" for job interviews.
  C. People who are "good risks" being unable to purchase as much insurance as they desire.
  D. People being "ripped off" by mechanics who perform unnecessary repairs.

_____ 34. What is meant by an efficiency wage?
  A. The equilibrium wage paid in an efficient market.
  B. A wage higher than the equilibrium wage that is used to address the principal-agent problem.
  C. The wage rate that a social planner would choose to maximize the economy's gains from trade.
  D. A relatively low wage used as a signal for people needing on-the-job training.

_____ 35. Suppose prices and wages both increase by 5%, but people base their decisions on the expectation that inflation is 8%. In this situation, the unemployment rate will
  A. fall, because people are "fooled" by low absolute wages.
  B. fall, because people are "fooled" by high absolute wages.
  C. rise, because people mistakenly believe that their wages have less purchasing power.
  D. rise, because people mistakenly believe that their wages have greater purchasing power.

REVIEW QUESTIONS

36.   Compare and contrast an economy that allocates resources through competitive prices with one where people are actively altruistic and cater to your every whim.

37.   What is rent? Why did the Fabian socialists believe that the government could appropriate rents with no social cost? Why were they wrong?

38.   Since insider trading of stocks is illegal and carries obvious risks, why is insider trading so tempting?

39.   What is a principal-agent problem? What are some possible remedies for principal-agent problems?

40.   Explain why employers might choose to pay workers wages that are higher than the market equilibrium wage. What are such wages called?

41.   Explain why unexpectedly low inflation may increase unemployment.

PROBLEMS

42. Consider the owner of a firm who has superior managerial skills that make his firm more efficient than most other firms in the industry, which is assumed to be competitive. The owner can supply at most 50 weeks of managerial services per year; the owner's marginal cost of providing managerial skills to his firm (MC) and the initial demand for those skills (D) are shown on the axes below.

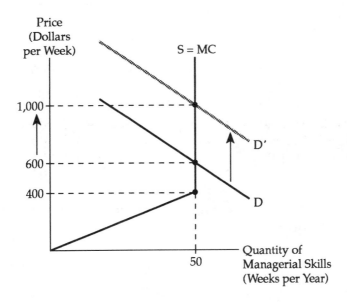

i. What is the minimum payment the owner would accept to supply 50 weeks of labor? What opportunity cost does the firm incur when the owner works at the firm for 50 weeks? How much of this opportunity cost is in the form of rent?

ii. Suppose the demand for the good produced by the firm increases, raising the price of the firm's product and causing new, less-efficient firms to enter the industry. In the long run, the demand for the owner's managerial skills increases to D' as shown in the above diagram. How does this change affect the owner's rent? Explain.

43. A city council determines that much of the city's air pollution is caused by its two major firms (call them A and B). The council wants to reduce the amount of particulate matter (soot and fly ash) that the firms emit daily by a total of 10 tons. The marginal costs that the firms face for reducing their emissions are given in the tables below.

Firm A		Firm B	
Reduction in Emissions	Marginal Cost	Reduction in Emissions	Marginal Cost
1 ton	$ 200 per ton	1 ton	$ 400 per ton
2	300	2	600
3	400	3	800
4	500	4	1,000
5	600	5	1,200
6	700	6	1,400
7	800	7	1,600
8	900	8	1,800
9	1,000	9	2,000
10	1,100	10	2,200

i.   What is the lowest possible cost required to achieve a 10-ton reduction in the firms' total daily emissions?

ii. Suppose the city council decides to treat the two firms equally and establishes a standard requiring each firm to reduce its daily emissions by 5 tons. Calculate the cost of achieving the council's goal under this plan.

iii. Suppose the city council instead imposes a tax on these firms equal to $800 per ton of particulate matter emitted. First use the equimarginal principle to describe how the firms will react to this tax, and then calculate the cost required to achieve the council's goal using this plan.

iv. Compare the efficiency of the two plans for reducing air pollution.

44. Suppose that two prisoners have jointly committed a crime and are awaiting trial. The district attorney has enough evidence to send both prisoners to jail for 5 years, but he would like to strengthen his case (and increase the prisoners' punishment) by obtaining a confession from one or both prisoners. The district attorney offers each prisoner the following deal. If a prisoner confesses and provides additional evidence against his partner, the attorney will let the confessor go free and the partner will get life imprisonment. If both prisoners confess, however, the deal is off, and the district attorney will now have enough evidence to send both prisoners to jail for 20 years. The prisoners are held in separate cells and are not allowed to discuss the deal offered by the district attorney.

   i. If a prisoner acts in his own self-interest, will he choose to confess? Why or why not?

   ii. If each prisoner acts in his own self-interest, is the outcome Pareto optimal? Why or why not?

   iii. Suppose the prisoners, communicating through their lawyers, strike a deal in which each one promises the other that he will not confess. What type of information problem do the prisoners face in enforcing their agreement? Explain.

45.   Jan and Jayce each receive 100 apples per year from a local orchard. Each places a marginal value of $0.40 on the 100th apple. Jan's elasticity of demand for apples is –1.6, and Jayce's elasticity of demand for apples is –0.8.

    i.   One year, the orchard produces an additional 12 apples. If you were a social planner, how should you allocate the additional 12 apples between Jan and Jayce in order to create the most social gain?

    ii.   How would a competitive price system achieve the allocation described in part i? What will be the new market price of apples?

SOLUTIONS

Completion Exercises

1. efficient market
2. rent
3. Fabian socialism
4. technical analysts
5. speculative bubble

6. adverse selection
7. signal
8. principal-agent problem
9. moral hazard
10. efficiency wages

True-False Exercises

11. TRUE.

12. FALSE. Hayek argues that the breadth of <u>specialized</u> knowledge makes social planning <u>less efficient than</u> competitive markets.

13. FALSE. The traditional measure of deadweight loss <u>fails to provide</u> an accurate measure of social losses <u>when allocation decisions are not made on the basis of price.</u>

14. FALSE. In an efficient market, knowledge of past price changes <u>is already reflected in the current market price.</u>

15. TRUE.

16. TRUE.

17. TRUE.

18. TRUE.

19. FALSE. The moral hazard problem occurs because <u>insured people tend to take more risks than uninsured people.</u>

20. FALSE. Principal-agent problems occur when employers cannot <u>fully monitor</u> their employees' work efforts.

Multiple Choice Questions

21. A. Rent is the producer's surplus received by the owner of a resource.

22. B. In competition, the marginal costs of firms will be equated. If a total of 6 units are produced, then all three firms will have a marginal cost of $3 per unit. Firm A will produce 2 units at a cost of $4, Firm B will produce 1 unit at a cost of $3, and Firm C will produce 3 units at a cost of $6. The total cost of the 6 units will be $13.

23.   C. If Firms A, B, and C each produce 2 units, then their costs will be $4, $10, and $3, respectively. The total cost of producing 6 units will be $17, which is $4 greater than the cost achieved by a competitive market.

24.   C. The social cost of the army is the opportunity cost of having men and women in military service instead of some other occupation. This opportunity cost is measured by the area under the supply curve.

25.   D. If the government drafts men and women with high opportunity costs instead of those with low opportunity costs, then the area B + D will underestimate the actual cost of the army.

26.   B. The rectangle B + C + D has the quantity supplied as the base and the price per unit as the width, so the area of this rectangle represents the total amount paid to the owner.

27.   D. Rent is the producer's surplus received by the owner of the resource.

28.   A. Although the confiscation of rents makes the producer's surplus equal to zero, the result can still be efficient if the resource is given to those consumers who place the highest value on the resource. Without the price system to give the owner the incentive to locate those consumers, however, the area under the demand curve (area A + B + C + D) will overestimate the total value created.

29.   D. This statement is simply the definition of an efficient market.

30.   C. The risks of an accident have changed because of the insurance, so the premiums must be adjusted to account for this moral hazard.

31.   A. Consumers use the brand name as a signal to distinguish high-quality goods from low-quality goods.

32.   B. When they cannot distinguish high-risk people from low-risk people, the insurance companies face an adverse selection problem and must limit the amount of insurance offered for low-risk people.

33.   D. The mechanic is the agent, and a person hiring the mechanic is the principal. The principal cannot fully monitor the agent's performance, so there is a principal-agent problem.

34.   B. The theory of efficiency wages argues that a wage high enough to create involuntary unemployment provides workers with an incentive to not shirk.

35.   C. Relative prices are actually unchanged, but people think prices are rising faster than wages. They are fooled into believing that their wages are not keeping up with inflation. Consequently, people cut back on their labor supply, and the unemployment rate rises.

Review Questions

36.   You would probably favor the world in which people cater to your every whim because your "share of the pie" will be very large in such a world. You will find it very difficult to communicate your desires in this world, however, because you lack the specialized knowledge of others. Consequently, the total "pie" will also be very small. The economy with competitive prices will be much more efficient and will create a much larger "pie," because prices are able to convey information and provide incentives for people to act on their own information.

37.   Rent is any payment for a resource in excess of the minimum amount necessary to call it into existence. The Fabian socialists argued that this surplus was an unnecessary incentive for resource owners, so the rent could go to the government without affecting the quantity supplied of resources. The problem with this argument is that it ignores the informational content of prices. Without the price system and the incentive of the rents it creates, resource owners would be unable to supply their resources to those people who place the highest value on them. In this case, the resources would not create the maximum possible value for consumers, causing a loss in efficiency even though the quantity supplied of the resources would not be affected.

38.   The stock market tends to be highly efficient; all available information is already reflected in the price of the stock. Only inside information may not yet be accounted for in the price of a stock. Therefore, inside information provides a far greater opportunity for someone to earn a profit than does public information.

39.   A principal-agent problem occurs when an employer (called the principal) is unable to fully monitor his employee (called the agent). This situation creates inefficiency, because if the principal could be certain of getting what he pays for, then higher wages could be paid to the agent for better work, making both employer and employee better off. Fringe benefits, profit sharing, and efficiency wages can be used to remedy the principal-agent problem.

40.   In order to address the principal-agent problem, employers need the ability to punish workers who are caught shirking. If the labor market is in equilibrium, then firing the

shirker is no punishment at all, because the shirker can simply move on to another job. If wages are above the market equilibrium, however, then there is a surplus of labor in the market and a fired worker takes the risk of being unable to find another job. In this case, workers have an incentive to provide good job performance. These higher-than-equilibrium wages are called efficiency wages.

41.   If inflation is lower than what people expect, people may be "fooled" by low absolute wages. People may think prices are rising more than their wages are, which causes people to reduce the amount of labor they provide and creates unemployment. If people had correctly realized that prices and wages were rising by the same percentage, they would have seen that relative prices were unchanged and would not have adjusted their work efforts.

Problems

42.   i.   The minimum payment that the owner would accept is given by the area beneath the supply curve. This area is a triangle with a base of 50 weeks per year and a height of $400 per week. The area of a triangle is calculated taking ½ times the base times the height, so ½ × 50 × 400 or $10,000 per year is the minimum payment the owner would accept to supply 50 weeks of managerial services.

The owner's managerial services command a price of $600 per week in the market. Thus, the firm could rent out 50 weeks of the owner's services for $600 per week × 50 weeks or $30,000, which is the opportunity cost the firm incurs for the owner's services. Rent is the portion of this payment in excess of the minimum amount the owner will accept, so rent in this situation equals $30,000 – $10,000 or $20,000.

ii.   The owner's managerial skills now command a price of $1,000 per week in the market, for a total of $50,000 for 50 weeks of work. The owner's rent is this amount minus the $10,000 minimum needed to get him to supply 50 hours of services, which equals $40,000. Thus, the long-run increase in demand raises the owner's rent by $20,000.

43.   i.   To achieve the lowest possible cost, each consecutive ton of reduced emissions should be undertaken by the firm with the lowest marginal cost. Firm A should reduce its emissions by 7 tons daily (costing $3,500), and Firm B should reduce its emissions by 3 tons daily (costing $1,800). Consequently, emissions can be reduced by 10 tons daily at a cost of $5,300.

ii. Firm A's cost of reducing emissions by 5 tons daily will be $2,000 ($200, $300, $400, $500, and $600 for the first, second, third, fourth, and fifth tons, respectively). Firm B's cost of reducing emissions by 5 tons daily will be $4,000 ($400, $600, $800, $1,000, and $1,200 for the first, second, third, fourth, and fifth tons, respectively). The cost of reducing air pollution under the proposed standard is $6,000.

iii. According to the equimarginal principle, each firm will reduce its emissions up to the point where the marginal cost of doing so equals the marginal benefit obtained from avoiding the tax. Therefore, each firm will reduce its emissions until the marginal cost exceeds $800 per ton. Firm A will reduce its emissions by 7 tons daily (costing $3,500), and Firm B will reduce its emissions by 3 tons daily (costing $1,800). The cost of reducing air pollution under the proposed tax is $5,300. (The tax revenue is a transfer of wealth from the firms to tax recipients and does not count as a social cost.)

iv. The city council does not have access to the specialized knowledge about the firms' costs, so the standard ignores the fact that Firm A has the lowest marginal cost of reducing its emissions. This situation creates a social loss, because the cost of reducing emissions is then higher than necessary ($6,000 instead of $5,300).

   The tax on emissions takes advantage of the incentives provided by the price system. The tax allows each firm to apply its specialized knowledge of its costs to its own advantage. Consequently, the cost of reducing emissions is as low as possible, and there is no social loss.

44. i. It is in a prisoner's self-interest to confess. If his partner does not confess, then the prisoner has the choice of remaining silent and getting 5 years in prison or confessing and going free. If his partner does confess, then the prisoner has the choice of remaining silent and getting life imprisonment or confessing and getting 20 years in prison. In either case, the prisoner's best option is to confess. (This situation is called the "Prisoners' Dilemma" and will be discussed in more detail in Chapters 11 and 12.)

   ii. When both prisoners act in their own self-interest, they both confess and get 20 years in prison. This outcome is not Pareto optimal. If both prisoners remained silent, then they would both get 5 years in prison, and both would be better off. However, the optimal situation for the prisoners is not an equilibrium situation, because each prisoner would be tempted to confess so that he could go free.

iii.   If the prisoners strike a deal and promise each other to remain silent, then both prisoners face a principal-agent problem. In essence, each prisoner is a principal who has "hired" his partner as an agent whose job is to remain silent. Just like the principal cannot fully monitor the agent's performance, the prisoner has no way of making sure his partner keeps the agreement. The principal-agent problem makes their agreement more difficult to enforce.

45. i.   For social gain to be at a maximum, Jan and Jayce must place the same marginal value on an additional apple. The elasticity coefficients show that for each 1% decline in marginal value, Jan's quantity demanded must rise by 1.6% and Jayce's quantity demanded must rise by 0.8%. Therefore, to create the most social gain, you must allocate twice as many apples to Jan as you do to Jayce. Since there are 12 additional apples to allocate, you should give 8 apples to Jan and 4 apples to Jayce.

ii.   Initially, the price of apples is $0.40 per apple, and Jan and Jayce each purchase 100 apples per year from the local orchard. The surplus of 12 apples causes the market price to fall by just enough to cause Jan to buy 8 more apples (an 8% increase) and Jayce to buy 4 more apples (a 4% increase). For each person, the elasticity coefficient times the percent change in price equals the percent change in quantity demanded. This equation shows that the price changes by –5% (notice that –1.6 × –5% = 8% for Jan and –0.8 × –5% = 4% for Jayce). Therefore, the price of apples will fall by $0.02 per apple (5% × $0.40), from $0.40 to $0.38 per apple.

CHAPTER 10

MONOPOLY

This chapter begins a two-chapter unit on noncompetitive goods markets with an introduction to the concepts of monopoly and market power. The first section of the chapter examines the monopoly equilibrium, the second section discusses the causes of monopoly, and the final section surveys the various pricing schemes that are used by monopolies.

KEY TERMS

- Market power (or monopoly power)
- Monopoly
- Rate-of-return regulation
- Natural monopoly

- Patent
- Legal barriers to entry
- Price discrimination
- First-degree price discrimination

- Second-degree price discrimination
- Third-degree price discrimination
- Two-part tariff

KEY IDEAS

- **Section 10.1.** A monopoly is any firm that faces a downward-sloping demand curve for its product. Consequently, marginal revenue is always smaller than price for a monopoly. In order to maximize its profit, the monopoly will produce the quantity for which marginal revenue equals marginal cost. The price charged by the monopoly will be determined by the demand curve for its product.

- **Section 10.2.** Sources of monopoly power include economies of scale, patents, control of resources, and legal barriers to entry. If economies of scale cause the average cost curve to still be decreasing when it crosses the industry demand curve, the monopoly is called a natural monopoly.

◆ **Section 10.3.** A monopoly can increase its profit by charging different prices for identical items. A monopoly practices first-degree price discrimination when it charges each consumer the maximum he is willing to pay. Second-degree price discrimination occurs when the monopoly offers different prices to the same customer, as is done with quantity discounts. If the monopoly can identify two separate groups of buyers and charge a different price to each group, this is called third-degree price discrimination. Finally, a monopoly is using a two-part tariff when it charges consumers an initial fee for the right to purchase its good.

COMPLETION EXERCISES

1. A firm has _____ when its decisions can affect the market price of its product.

2. A monopoly is forced to set prices in such a way that it earns zero economic profit when _____ is imposed.

3. When a firm has a new invention, it can apply for a _____ and receive a legally protected monopoly for 17 years.

4. When a firm's average cost curve is still declining at the point where it crosses the market demand curve, the firm is classified as a _____.

5. The traditional measure of deadweight loss underestimates the social cost of a monopoly created by _____, because resources are wasted in lobbying efforts geared towards obtaining the monopoly.

6. A seller must have some monopoly power and be able to control resales of its product in order for any form of _____ to be profitable.

7. A monopoly is practicing _____ when it charges the same consumer different prices for the same item.

8. When a monopoly uses a _____, it should charge the competitive price for its product and attempt to collect the entire consumers' surplus for the entry fee.

9. When a monopoly practices _____, it charges a lower price to the group with the more elastic demand.

10. When a monopoly can charge each consumer the maximum amount that he is willing to pay, the pricing scheme is called _____.

TRUE-FALSE EXERCISES

_____ 11. For a monopolist, marginal revenue is less than the price charged.

_____ 12. A monopolist's marginal revenue will be negative whenever demand is downward sloping.

_____ 13. A monopolist charges a price equal to its marginal cost.

_____ 14. A monopoly's supply curve is always unit elastic.

_____ 15. An effective price ceiling causes a monopoly to reduce its output.

_____ 16. When conditions for natural monopoly exist, competition cannot provide any increases in social gain.

_____ 17. If a simple monopoly begins to practice first- or second-degree price discrimination, social welfare will fall.

_____ 18. First-degree price discrimination benefits both the monopoly and the consumers.

_____ 19. Second-degree price discrimination benefits both the monopoly and the consumers.

_____ 20. Any producer selling in two different markets will choose quantities so that the elasticity of demand is the same in each market.

MULTIPLE CHOICE QUESTIONS

_____ 21. Which of the following equations holds for a simple profit-maximizing monopoly?
  A. Marginal revenue equals marginal cost.
  B. Price equals marginal revenue.
  C. Price equals marginal cost.
  D. Price equals average cost.

_____ 22. For a simple, profit-maximizing monopoly, if demand is elastic then
   A.   the monopoly is guaranteed a positive economic profit.
   B.   the monopoly's marginal revenue must be positive.
   C.   the monopoly should increase its output until demand becomes inelastic.
   D.   the monopoly can still take advantage of economies of scale.

_____ 23. Suppose a monopoly has constant marginal and average costs. An excise tax of $1 per unit will increase a monopoly's equilibrium price by
   A.   the same amount as it would increase the long-run equilibrium price in a competitive constant-cost industry.
   B.   exactly $1 per unit.
   C.   more than $1 per unit.
   D.   less than $1 per unit.

_____ 24. A monopoly's supply curve
   A.   is that portion of its marginal cost curve that lies above its average variable cost curve.
   B.   is that portion of its marginal cost curve that lies above its average cost curve.
   C.   does not exist.
   D.   coincides with its marginal revenue curve.

_____ 25. Which of the following *cannot*, in general, be used to eliminate the deadweight loss due to monopoly?
   A.   An excise subsidy.
   B.   An effective price ceiling.
   C.   Rate-of-return regulation.
   D.   First-degree price discrimination.

_____ 26. Consider a price ceiling imposed on a simple, profit-maximizing monopoly. For what quantities will the monopoly's new marginal revenue schedule be equal to the ceiling price?
   A.   For those quantities where consumers are willing to pay more than the ceiling price.
   B.   For those quantities where demand is price elastic.
   C.   For those quantities where the monopoly's marginal cost is falling.
   D.   For those quantities where the price ceiling is ineffective.

_____ 27. Suppose regulators require a monopoly to produce the quantity where its average cost curve crosses the demand curve. In this situation,
   A.   the monopoly will have to be subsidized, because the price it will receive is too low for it to avoid economic losses.
   B.   the deadweight loss due to monopoly will be eliminated.
   C.   the monopoly will earn a zero economic profit.
   D.   the regulation will be ineffective and the monopoly's price and output will remain unchanged.

_____ 28. Which of the following statements about natural monopoly is *false?*
   A. For a natural monopoly, the average cost curve is decreasing at the point where it crosses the demand curve.
   B. A natural monopoly is likely to exist when production exhibits low fixed costs and high marginal cost.
   C. If a natural monopoly charges the competitive price, it will suffer economic losses.
   D. The welfare consequences of natural monopoly are uncertain, because comparison with competition is invalid.

_____ 29. The area showing deadweight loss in a monopoly diagram underestimates the actual welfare cost of monopoly when the source of monopoly power is
   A. economies of scale.
   B. patents.
   C. ownership of an essential resource.
   D. a legal barrier to entry.

_____ 30. Which of the following is the best example of second-degree price discrimination?
   A. Colleges use financial aid to charge different prices to different students.
   B. Retail stores advertise "Buy one, get the second at half price."
   C. Movie theaters give senior citizens a 20% discount on admission.
   D. Natural food stores offer lower prices to customers who purchase a $20 "frequent customer" discount card.

_____ 31. Furniture stores often set prices significantly higher than the competitive level and allow their salespersons to offer discounts depending on their perceptions of a customer's willingness to pay. This pricing strategy is an attempt to implement
   A. first-degree price discrimination.
   B. second-degree price discrimination.
   C. third-degree price discrimination.
   D. a two-part tariff.

_____ 32. When a two-part tariff is used,
   A. regulators allow the monopoly to charge lower prices to its industrial customers than to its residential customers.
   B. the monopoly's market is divided into two noncompeting submarkets.
   C. the monopoly lowers its usual prices whenever a potential rival threatens to enter the market.
   D. the monopoly attempts to appropriate the consumers' surplus by charging customers an entry fee.

_____ 33. When a monopoly practices third-degree price discrimination, it charges the highest price to the group that
   A. has the most elastic demand.
   B. has the most inelastic demand.
   C. purchases the highest quantity.
   D. purchases the lowest quantity.

_____ 34. Which of the following is *not* a good example of third-degree price discrimination?
   A.   Lower prices for people who use manufacturers' coupons.
   B.   Discounts for senior citizens buying prescription drugs.
   C.   Lower airline prices for travelers who are staying over a Saturday night.
   D.   Lower salad bar prices for people who purchase an entree.

_____ 35. Which of the following pricing practices may *not* increase the social gain created by a simple profit-maximizing monopoly?
   A.   First-degree price discrimination.
   B.   Second-degree price discrimination.
   C.   Third-degree price discrimination.
   D.   A two-part tariff.

REVIEW QUESTIONS

36.   Explain why a simple profit-maximizing monopoly charges a price higher than its marginal cost. What does this fact imply about a monopolized market as compared to a competitive market?

37.   Explain why a simple profit-maximizing monopoly always operates on the elastic portion of the demand curve.

38.   List four sources of monopoly power. For each source, indicate how the basic welfare analysis of deadweight loss under monopoly should be modified.

39.   What is a natural monopoly? Why can't the market support a competitive industry under the conditions of natural monopoly?

40.   Is price discrimination ever beneficial for consumers? Does price discrimination ever improve the market's efficiency?

41.   Compare and contrast a two-part tariff and first-degree price discrimination.

PROBLEMS

42. i.   Consider two market structures: a monopoly with constant long-run average and
          marginal costs and a competitive constant-cost industry in the long run. Suppose the
          government places an excise tax on the producers in these industries. Complete the
          diagrams below to show the effects of this taxation. Label the following in your
          diagrams:

          a.   the pretax and post-tax equilibria,
          b.   consumers' surplus after the tax,
          c.   tax revenue collected by the government,
          d.   the monopoly's after-tax profit, and
          e.   the deadweight loss due to the tax.

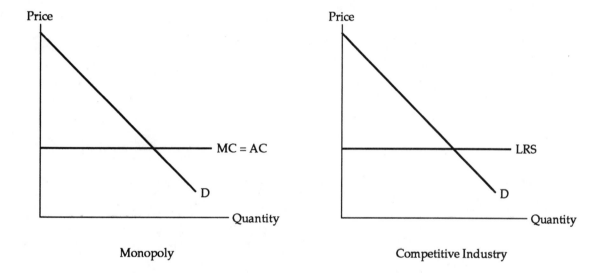

          Monopoly   Competitive Industry

     ii. As costs rise and fall, which price will fluctuate more: the long-run monopoly price or
          the long-run competitive price? Explain, using your answer to part i.

     iii. As demand rises and falls, which price do you think will fluctuate more: the long-run
          monopoly price or the long-run competitive price? Justify your conjecture.

43.   Suppose a monopoly practices third-degree price discrimination by separating its customers into two groups: consumers under 65 and senior citizens. The monopoly's marginal cost is given by $MC = \frac{1}{20}Q$, where Q is the total output produced by the monopoly. The demand and marginal revenue for consumers under 65 are given by $P_1 = 25 - \frac{1}{6}Q_1$ and $MR_1 = 25 - \frac{1}{3}Q_1$, respectively, where Q_1 is the quantity demanded by consumers under 65 and P_1 is the price the monopoly charges to this group. The demand and marginal revenue for senior citizens are given by $P_2 = 15 - \frac{1}{8}Q_2$ and $MR_2 = 15 - \frac{1}{4}Q_2$, respectively, where Q_2 is the quantity demanded by senior citizens and P_2 is the price the monopoly charges them.

   i.   Use the equilibrium condition $MR_1 = MR_2 = MC$ to solve for the equilibrium quantities Q_1, Q_2, and Q. (*Hint* – First substitute $Q = Q_1 + Q_2$ into the formula for marginal cost. The equilibrium condition then gives you two equations in two unknowns, which can be solved using standard techniques.)

   ii.   Use the demand formulas and your answers to part i to find the price that the monopoly charges in each market.

   iii.   Use your answers to part i to find the common equilibrium value of MR_1 and MR_2. Use this value, your answers to part ii, and the equation $MR = P \cdot (1 - \frac{1}{|\eta|})$ to find the price elasticity coefficient η for each market. Verify that the monopoly charges the lower price to the group with the more elastic demand.

44. Determine whether each of the following situations is an example of first-degree price discrimination, second-degree price discrimination, third-degree price discrimination, a two-part tariff, or none of these. Justify your choices.

   i.   Airlines have "frequent flier" plans, in which the consumer is given a free or discounted flight after compiling a certain level of mileage in flights with the airline.

   ii. A car salesperson typically works with a 15 percent profit margin. A good salesperson "sizes up the customer" and determines how much of this profit margin can be given away to land the sale.

   iii. Many pizza restaurants charge $8.99 for the first pizza ordered and only $4.00 more for each additional pizza.

   iv. Many video stores offer consumers two alternative payment plans for renting videos. Consumers may join the store's video club for an annual membership fee; club members are charged a small fee for each video rental. Consumers who choose not to join the store's video club pay higher rental fees. (*Hint* – The video stores are combining two different pricing schemes in this situation.)

45.   Sumatran coffee beans are produced by a simple profit-maximizing monopoly. The marginal cost to produce Sumatran coffee beans is constant at $4 per pound. The elasticity of demand for Sumatran coffee beans is constant at –1.4.

    i.   Calculate the price charged for Sumatran coffee beans.

    ii.   Poor weather conditions cause the marginal cost of production to rise by $1 per pound. What happens to the price of Sumatran coffee beans?

    iii.   The development of a popular new variety of coffee bean makes demand for Sumatran coffee beans more elastic. What happens to the price of Sumatran coffee beans?

SOLUTIONS

Completion Exercises

1.   market power
2.   rate-of-return regulation
3.   patent
4.   natural monopoly
5.   legal barriers to entry

6.   price discrimination
7.   second-degree price discrimination
8.   two-part tariff
9.   third-degree price discrimination
10.   first-degree price discrimination

True-False Exercises

11.   TRUE.

12.   FALSE. A monopolist's marginal revenue will be negative whenever demand is <u>inelastic</u>.

13.   FALSE. A monopolist charges a price <u>greater than</u> its marginal cost.

14.   FALSE. A monopoly's supply curve <u>is a meaningless concept</u>.

15.   FALSE. An effective price ceiling causes a monopoly to <u>increase</u> its output.

16.   FALSE. When conditions for natural monopoly exist, competition <u>can stimulate product improvements that have social value.</u>

17.   FALSE. If a simple monopoly begins to practice first- or second-degree price discrimination, social welfare will <u>rise</u>.

18.   FALSE. First-degree price discrimination benefits <u>the monopoly but reduces consumers' surplus to zero.</u>

19.   TRUE.

20.   FALSE. Any producer selling in two different markets will choose quantities so that the <u>marginal revenue</u> is the same in each market.

Multiple Choice Questions

21.   A. The monopoly maximizes its profit by choosing the quantity where marginal revenue equals marginal cost.

22.   B. Recall that $MR = P \cdot (1 - 1/|\eta|)$ where η is the price elasticity of demand. If demand is elastic, then $|\eta| > 1$ and $MR > 0$.

23.   D. If marginal cost increases by $1 per unit, then a profit-maximizing monopoly must reduce its output so that marginal revenue also increases by $1 per unit. The resulting

increase in price will therefore be less than $1 per unit, since the demand curve is flatter than the marginal revenue curve.

24.   C. When we use a supply curve, we presume that the firm determines its output level based on a given market price. The monopoly's actions, however, determine the price it charges. Consequently, there is no pre-established market price, and the concept of a supply curve is meaningless for a monopoly.

25.   C. When rate-of-return regulation is used, a price ceiling is set at the price where the demand curve crosses the average cost curve. For the deadweight loss to be zero, the price ceiling must be set at the price where the demand curve crosses the marginal cost curve. These two prices are almost never identical.

26.   A. When consumers are willing to pay more than the ceiling price, the demand curve lies above the ceiling price and the price ceiling is effective. The monopoly cannot affect the market price when the price ceiling is effective, so the monopoly's marginal revenue curve is horizontal like a competitive firm's at these quantities.

27.   C. Zero profit occurs when price equals average cost.

28.   B. Natural monopoly is likely to occur when production exhibits high fixed costs and low marginal cost. This situation is common in public utilities.

29.   D. Firms will spend resources lobbying legislators to obtain a monopoly created by a legal barrier to entry. The deadweight loss does not include these lobbying costs, so it underestimates the welfare cost of monopoly.

30.   B. In second-degree price discrimination, the monopoly charges different prices to the same consumer. This type of pricing scheme usually takes the form of quantity discounts. (Quantity discounts do not always indicate second-degree price discrimination; they can also be a result of lower production costs.)

31.   A. In first-degree price discrimination, the monopoly charges each consumer the maximum he is willing to pay. The furniture stores' strategy allows it to estimate an individual customer's willingness to pay and charge appropriately.

32.   D. In a two-part tariff, the consumer must pay a fee in exchange for the right to purchase the good.

33.   B. Recall that $MR = P \cdot (1 - 1/|\eta|)$ where η is the price elasticity of demand. When third-degree price discrimination is used, all groups must have the same marginal revenue

for the monopoly's profit to be maximized. The value of $|\eta|$ is smallest for the group with the most inelastic demand, so the value of P must also be the highest for this group.

34.   D. People who order an entree will generally eat less from a salad bar than people who have the salad bar for a meal, so the restaurant is not actually charging different prices for the same good. The "salad bar with entree" has a lower price because it costs the restaurant less than a "salad bar without entree."

35.   C. When a simple profit-maximizing monopoly begins to use third-degree price discrimination, total output and social gain may either increase or decrease.

Review Questions

36.   The monopoly's price is always larger than its marginal revenue, since the sale of an additional unit requires the monopoly to lower its price on all previous units. The profit-maximizing monopoly produces the quantity where marginal revenue equals marginal cost, so its price must also be larger than its marginal cost. This inequality indicates that a deadweight loss exists in the monopolized market, since a competitive industry would produce the quantity where price equals marginal cost.

37.   Marginal revenue is positive when demand is elastic and negative when demand is inelastic. A simple profit-maximizing monopoly will produce the quantity where marginal revenue equals marginal cost. The monopoly's marginal cost is always positive, so the profit-maximizing quantity must occur where marginal revenue is also positive. Therefore, demand must be elastic at the profit-maximizing quantity.

38.   Four sources of monopoly power are economies of scale, patents, control of an essential resource, and legal barriers to entry. When economies of scale create a natural monopoly, a competitive industry is not a viable alternative. Therefore, it is uncertain whether the deadweight "loss" is actually a loss in this case. The monopoly power granted by patents provides an incentive for firms to pursue the development of some inventions and not others, so the effect that the length of a patent has on deadweight loss is also uncertain. In the case of a resource monopoly, no serious alterations to the welfare analysis are needed. Finally, when legal barriers to entry are available, the deadweight loss underestimates the true social cost of monopoly, because firms spend resources on lobbying efforts to obtain the right to operate in the entry-restricted market.

39. A natural monopoly exists when the average cost curve is still decreasing as it crosses the demand curve. The point where the marginal cost curve crosses the demand curve must therefore lie beneath the average cost curve. The competitive price equals firms' marginal costs, and so it must be less than firms' average costs in this case. A competitive industry cannot be supported under the conditions of natural monopoly, because all firms would earn negative profits.

40. There are two situations in which price discrimination is beneficial for consumers. Second-degree price discrimination benefits consumers, because they are allowed to purchase additional units of the good at a discounted price which increases the consumers' surplus. Third-degree price discrimination benefits the consumers with the more elastic demand, because they will pay a lower price and earn more consumers' surplus than if they paid the standard monopoly price. (However, the group of consumers with the more inelastic demand is hurt by third-degree price discrimination.)

   Two types of price discrimination always improve the market's efficiency. Both first- and second-degree price discrimination cause social gain to increase, because the monopoly increases its output under these pricing schemes. In fact, there is no deadweight loss when first-degree price discrimination is perfectly implemented (although all social gain goes to the monopoly in this case). The effect that third-degree price discrimination has on social gain is uncertain, because the monopoly may or may not increase its total output in this case.

41. The prices that consumers pay are different under a two-part tariff and first-degree price discrimination. In a two-part tariff, all consumers pay the same price, but they must also pay an entry fee for the right to purchase the monopoly's product. Each consumer pays a different price in first-degree price discrimination, because each consumer is charged the maximum amount that he is willing to pay for the good. Also notice that a two-part tariff is not a form of price discrimination, because all consumers pay the same price. A two-part tariff and first-degree price discrimination, if perfectly implemented, have identical effects on the monopoly's output and the gains from trade. In both cases, the monopoly will produce the competitive quantity. The social gain will be as large as possible and go entirely to the monopoly, while the consumers' surplus will be zero.

Problems

42.   i.

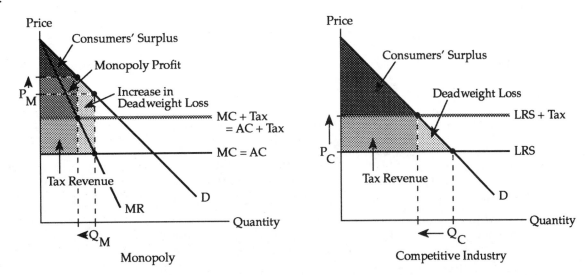

Monopoly

Competitive Industry

ii.   The long-run competitive price is more sensitive to changes in cost than is the long-run monopoly price. As shown in the above graphs, the competitive price rises more than does the monopoly price when marginal costs rise. Similarly, if marginal costs fall, more of the price decrease will be passed on to the consumers of a competitive industry's product than to the consumers of a monopoly's product. (If the competitive industry is a constant-cost industry like that shown, changes in marginal cost will be entirely passed on to consumers in the long run.)

iii.   The long-run monopoly price is more sensitive to changes in demand than is the long-run competitive price. In a competitive market, the long-run equilibrium price is determined entirely by firms' break-even prices. For example, in a competitive constant-cost industry, the long-run price does not change as demand rises or falls, because all firms have the same break-even price. On the other hand, in a monopoly market, changes in demand will affect the monopoly's marginal revenue, which can easily alter the equilibrium price and quantity. In fact, it can be shown that the monopoly price will increase when demand increases, as long as the new demand curve is not too elastic.

43.   i.   First notice that the marginal cost equation can be rewritten as $MC = \frac{1}{20}(Q_1 + Q_2)$. The equilibrium condition gives us two equations in two unknowns: $MR_1 = MR_2$ and $MR_2 = MC$. Solving the latter equation for Q_1 yields $15 - \frac{1}{4}Q_2 = \frac{1}{20}(Q_1 + Q_2)$ $\Rightarrow 300 - 5Q_2 = Q_1 + Q_2 \Rightarrow Q_1 = 300 - 6Q_2$. Substitute this equation into $MR_1 = MR_2$

and solve for Q_2: $25 - \frac{1}{3}Q_1 = 15 - \frac{1}{4}Q_2 \Rightarrow 25 - \frac{1}{3}(300 - 6Q_2) = 15 - \frac{1}{4}Q_2 \Rightarrow$

$25 - 100 + 2Q_2 = 15 - \frac{1}{4}Q_2 \Rightarrow 90 = \frac{9}{4}Q_2 \Rightarrow Q_2 = 40$ units of output. Substitute this

value into the previous equation for Q_1 to find the amount sold in the other market:

$Q_1 = 300 - 6Q_2 = 300 - 6 \cdot 40 = 300 - 240 = 60$ units of output. Thus, the monopoly's

total output is $Q = Q_1 + Q_2 = 60 + 40 = 100$ units of output.

ii. Simply substitute the quantities found in part i into the demand equations: $P_1 =$

25 $- \frac{1}{6}Q_1 = 25 - \frac{1}{6} \cdot 60 = 25 - 10 = 15$ dollars per unit, and $P_2 = 15 - \frac{1}{8}Q_2 =$

$15 - \frac{1}{8} \cdot 40 = 15 - 5 = 10$ dollars per unit.

iii. Substituting Q_1 into the formula for MR_1 shows $MR_1 = 25 - \frac{1}{3}Q_1 = 25 - \frac{1}{3} \cdot 60 =$

$25 - 20 = 5$ dollars per unit. Substituting Q_2 into the formula for MR_2 shows

$MR_2 = 15 - \frac{1}{4}Q_2 = 15 - \frac{1}{4} \cdot 40 = 15 - 10 = 5$ dollars per unit. Substituting $MR_1 = 5$ and

$P_1 = 15$ into the equation $MR = P \cdot (1 - \frac{1}{|\eta|})$ gives $5 = 15 \cdot (1 - \frac{1}{|\eta|}) \Rightarrow \frac{1}{3} = 1 - \frac{1}{|\eta|}$

$\Rightarrow \frac{1}{|\eta|} = \frac{2}{3} \Rightarrow |\eta| = \frac{3}{2} = 1\frac{1}{2}$ is the elasticity coefficient in the market for consumers

under 65. Substituting $MR_2 = 5$ and $P_2 = 10$ into the same equation gives $5 = 10 \cdot (1 -$

$\frac{1}{|\eta|}) \Rightarrow \frac{1}{2} = 1 - \frac{1}{|\eta|} \Rightarrow \frac{1}{|\eta|} = \frac{1}{2} \Rightarrow |\eta| = 2$ is the elasticity coefficient in the market

for senior citizens. Larger absolute values indicate more elastic demand, so senior

citizens have the more elastic demand, and as shown in the previous part, they are

indeed charged the lower price.

44. i. The "frequent flier" program is an example of second-degree price discrimination. The

same consumer is being charged different prices for the same good.

ii. A good car salesperson uses first-degree price discrimination. If the salesperson

correctly "sizes up the customer," each consumer is charged the maximum he is

willing to pay.

iii. The pizza prices most likely represent the restaurant's costs and are not an example of

price discrimination. When a customer orders a second pizza, he does not need a

second waiter, a second table, or a second attendant at the cash register. These factors

make the second pizza genuinely cheaper for the restaurant to produce.

iv. The payment for members of the video club is a two-part tariff. The video store is

using the membership fee to appropriate some of the consumers' surplus. The video

club serves a second purpose; it allows the video store to use third-degree price

discrimination. People who watch lots of movies will have more elastic demand than

people who only watch occasional movies. The video club allows the store to identify these two groups and charge them appropriate prices. The video store will have difficulty preventing resale, but the membership fee helps it to recoup any proceeds it loses from club members renting videos for non-club members.

45. i. To maximize profit, the monopoly must choose its price so that marginal revenue equals $4 per pound. Substitute $MR = 4$ and $|\eta| = 1.4$ into the equation $MR = P \cdot (1 - 1/|\eta|)$ and solve for P: $4 = P \cdot (1 - 1/1.4) \Rightarrow 2/7\, P = 4 \Rightarrow P = \$14$ per pound.

ii. The monopoly must raise its price so that marginal revenue equals $5 per pound – a 25% increase. The elasticity coefficient $|\eta|$ is constant, so the equation $MR = P \cdot (1 - 1/|\eta|)$ shows that the price must also rise by 25%, from $14 to $17.50 per pound.

iii. Since marginal cost is unchanged, the monopoly must choose its price so that marginal revenue is unchanged. Thus, the right-hand side of the equation $MR = P \cdot (1 - 1/|\eta|)$ must also remain unchanged. When demand becomes more elastic, $|\eta|$ becomes larger, and the value $1 - 1/|\eta|$ also becomes larger. The monopoly must therefore reduce its price to obtain the maximum profit.

CHAPTER 11

MARKET POWER, COLLUSION, AND OLIGOPOLY

This chapter concludes a two-chapter unit on noncompetitive goods markets. The focus for the chapter is the acquisition and exploitation of monopoly power by firms. Several different models of firms with market power are surveyed, providing insight into mergers, cartels, regulation, oligopoly, and monopolistic competition.

KEY TERMS

- Horizontal integration
- Vertical integration
- Antitrust laws
- Tournament
- Predatory pricing
- Buy-outs

- Resale price maintenance (or fair trade)
- Collusion
- Cartel
- Prisoners' Dilemma
- Blue laws

- Creative response
- Oligopoly
- Contestable market
- Cournot model
- Bertrand model
- Product differentiation
- Monopolistic competition

KEY IDEAS

- **Section 11.1.** Firms are often accused of using horizontal mergers, vertical mergers, predatory pricing, buy-outs, and resale price maintenance in their attempts to gain monopoly power. Economic analysis shows that the profitability of predatory pricing and buy-outs is severely limited and that social gain can actually increase because of horizontal mergers, vertical mergers, and resale price maintenance. Nevertheless, U.S. antitrust laws (as interpreted by the courts) limit many of these practices, even when they do improve economic welfare.

- **Section 11.2.** A cartel is formed when the firms in an industry collude to set prices and output. The Prisoners' Dilemma shows that each member of a cartel has the incentive to cheat on the cartel agreement, and so some form of outside enforcement is needed for a cartel to be successful.

◆   **Section 11.3.** Government and its regulatory agencies can sometimes lessen competition in an industry by becoming the outside enforcer of a *de facto* cartel. Examples of such regulation include professional licensing, minimum quality standards, minimum prices, and blue laws. Some studies, however, show that regulation has limited effects on economic behavior.

◆   **Section 11.4.** An oligopoly is an industry in which the number of firms is sufficiently small that any one firm's actions can affect market conditions. Models of oligopoly include contestable markets, the Cournot model, and the Bertrand model. These models show that economic results are quite sensitive to the assumptions made about a firm's perceptions of other firms' behavior.

◆   **Section 11.5.** In monopolistic competition, a large number of firms produce similar but differentiated products. In the long run, firms in monopolistic competition do not minimize the average cost of production. This social loss must be weighed against the benefits of having differentiated products when examining the welfare consequences of monopolistic competition.

COMPLETION EXERCISES

1.   When one firm produces an input used by another firm, a merger of the two firms is called

      _____.

2.   A _____ can lead to inefficiency, because a firm may make large investments to create only slight improvements over a rival's product.

3.   A firm is using _____ when it tries to drive rivals out of the industry by setting prices so low that losses are created.

4.   A disadvantage of _____ is that they attract new entrants who are hoping to earn a quick profit by selling their assets to the acquiring firm.

5.   Analysis of the _____ game shows that each firm in a cartel has an incentive to "cheat" by increasing its output beyond its allotted share.

6.   Regulation can serve to lessen competition by making government the enforcer of a *de facto* _____ agreement.

7. Regulation can have minimal or unexpected effects because firms often engage in

    _____, in which they devise policies that conform to the letter—but

    not the spirit—of the law.

8. It is assumed that each firm takes its rivals' output levels as given in the

    _____ of oligopoly.

9. In the _____ model of oligopoly, the threat of costless entry by new

    rivals forces firms to behave as competitors.

10. In monopolistic competition, firms attempt to gain some degree of monopoly power by

    engaging in _____.

TRUE-FALSE EXERCISES

_____ 11. Judge Robert Bork argues that antitrust laws should be interpreted so as to promote
           small businesses and competition.

_____ 12. In a tournament, the social cost of product improvements can exceed their value.

_____ 13. The Axelrod experiment suggests that "always confess" is the most successful
           strategy to use in a repeated Prisoners' Dilemma game.

_____ 14. If a cartel is to succeed, it needs an enforcement mechanism.

_____ 15. Regulations that set minimum quality standards always benefit consumers.

_____ 16. The Benham study has convinced many economists that restrictions on advertising
           help to keep prices low.

_____ 17. In a contestable market with room for several firms, the threat of entry by rivals will
           force those firms to form a cartel.

_____ 18. Industry output in a Cournot oligopoly is equal to the competitive quantity.

_____ 19.   Firms in monopolistic competition produce a homogeneous product.

_____ 20.   Firms in monopolistic competition earn zero profit in long-run equilibrium.

MULTIPLE CHOICE QUESTIONS

_____ 21.   The horizontal merger shown in the diagram on the right will increase economic efficiency if
   A.   area A + C outweighs area B + D + E.
   B.   area C + D + F + G outweighs area A + B.
   C.   area C + D outweighs area F + G.
   D.   area F + G outweighs area E.

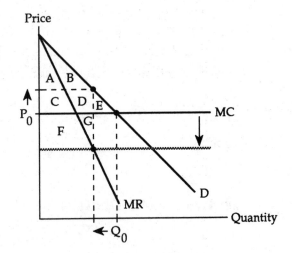

_____ 22.   Consider a vertical merger between a computer manufacturer and a memory chip supplier, where both firms are monopolies. This merger causes social gain to increase, because the new firm
   A.   gets both consumer's surplus from buying memory chips and producer's surplus from selling memory chips.
   B.   earns monopoly profits in both the memory chip market and the computer market.
   C.   can force the memory chip supplier to sell at below cost to the computer manufacturer.
   D.   will behave competitively in the market for computers.

_____ 23.   Which of the following is the best example of a horizontal merger?
   A.   A merger of a lumber mill and a furniture manufacturer.
   B.   A merger of a popcorn company and a book publisher.
   C.   A merger of two local grocery store chains.
   D.   A merger of a spark plug producer and an automobile manufacturer.

_____ 24.   Borrowing funds, "laying low," and future reentry are strategies that a firm can use to counter
   A.   the effects of regulation.
   B.   a supplier's imposition of resale price maintenance.
   C.   predatory pricing.
   D.   a proposed buy-out.

_____ 25. Why might a firm practice resale price maintenance?
   A.   To guarantee high monopoly prices.
   B.   To guarantee that retailers will supply customer services.
   C.   To prevent retailers from appropriating part of the firm's monopoly profit.
   D.   To force retailers to absorb the costs of selling the good.

_____ 26. Which model highlights the effects that costless entry and exit have on firms' behavior?
   A.   The Prisoners' Dilemma model of cartels.
   B.   The contestable market model of oligopoly.
   C.   The Cournot oligopoly model.
   D.   The predatory pricing model.

_____ 27. Which of the following is the key defining feature of monopolistic competition?
   A.   Tit-for-tat strategies.
   B.   High levels of vertical integration.
   C.   Price-taking behavior.
   D.   Product differentiation.

_____ 28. Which of the following is the best example of a contestable market?
   A.   The FDA and the market for pharmaceutical drugs.
   B.   The toothpaste industry.
   C.   Schwinn and the bicycle market.
   D.   Airline service on a particular route.

_____ 29. Which of the following statements about cartels is *false?*
   A.   A member has the incentive to cheat on the cartel agreement only when it fears that other members will also cheat.
   B.   A member can cheat on the cartel agreement and greatly increase its profit by increasing its output above the allotted level.
   C.   If all members cheat on the cartel agreement, the cartel will break down and output will eventually rise to the competitive level.
   D.   Government regulation can be used as outside enforcement for the cartel agreement.

_____ 30. Which of the following statements about the Prisoners' Dilemma is *false?*
   A.   If both prisoners act in their own self-interest, the result of the Prisoners' Dilemma will not be Pareto optimal.
   B.   The Prisoners' Dilemma is another situation in which the Invisible Hand Theorem is true.
   C.   Coercion could be used to make both prisoners better off.
   D.   Tit-for-Tat has proven to be a successful strategy in the repeated Prisoners' Dilemma game.

_____ 31. What conclusion about oligopoly can be reached from comparing the Cournot and Bertrand models?
- A. The equilibrium in an oligopoly market is always less efficient than the competitive equilibrium.
- B. Free entry and exit forces oligopoly firms to have excess capacity in the long run.
- C. The market outcome in oligopoly is quite sensitive to the assumptions made about firms' reactions to rivals' behavior.
- D. Oligopoly firms will find tit-for-tat to be a superior strategy to predatory pricing, buy-outs, and collusion.

_____ 32. In the Bertrand model of oligopoly, firms produce
- A. the competitive quantity.
- B. the monopoly quantity.
- C. more than the monopoly quantity, but less than the competitive quantity.
- D. less than the monopoly quantity.

_____ 33. In the Cournot model of oligopoly, each firm chooses its output assuming that its rivals
- A. do not change their price.
- B. do not change their output.
- C. can enter and exit the industry costlessly.
- D. use the Tit-for-Tat strategy.

_____ 34. Which of the following statements about monopolistic competition is *false?*
- A. Firms in monopolistic competition, like competitive firms, earn zero profits in the long run because of entry and exit.
- B. The industry's output in monopolistic competition, like that in competition, is produced at the lowest possible cost.
- C. Firms in monopolistic competition, like monopolies, face downward-sloping demand curves for their products.
- D. Firms in monopolistic competition, like monopolies, charge prices higher than their marginal costs.

_____ 35. What are the welfare consequences of monopolistic competition?
- A. The Invisible Hand Theorem shows that monopolistic competition, like competition, makes social gain as large as possible.
- B. Social welfare would be improved if a monopolistically competitive industry were replaced by a competitive industry.
- C. The welfare consequences of monopolistic competition, like those of monopoly, depend on the firms' source of market power.
- D. The welfare consequences of monopolistic competition are ambiguous, because its inefficiencies must be weighed against the benefits of having differentiated products.

REVIEW QUESTIONS

36. What is resale price maintenance? How does it benefit the producer? How does it benefit consumers?

37. According to game theory, why are cartels subject to breaking down? What name is given to this situation and how can it be remedied?

38. List some specific ways that government regulation is used to direct the activities of firms. Provide some examples of these types of regulation.

39.   Describe two situations in which an oligopoly market reaches the competitive outcome.

40.   Compare and contrast the Cournot and Bertrand models of oligopoly.

41.   Firms in monopolistic competition earn zero profits in long-run equilibrium, yet the cost of producing the industry's output is not as low as possible. Explain why this is the case.

PROBLEMS

42.   Suppose the demand and marginal revenue curves for a firm's product are given by the formulas $P = 40 - \frac{1}{2}Q$ and $MR = 40 - Q$, where Q is the quantity produced and P is the price charged. Also suppose that the firm's marginal cost is constant at $MC = 20$.

   i.   Find the equilibrium quantity, equilibrium price, the consumers' and producer's surpluses, and the social gain if the firm behaves competitively.

   ii.   Suppose the firm undertakes a horizontal merger that lowers its marginal cost, and let x be the fraction by which marginal cost falls after the merger. Also suppose the merger gives the firm enough market power that it begins to charge the monopoly price. Find a formula in terms of x which gives the social gain after the merger.

   iii.   By what percentage must marginal cost fall for the merger to create an increase in social gain? (*Note* – This problem requires use of the quadratic formula, which says that the equation $ax^2 + bx + c = 0$ has the solution $x = (-b \pm \sqrt{b^2 - 4ac})/2a$.)

43. Two identical firms have access to a copper mine that is, for all practical purposes, inexhaustible. Their marginal cost of extracting copper from the mine is constant at $20 per ton. The annual market demand for copper is $P = 200 - 3Q$, where P is the price (in dollars per ton) and Q is the quantity demanded (in thousands of tons).

   i. Suppose the two firms form a successful cartel. How much copper will the firms produce, and what price will they charge?

   ii. Suppose the firms behave as in the Bertrand model of oligopoly. How much copper will the firms produce, and what price will they charge?

   iii. Suppose the firms behave as in the Cournot model of oligopoly. How much copper will the firms produce, and what price will they charge?

44. Consider a monopoly producer's use of resale price maintenance. Let P_0 equal the price that the producer charges retailers, P_1 equal the price that retailers are required to charge to consumers, V equal the value per unit that consumers place on retailers' services, and C equal the cost per unit that retailers incur to provide services to consumers. Assume that retailers have no other costs besides the purchase of the good from the producer and the services provided to consumers. The diagram on the right shows the typical retailer's market. The retailer's demand and marginal cost are D and MC, respectively; the imposition of resale price maintenance shifts these curves to D' and MC'.

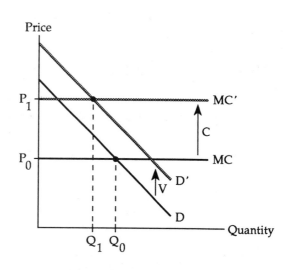

i. On the diagram, label the consumers' surpluses obtained before and after resale price maintenance. Did consumers' surplus rise or fall in this situation? What is causing this result?

ii. Why does resale price maintenance hurt the monopoly supplier in this situation? What must happen for resale price maintenance to be worthwhile to the monopoly producer?

iii. Suppose the monopoly supplier finds that when retailers increase C by an additional dollar, V increases by more than one dollar. Assuming that it continues to use resale price maintenance, should the monopoly producer raise or lower the retail price P_1? When will the monopoly supplier get the most profit from resale price maintenance? Explain, using the equimarginal principle.

45.   Consider a Cournot oligopoly containing N firms; each firm chooses its production level assuming that its rivals' outputs are fixed. Marginal cost is assumed to be constant and identical for the N firms, and the industry demand curve is assumed to be linear. Let Q_A represent the quantity produced by an arbitrarily chosen firm (call it Firm A), let Q_B represent the quantity produced by each of this firm's rivals (who are assumed to be producing equal amounts), and let Q_C be the quantity that the industry would produce if it were competitive.

   i.   What is the total quantity produced by Firm A's rivals? Assuming that it chooses to maximize its profit, what quantity will Firm A choose to produce? Explain.

   ii.   Suppose all N firms in the Cournot oligopoly are identical. Use this assumption and your answer to part i to find the amount produced (relative to the competitive quantity Q_C) by each firm and by the industry in a Cournot equilibrium.

   iii. What happens to the market outcome in a Cournot oligopoly as the number of firms in the industry get large? Explain, using your answer to part ii.

SOLUTIONS

Completion Exercises

1. vertical integration
2. tournament
3. predatory pricing
4. buy-outs
5. Prisoners' Dilemma
6. cartel
7. creative response
8. Cournot model
9. contestable market
10. product differentiation

True-False Exercises

11. FALSE. Judge Robert Bork argues that antitrust laws should be interpreted so as to promote <u>economic efficiency</u>.
12. TRUE.
13. FALSE. The Axelrod experiment suggests that <u>"Tit-for-Tat"</u> is the most successful strategy to use in a repeated Prisoners' Dilemma game.
14. TRUE.
15. FALSE. Regulations that set minimum quality standards <u>can lead to higher prices and fewer choices for consumers</u>.
16. FALSE. The Benham study has convinced many economists that <u>the net effect of advertising is often to lower prices</u>.
17. FALSE. In a contestable market with room for several firms, the threat of entry by rivals will force those firms to <u>behave as competitors</u>.
18. FALSE. Industry output in a Cournot oligopoly is <u>less than the competitive quantity but more than the monopoly quantity</u>.
19. FALSE. Firms in monopolistic competition produce <u>many similar but differentiated products</u>.
20. TRUE.

Multiple Choice Questions

21. D. The merger gives the firm lower costs, which increase social gain by area F + G. The merger also gives the firm monopoly power, which causes the firm to restrict its output and lowers social gain by area E.

22. A. The new firm's profit includes both the consumer's and producer's surplus from memory chips, so the new firm instructs the memory chip supplier to produce the competitive output level.

23. C. Horizontal integration refers to a merger of firms that produce the same product.

24. C. These strategies make economists skeptical about the profitability of predatory pricing.

25. B. Resale price maintenance forces retailers to compete on a non-price basis, such as through the quality of customer services offered.

26. B. A contestable market is defined as one with costless entry and exit.

27. D. Monopolistic competition occurs when there are many similar but differentiated products.

28. D. Airlines can easily add or abandon the route, so entry and exit are virtually costless.

29. A. The Prisoners' Dilemma shows that it is in each member's self-interest to cheat whether or not other cartel members also cheat.

30. B. If both prisoners act in their own self-interest, the result of the Prisoners' Dilemma will not be Pareto optimal, so the Invisible Hand Theorem is not true in this case.

31. C. In the Cournot model, firms base their decisions on the assumption that their rivals' outputs are fixed, while in the Bertrand model, firms act as though their rivals' prices are fixed. The Cournot equilibrium output is between the competitive and monopoly outcomes, while the Bertrand equilibrium output coincides with the competitive outcome. Thus, different assumptions about firm behavior lead to vastly different equilibria.

32. A. After it takes its rivals' price into account, a firm in the Bertrand model of oligopoly undercuts that price to try to increase its market share. This behavior results in a "price war" which continues until the price equals the firms' marginal cost, which is the competitive outcome.

33. B. Each firm acts as if its rivals' outputs are fixed in the Cournot model of oligopoly.

34. B. The monopolistic competitor's demand curve is downward sloping and tangent to its average cost curve in long-run equilibrium. Therefore, the monopolistic competitor does not produce at the lowest possible average cost as would a competitive firm.

35. D. Economists have not developed any good general theory for dealing with the welfare consequences of monopolistic competition.

Review Questions

36. Resale price maintenance occurs when a monopoly supplier sets the retail price for its product and forbids retailers to undercut this price. Consequently, retailers compete by offering high-quality customer services instead of competing by lowering price. The supplier benefits from this scheme because the customer services provided by retailers increase demand for the product and the resulting producer's surplus. When the value consumers receive from retailers' services is greater than the retailers' required markup, consumers' surplus also increases when resale price maintenance is used.

37. The Prisoners' Dilemma from game theory shows that cartels can easily break down, because each member of the cartel has the incentive to cheat on the cartel agreement, regardless of the actions of other cartel members. Cheating on the cartel agreement will greatly increase the cheater's market share and profit when other cartel members hold to the agreement. On the other hand, cheating will keep a firm from having severe losses when other cartel members are also cheating. The cartel will break down and monopoly profits will no longer be attainable if all cartel members succumb to the incentive to cheat on the agreement. For a cartel to avoid the Prisoners' Dilemma, it needs some way to enforce the cartel agreement and punish members who are in violation.

38. Regulation can be used to control the entry of new firms and the specific production activities and expansion of existing firms (like the Interstate Commerce Commission's regulation of the trucking industry). Regulation can also establish minimum quality standards (like those imposed by the Food and Drug Administration and professional licensing), restrict advertising (as is done by the medical and legal professions), establish minimum prices (like the minimum wage law), and dictate the times of business (as is done using blue laws).

39. The contestable market model and the Bertrand model are two oligopoly situations in which the competitive outcome is achieved. In the contestable market model, entry and exit are completely costless. In this case, potential entry can force firms to behave as competitive firms, even when there are few firms in the market. In the Bertrand model, firms make their pricing and output decisions assuming their rivals' prices will remain unchanged. This behavior causes firms to repeatedly undercut each other's price, ultimately resulting in the competitive price and quantity.

40. The Cournot and Bertrand models of oligopoly both emphasize firms' perceptions about their rivals' behavior. In the Cournot model, each firm makes its decisions based on the assumption that its rivals will not change their output. In the Bertrand model, a firm chooses its price and quantity based on the assumption that its rivals will not change the prices they charge. The two models result in different market outcomes. Firms produce more than the monopoly quantity but less than the competitive quantity in the Cournot model, while firms produce the competitive quantity in the Bertrand model.

41. Firms in monopolistic competition produce differentiated products, and so they face downward-sloping demand curves for their products. If each firm's demand curve lies above its average cost curve, then firms are earning positive profits. New firms will enter the industry, and each firm's demand curve will shift to the left. On the other hand, if each firm's demand curve lies entirely below its average cost curve, then firms have economic losses. Some firms will exit the industry, and each remaining firm's demand curve will shift to the right. Therefore, each firm is earning zero economic profit in long-run equilibrium, and the firm's demand curve is tangent to its average cost curve in this situation. This tangency cannot occur at the minimum point of the average cost curve, because the firm's demand curve is downward sloping. Therefore, the cost of the industry's output is not as low as possible in monopolistic competition.

Problems

42. i. First solve the equation $P = MC$ to find the equilibrium quantity: $40 - \frac{1}{2}Q = 20$ $\Rightarrow 20 = \frac{1}{2}Q \Rightarrow Q = 40$ units. Substitute this quantity back into the demand formula to find the equilibrium price: $P = 40 - \frac{1}{2} \cdot 40 = 40 - 20 = 20$ dollars per unit.

   Consumer's surplus is measured by the triangular area between the demand curve and the price paid. This triangle has a base of 40 units. The vertical intercept of the demand curve is at 40 and the price is at 20, so the height of the triangle is 20. The formula for the area of a triangle is $\frac{1}{2}$ times base times height, so consumers' surplus equals $\frac{1}{2} \cdot 40 \cdot 20 = \$400$.

   When marginal cost is constant, producer's surplus is zero for a competitive firm. Social gain consists solely of consumers' surplus in this case, so the social gain is $400.

   ii. The new marginal cost is $(1 - x) \cdot 20$ or $20 - 20x$ dollars per unit. First solve the equation $MR = MC$ for the monopoly quantity: $40 - Q = 20 - 20x \Rightarrow Q =$

$40 - 20 + 20x = 20 + 20x$ units of output. Substitute this quantity into the demand curve to find the monopoly price: $P = 40 - \frac{1}{2}(20 + 20x) = 40 - 10 - 10x = 30 - 10x$ dollars per unit.

The triangle which measures consumers' surplus has a base of $20 + 20x$ and a height of $40 - (30 - 10x)$ or $10 + 10x$. Therefore, consumers' surplus is

$\frac{1}{2} \cdot (20 + 20x) \cdot (10 + 10x) = \frac{1}{2} \cdot (200 + 400x + 200x^2) = 100 + 200x + 100x^2$ dollars.

When a monopoly's marginal cost is constant, its producer's surplus will be measured by a rectangular area. The base of this rectangle is the equilibrium quantity, which is $20 + 20x$. The width of the rectangle is the difference between price and marginal cost, which is $(30 - 10x) - (20 - 20x) = 10 + 10x$. The area of a rectangle is its base times its height, so producer's surplus is $(20 + 20x) \cdot (10 + 10x) = 200 + 400x + 200x^2$ dollars.

Social gain is the sum of consumers' and producer's surpluses, so social gain equals $(100 + 200x + 100x^2) + (200 + 400x + 200x^2) = 300 + 600x + 300x^2$ dollars.

iii.   If the merger increases social gain, then the formula found in part ii must be larger than the \$400 social gain in part i. First find the value of x which makes the two social gains equal: $300 + 600x + 300x^2 = 400 \Rightarrow 300x^2 + 600x - 100 = 0 \Rightarrow 3x^2 + 6x - 1 = 0$. Use the quadratic equation to solve this formula for x. The resulting solutions are $x = -1 - \sqrt[2]{3}/3$ and $x = -1 + \sqrt[2]{3}/3$, which are approximately -2.155 and 0.155. The negative solution is superfluous. Therefore, the decrease in marginal cost must be larger than 15.5% for the merger to increase social gain.

43.   i.   When demand is linear, marginal revenue has the same vertical intercept and double the slope, so the formula for marginal revenue is $MR = 200 - 6Q$. When the firms form a cartel, industry output will equal the monopoly output. Solve the equation $MR = MC$ to find industry output: $200 - 6Q = 20 \Rightarrow 6Q = 180 \Rightarrow Q = 30$. Substituting this value into the demand formula shows $P = 200 - 3 \cdot 30 = 200 - 90 = 110$. Each firm produces 15 thousand tons, and the cartel charges a price of \$110 per ton.

ii.   The result of a Bertrand oligopoly is the same as the competitive equilibrium. The competitive price equals the marginal cost of \$20 per ton. Use the demand formula to find industry output: $20 = 200 - 3Q \Rightarrow 3Q = 180 \Rightarrow Q = 60$. Each firm produces 30 thousand tons and charges a price of \$20 per ton.

iii. When there are two firms, industry output in the Cournot equilibrium is two-thirds of the competitive quantity, so $Q = \frac{2}{3} \cdot 60 = 40$. Use the demand formula to find the price: $P = 200 - 3 \cdot 40 = 200 - 120 = 80$. Each firm produces 20 thousand tons and charges a price of $80 per ton.

44. i. As shown in the diagram below, consumers' surplus falls after resale price maintenance is imposed. The problem is that the retailers' cost per unit of providing services (C) exceeds the value per unit that consumers receive from those services (V).

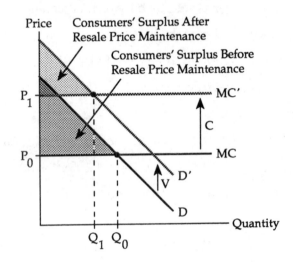

ii. The monopoly supplier is hurt because its sales (through the retailer) fall from Q_0 to Q_1 as shown in the above diagram. For resale price maintenance to be worthwhile, V must exceed C so that sales will rise. Notice that this will also cause consumers' surplus to rise as shown in part i.

iii. The monopoly supplier should increase its retail price P_1. This will cause retailers to increase the amount per unit they spend on providing services (C), since competition among retailers forces them to spend the entire difference between the wholesale and retail prices on these services (i.e., since $C = P_1 - P_0$). This change will cause an even larger vertical shift in the demand curve, which raises the quantity sold and thus the monopoly supplier's profit.

The monopoly producer gets the most possible profit out of resale price maintenance when C exceeds V by the greatest amount. This optimum occurs when an additional dollar added to C causes V to rise by exactly one dollar. According to the equimarginal principle, the optimal retail price will occur when the marginal cost of raising C just equals the marginal benefit from the resulting increase in V.

45.   i.   Since there are N firms in the industry, Firm A has N – 1 rivals. Each rival produces Q_B, for a total amount of $(N – 1) \times Q_B$.

   If Firm A behaved competitively, it would produce enough to raise industry output to the competitive level, so Firm A would produce the difference between the competitive output and its rivals' output $(Q_C – (N – 1)Q_B)$. However, Firm A will behave like a monopoly facing the residual demand (i.e., the demand left over after its rivals' output has been taken into account). Since the demand curve is linear, a monopoly producer's output will be exactly half of a competitive producer's output. Thus, Firm A chooses to produce $\frac{1}{2}(Q_C – (N – 1)Q_B)$ units of output.

   ii.   Part i shows that $Q_A = \frac{1}{2}(Q_C – (N – 1)Q_B)$. If all firms are identical, then we also have $Q_A = Q_B$. Substitute the latter equation into the former and then solve for Q_A:

   $Q_A = \frac{1}{2}(Q_C – (N – 1)Q_A) \Rightarrow 2Q_A = Q_C – (N – 1)Q_A \Rightarrow (N + 1)Q_A = Q_C \Rightarrow Q_A = \frac{1}{N+1}Q_C$. Thus, each firm produces $\frac{1}{N+1}$ of the competitive quantity. There are N total firms, so the industry output is $N \times \frac{1}{N+1}Q_C$ or $\frac{N}{N+1}Q_C$.

   iii.   As N gets large, the fraction $\frac{N}{N+1}$ gets close to 1. Thus, the Cournot market outcome $\left(\frac{N}{N+1}Q_C\right)$ approaches the competitive outcome (Q_C) as the number of firms gets large.

CHAPTER 12

THE THEORY OF GAMES

Strategic behavior is common in many economic situations, as shown by the oligopoly models examined in the previous chapter. A branch of mathematics known as game theory provides several tools that can be used to analyze strategic situations and their outcomes. This chapter introduces some of the concepts from game theory that are commonly used in economic analysis.

KEY TERMS

- Theory of games (or game theory)
- Game matrix
- Nash equilibrium
- Dominant strategy

- Solution concept
- Mixed strategy
- Pure strategy
- Pareto optimal outcome

- Pareto improvement (or Pareto preferred outcome)
- Sequential game
- Stackelberg equilibrium

KEY IDEAS

- **Section 12.1.** A strategic situation can be modeled using a game matrix, which shows the outcomes that result from each combination of strategies available to the players. The most commonly used equilibrium concept for a game is a Nash equilibrium, which is an outcome from which neither player would deviate, taking the opponent's behavior as given. Games may have zero, one, or many Nash equilibria, which may or may not be Pareto optimal.

- **Section 12.2.** Sequential games are games in which the players take turns choosing their strategies instead of selecting them simultaneously. Either the first player or the second player may have an advantage in a sequential game, depending on the particular game being played. A Stackelberg equilibrium occurs in a sequential game when the first player chooses the strategy with the highest payoff, taking into account an optimal response from the second player.

COMPLETION EXERCISES

1. The _____ for a two-player game shows the outcomes from every possible combination of strategies.

2. A rule for predicting the outcome of a game is called a _____.

3. Players have reached a _____ when neither player wants to change his strategy, given the strategy chosen by the other player.

4. If it is impossible to improve one player's welfare without simultaneously reducing the other player's welfare, the players have reached a _____.

5. If a player chooses and commits to a single row or column in the game matrix, we say he is playing a _____.

6. A player is using a _____ when he makes a random selection at certain fixed probabilities among pure strategies.

7. A strategy that results in a superior outcome regardless of the other player's behavior is called a _____.

8. A change is a _____ if nobody objects to it.

9. A game in which players take turns in playing their strategies is called a _____.

10. A common solution concept for sequential games is the _____.

TRUE-FALSE EXERCISES

_____ 11. A Nash equilibrium must also be a Pareto optimal outcome.

_____ 12. Nash equilibrium is a positive concept, while Pareto optimality is a normative concept.

_____ 13. Once a Nash equilibrium is reached, it tends to be stable.

_____ 14. In the Copycat Game, no outcome is Pareto optimal.

_____ 15. The Prisoners' Dilemma game has a single Nash equilibrium that is not Pareto optimal.

_____ 16. In the Battle of the Sexes game, any outcome where the players have chosen the same strategy will be both a Nash equilibrium and a Pareto optimal outcome.

_____ 17. A strategy that involves a player making a random choice among pure strategies is called a dominant strategy.

_____ 18. The Stackelberg equilibrium is the natural solution concept when games are played simultaneously.

_____ 19. In a Stackelberg equilibrium, the first player chooses a strategy taking the second's players optimal response into account.

_____ 20. In a sequential game, the first player always has an advantage over the second player.

MULTIPLE CHOICE QUESTIONS

_____ 21. In a game, any outcome in which neither player wants to change his strategy given the strategy chosen by the other player is called a
   A. Nash equilibrium.
   B. Stackelberg equilibrium.
   C. Prisoners' Dilemma.
   D. Pareto optimal outcome.

_____ 22. When will a game's outcome be Pareto optimal?
   A. When it is a Nash equilibrium.
   B. When the total payoff to the players is positive.
   C. When any attempt to improve one player's payoff lowers the other player's payoff.
   D. When the players are able to commit to a strategy, even if better options become available.

_____ 23. When both players in a game have a dominant strategy,
  A.   a Nash equilibrium exists and is unique.
  B.   no Nash equilibrium exists.
  C.   any Nash equilibrium is also Pareto optimal.
  D.   all entries in the game matrix will be Nash equilibria.

_____ 24. Which of the following is *not* a solution concept for a game?
  A.   A Nash equilibrium.
  B.   A Pareto optimal outcome.
  C.   A Stackelberg equilibrium.
  D.   Nash equilibria, Pareto optimal outcomes, and Stackelberg equilibria are all commonly used solution concepts for games.

_____ 25. Consider an outcome for which one player finds that it would be advantageous to switch strategies. We can then conclude that this outcome
  A.   cannot be a Nash equilibrium.
  B.   must be Pareto optimal.
  C.   will not occur when the players use mixed strategies.
  D.   is a Stackelberg equilibrium.

_____ 26. A player is using a mixed strategy when
  A.   his chosen strategy provides a better outcome than any other strategy.
  B.   he must commit to using a single strategy 100% of the time.
  C.   in a sequential game, he takes the other player's optimal response into account.
  D.   he randomly chooses the strategy to play, with each strategy having a fixed probability of being chosen.

_____ 27. In which of the following games do both players have a dominant strategy?
  A.   The "pigs in a box" game.
  B.   The Prisoners' Dilemma game.
  C.   The Battle of the Sexes game.
  D.   The Copycat Game.

_____ 28. In the Copycat Game, when both players are restricted to pure strategies,
  A.   there is no Nash equilibrium.
  B.   there are two Nash equilibria, and both are Pareto optimal.
  C.   each player will resist the temptation to play his dominant strategy.
  D.   no Pareto optimal outcome exists.

_____ 29. In the Prisoners' Dilemma game, the Nash equilibrium is
  A.   unique and Pareto optimal.
  B.   the only outcome that is not Pareto optimal.
  C.   unstable.
  D.   only attained when both players refuse to play their dominant strategies.

◆◆◆ Questions 30–33 refer to the following game matrix. Player A can play the strategies ♣ and ♠, and Player B can play the strategies ♦ and ♥.

		Player B's Strategies	
		♦	♥
Player A's Strategies	♣	A gets 0 B gets 2	A gets 6 B gets 4
	♠	A gets 5 B gets 3	A gets 7 B gets 1

_____ 30. Does either player have a dominant strategy in this game?
   A.   No, neither player has a dominant strategy.
   B.   Player A has a dominant strategy.
   C.   Player B has a dominant strategy.
   D.   Both players have dominant strategies.

_____ 31. Which outcomes in this game are Nash equilibria?
   A.   This game does not have any Nash equilibria.
   B.   The upper right-hand, lower left-hand, and lower right-hand corners are all Nash equilibria.
   C.   Only the upper right-hand corner is a Nash equilibrium.
   D.   Only the lower left-hand corner is a Nash equilibrium.

_____ 32. Which outcomes are Pareto preferred to the upper left-hand corner?
   A.   No change would be a Pareto improvement over the upper left-hand corner.
   B.   Only the lower right-hand corner.
   C.   Both the upper right-hand and lower left-hand corners.
   D.   All other outcomes are Pareto preferred to the upper left-hand corner.

_____ 33. Which outcomes in this game are Pareto optimal?
   A.   Only the upper right-hand corner is Pareto optimal.
   B.   Both the upper right-hand and lower left-hand corners are Pareto optimal.
   C.   Both the upper and lower right-hand corners are Pareto optimal.
   D.   Both the lower left-hand and lower right-hand corners are Pareto optimal.

_____ 34. When the Battle of the Sexes game is played sequentially,
   A.   it is advantageous to be the first player.
   B.   it is advantageous to be the second player.
   C.   neither player gains an advantage over the other.
   D.   a Pareto optimal outcome will not be achieved.

_____ 35. In a sequential game, when is it advantageous to be the first player?
   A.   Always, because the first player can take into account the second player's optimal response.
   B.   Almost always, as long as the game has a Stackelberg equilibrium.
   C.   Sometimes, depending on the particular game being played.
   D.   Never, because the second player always knows the first player's move.

REVIEW QUESTIONS

36.   What is meant by a dominant strategy? What can be said about Nash equilibria when both players have dominant strategies?

37.   What is meant by a solution concept? Describe the solution concepts typically used for games where the players choose strategies simultaneously and for sequential games.

38.   Can a game have more than one Nash equilibrium? Can a game have more than one Pareto optimal outcome? If yes, provide an example; if no, explain why not.

39.   In the Copycat Game, which outcomes are Nash equilibria? Which are Pareto optimal?

40.   How does a mixed strategy differ from a pure strategy? What can be said about the existence of Nash equilibria when mixed strategies are allowed?

41.   What type of game (simultaneous or sequential) is Tic-Tac-Toe? What type of game is "scissors, paper, rock"? For both games, indicate whether the first player or the second player would have the advantage if the game were played sequentially.

PROBLEMS

42.   Consider the following game matrix, in which the players choose between the strategies "Hi" and "Lo."

		Player B's Strategies	
		Lo	Hi
Player A's Strategies	Lo	A gets 3 B gets 4	A gets 1 B gets 2
	Hi	A gets 4 B gets 1	A gets 2 B gets 3

i.   Does either player have a dominant strategy? Justify your responses.

ii.   Does this game have any Nash equilibria? Are these equilibria, if any exist, also Pareto optimal? Justify your responses.

iii.   Suppose the game is played sequentially, with Player A being first. What is the Stackelberg equilibrium for this game? Is it Pareto optimal? Justify your responses.

43.   A *zero-sum game* is one in which the payoffs to the two players always add to zero. (So, for instance, if one player gets 5, then the other player gets –5.) Typically, the player who gets the positive score is the "winner," and the player who gets the negative score is the "loser."

   i.   Must a zero-sum game have a Nash equilibrium in pure strategies? If yes, explain why. If no, provide a counterexample.

   ii.   Explain why all outcomes will be Pareto optimal in a zero-sum game.

   iii.   Do you believe zero-sum games arise frequently or rarely in economic analysis? Justify your viewpoint.

44. Two firms have access to a spring. Their marginal cost of bottling water from the spring is a constant 8¢ per bottle, respectively, and there are no fixed costs. The firms each have the option of producing 300, 400, or 600 bottles of spring water. The demand for bottled spring water is P = 32 – 2Q, where P and Q are the price (in cents per bottle) and quantity demanded (in hundreds of bottles) of spring water, respectively. The firms' possible profits for various outcomes are summarized in the game matrix below.

		Firm B's Strategies		
		300 bottles	400 bottles	600 bottles
	300 bottles	A gets ___ B gets ___	A gets $30 B gets $40	A gets $36 B gets $18
Firm A's Strategies	400 bottles	A gets $40 B gets $30	A gets ___ B gets ___	A gets $24 B gets $16
	600 bottles	A gets $36 B gets $18	A gets $24 B gets $16	A gets ___ B gets ___

i.   Determine the firms' profits when they sell a total of 600, 800, and 1,000 bottles, and use these numbers to complete the outcomes on the diagonal of the above game matrix.

ii. If the two firms behave competitively, what will be the outcome of this game? Is this outcome Pareto optimal for the firms?

iii.   If the two firms form a cartel and produce the monopoly output level, what will be the outcome of this game? Is this outcome Pareto optimal for the firms?

iv.   If the two firms achieve the Nash equilibrium, what will be the outcome of this game? Is this outcome Pareto optimal for the firms? How does the Nash equilibrium compare with the competitive and monopoly equilibria?

v.   Suppose this game is played sequentially, with Firm A as the first player. What will be the Stackelberg equilibrium in this situation? Is it Pareto optimal?

45.   Suppose there are two countries, the U.S. and Japan. By imposing a tariff, either country can tilt the terms of trade in favor of its export good, resulting in higher welfare for itself at the cost of hurting its trading partner. The trading partner can retaliate by imposing its own tariff, recovering some of its lost utility and reducing the other country's welfare. The possible situations are summarized in the table below, where ++, +, 0, and – represent the best, second best, third best, and worst levels of utility, respectively.

| | | Japan's Strategies | |
		Tariff	Free Trade
	Tariff	U.S. gets 0 Japan gets 0	U.S. gets ++ Japan gets –
U.S.'s Strategies			
	Free Trade	U.S. gets – Japan gets ++	U.S. gets + Japan gets +

i.   What type of game is the above? What are the countries' dominant strategies and what outcome is the Nash equilibrium? Is the Nash equilibrium Pareto optimal?

ii.   How might the U.S. and Japan achieve the Pareto improvement from the upper left-hand corner to the lower right-hand corner?

SOLUTIONS

Completion Exercises

1. game matrix
2. solution concept
3. Nash equilibrium
4. Pareto optimal outcome
5. pure strategy

6. mixed strategy
7. dominant strategy
8. Pareto improvement
9. sequential game
10. Stackelberg equilibrium

True-False Exercises

11. FALSE. A Nash equilibrium <u>may or may not</u> be a Pareto optimal outcome.

12. TRUE.

13. TRUE.

14. FALSE. In the Copycat Game, <u>all outcomes are</u> Pareto optimal.

15. TRUE.

16. TRUE.

17. FALSE. A strategy that involves a player making a random choice among pure strategies is called a <u>mixed</u> strategy.

18. FALSE. The Stackelberg equilibrium is the natural solution concept when games are played <u>sequentially</u>.

19. TRUE.

20. FALSE. In a sequential game, the first player <u>sometimes</u> has an advantage over the second player <u>and the second player sometimes has an advantage over the first player</u>.

Multiple Choice Questions

21. A. In a Nash equilibrium, neither player wants to switch strategies under the assumption that the other player's strategy remains unchanged.

22. C. In a Pareto optimal outcome, it is impossible to improve one player's welfare without hurting the other player.

23. A. Only when both players choose their dominant strategies will there be an outcome where neither player wants to change his strategy.

24. B. Pareto optimality is a normative concept; it is not used to predict the outcome of a game.

25.   A. If either or both players wish to switch strategies, the outcome is ruled out as a Nash equilibrium.

26.   D. One example of a mixed strategy is a player with two strategies who chooses his play by flipping a fair or unfair coin.

27.   B. Confessing is the dominant strategy for both players in the Prisoners' Dilemma game.

28.   A. In each outcome of the Copycat Game, one of the two players wants to switch strategies.

29.   B. When both players choose to confess, they are both worse off than the outcome where both do not confess.

30.   B. Strategy ♠ gives Player A an outcome superior to strategy ♣ regardless of Player B's strategy.

31.   D. Player A will not deviate from the dominant strategy ♠. Given Player A's strategy, Player B will not switch from strategy ♦.

32.   C. The upper right-hand and lower left-hand corners give both players higher payoffs than does the upper left-hand corner.

33.   C. Any switch from the upper right-hand corner makes Player B worse off. Any switch from the lower right-hand corner makes Player A worse off.

34.   A. It is optimal for the second player to follow the first, which allows the first player to attend the event that he or she prefers.

35.   C. The first player has the advantage in the Battle of the Sexes game, but the second player has the advantage in the Copycat Game.

Review Questions

36.   A strategy is a dominant strategy if, for any given strategy played by the opponent, it provides a payoff higher than any other available strategy. If both players have a dominant strategy, then there is one and only one Nash equilibrium—the outcome that results when each player chooses his dominant strategy. No other outcome can be a Nash equilibrium in this case, because players would want to switch to their dominant strategies in these situations.

37.   A solution concept is a rule for predicting the outcome of a game to be played. Nash equilibrium, in which no player wants to switch strategies given the strategy played by the

opponent, is the most frequently used solution concept when the players simultaneously choose their strategies. Stackelberg equilibrium, in which the first player chooses the strategy with the highest payoff taking into account an optimal response by the second player, is commonly used to analyze sequential games.

38. A game can have more than one Nash equilibrium. For instance, the Battle of the Sexes game has two Nash equilibria (the two situations where both players attend the same event). A game can also have more than one Pareto optimal outcome. The Battle of the Sexes game has two Pareto optimal outcomes (the two situations where both players attend the same event), the Prisoners' Dilemma game has three Pareto optimal outcomes (the three situations in which at least one player does not confess), and the Copycat Game has all four outcomes being Pareto optimal.

39. None of the outcomes in the Copycat Game are Nash equilibria. Whatever the outcome is, one player always wants to switch strategies in order to obtain a higher payoff. On the other hand, all outcomes in the Copycat Game are Pareto optimal. Any change that makes one player better off will simultaneously make the other player worse off.

40. A pure strategy is one where the player chooses to play a single strategy 100% of the time. When a player uses a mixed strategy, he randomly selects a strategy each time the game is played, with each strategy assigned a certain probability of being selected. When mixed strategies are allowed, it can be proven under rather general circumstances that a game will have a Nash equilibrium. This is not true if only pure strategies are allowed.

41. Tic-Tac-Toe is a sequential game—the players take turns in selecting their strategies. Neither the first player nor the second player has an advantage in Tic-Tac-Toe, because optimal moves by both players will guarantee that the game will end in a draw. Players choose their strategies simultaneously in "scissors, paper, rock." If the game were played sequentially, the second player could always choose a winning strategy.

Problems

42. i. Player A's dominant strategy is Hi. Each payoff for Player A in the Hi row is larger than the corresponding entry in the Lo row. Player B does not have a dominant strategy. If A has played Lo, then B prefers playing Lo; if A has played Hi, then B prefers playing Hi.

    ii.   This game has one Nash equilibrium: when A and B both play Hi. A will not want to deviate from the dominant strategy. When A plays Hi, B will not want to switch to Lo from Hi. This Nash equilibrium is not Pareto optimal. The outcome when A and B both play Lo is Pareto preferred to the Nash equilibrium.

    iii.   If A plays the dominant strategy Hi, then B will also play Hi, and A will get 2 points. If A plays Lo, then B will also play Lo, and A will get 3 points. The latter possibility is the better for A, so the Stackelberg equilibrium is when A and B both play Lo. The Stackelberg equilibrium is Pareto optimal in this game. The equilibrium outcome gives B more points than any other outcome. Therefore, A cannot be made better off without also making B worse off.

43.   i.   A zero-sum game can fail to have a Nash equilibrium in pure strategies. For example, consider the Copycat Game of Exhibit 12-4 of the textbook with the score of 0 replaced with –5 throughout the game matrix.

    ii.   If one player is made better off (i.e., wins more) in a zero-sum game, the other player is automatically made worse off (i.e., loses more). It is never possible to improve one player's payoff without simultaneously harming the other player, so all outcomes must be Pareto optimal.

    iii.   Zero-sum games rarely arise in economic analysis. Most economic situations involve gains from trade—situations where a proper change in incentives will increase social welfare. Much of economic analysis describes how to obtain a Pareto optimal outcome, not situations where all options are Pareto optimal. Thus, economic analysis primarily focuses on situations where there are "winners and winners," not "winners and losers."

44.   i.   If 600 bottles are produced, the price will be $32 - 2 \times 6 = 32 - 12 = 20$¢ per bottle. Each firm's cost is 8¢ per bottle, leaving 12¢ per bottle in profit. Thus, each firm earns 300 bottles $\times$ 12¢ per bottle, which equals $36. If 800 bottles are produced, each firm earns 8¢ per bottle (a price of 16¢ per bottle minus a cost of 8¢ per bottle), so each firm makes $32. If 1,000 bottles are produced, the price equals the marginal cost of 8¢ per bottle, so profits have fallen to 0. These results are summarized in the table at the top of the following page.

    ii.   When firms behave competitively, price and marginal cost are equal. This occurs when the total quantity produced is 1,200 bottles (both price and marginal cost equal 8¢ per

	Firm B's Strategies		
	300 bottles	400 bottles	600 bottles
300 bottles	A gets $36 B gets $36	A gets $30 B gets $40	A gets $36 B gets $18
Firm A's Strategies 400 bottles	A gets $40 B gets $30	A gets $32 B gets $32	A gets $24 B gets $16
600 bottles	A gets $36 B gets $18	A gets $24 B gets $16	A gets $0 B gets $0

bottle). Thus the competitive equilibrium is the lower right-hand corner, with both firms earning a zero profit. This is not Pareto optimal for the firms—moving to the northwest improves both firms' profits. (However, the situation is Pareto optimal from the social viewpoint when consumer surplus is included.)

iii. The total profit earned is $(P - MC) \times Q = (32 - 2Q - 8)Q = Q(24 - 2Q) = 2Q(12 - Q)$. This quadratic is a maximum when $Q = 6$, for a profit of $72. Thus, the upper left-hand corner is the monopoly equilibrium. It is Pareto optimal, because any increase in one firm's profits will also cause a reduction in the rival's profits.

iv. The Nash equilibrium occurs when both firms produce 400 bottles. In this situation, Firm A cannot increase its profits, given that Firm B is producing 400 bottles (A's alternatives are $30 and $24, both lower than the equilibrium's $32). Furthermore, Firm B cannot raise its profits while Firm A continues to produce 400 bottles. In all other outcomes, one firm or the other wants to switch its production level, so no other Nash equilibrium exists. The Nash equilibrium is not Pareto optimal—both firms would receive higher profits if they both cut production to 300 bottles. As was shown with the Cournot oligopoly model in the previous chapter, the Nash equilibrium lies between the competitive and monopoly equilibria.

v. If Firm A produces 300 bottles, then Firm B will earn the highest profit ($40) by producing 400 bottles, leaving Firm A a profit of $30. If Firm A produces 400, then Firm B will earn the highest profit ($32) by producing 400 bottles, which gives Firm A a profit of $32. Finally, if Firm A chooses 600 bottles, Firm B's best response is to produce 300 bottles for a profit of $18, which gives Firm A a profit of $36. Of the three possibilities, the latter gives Firm A the highest profit, so the lower left-hand corner is the Stackelberg equilibrium. This situation is not Pareto optimal for the firms, because both would earn higher profits if Firm A would reduce its production.

45. i.   This game is a Prisoners' Dilemma game—replace "Tariff" with "Confess" and "Free Trade" with "Do Not Confess" to see the similarity. The dominant strategy for both countries is to levy a tariff, and thus both receive a payoff of 0 in the Nash equilibrium. This outcome is not Pareto optimal, however, since both could receive the payoff + if both had opted for free trade.

     ii.   The U.S. and Japan could make a Pareto improvement by behaving cooperatively instead of competitively. Through trade negotiations, such as the General Agreement of Tariffs and Trade (GATT), the two countries could agree to lower or reduce tariffs and other trade barriers, moving the countries from the upper left-hand corner towards the lower right-hand corner. However, since the outcome under free trade is not a Nash equilibrium, each party will have the incentive to cheat on the agreement, so some type of outside enforcement would be beneficial.

CHAPTER 13

EXTERNAL COSTS AND BENEFITS

Previous chapters have analyzed markets in which buyers and sellers voluntarily participate in trade. When property rights are incomplete, markets can also have involuntary participants who receive costs or benefits from transactions in which they were not involved. This chapter begins a two-chapter unit examining how incomplete property rights can cause inefficiency, starting with an introduction to the basic theory of externalities.

KEY TERMS

- External costs
- External benefits
- Externalities
- Negative externalities
- Positive externalities
- Private marginal costs
- Social marginal costs
- Internalize

- Pigou tax (or Pigovian tax)
- Liable
- Property right
- Transactions cost
- Strong Coase Theorem
- Weak Coase Theorem
- Free riders

- Common law
- Torts
- Negligence
- Contributory negligence
- Strict liability
- Punitive damages
- General average
- Respondeat superior
- Good Samaritan Rule

KEY IDEAS

- **Section 13.1.** An externality exists when trade imposes costs or benefits on people who were not participants in the trade. External costs can cause economic inefficiency, because social marginal cost may differ from private marginal cost. An analysis by A. C. Pigou suggests that a tax can be used to achieve efficiency when a negative externality exists. This analysis was accepted by economists for many years, but more recent analysis by Ronald Coase shows that Pigou's reasoning is flawed.

◆ **Section 13.2.** A transactions cost is any cost required to negotiate or enforce a contract. Coase's analysis shows that, in the absence of transactions costs, externalities are automatically internalized when property rights are clearly defined. Moreover, the precise assignment of property rights will have no effect on social welfare.

◆ **Section 13.3.** Coase's analysis also shows that Pigou's analysis of externalities is incomplete when transactions costs are present. When a Pigou tax is imposed, only the liable party will have an incentive to find a less costly solution to the externality. Therefore, a Pigou tax will not lead to an efficient result if some other party has access to the least-cost solution to the externality.

◆ **Section 13.4.** The common law and the courts can promote economic efficiency by an appropriate assignment of property rights. Judge Richard Posner argues that the common law has evolved to promote economic efficiency. The negligence standard, the doctrine of general average, and the doctrine of respondeat superior provide support for Posner's claim.

COMPLETION EXERCISES

1.   When trading imposes damages on third parties, the damages are called

   _____.

2.   An _____ exists when people are involuntarily affected by others' market activities.

3.   Whether or not an externality exists, firms base their supply decisions on their

   _____.

4.   A negative externality is _____ when all external costs are treated as private costs.

5.   Any cost required to negotiate or enforce a contract is called a

   _____.

6.   The Weak Coase Theorem states that, in the absence of transactions costs, the assignment of _____ does not affect the efficiency of resource allocation.

7.   Sources of transactions costs include the principal-agent problem, incomplete property rights, and _____.

8. The system of legal precedents which has evolved from court decisions is known as the

_____.

9. The law of _____ deals with cases in which one party does unrectifiable damage to another.

10. The doctrine of _____ makes an employer liable for torts committed by his employees.

TRUE-FALSE EXERCISES

_____ 11. According to Pigovian analysis, external costs cause a good to be overproduced relative to the social optimum.

_____ 12. According to Pigovian analysis, when a negative externality exists, the government should impose a tax equal to the deadweight loss created.

_____ 13. Coase's analysis shows that private costs and social costs are always equal.

_____ 14. When transactions costs are zero, the assignment of property rights has no effect on social welfare.

_____ 15. When transactions costs are zero, the assignment of property rights has no effect on the allocation of resources.

_____ 16. To achieve economic efficiency when transactions costs are present, liability should be assigned to the party who can solve the problem at the least possible cost.

_____ 17. To achieve economic efficiency when a principal-agent problem exists, the Coase Theorem suggests that only the principal should be assigned liability.

_____ 18. Free riders choose not to pay for a service because they receive no benefit from it.

_____ 19. Posner's positive theory of the common law asserts that the law seeks to ensure that gains and losses are equitably distributed.

_____ 20. Epstein argues that the negligence system should be largely replaced by a system of strict liability.

MULTIPLE CHOICE QUESTIONS

_____ 21. Suppose firms' production activities create external costs. According to Pigou's analysis of externalities,
A. complete property rights have not yet been assigned.
B. competitive behavior will result in underproduction of the firms' product relative to the social optimum.
C. social marginal cost will be higher than private marginal cost.
D. the social marginal cost of the firms' product will equal its social marginal benefit at the competitive equilibrium.

_____ 22. According to the Weak Coase Theorem, in the absence of transactions costs, economic efficiency is unaffected by
A. changes in property rights.   C. private bargaining.
B. Pigou taxes.   D. incomplete liability rules.

◆◆◆ Questions 23–25 refer to the following situation. A factory's production of goods also creates smoke. The smoke makes it harder to clean clothes and increases the costs of the neighboring dry cleaner by $400 per week. The factory can install an air-cleaning system that costs $200 per week, and the dry cleaner can install a new ventilation system that costs $100 per week. Both systems would eliminate the smoke damage at the dry cleaners.

_____ 23. Suppose transactions costs are zero. If the factory is not liable for the dry cleaner's damages and can continue to produce smoke, then
A. the factory will pay the cleaners $400 per week in smoke damages.
B. the dry cleaner will bear the $400 per week cost of smoke damages.
C. the factory will install the air-cleaning system.
D. the dry cleaner will install the ventilation system.

_____ 24. Suppose transactions costs are zero. If the factory is assigned liability for the dry cleaner's smoke damages, then
A. the factory will pay the cleaners $400 per week in smoke damages.
B. the dry cleaner will bear the $400 per week cost of smoke damages.
C. the factory will install the air-cleaning system.
D. the dry cleaner will install the ventilation system.

_____ 25. Suppose transactions costs preclude the possibility of private bargaining between the factory and the dry cleaner. If a Pigou tax is levied on the factory with the proceeds given to the dry cleaner, then
A. the factory will pay the cleaners $400 per week in smoke damages.
B. the dry cleaner will bear the $400 per week cost of smoke damages.
C. the factory will install the air-cleaning system.
D. the dry cleaner will install the ventilation system.

◆◆◆ Questions 26–29 refer to the diagram below, which shows the effects of a negative externality created by an industry's production. The equilibrium quantity in the absence of any attempt to internalize the externality is Q_E. The optimal quantity according to a Pigovian analysis of the externality is Q_O.

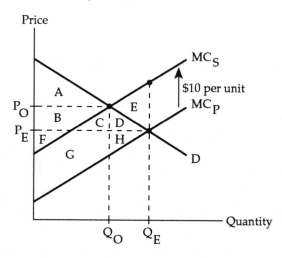

26. Suppose there is no attempt to internalize the externality. If the industry behaves competitively, the total value of the external costs it creates is measured by
    A. area A + B + F.
    B. area B + C.
    C. area C + G.
    D. area C + D + E + G + H.

27. Suppose a Pigou tax of $10 per unit is imposed on the firms. Pigou's analysis of externalities claims that social gain will increase by
    A. area C + D + E + G + H.
    B. area E.
    C. area D + E + H.
    D. area D + H.

28. Suppose there are no transactions costs. Also suppose the externality is internalized when the damaged parties offer producers a bribe of $10 per unit to reduce their production. In this situation, the damaged parties will pay bribes equal to
    A. area C + D + E + G + H.
    B. area C + D + G + H.
    C. area D + E + H.
    D. area E.

29. Suppose transactions costs prevent private bargaining between the firms and the damaged parties. Also suppose that the externality can be eliminated by relocating the damaged parties. Assigning liability to the firms would create inefficiency if the cost of relocation is smaller than
    A. area D + E + H.
    B. area C + D + G + H.
    C. area C + G.
    D. area E.

30. A firm uses a lake for cooling. This activity makes the lake warmer, which damages the quality of fishing at the lake. When the dispute between the firm and the fishers over the use of the lake is resolved in court, liability is assigned to the firm. The firm wishes to negotiate with the fishers, but it finds this difficult because of the continual entry of new fishers at the lake. This situation is an example of
    A. the Coase Theorem.
    B. the principal-agent problem.
    C. incomplete property rights.
    D. the free-rider problem.

_____ 31. Suppose a firm's production imposes external costs on neighboring households. There are no transactions costs to prevent private bargaining between the firm and the households. When could a Pigou tax lower economic efficiency?
   A.   When transactions costs prevent tax recipients from bargaining with the firm and households.
   B.   When tax recipients can enter negotiations with the firm and the households.
   C.   When the revenues from the Pigou tax are given to the households.
   D.   According to the Coase Theorem, a Pigou tax cannot lower economic efficiency in this situation.

_____ 32. Which of the following statements about the Coase Theorem is *false?*
   A.   The Strong and Weak Coase Theorems apply to situations where transactions costs are zero.
   B.   The Weak Coase Theorem guarantees that efficiency will be unaffected by the reassignment of property rights.
   C.   The Strong Coase Theorem guarantees that the distribution of income will be unaffected by the reassignment of property rights.
   D.   The Strong Coase Theorem does not hold when the reassignment of property rights has significant effects on market demand curves.

_____ 33. Which of the following situations is the best example of a free-rider problem?
   A.   Positive externalities cause beekeepers and orchard growers to establish elaborate contracts.
   B.   Property rights to a smoke-free workplace are given nonsmokers in general instead of to a specific group of nonsmokers.
   C.   Mine owners are unable to observe if their workers follow safety guidelines.
   D.   Only about 10% of the viewers of public television contribute money to pay for its costs.

_____ 34. A principal-agent problem occurs when
   A.   transactions costs are too high to permit private bargaining.
   B.   an employer is unable to fully monitor an employee's behavior.
   C.   an agent attempts to avoid paying for benefits received from the principal.
   D.   property rights are assigned to vague groups instead of to specific people.

_____ 35. What is the most efficient liability rule when transactions costs are created by a principal-agent problem?
   A.   The agent should be made liable for all damages resulting from the interaction of the principal and agent.
   B.   The principal should be made liable for all damages resulting from the interaction of the principal and agent.
   C.   The principal and the agent should be made equally liable for any damages resulting from the interaction of the principal and agent.
   D.   The assignment of liability does not affect efficiency according to the Coase Theorem.

REVIEW QUESTIONS

36.   What is an externality? Why can an externality be viewed as a dispute over the use of a resource?

37.   What is the difference between the Strong and Weak Coase Theorems? In what circumstances are the Strong and Weak Coase Theorems applicable?

38.   What are transactions costs? What are some sources of transactions costs?

39.   Why is the Pigovian analysis of externalities incorrect when transactions costs are present? How can the common law promote economic efficiency in this case?

40.   Discuss Posner's and Epstein's views on the relationship between law and economic efficiency. Provide examples that support each person's view.

41.   How do the standards of negligence and contributory negligence affect economic efficiency? How would an assessment of punitive damages in addition to actual damages affect economic efficiency?

PROBLEMS

42. Consider the market for vaccinations, which is shown in the diagram below. Vaccinations are produced by a competitive industry at a constant cost of $4 per dose. The demand for vaccinations coincides with households' private marginal value curve. However, each vaccination creates $2 in external benefits for others, which makes the social marginal value curve higher than households' demand.

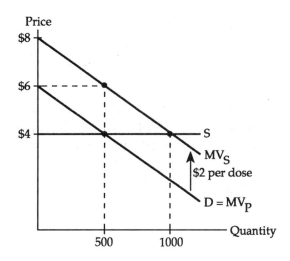

i.   Explain why the consumption of vaccinations creates external benefits for others.

ii. Consider a Pigovian analysis of this positive externality. What would be the equilibrium quantity and social gain if no attempt is made to internalize the externality?

iii. What Pigovian policy would be appropriate for this situation? According to Pigovian analysis, what will be the quantity and social gain after this policy is implemented?

iv. Should the Coase Theorem be applied to this situation? Why or why not?

43.   This problem reexamines the externality between Bridgman the confectioner and Sturges the doctor. The graph below shows the costs of Bridgman's candy production. Bridgman can sell his candy at the price of $5 per pound. Assume that Bridgman has been given the property right to make noise.

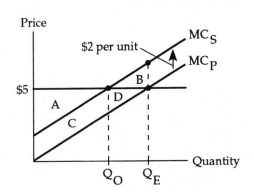

i.   What are Bridgman's gains, Sturges's losses, and social gain if no attempt is made to internalize the externality?

ii.   Suppose Bridgman and Sturges reach an agreement. Sturges agrees to pay Bridgman a bribe of ½B + D, and in return, Bridgman agrees to reduce his candy production from Q_E to Q_O. What are Bridgman's gains, Sturges's losses, and social gain if both abide by the agreement? Who is made better off: Bridgman, Sturges, or both?

iii.   Suppose Bridgman reneges on his agreement with Sturges. Sturges pays Bridgman the bribe, but Bridgman does not reduce the level of his candy production. What are Bridgman's gains, Sturges's losses, and social gain in this situation? Who is made better off: Bridgman, Sturges, or both?

iv. Suppose instead that Sturges reneges on the agreement. Bridgman reduces the level of his candy production to Q_O, but Sturges does not pay him the bribe. What are Bridgman's gains, Sturges's losses, and social gain in this situation? Who is made better off: Bridgman, Sturges, or both?

v. Suppose that the agreement in part ii is unenforceable and that either party can renege on the agreement without repercussions. In this case, there are four possible outcomes: both abide by the agreement, only Bridgman abides by the agreement, only Sturges abides by the agreement, and both renege on the agreement. Use your answers to parts i–iv to determine Bridgman's gains and Sturges's losses in each of these four situations, and summarize your answers in the table below.

	Bridgman Reneges on Agreement	Bridgman Abides by Agreement
Sturges Reneges on Agreement	Bridgman gains _____. Sturges loses _____.	Bridgman gains _____. Sturges loses _____.
Sturges Abides by Agreement	Bridgman gains _____. Sturges loses _____.	Bridgman gains _____. Sturges loses _____.

If each person acts in his own self-interest, will Bridgman and Sturges choose to abide by or renege on the agreement? Explain.

vi. What limitation of the Coase Theorem is illustrated by the result in part v?

44. Suppose that reckless driving imposes costs (in the form of medical bills) on both the drivers themselves and on pedestrians. Each mile of reckless driving costs drivers $1.50 and pedestrians $0.50. The marginal value of reckless driving to a typical driver is shown in the following diagram.

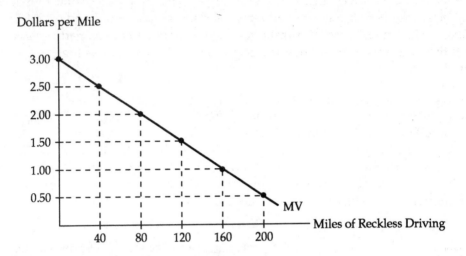

Drivers can acquire airbags which reduce the cost (to them) of their reckless driving from $1.50 to $0.50 per mile. The cost to pedestrians remains $0.50 per mile regardless of whether drivers use airbags, and pedestrians pay their own medical bills.

i.   If a driver does not have an airbag, what is the social gain from reckless driving? If a driver does have an airbag, what is the social gain from reckless driving?

ii.   How much is a driver willing to pay for an airbag?

iii. Suppose your goal is to maximize social welfare, so that you want a driver to buy an airbag if and only if the social benefit exceeds its cost. You cannot tax reckless driving, but you can tax airbags. How large of a tax should you place on airbags?

45.   In recent years, the use of "900" telephone numbers has become widespread. When a person dials a "900" number, the telephone company automatically bills the charge to the telephone number from which the call is made. Charges vary widely but usually range from 95¢ per minute to $35 per call. Firms use "900" numbers to provide consumers with a wide variety of services, including horoscopes, contests, and sexually-explicit messages. These "900" numbers are widely advertised, both in magazines and on television.

A major problem with "900" numbers is that minors have been getting access to them, leaving their parents with tremendous phone bills. Phone bills as high as $20,000 have been reported.

i.   What is the missing market causing this externality?

ii.   Discuss the possibilities in assigning liability to promote economic efficiency in this situation.

iii. Suppose access to sexually explicit "900" numbers is restricted by providing a subscription service. Persons desiring the use of a "900" number would be required to pay a membership fee; in return, they would receive an exclusive authorization code that must be used to obtain the "900" number's services. Operators of these "900" numbers would be required to restrict membership to those persons 21 years of age and older. Discuss the principal-agent problems involved in such a scheme and the implications these problems have for assigning liability when a minor uses a sexually explicit "900" number.

SOLUTIONS

Completion Exercises

1. external costs
2. externality
3. private marginal costs
4. internalized
5. transactions cost

6. property rights
7. free riders
8. common law
9. torts
10. respondeat superior

True-False Exercises

11. TRUE.

12. FALSE. According to Pigovian analysis, when a negative externality exists, the government should impose a tax equal to the <u>external costs</u>.

13. FALSE. Coase's analysis shows that private costs and social costs are <u>equal when there are no transactions costs</u>.

14. TRUE.

15. FALSE. When transactions costs are zero, the assignment of property rights has no effect on the allocation of resources <u>as long as the resulting redistribution of income has negligible effects on market demand curves</u>.

16. TRUE.

17. FALSE. To achieve economic efficiency when a principal-agent problem exists, the Coase Theorem suggests that only the <u>agent</u> should be assigned liability.

18. FALSE. Free riders choose not to pay for a service because they receive <u>the benefits whether or not they choose to pay</u>.

19. FALSE. Posner's positive theory of the common law asserts that the law seeks to <u>promote economic efficiency</u>.

20. TRUE.

Multiple Choice Questions

21. C. The external costs must be added to the private marginal cost of production in order to obtain the social marginal cost.

22. A. The Weak Coase Theorem states that, in the absence of transactions costs, the reassignment of property rights will have no effect on the efficiency of resource allocation.

23.   D. The dry cleaner will offer the factory up to $100 per week to eliminate the smoke. The factory will turn down this offer, because it cannot eliminate the smoke for less than $200 per week. Consequently, the dry cleaner will install the ventilation system. Notice that this is the most efficient choice.

24.   D. The factory will offer the dry cleaner up to $200 per week for the right to produce smoke. The dry cleaner will find this offer acceptable, because the dry cleaner can deal with the smoke for only $100 per week. The two will strike a deal somewhere between $100 and $200 per week, and the dry cleaner will install the ventilation system. Notice that the result will be efficient. The only difference between the situations in questions 8 and 9 is the distribution of income — the dry cleaner is better off when the factory has liability for the smoke damage and *vice versa*.

25.   C. The Pigou tax assigns liability to the factory, so the dry cleaner has no incentive to deal with the smoke damage when private bargaining is not possible. In this situation, the outcome under the Pigou tax is not efficient.

26.   D. The vertical distance between the private and social marginal cost curves represents the external cost of the externality.

27.   B. Before any attempt to internalize the externality, the social gain is A + B + F − E. According to Pigou's analysis, the Pigou tax will increase social gain to A + B + F.

28.   C. The damaged parties are willing to offer up to C + D + E + G + H in bribes. The producers will forgo area C + G in bribes, because they are earning more profit than $10 per unit on the first Q_O units. The producers will accept the difference, area D + E + H, for reducing production from Q_E to Q_O units.

29.   B. If liability is assigned to the firms, social gain will equal area A + B + F. If instead the damaged parties are relocated, then the social marginal cost curve will be shifted down and will coincide with the private marginal cost curve. In this situation, social gain will equal area A + B + C + D + F + G + H minus the costs of relocation. This social gain will be larger than area A + B + F if the costs of relocation are smaller than area C + D + G + H.

30.   C. This liability rule did not give the property right to specific fishers, but to all fishers in general. This incomplete property right creates a transactions cost for the firm wishing to negotiate.

31.   A. The firm would have a double incentive to reduce production — one incentive from households' bribes and another incentive from the Pigou tax. This double incentive forces

output below the efficient level. The Coase Theorem cannot resolve the situation when tax recipients cannot enter the negotiations.

32.   C. The Strong Coase Theorem states that the reassignment of property rights does not affect resource allocation. The Coase Theorem makes no claims about the distribution of income.

33.   D. Most viewers are attempting to take a "free ride" and enjoy the benefits of public television without helping to pay the costs.

34.   B. The employee's unobservable behavior constitutes a transactions cost that prevents the enforcement of an optimal contract.

35.   A. The agent's actions are unobservable, so there is no incentive for the agent to prevent damage caused by his interaction with the principal. According to the Coase Theorem, private negotiations between the agent and the principal provide incentive for the principal to prevent these damages.

Review Questions

36.   An externality exists when people are involuntarily affected by external costs or benefits created by others' market activities. Externalities occur when no market exists to allocate the use of a resource. Without a market to determine the most valuable use of the resource, different parties have conflicting uses for the resource, and external costs and benefits are created. If markets exist for *all* resources, then all costs and benefits are subject to market forces and no externalities can exist.

37.   The Weak Coase Theorem states that, in the absence of transactions costs, the reassignment of property rights has no effect on the efficiency of resource allocation. The Strong Coase Theorem states that, in the absence of transactions costs, the allocation of resources itself is unaffected by the reassignment of property rights. The Weak Coase Theorem is always true, as long as transactions costs are zero. The Strong Coase Theorem is only true when the income effects caused by the reassignment of property rights do not shift market demand curves.

38.   Transactions costs are any costs associated with the negotiation or enforcement of a contract. The principal-agent problem creates transactions costs, because the principal has no way of guaranteeing that the agent performs his obligations in a contract. Incomplete property rights, which occur when property rights are ill-defined or nonexistent, create

transactions costs because a contract concerning the use of a resource cannot be negotiated when the resource has no identifiable owner. The problem of free riders can create transactions costs when a large group is a party to a contract, because some people will choose not to contribute to the costs of negotiation and instead rely on others' efforts.

39.   Traditional Pigovian analysis is incomplete because it ignores the possibility of alternative low-cost solutions to the externality problem. A Pigou tax assigns liability to the party paying the tax, so only that party has the incentive to search for a low-cost solution to the externality problem. If some other party has access to the optimal solution, and if transactions costs prevent the liable party from purchasing this solution, then the Pigou tax will not achieve an efficient outcome. When transactions costs are present, the common law can promote economic efficiency by creating incentives to solve externality problems at the lowest cost and by reducing transactions costs so that private bargaining can achieve low-cost solutions to externalities.

40.   Posner believes that the common law has been successful in providing doctrines that promote economic efficiency. Examples of Posner's views include the negligence standard in the law of torts, the doctrine of general average used to determine losses from disasters at sea, and the doctrine of respondeat superior used to determine an employer's liability for torts committed by his employees. Epstein believes that goals other than economic efficiency should be given greater weight, because in his opinion the cause of an injury can be identified and should be used to assign liability. One example of Epstein's view is given by the Good Samaritan Rule, which states that a bystander has no obligation to rescue a stranger in trouble.

41.   The negligence standard promotes economic efficiency because it gives the person who may cause an accident the incentive to avoid and prevent the accident. The negligence standard may lead to an inefficient outcome, however, because the damaged party has no incentive to seek prevention of the accident at a lower cost. The standard of contributory negligence provides the damaged party with this incentive. However, it too can lead to an inefficient outcome because it provides no incentive for other involved parties to seek solutions which can prevent the accident at still lower costs. If punitive damages are assessed in addition to liability, then private costs will be driven above social costs. Consequently, less of an activity than is socially optimal will be undertaken.

Problems

42. i.   When a person consumes a vaccination, he receives benefits because he has a smaller chance of catching a disease. Other people also receive benefits, because they have a smaller chance of catching a disease from the vaccinated person.

   ii.   If no attempt is made to internalize the externality, then the outcome is the competitive equilibrium occurring at the intersection of the supply and demand curves. Thus, 500 doses will be purchased. Social gain is the area between the social marginal value curve and the marginal cost curve out to the quantity consumed. This area consists of 3 identical triangles, each with a base of 500 doses and a height of $2 per dose. The area of a triangle is ½ times the base times the height, so each of these triangles has an area of ½ × 500 doses × $2 per dose or $500. Thus, social gain is 3 times this amount, or $1500.

   iii. The appropriate Pigovian policy is a subsidy (i.e., a negative tax) of $2 per dose. This subsidy would shift the demand curve to coincide with the social marginal value curve. The new equilibrium quantity would be 1000 doses. Social gain will now be the entire consumers' surplus out to 1000 doses. This triangular area has a base of 1000 doses and a height of $4 per dose, so social gain equals ½ × 1000 doses × $4 per dose or $2000. (The subsidy itself is a transfer from taxpayers to the consumers of vaccinations, and so it makes no net contribution to social gain.)

   iv.   The Coase Theorem probably cannot apply to this situation unless the number of households in the community is relatively small. Otherwise, the transactions costs incurred for the households to reach and enforce an optimal contract would be prohibitive.

43. i.   Bridgman gains the producer's surplus, which is area A + C + D. Sturges's losses consist of the noise damage he suffers, which is measured by area B + C + D. The social gain is the difference between these two, which is area A – B.

   ii.   Bridgman's gains consist of his producer's surplus, which is area A + C when he produces Q_O, and the bribe he receives from Sturges, which equals ½ B + D. Bridgman's total gains are A + ½ B + C + D. Sturges's losses consist of the noise damage, which is measured by area C when Bridgman produces Q_O, and the bribe he pays to Bridgman, which is ½ B + D. Sturges's total losses are ½ B + C + D. The social gain is the difference between Bridgman's gains and Sturges's losses, which equals area A. Bridgman's gains are larger and Sturges's losses are smaller than those in part i, so both parties are better off.

iii. When Bridgman reneges on the agreement, he produces Q_E pounds of candy. His producer's surplus is area $A + C + D$, and he also receives the bribe of $\frac{1}{2}B + D$ from Sturges. Sturges has noise damage of area $B + C + D$, and he also loses the bribe of $\frac{1}{2}B + D$. Bridgman's total gains are $A + \frac{1}{2}B + C + 2D$, and Sturges's losses are $\frac{3}{2}B + C + 2D$, so the social gain is area $A - B$. Bridgman's gains and Sturges's losses are larger than those in parts i and ii, so Bridgman is better off and Sturges is worse off.

iv. If Sturges fails to pay the bribe, Bridgman's gains consist solely of his producer's surplus, which is area $A + C$ when he reduces production to Q_O pounds of candy. Sturges's only loss is the noise damage, which is area C. Social gain is therefore measured by area A. Bridgman's gains and Sturges's losses are smaller than those in parts i and ii, so Bridgman is worse off and Sturges is better off.

v. The following table summarizes the results found in parts i–iv.

	Bridgman Reneges on Agreement	Bridgman Abides by Agreement
Sturges Reneges on Agreement	Bridgman gains $A + C + D$. Sturges loses $B + C + D$.	Bridgman gains $A + C$. Sturges loses C.
Sturges Abides by Agreement	Bridgman gains $A + \frac{1}{2}B + C + 2D$. Sturges loses $\frac{3}{2}B + C + 2D$.	Bridgman gains $A + \frac{1}{2}B + C + D$. Sturges loses $\frac{1}{2}B + C + D$.

This situation is identical to the Prisoners' Dilemma game. Whether or not Sturges abides by the agreement, Bridgman is better off if he chooses to renege on the agreement. Whether or not Bridgman abides by the agreement, Sturges's losses are smaller when he reneges on the agreement. If the agreement is unenforceable, each party has the incentive to renege on the agreement.

vi.   The Prisoners' Dilemma game in part v shows that the Coase Theorem does not hold when transactions costs make the optimal contract unenforceable.

44.   i.   If a driver does not have an airbag, the marginal social cost of reckless driving is $2.00 per mile ($1.50 per mile cost to the driver plus $0.50 per mile cost to pedestrians). The diagram shows that, at the private marginal cost of $1.50 per mile, the driver will drive recklessly for 120 miles. The consumer's surplus triangle has a height of $1.50 per mile and a base of 120 miles, so the driver receives $90 of value from reckless driving (½ × 120 miles × $1.50 per mile). The driver imposes $60 of external costs on pedestrians (120 miles × $0.50 per mile). Social gain from reckless driving is thus $30 when the driver does not have an airbag.

If the driver does have an airbag, the marginal social cost of reckless driving falls to $1.00 per mile ($0.50 per mile cost to the driver plus $0.50 per mile cost to pedestrians). Social gain is $150 ($250 of value to the driver minus $100 of external cost imposed on pedestrians).

ii.   Part i shows that a driver without an airbag receives $90 of value from reckless driving, while a driver with an airbag receives $250 of value. A driver is thus willing to pay up to $250 – $90 or $160 for an airbag.

iii.   Part i shows that an airbag adds $150 – $30 or $120 to the social gain from reckless driving, so you do not want the driver to purchase the airbag if it costs more than $120. Part ii shows that the driver is willing to pay up to $160 for the airbag. Thus, you should place a $40 tax on the airbag ($160 – $120).

45.   i.   There is no market to allocate the access to the "900" numbers. Every parent's phone can be used to access a "900" number whether or not the parent wants to purchase that service.

ii.   The optimal assignment of liability depends on which group may have the low-cost solution to the problem. Parents should be assigned liability if tighter control over their children's behavior appears to be the optimal solution. The telephone company should be assigned liability if it can provide parents a service to block access to "900" numbers from their telephones at a low cost. The operators of "900" numbers should be assigned liability if they can easily switch to a subscription service or to payment by credit card. If possible, transactions costs among these groups should be reduced to allow private bargaining to determine the solution with the lowest cost.

iii. The operators of sexually explicit "900" numbers have contracted with parents to prevent minors from subscribing. The operators' behavior is largely unobservable to parents, so the operators should be held liable for any damages that result when minors subscribe to a "900" number's services. Subscribers to the "900" number have contracted with the operators to prevent minors from having access to their authorization codes. Subscribers' behavior is unobservable to the operators, so subscribers should be held liable for any damages that result when minors get access to their authorization codes.

CHAPTER 14

COMMON PROPERTY AND PUBLIC GOODS

This chapter concludes a two-chapter unit examining how incomplete property rights create inefficiency. Two special cases of the externality problem are considered. The first half of the chapter introduces the concept of common property, which is property that has no owner. The second half of the chapter examines public goods, which are goods that, once produced, are costlessly available for use by others.

KEY TERMS

- Common property
- Dissipation of rents (or tragedy of the commons)
- Fishery

- Public good
- Nonexcludable good
- Nonrivalrous good
- Market failure

- Free riding
- Clarke tax

KEY IDEAS

- **Section 14.1.** When a property has no owner and can be used by anyone who so chooses, it is called a common property. Competitive behavior will cause a common property to be overused, reducing the economic rent created by the property. If all users are identical, then the rent earned from the use of the common property will be driven to zero. This result is known as the dissipation of rents or the tragedy of the commons.

- **Section 14.2.** A public good is one for which one person's consumption increases the amount available to everyone else. Public goods are nonexcludable, nonrivalrous, or both. The government frequently provides public goods, because competitive markets fail to produce these goods in socially efficient quantities. People may have incentives to overstate or understate their preferences for a public good, so the government must design incentives like the Clarke tax to get people to reveal their true preferences in order to determine if a public good should be provided.

COMPLETION EXERCISES

1. When a property has no well-defined owner and is open to people to use as they choose, it is called a _____.

2. A common property is one example of a _____, because anyone can use the property.

3. A fishery is not a _____, because one person's use of the property reduces the value that others receive from it.

4. Competitive behavior causes a common property to be overused; this result is known as the _____.

5. A _____ occurs when private markets fail to provide a commodity in socially efficient quantities.

6. If one person's consumption of a good increases the amount available to everyone, then it is called a _____.

7. Computer software is a _____, because once it has been created, it can be provided to others at no additional cost.

8. A producer cannot force people to pay for a _____ because people have use of the good whether they pay for it or not.

9. A tax designed to give people the incentive to truthfully reveal their preferences for a public good is called a _____.

10. A _____ problem occurs when people receive the benefits from a nonexcludable good but choose not to contribute to its cost.

TRUE-FALSE EXERCISES

_____ 11. People enter a common property as long as their social marginal benefit exceeds the opportunity cost of a visit.

_____ 12. Social gain from an orchard is largest when people are allowed free entry into the orchard.

_____ 13. If people have identical tastes, then they will use a common property until the rents fall to zero.

_____ 14. If people have identical tastes, then everyone has an incentive to maintain and improve a common property.

_____ 15. The marginal user of a common property receives the greatest net value from its use.

_____ 16. Nonexcludability can lead to free riding.

_____ 17. The efficient price for a nonexcludable good is zero.

_____ 18. Whenever a public good increases the desirability of living in a certain area, its benefits tend to be evenly shared among the residents.

_____ 19. When a Clarke tax is used to finance a public good, people have the incentive to understate the value they receive from it.

_____ 20. The revenue raised from a Clarke tax will exactly cover the cost of a public good.

MULTIPLE CHOICE QUESTIONS

_____ 21. Which of the following is *not* an example of a common property?
   A. A lake that residents freely use to catch fish.
   B. A forest that is open to any loggers who wish to use it.
   C. A grassland that all members of a tribe use for grazing.
   D. A satellite transmission that can be received by anyone who has a satellite dish.

_____ 22. When is the social gain that people obtain from a common property maximized?
   A.   When their marginal cost equals the social marginal benefit.
   B.   When their marginal cost equals the value they receive, on average, from the common property.
   C.   When the social marginal benefit of the property equals the average value they receive from the property.
   D.   When the entrance fee that a private owner can charge users is as large as possible.

_____ 23. Suppose that people's use of a common property is unrestricted. People will increase their usage of the common property as long as their marginal cost is smaller than
   A.   the social marginal benefit of the common property.
   B.   the competitive entrance fee that a private owner would charge.
   C.   the rent created by the common property.
   D.   the value they receive from using the common property.

_____ 24. When will a property create zero economic rent?
   A.   When the property has a private owner who charges a monopoly entrance fee.
   B.   When the property has a private owner who charges a competitive entrance fee.
   C.   When the property is commonly owned and the opportunity cost of using it is the same for everyone.
   D.   When the property is commonly owned and the opportunity cost of using it is different for different people.

_____ 25. Consider a lake stocked with fish that is common property. Suppose that some fishers face higher opportunity costs than others when they use the lake. The social gain created by the lake is
   A.   as large as possible.
   B.   positive, but less than the maximum amount possible.
   C.   equal to the difference between the fishers' average and marginal catches.
   D.   zero.

_____ 26. Consider a public zoo at which crowding affects the value received by the typical visitor. In order to maximize the economic rent created by the zoo, the local authorities should
   A.   charge a competitive admission fee.
   B.   allow visitors to have free admission to the zoo.
   C.   accept voluntary contributions from zoo visitors.
   D.   charge the same entrance fee that a monopoly owner would charge.

_____ 27. A common property is best classified as
   A.   a nonexcludable good.
   B.   a nonrivalrous good.
   C.   both a nonexcludable good and a nonrivalrous good.
   D.   neither a nonexcludable good nor a nonrivalrous good.

◆◆◆ Questions 28–31 refer to the following diagram, which shows the benefits and costs associated with the use of a common property.

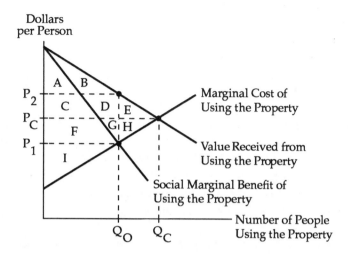

_____ 28. If access to the common property cannot be prohibited, the resulting social gain is measured by
A.   area I.
B.   area F + G + H + I.
C.   area C + D + F + G + I.
D.   area A + B + C + D + E + F + G + H + I.

_____ 29. The maximum social gain that can be obtained from the common property is measured by
A.   area I.
B.   area F + G + H + I.
C.   area C + D + F + G + I.
D.   area A + B + C + D + E + F + G + H + I.

_____ 30. Suppose the common property becomes privately owned. The owner behaves competitively and charges people an entrance fee for the right to use the property. The total entrance fees earned by the owner are measured by
A.   area I.
B.   area F + G + H + I.
C.   area C + D + F + G.
D.   area A + B + C + D + E.

_____ 31. Suppose the common property becomes privately owned. The owner behaves competitively and charges people an entrance fee for the right to use the property. The surplus value that people earn from using the property is measured by
A.   area I.
B.   area F + G + H + I.
C.   area C + D + F + G.
D.   area A + B + C + D + E.

_____ 32. Which of the following is the best example of a public good that is both
nonexcludable and nonrivalrous?
  A.   The Mona Lisa.
  B.   Computer software.
  C.   Fish in the ocean.
  D.   National defense.

_____ 33. A fireworks display for a community is worth $10 to each of 100 residents. The
display costs $750. Which of the following statements is *false?*
  A.   The social value of the fireworks display exceeds its cost.
  B.   No one individual is willing to purchase the fireworks display.
  C.   A private group could provide the fireworks display by asking each resident for
       a contribution of $7.50.
  D.   The government could provide the fireworks display and increase social welfare
       by imposing a tax of $7.50 per person.

_____ 34. When do people have an incentive to understate their preferences for a public good?
  A.   When a Clarke tax is used.
  B.   When their tax shares are proportional to their revealed preferences for the
       public good.
  C.   When a vote is used to determine if the public good should be provided.
  D.   When a poll is used to determine the value that people receive from the public
       good.

_____ 35. Which of the following statements provides the best description of a Clarke tax?
  A.   Each person's tax share is proportional to his revealed preference for the public
       good.
  B.   The tax burden for the public good is divided evenly among the taxpayers.
  C.   Taxes to finance the public good are levied only on those people who report that
       the value they place on the public good is higher than its cost.
  D.   Each person's tax equals the cost of the public good minus other people's
       revealed preferences for the public good.

REVIEW QUESTIONS

36. Why does the value that people receive, on average, from a common property decline as the number of users increases? Why is the social marginal benefit of a common property smaller than the value that people, on average, receive from it?

37. Why does unrestricted use of a common property lead to its overuse?

38. When are the rents created by a common property totally dissipated? Why does this phenomenon occur?

39.   What entrance fee can a private owner charge for the right to use a common property? How can this entrance fee prevent the dissipation of rents?

40.   Explain why computer software is a nonrivalrous good but is not a nonexcludable good.

41.   How does free riding affect the government's provision of a public good? How can this problem be overcome?

PROBLEMS

42.   Consider miners working in a gold mine. The daily marginal cost of working in the gold mine and the total value of the gold that can be mined daily depend on the number of miners, as summarized in the table below.

Number of Miners	Marginal Cost of Mining	Number of Miners	Total Value of Gold Mined	Value per Miner	Social Marginal Benefit
0 miners	—	0 miners	$ 0	—	—
1	$ 5 per miner	1	20		
2	6	2	36		
3	7	3	48		
4	8	4	56		
5	9	5	60		
6	10	6	60		
7	11	7	56		
8	12	8	48		

i.   Complete the above table by calculating the value that each miner, on average, receives from working in the mine and the social marginal benefit created by the mine.

ii.   Suppose the mine is common property. How many miners will choose to work in the mine? How much social gain is created by the existence of the mine?

iii. Suppose the mine is private property, where the owner charges miners a competitive entrance fee for the right to access the mine. What is the optimal number of miners? What is the maximum social gain created by the existence of the mine? What is the competitive entrance fee that leads to the optimal outcome? How is the social gain divided between the owner and the miners in this situation?

43. The diagram below shows the values and costs associated with catching fish from a lake. The quantity variable is the number of fishers who choose to use the lake, shown on the horizontal axis. The fishers' opportunity cost of using the lake is shown by the curve labeled "Fishers' Marginal Cost." The value that a fisher receives from the lake is the value of the fish he catches, shown by the curve labeled "Fishers' Average Catch." The social marginal benefit created by the lake is the value of the fish attributable to the last fisher working in the lake, shown by the curve labeled "Fishers' Marginal Catch."

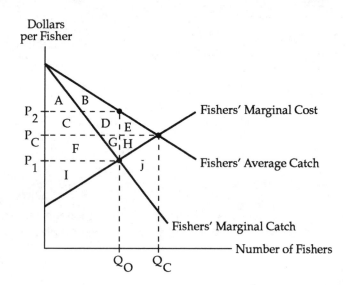

i.   Suppose the lake is privately owned. Instead of charging fishers an entrance fee, the owner of the fishery has decided to hire fishers to catch the fish for him. The owner retains all fish caught by the fishers. In the diagram, what curve represents the owner's demand curve for fishers? What curve represents the supply curve of fishers? If the owner and the fishers behave competitively, what wage will the owner pay the fishers? How many fishers will the owner hire? Calculate the surplus value earned by the owner, the surplus value earned by the fishers, and the social gain.

ii.   Show that if the owner hires fishers to catch fish for him, he earns the same amount that he would earn from charging fishers a competitive entrance fee for the right to use the fishery. (*Hint* – Use the fact that the marginal catch curve is exactly twice as steep as the average catch curve.)

iii.   Use the Invisible Hand Theorem to explain why the result in part ii is not surprising.

iv.   Show that area J represents the deadweight loss created if fishers have unrestricted access to the fishery.

44.   Cleantown and Grimyville are identical except for the inferior air quality in Grimyville. The quantity of apartments in each town is fixed, and everyone values a Cleantown apartment at $500 per month. Apartments in Cleantown and Grimyville rent for $500 and $300 per month, respectively. The market for Grimyville apartments is shown in the diagram below.

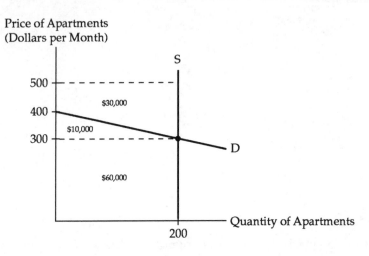

i.   What are residents' costs of breathing the polluted Grimyville air? How much consumers' surplus is created for Grimyville residents, and how much producers' surplus is created for Grimyville landlords?

ii.   Suppose that Grimyville can have the same air quality as Cleantown by installing filters on area factory smokestacks. If the filters are installed, what will apartments rent for in Grimyville? Who benefits and who loses?

iii. Suppose the filters in part ii cost $35,000 a month. If the Grimyville government wishes to maximize social gain, should it provide this public good? Why or why not?

iv.   Again suppose the filters in part ii cost $35,000 a month. Also suppose that the numbers of Grimyville landlords and factories are sufficiently small that the filters can be provided by private action. Will the Grimyville landlords provide this public good? How will social gain be affected?

45.   i.   The theory of common property is a special case of the theory of externalities. Could the Coase Theorem be applied to resolve the tragedy of the commons? If yes, describe the possible results of private bargaining. If no, describe the transactions costs that prevent the Coase Theorem from being applied.

ii.   The theory of public goods is also a special case of the theory of externalities. Could the Coase Theorem be applied to resolve the market's suboptimal provision of public goods? As in part i, describe the possible results of private bargaining or the transactions costs which prevent private bargaining.

SOLUTIONS

Completion Exercises

1. common property
2. nonexcludable good
3. nonrivalrous good
4. dissipation of rents
5. market failure

6. public good
7. nonrivalrous good
8. nonexcludable good
9. Clarke tax
10. free riding

True-False Exercises

11. FALSE. People enter a common property as long as their <u>private</u> marginal benefit exceeds the opportunity cost of a visit.

12. FALSE. Social gain from an orchard is largest when people are <u>charged a competitive entrance fee for using</u> the orchard.

13. TRUE.

14. FALSE. If people have identical tastes, then <u>no one</u> has an incentive to maintain and improve a common property.

15. FALSE. The marginal user of a common property receives <u>no</u> net value from its use.

16. TRUE.

17. FALSE. The efficient price for a <u>nonrivalrous</u> good is zero.

18. FALSE. Whenever a public good increases the desirability of living in a certain area, its benefits tend to be <u>concentrated among landlords</u>.

19. FALSE. When a Clarke tax is used to finance a public good, people have the incentive to <u>honestly reveal</u> the value they receive from it.

20. FALSE. The revenue raised from a Clarke tax <u>may or may not</u> cover the cost of a public good.

Multiple Choice Questions

21. D. A common property is a rivalrous, nonexcludable good. A satellite transmission is a nonrivalrous good, because when it is broadcast to one person, that same transmission is also available for others to see. The satellite transmission is an excludable good, however, because the broadcast can be scrambled to prevent others from seeing it.

22.   A. This result is simply an application of the equimarginal principle.

23.   D. People will continue to use a common property as long as they can earn rent from it. Consequently, a person will choose to use the common property when the value he receives from it exceeds his opportunity cost.

24.   C. When property is commonly owned, it will be overused and the rent it creates will not be as large as possible. When the marginal cost of using the property is constant, the rent will be totally dissipated.

25.   B. When the marginal cost of using the lake increases with the number of fishers, then the rent is suboptimal but is not totally dissipated.

26.   A. The admission fee serves as a proxy for the external costs of crowding. The fee must be set competitively in order to maximize social gain.

27.   A. Use of a common property is unrestricted, so a common property is a nonexcludable good. However, one person's use of a common property affects the value that others receive from it, so a common property is a rivalrous good.

28.   B. When access to the common property cannot be prohibited, Q_C people will choose to use the property. Each person will receive, on average, a value of P_C dollars from his use of the property. The social gain is measured by the difference between P_C and the marginal cost.

29.   C. Social gain will be maximized at the quantity Q_O where social marginal value equals the users' marginal cost. The value each person receives, on average, from the common property will be P_2. The social gain is measured by the difference between P_2 and the marginal cost.

30.   C. The owner can charge an entrance fee equal to the difference between the value received by the typical person and the marginal cost of using the property. When the owner behaves competitively, Q_O people will be charged an entrance fee of $P_2 - P_1$. Therefore, the rectangular area $C + D + F + G$ measures the entrance fees collected by the owner.

31.   A. People's benefits equal the value they receive from using the property minus the entrance fee. When the owner charges a competitive entrance fee, this difference equals P_1. The surplus value people earn is thus the difference between P_1 and their marginal cost.

32.   D. National defense is nonexcludable because it would be prohibitively costly to prevent any individual from sharing in its benefits. National defense is also nonrivalrous because one person's consumption does not reduce the amount available for other people.

33.   C. Each resident would have an incentive to take a "free ride" and attempt to enjoy the benefits of the fireworks display without sharing in its cost.

34.   B. If people realize that their tax payments are connected to their revealed preferences for the public good, then they will understate their preferences in an attempt to share in the benefits but not the costs of the public good.

35.   D. A Clarke tax gives people an incentive to truthfully reveal their preferences, because the tax they pay is unrelated to their revealed preferences.

Review Questions

36.   If an additional person chooses to use the common property, then the resulting congestion lowers the value that each person, on average, receives from the property. In other words, consumption of a common property is rivalrous, so the value people get from the property falls as the number of users increases. Consequently, each user imposes external costs on others when he chooses to use the common property. These external costs make the social marginal benefit smaller than the private value that people receive, on average, from the common property.

37.   People will choose to use a common property as long as the value they receive from it exceeds their opportunity cost of using it. Consequently, the *average* value received must equal the marginal cost for the last person using the common property. The social optimum, however, occurs when the social *marginal* value of the property equals the marginal cost. The common property's social marginal value is smaller than its average value, so the socially optimal level of usage is smaller than the competitive level of usage.

38.   The rents created by a common property are totally dissipated when the marginal cost of using the property is constant and identical for all people. People will continue to use a common property as long as they can earn rent from it, therefore the last person who chooses to use a common property earns zero rent from its use. The rent each person earns is equal to the value he receives from the property minus the opportunity cost he incurs from using it, and this rent equals zero for the last person. If everyone has the same opportunity cost, then everyone earns zero rent just like the last person, and so the rents are totally dissipated.

39.   A private owner can charge an entrance fee equal to the difference between the value a person receives, on average, from the common property and the person's opportunity cost

of using it. An entrance fee prevents the dissipation of rents because it limits entry. People will choose to use the property as long as the value they receive exceeds the entrance fee plus their opportunity cost. The entrance fee keeps the value that people receive from the property above their marginal cost, which prevents the rents from falling to zero.

40.   When one person uses a computer software package, it does not reduce the availability of that software to other people, thus it is a nonrivalrous good. However, people can be prevented from using the software package by various copy protection schemes, so computer software fails to be a nonexcludable good.

41.   To decide if a public good should be provided, the government must determine the value of the public good to citizens. The government must also raise tax revenues to finance the provision of the public good. If citizens realize that their stated preferences for the public good are related to the tax shares they pay, then a free rider problem will be created. They will have an incentive to understate their preferences for the public good in an attempt to receive the benefits from it without fully sharing in its costs. To overcome this problem, the government needs to change the incentives so that each person's tax share is unrelated to his revealed preference for the public good. The Clarke tax is one example of this approach.

Problems

42.   i.   To calculate the value that each miner, on average, receives from working in the mine, divide the total value of the gold mined by the number of miners. To calculate the social marginal benefit of the mine's existence, find the additional value of gold attributable to the last miner. These calculations are summarized in the table below.

Number of Miners	Marginal Cost of Mining	Number of Miners	Total Value of Gold Mined	Value per Miner	Social Marginal Benefit
0 miners	—	0 miners	$ 0	—	—
1	$ 5 per miner	1	20	$20 per miner	$20 per miner
2	6	2	36	18	16
3	7	3	48	16	12
4	8	4	56	14	8
5	9	5	60	12	4
6	10	6	60	10	0
7	11	7	56	8	−4
8	12	8	48	6	−8

ii.   When the mine is common property, miners will continue to work the mine until the value they receive, on average, equals their marginal cost. Thus 6 miners will choose to work the mine, because both the marginal cost of mining and the value per miner equal $10 per miner. The miners receive all the social gain in this case, which equals the difference between the value they receive and their marginal cost. The first miner receives a gain of $5 (the value of $10 minus the marginal cost of $5), the second miner receives a gain of $4 (the value of $10 minus the marginal cost of $6), the third miner receives a gain of $3, the fourth miner receives a gain of $2, the fifth miner receives a gain of $1, and the last miner receives a gain of $0. The social gain created by the existence of the mine is thus $5 + $4 + $3 + $2 + $1 + $0, or $15.

iii.   The optimal number of miners is 4, because this quantity is where the marginal cost of mining equals the social marginal benefit created by the mine (both equal $8 per miner). In this case, each miner receives, on average, a value of $14. The social gain created by the mine's existence equals the difference between this value and marginal cost, so the maximum social gain is ($14 – $5) + ($14 – $6) + ($14 – $7) + ($14 – $8) = $9 + $8 + $7 + $6 = $30. The competitive entrance fee equals the difference between the value the miners receive and the social marginal benefit in this optimal situation, so the owner changes $14 – $8, or $6 per miner. Since 4 miners choose to work the mine, the owner receives a total of $6 per miner × 4 miners, or $24. Thus, the social gain of $30 is split into $24 for the owner and $6 for the miners.

43.   i.   The owner's demand curve for fishers is determined by the marginal value he receives from hiring the last fisher. The owner keeps the entire catch, so the marginal value of a fisher equals the marginal catch that the owner receives from hiring an additional fisher. The supply of fishers is determined by their marginal cost of using their time to catch fish for the owner.

If the owner and the fishers behave competitively, the owner will pay fishers a wage of P_1, because the owner's demand curve intersects the fishers' supply curve at this price. The owner will hire Q_0 fishers. The owner's surplus value will be the area beneath his demand curve and above the wage paid to the fishers, which is area A + C + F. The fishers' surplus value will be the area above their supply curve and below the wage they receive, which is area I. The social gain is the sum of these two surplus values, which equals area A + C + F + I.

ii.   If the owner charges fishers a competitive entrance fee for the right to use the fishery, then the owner will collect area C + D + F + G in entrance fees and the fishers will earn area I in surplus value. Area A equals area D + G, because the marginal catch curve is twice as steep as the average catch curve. Therefore, area A + C + F equals area C + D + F + G, and so the owner earns the same amount in the two situations.

iii. The Invisible Hand Theorem guarantees that competitive markets will create the most social gain possible, so it is no surprise that the maximum social gain (area A + C + F + I or area C + D + F + G + I) is created whether the owner charges fishers a competitive entrance fee or hires fishers at a competitive wage.

iv.   If fishers have unrestricted access to the fishery, then their surplus value and the social gain both equal area F + G + H + I. Area A + C equals area G + H + J, because the marginal catch curve is twice as steep as the average catch curve. Therefore, area G + H equals area A + C – J, and the social gain equals area A + C + F + I – J. The maximum social gain is measured by area A + C + F + I, so area J equals the deadweight loss.

44. i.   Residents' costs of breathing Grimyville air range from $100 to $200 per month (the difference between the demand curve and the $500 per month value placed on a Cleantown apartment). Grimyville residents receive $10,000 in consumers' surplus, and Grimyville landlords receive $60,000 in producers' surplus.

ii.   If the filters are installed, then Grimyville apartments will be identical to Cleantown apartments and will rent for $500 per month. Producers' surplus will rise to $100,000, so Grimyville landlords benefit from the cleaner air. Consumers' surplus will fall to zero, so Grimyville residents lose.

iii. Social welfare is $70,000 without the filters and $100,000 with the filters. The $35,000 cost of the filters outweighs the $30,000 increase in social welfare, so the Grimyville government should choose not to provide the filters.

iv.   Grimyville landlords will provide the public good, because the $35,000 cost of the filters is smaller than the $40,000 increase in their producers' surplus. Social gain will fall from $70,000 to $65,000, because the loss of consumers' surplus offsets some of the landlords' gains.

45. i.   The Coase Theorem can be applied to resolve the tragedy of the commons if two conditions are met. First, the property right to the common property must be clearly

defined. Second, there must be a way of prohibiting and punishing unauthorized use of the common property. A competitive entrance fee could be one result of private bargaining. If the two conditions cannot be met, then the transactions costs of enforcing the optimal contract prevent the Coase Theorem from being applicable. This could occur if the perimeter of the common property is too vast to be effectively patrolled. (For example, use of an ocean fishing ground probably cannot be prohibited.) Transactions costs could also be created if the agents' use of the common property is largely unobservable. (For example, it may be too costly to count each hunter's kills or every fisher's catch.)

ii.   Transactions costs prevent the Coase Theorem from resolving problems with most public goods. If the public good is a nonexcludable good, then property rights to the public good cannot be clearly established. Public goods generally involve large numbers of people, so principal-agent problems may arise. Free riding by consumers also constitutes a transactions cost of negotiation which can prevent the Coase Theorem from being applicable. On the other hand, when the benefits of the public good are concentrated among a small number of people, then there is a better chance that the Coase Theorem can be applied. For instance, if a public good increases the desirability of living in a certain area, the benefits tend to be completely captured by an increase in land values. If the number of landlords is sufficiently small, then the public good may be provided by private action.

CHAPTER 15

THE DEMAND FOR FACTORS OF PRODUCTION

Previous chapters have analyzed the markets for consumption goods. This chapter begins a three-chapter unit examining the markets for factors of production. The fundamental concepts needed to understand the demand for factors of production are the focus for this chapter.

KEY TERMS

- Marginal revenue product of labor (MRP_L)
- Marginal product of labor (MP_L)
- Complements in production

- Substitutes in production
- Derived demand
- Substitution effect
- Scale effect
- Regressive factor
- Monopsonist

- Marginal labor cost (MLC)
- Quasi-rents

KEY IDEAS

- **Section 15.1.** The marginal revenue product of labor is the revenue attributable to the last unit of labor employed. The firm's short-run demand curve for labor coincides with the downward-sloping portion of its marginal revenue product of labor curve.

- **Section 15.2.** When the wage rate changes, the firm's long-run use of labor changes for two reasons: the substitution effect and the scale effect. The substitution effect always works in the same direction as the law of demand. The scale effect also works in the same direction as the law of demand if labor is not a regressive factor. The law of demand always holds for a firm's long-run use of labor, even if labor is a regressive factor.

- **Section 15.3.** An industry's demand curve for a factor of production is less elastic than the horizontal sum of individual firms' demand curves, because changes in the price of the industry's output must be taken into account. A monopsonist is a firm that has market power in the input market. The marginal labor cost is always higher than the wage rate for a monopsony demander, so a monopsonist hires less labor and pays a lower wage than if it behaved competitively.

◆ **Section 15.4.** The producer's surplus earned by a factor of production is called rent. Factors with inelastic supply earn more rents as a percentage of income than do factors with elastic supply, so factors with inelastic supply stand to gain or lose the most from changes in the industry.

COMPLETION EXERCISES

1. A firm's factor demand is called a _____, because it depends in part on the demand for the firm's product.

2. A profit-maximizing firm in a competitive labor market hires labor to the point where the wage rate equals the _____.

3. The marginal revenue product of labor equals a firm's marginal revenue times the

    _____.

4. If labor and capital are _____, then greater capital usage leads to a fall in the marginal product of labor.

5. If labor and capital are _____, then greater capital usage leads to a rise in a firm's short-run demand for labor.

6. If a higher wage leads to a decline in a firm's long-run marginal costs, then labor is called a

    _____.

7. In the long run, an increase in the wage rate will affect a firm's long-run marginal costs, which leads to adjustments in production and labor usage—this change in labor usage is known as the _____.

8. In the long run, an increase in the wage rate will cause a firm to use more capital and less labor to produce any given level of output—this change in labor usage is known as the

    _____.

9. A _____ can affect the price paid for a factor and thus faces an upward-sloping supply curve for the factor.

10. When the price of a firm's output rises, factors with highly inelastic supply earn temporary short-run rents called _____.

TRUE-FALSE EXERCISES

_____ 11. A firm's short-run demand for labor coincides with the downward-sloping portion of the marginal labor cost curve.

_____ 12. The marginal revenue product of labor equals the wage rate times the marginal product of labor.

_____ 13. An increase in capital always reduces a firm's short-run demand for labor.

_____ 14. When a firm is faced with a wage increase in the long run, the substitution effect always reduces the firm's employment of labor.

_____ 15. When a firm is faced with a wage increase in the long run, the scale effect always reduces the firm's employment of labor.

_____ 16. A firm's long-run labor demand curve will fail to be downward-sloping when labor is a regressive factor.

_____ 17. An industry's demand curve for a factor is more elastic than the sum of the individual firms' factor demand curves.

_____ 18. A monopsonist pays a wage rate equal to labor's marginal revenue product.

_____ 19. In a competitive long-run equilibrium, factor shares add up to more than a firm's revenue when production exhibits decreasing returns to scale.

_____ 20. Factors with relatively inelastic supply tend to earn more rent than factors with relatively elastic supply.

MULTIPLE CHOICE QUESTIONS

_____ 21. Suppose a firm hires labor in a competitive labor market. If the marginal revenue product of labor is less than the wage rate, then
   A.   the firm can increase its profit by hiring less labor.
   B.   the firm can increase its profit by hiring more labor.
   C.   the firm's profit is maximized.
   D.   the firm has losses in the short run.

_____ 22. How will an increase in the price of a competitive firm's output affect its short-run demand curve for labor?
   A.   The demand curve may shift either to the left or to the right, depending on whether or not labor is a regressive factor.
   B.   The demand curve will become more elastic.
   C.   The demand curve will shift to the right.
   D.   The demand curve is unaffected by changes in output prices.

_____ 23. If an increase in the amount of capital causes the marginal product of labor to rise, then
   A.   labor and capital are complements in production.
   B.   labor and capital are substitutes in production.
   C.   labor is a regressive factor.
   D.   labor usage is independent of scale effects.

_____ 24. Suppose labor and capital are substitutes in production. How will an increase in the amount of capital affect the total product of labor curve?
   A.   There will be no shift in the total product of labor curve.
   B.   There will be a parallel shift upwards in the total product of labor curve.
   C.   The total product of labor curve will become steeper at every level of labor usage.
   D.   The total product of labor curve will rise, but it will become shallower at every level of labor usage.

_____ 25. Which of the following is _not_ held fixed when the firm's long-run demand curve for labor is derived?
   A.   The technology available to the firm.
   B.   The rental rate of capital.
   C.   The amount of capital that the firm employs.
   D.   The market price of the firm's output.

_____ 26. If labor is a regressive factor, then an increase in the wage rate will
   A.   increase the marginal product of labor.
   B.   decrease the firm's long-run marginal cost of production.
   C.   cause the firm to reduce its output in the long run.
   D.   increase the quantity of labor demanded by the firm.

_____ 27. Suppose the wage rate falls,
causing the firm to increase the
amount of labor it hires from L_0 to
L_1 in the long run. In the diagram
on the right, what are the
substitution and scale effects of
this change in the wage rate?
   A.   The movement from A to B is
        the substitution effect, and the
        movement from B to D is the
        scale effect.
   B.   The movement from A to C is
        the substitution effect, and the
        movement from C to D is the
        scale effect.
   C.   The movement from A to D is
        the substitution effect, and the
        movement from D to B is the
        scale effect.
   D.   The movement from A to B is
        the substitution effect, and the
        movement from B to C is the
        scale effect.

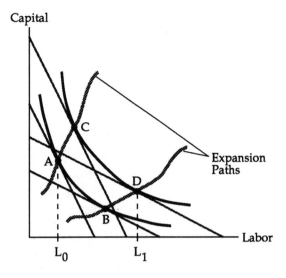

_____ 28. If the substitution and scale effects are in opposite directions, then
   A.   the scale effect must outweigh the substitution effect.
   B.   the firm's long-run demand curve for labor is upward sloping.
   C.   labor and capital are complements in production.
   D.   labor is a regressive factor.

_____ 29. Assume that labor is not a regressive factor. Why is the industry's demand curve for
labor less elastic than the horizontal sum of individual firms' demand curves?
   A.   Because changes in the firms' use of capital must be taken into account.
   B.   Because changes in the market price of the firms' output must be taken into
        account.
   C.   Because firms' interdependence and their use of strategic behavior must be
        taken into account.
   D.   Because shifts in the firms' marginal product of labor curves must be taken into
        account.

_____ 30. A profit-maximizing monopsonist hires labor up to the point where the marginal
revenue product of labor equals
   A.   the wage rate.
   B.   the marginal product of labor.
   C.   the marginal labor cost.
   D.   the rent paid to labor.

_____ 31. In long-run competitive equilibrium, if production exhibits constant returns to scale, factor shares add up to
   A.   zero.
   B.   the firm's variable cost.
   C.   the firm's revenues.
   D.   producer's surplus.

_____ 32. What factors earn the largest proportion of their income in the form of rent?
   A.   Fixed factors of production.
   B.   Regressive factors of production.
   C.   Factors of production that are paid a high price.
   D.   Factors of production that have highly elastic supply.

◆◆◆ Questions 33–35 refer to the diagram on the right, which shows an industry's labor demand and labor supply. Firms' demand is determined by labor's marginal revenue product (MRP_L). The equilibrium quantity of labor is denoted by L, and the equilibrium wage rate is denoted by P_L.

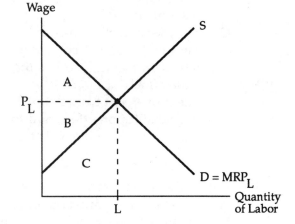

_____ 33. The total revenue collected by firms in the industry is equal to
   A.   area A.
   B.   area A + B.
   C.   area B + C.
   D.   area A + B + C.

_____ 34. The income earned by laborers is measured by
   A.   area A + B.
   B.   area B.
   C.   area C.
   D.   area B + C.

_____ 35. The rent earned by laborers is measured by
   A.   area A + B.
   B.   area B.
   C.   area C.
   D.   area B + C.

REVIEW QUESTIONS

36.   Explain why a firm in a competitive labor market should hire labor so that its marginal revenue product equals the wage rate. What does this result imply about the firm's short-run demand curve for labor?

37.   What can cause a firm's short-run demand curve for labor to shift to the right?

38.   Describe how additional capital can affect the total and marginal products of labor. Consider both the cases of complements and substitutes in production. Which of these two cases is the more likely?

39. Describe the substitution and scale effects of a wage increase. What roles do these effects play in determining the slope of a firm's long-run demand curve for labor?

40. Assume that labor is not a regressive factor. Explain why the industry's demand curve for labor is less elastic than the horizontal sum of individual firms' demand curves.

41. How does a monopsonist's demand curve for labor differ from that for a firm that is competitive in the labor market?

PROBLEMS

42. Angie's Pizza is one of many pizza restaurants serving a local college campus. How will each of the following affect the short-run demand for labor at Angie's? Justify your responses.

   i.   Angie expands her restaurant, adding a new oven and a new seating area.

   ii. Angie's refrigerator is accidentally unplugged, and $500 worth of food is spoiled.

   iii. Everyone is surprised to learn that this year the university has admitted 300 more students than last year.

43.　Suppose a competitive firm's technology is described by the formula $Q = 2\sqrt{L \cdot K}$, where Q is the quantity of output, L is the quantity of labor, and K is the quantity of capital. The marginal product of labor is given by the formula $MP_L = \sqrt{K/L}$, and the marginal product of capital is given by $MP_K = \sqrt{L/K}$. Let W be the wage rate paid to labor, R be the rental rate paid to capital, and P be the price of the firm's output.

i.　Show that the firm's short-run demand for labor is given by $L = K_0 P^2 \cdot 1/w^2$, where K_0 is the fixed level of short-run capital. Verify that this demand curve for labor is indeed downward sloping.

ii.　Find a formula for the marginal rate of technical substitution of labor for capital ($MRTS_{LK}$). Use this formula to prove that the expansion path is a straight line from the origin with slope W/R.

iii. Use the formulas for the production function and the expansion path to show that $L = \frac{1}{2} \cdot \sqrt{R/W} \cdot Q$ and $K = \frac{1}{2} \cdot \sqrt{W/R} \cdot Q$ in the long run.

iv. Use your answer to part iii to find formulas which express the firm's long-run total cost (TC) and long-run marginal cost (MC) in terms of R, W, and Q.

v. Find a formula for this firm's long-run demand for labor in terms of the price of output P and the rental rate for capital R.

44. Suppose that a firm's isoquants are right-angled as shown in the diagram on the right.

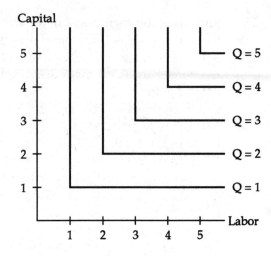

   i.   Describe the firm's expansion path. How does the expansion path change if the wage rate or the rental rate changes?

   ii.   Show that the firm's long-run marginal cost is given by the formula $LRMC = W + R$, where W is the wage rate and R is the rental rate.

   iii. Use your answer to part ii to determine whether or not labor is a regressive factor.

   iv.   Describe the substitution and scale effects that would be caused by a rise in the wage rate.

   v.   Are labor and capital complements or substitutes in production?

45. Suppose labor and capital are the only
factors of production. Capital is fixed
and has a perfectly inelastic supply in
the short run, so all income earned by
capital is rent.

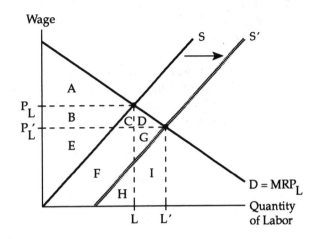

   The diagram on the right shows the
short-run demand and supply curves for
labor in the United States. Suppose a
group of immigrants enters the U.S. The
immigrants' supply of labor is perfectly
inelastic, so there is a parallel shift from
S to S' as shown in the diagram. After
the immigrants' arrival, the wage rate
falls from P_L to P_L', and employment
rises from L to L'. Furthermore, suppose
the immigrants own no factors of
production other than labor. All capital
and all firms are owned by U.S. citizens.

i. What area represents the rents earned by American laborers before the arrival of
immigrants? What area represents the sum of the rents earned by owners of capital
and the profits earned by firms before the arrival of immigrants?

ii. What area represents the rents earned by American laborers after the arrival of
immigrants? What area represents the rents earned by immigrants? What area
represents the sum of the rents earned by owners of capital and the profits earned by
firms after the arrival of immigrants?

iii. Does the immigrants' arrival make American laborers better off or worse off in the
short run? Does it make owners of capital and owners of firms better off or worse off?
Are Americans overall better off or worse off from the immigrants' arrival?

SOLUTIONS

Completion Exercises

1. derived demand
2. marginal revenue product of labor
3. marginal product of labor
4. substitutes in production
5. complements in production

6. regressive factor
7. scale effect
8. substitution effect
9. monopsonist
10. quasi-rents

True-False Exercises

11. FALSE. A firm's short-run demand for labor coincides with the downward-sloping portion of the <u>marginal revenue product of labor</u> curve.

12. FALSE. The marginal revenue product of labor equals the <u>price of the firm's output</u> times the marginal product of labor.

13. FALSE. An increase in capital reduces a firm's short-run demand for labor <u>when capital and labor are substitutes in production</u>.

14. TRUE.

15. FALSE. When a firm is faced with a wage increase in the long run, the scale effect reduces the firm's employment of labor <u>only if labor is a regressive factor</u>.

16. FALSE. A firm's long-run labor demand curve <u>is always downward-sloping</u>.

17. FALSE. An industry's demand curve for a factor is <u>less</u> elastic than the sum of the individual firms' factor demand curves.

18. FALSE. A monopsonist pays a wage rate <u>less than</u> labor's marginal revenue product.

19. FALSE. In a competitive long-run equilibrium, factor shares add up to more than a firm's revenue when production exhibits <u>increasing</u> returns to scale.

20. TRUE.

Multiple Choice Questions

21. A. The last unit of labor hired does not generate enough revenue to cover its cost, so the firm should reduce its labor usage until the marginal revenue product is equal to the wage rate.

22. C. The firm's short-run demand curve for labor coincides with the marginal revenue product of labor curve. When the price of output rises, the firm's marginal revenue also

rises. This causes marginal revenue product, and hence the firm's demand for labor, to also rise.

23.   A. When labor and capital are complements in production, additional capital will increase the productivity of labor at the margin.

24.   D. When labor and capital are substitutes in production, additional capital will decrease the marginal product of labor.

25.   C. In the long run, the firm can alter the levels of both labor and capital, so the long-run demand for labor takes into account changes in the firm's use of both inputs.

26.   B. If labor is a regressive factor, lower marginal costs allow the firm to increase its output when the wage rate rises.

27.   A. The substitution effect is the change in labor usage caused by the change in the relative wage while keeping the output level constant. The points used to find the substitution effect must be on the same isoquant. The scale effect is the change in labor usage caused by the change in the firm's output level. The points used to find the scale effect must lie on the same expansion path.

28.   D. If the wage rate increases, the substitution effect leads to a fall in the firm's labor usage. If labor is a regressive factor, the firm's output will increase when the wage rate increases, so the scale effect leads to a rise in the firm's use of labor.

29.   B. The firms' demand curves for labor are derived under the assumption that the market price of output is fixed. However, if the wage rate rises and the industry's supply decreases, then the price of output will rise. This complication must be considered when deriving the industry's labor demand.

30.   C. Labor is worth hiring as long as its marginal revenue product exceeds its marginal cost.

31.   C. Competitive firms earn zero profit in long-run equilibrium, so the firm's entire revenues must be paid out to the factors.

32.   A. Fixed factors of production have highly inelastic supply, and therefore a higher percentage of their income is in the form of rent.

33.   D. The marginal revenue product of labor curve shows the revenue that each hour of labor generates for firms, so the area beneath the MRP_L curve measures the firms' total revenue.

34.   D. The base of the rectangular area B + C equals the number of hours worked, and its width equals the hourly wage. Therefore, the rectangle's area equals laborers' total income.

35.   B. The rent equals the producers' surplus earned by laborers.

Review Questions

36.   The equimarginal principle shows that a firm should hire labor to the point where the marginal revenue product of labor equals the wage rate. If the marginal revenue product exceeds the wage, then additional labor increases a firm's profit because it adds more to revenues than to costs. If the marginal revenue product is smaller than the wage, then the last hour of labor hired does not generate enough revenue to cover its cost, so the firm should hire less labor in order to increase its profit. We can conclude that the firm's demand curve for labor coincides with its marginal revenue product of labor curve, because the latter indicates the amount of labor the firm should hire at any given wage rate. (Capital is implicitly held constant in this argument, because changes in capital usage shift the marginal revenue product of labor curve. Therefore, the marginal revenue product of labor curve coincides with the firm's *short-run* demand curve for labor.)

37.   The firm's short-run demand curve for labor coincides with its marginal revenue product of labor curve, and the marginal revenue product of labor equals the firm's marginal revenue times the marginal product of labor. Consequently, anything (other than the wage rate and the amount of labor hired) that increases either the firm's marginal revenue or labor's marginal product will shift the demand curve for labor to the right. An increase in the demand for the firm's product, an increase in the amount of a complementary factor of production, or a nonregressive technological advance will increase the firm's demand for labor.

38.   Additional capital will cause the total product of labor to rise, but the marginal product of labor could either rise or fall. If labor and capital are complements in production, then additional capital causes the total product of labor curve to shift up so that it becomes steeper at every quantity of labor, and the marginal product of labor rises. If labor and capital are substitutes in production, then additional capital shifts up the total product of labor curve so that it becomes shallower at all quantities, so the marginal product of labor falls. Labor and capital are usually complementary factors of production.

39.   When the wage rate increases, the expansion path shifts and the firm uses less labor and more capital to produce any particular amount of output. The substitution effect is the decrease in labor usage caused by the increased wage, assuming that the output level is held fixed. The substitution effect always helps to make the firm's long-run demand curve for labor slope downwards.

When the wage rate increases, the firm's long-run marginal cost curve also shifts and so the firm changes its level of output. The scale effect is the change in labor usage attributable to the change in the firm's output. In most cases, the scale effect works with the substitution effect to make the long-run demand curve for labor slope downwards. If labor is a regressive factor, however, the scale effect works against the substitution effect. The substitution effect outweighs the scale effect in this situation, so the firm's long-run demand curve for labor is guaranteed to be downward sloping.

40.   If the wage rate increases and labor is not a regressive factor, then both the substitution and scale effects cause firms to use less labor. However, the higher wage also increases firms' marginal costs, so market supply decreases and the price of output rises. The higher market price encourages firms to increase their production, which in part offsets the scale effect. Therefore, the quantity demanded of labor falls by less than would be indicated by the horizontal sum of individual firms' demand curves.

41.   A monopsonist does not have a demand curve for labor, because there is no going market wage to which the monopsonist reacts. Instead, the monopsonist uses the labor supply curve to calculate the marginal labor cost, and it chooses the quantity of labor so that the marginal revenue product of labor equals the marginal labor cost. The monopsonist then chooses the appropriate wage rate from the labor supply curve. In contrast, a firm in a competitive labor market takes the wage rate as given, and then chooses the quantity of labor so that its marginal revenue product equals the wage rate.

Problems

42.   i.   Most likely, labor would be a complement for the new oven and seating area. The additional capital would increase the marginal product of labor, which in turn causes an increase in the firm's short-run demand for labor.

       ii.   The $500 worth of spoiled food is a sunk cost that cannot be recovered. The entire loss comes out of the firm's profit; the firm cannot benefit from any change in its operations. The short-run demand for labor thus remains unchanged.

       iii.   The price of pizza will rise in response to the increased demand. Labor has a higher marginal revenue product, and thus the firm's short-run demand for labor rises.

43.   i.   In the short run, a profit-maximizing competitive firm hires labor so that

$W = MRP_L = MR \times MP_L = P \times MP_L$. Substituting $MP_L = \sqrt{K_0/L}$ into this equilibrium condition yields $W = P \cdot \sqrt{K_0/L} \Rightarrow W^2 L = P^2 K_0 \Rightarrow L = K_0 P^2 \cdot 1/w^2$. If W increases, then $1/w^2$ falls, thus L falls and the demand curve for labor is downward sloping.

ii.   Calculate the $MRTS_{LK}$ by taking the ratio of marginal products: $MRTS_{LK} = MP_L/MP_K$ $= \sqrt{K/L} / \sqrt{L/K} = K/L$. The $MRTS_{LK}$ equals W/R for all points on the expansion path, so $K/L = W/R$ gives the formula for the expansion path. This formula can be rewritten as $K = W/R \cdot L$, which is the equation of a straight line from the origin with slope W/R.

iii. The formula for the expansion path can be written as $K = W/R \cdot L$ or as $L = R/W \cdot K$. To get an expression for L in terms of R, W, and Q, substitute the first formula for the expansion path into the production function and solve for L: $Q = 2\sqrt{L \cdot K} \Rightarrow$ $Q = 2\sqrt{L \cdot W/R \cdot L} = 2\sqrt{W/R} \cdot L \Rightarrow L = \frac{1}{2} \cdot \sqrt{R/W} \cdot Q$. To get an expression for K in terms of R, W, and Q, substitute the second formula for the expansion path into the production function and solve for K: $Q = 2\sqrt{L \cdot K} \Rightarrow Q = 2\sqrt{R/W \cdot K \cdot K} = 2\sqrt{R/W} \cdot K \Rightarrow$ $K = \frac{1}{2} \cdot \sqrt{W/R} \cdot Q$.

iv.   The firm's long-run total cost is given by the formula WL + RK. Substitute the equations from part iii into this formula for total cost and simplify: $TC = WL + RK = $ $W \cdot \frac{1}{2} \cdot \sqrt{R/W} \cdot Q + R \cdot \frac{1}{2} \cdot \sqrt{W/R} \cdot Q = \frac{1}{2} \cdot \sqrt{WR} \cdot Q + \frac{1}{2} \cdot \sqrt{WR} \cdot Q = \sqrt{WR} \cdot Q$. If Q increases 1 unit, then long-run total cost increases by $\sqrt{WR}$ dollars, so the formula for long-run marginal cost is given by $MC = \sqrt{WR}$.

v.   A competitive firm sets price equal to marginal cost to choose its output, so solve the equation P = MC for W: $P = \sqrt{WR} \Rightarrow W = P^2/R$. This formula does not depend on the quantity of labor L, so the long-run demand for labor is perfectly elastic at the wage P^2/R.

44.   i.   The "tangencies" between the isocosts and the isoquants will be at the corners of the isoquants, so the expansion path is a 45° line from the origin. The locations of the "tangencies" do not change when the slope of the isocosts changes, so the expansion path does not shift when the wage rate or the rental rate changes.

      ii. Production of the last unit of output always requires 1 hour of labor and 1 hour of capital. Consequently, the firm must spend $W on labor and $R on capital in order to produce the last unit of output, so its long-run marginal cost equals W + R dollars per unit.

iii. If the wage rate increases, then the firm's long-run marginal cost W + R also increases. Therefore, labor is not a regressive factor.

iv. When the wage rate increases, the expansion path does not shift. The firm uses the same combination of labor and capital to produce any particular level of output, so the substitution effect is zero. When the wage rate increases, the firm's long-run marginal cost increases and the firm reduces its output level. Therefore, the scale effect causes the firm to reduce the amounts of labor and capital it hires.

v. Labor and capital are complements in production. For example, when there are 2 hours of capital, the 3rd hour of labor has a marginal product of zero because it adds nothing to the firm's output. If capital usage increases to 3 hours of capital, then the marginal product of the 3rd hour of labor increases to 1 unit of output per hour, because the 3rd hour of labor and the 3rd hour of capital combine to produce 1 additional unit of output. Increased capital usage raises the marginal product of labor, so labor and capital are complements in production.

45. i. Before the arrival of immigrants, American laborers are paid area B + C + E + F + H, and area B + E of that income is in the form of rent. The area beneath the MRP_L curve, area A + B + C + E + F + H, represents the firms' revenues. Area B + C + E + F + H is paid to laborers, so area A remains for firms' profits and capital owners' rents.

ii. After the immigrants arrive, laborers earn rents equal to area E + F + G. Area E measures the rents earned by American laborers, and area F + G measures the rents earned by the immigrant laborers. The total revenues earned by firms are measured by area A + B + C + D + E + F + G + H + I, and area E + F + G + H + I of this amount is paid to laborers. Therefore, area A + B + C + D is left for the rents earned by owners of capital and the profits earned by firms.

iii. The rents earned by American laborers fall from area B + E to area E, so the immigrants' arrival makes American laborers worse off in the short run because they lose area B in rents. The rents earned by owners of capital and the profits earned by firms increase from area A to area A + B + C + D, so these groups gain area B + C + D and are made better off. Immigrants do not own capital or firms, so in the short run, Americans overall are made better off from the immigrants' arrival. The gains received by the owners of capital and the owners of firms outweigh the losses incurred by American laborers.

CHAPTER 16

THE MARKET FOR LABOR

This chapter is the second of three chapters examining the markets for factors of production. The first half this chapter focuses on the individual's supply of labor and the market for labor. The second half of the chapter examines two special topics related to labor markets: differences in wages and discrimination.

KEY TERMS

- Leisure
- Marginal value of leisure
- Consumption
- Nonlabor income

- Substitution effect
- Income effect
- Backward bending
- Intertemporal substitution

- Human capital
- Compensating differential
- Discrimination

KEY IDEAS

- **Section 16.1.** Indifference curves showing an individual's tastes for leisure and consumption are used to derive his labor supply. When the wage rate rises, the substitution effect causes the individual to increase his work effort, but the income effect works in the opposite direction. Therefore, the individual's labor supply curve may be backward bending.

- **Section 16.2.** An increase in nonlabor income causes labor supply to fall. An increase in productivity leads to an increased demand for labor, and if widespread, also leads to higher nonlabor incomes and a decreased supply of labor. Intertemporal substitution by laborers must be taken into account when examining the effects of temporary changes in the market.

- **Section 16.3.** Differences in human capital, compensating differentials, and differing access to capital can be used to explain the differences observed in people's wages.

◆   **Section 16.4.** Explanations for the wage differences between men and women and between blacks and whites include discrimination, differences in human capital, and workers' preferences. These factors are difficult to measure, so there is no consensus among economists on the significance of discrimination in the labor market.

COMPLETION EXERCISES

1.   To study labor supply, economists use indifference curves which show an individual's tastes for labor and _____ .

2.   By definition, _____ represents all uses of the individual's time other than labor.

3.   Income earned from an individual's assets is classified as _____ .

4.   The slope of an indifference curve measures the _____ , which must equal the wage rate at the optimum.

5.   At relatively high wages, the income effect may outweigh the substitution effect and cause an individual's labor supply curve to be _____ .

6.   When the wage rate increases, the _____ causes the individual to demand more consumption and less leisure because the marginal hour of leisure is now more expensive.

7.   When the wage rate increases, the _____ makes suppliers of labor better off, which leads to them to choose more consumption and more leisure.

8.   When workers use _____ , they adjust their work schedules and vacation times so that they are working when wages are highest.

9.   Productive skills resulting from education and training are called _____ .

10.   Worker compensation for particularly unpleasant or risky aspects of a job is called a _____ .

TRUE-FALSE EXERCISES

_____ 11. When the wage rate falls, the substitution effect causes the worker to supply more hours of labor.

_____ 12. When the wage rate falls, the income effect causes the worker to supply more hours of labor.

_____ 13. The income effect may outweigh the substitution effect when wages are relatively low.

_____ 14. An individual's labor supply curve must slope upwards.

_____ 15. An increase in nonlabor incomes leads to a reduction in the wage rate.

_____ 16. When workers own capital, an increase in their marginal productivity is offset by a decrease in their nonlabor income.

_____ 17. Workers engage in intertemporal substitution when faced with a permanent increase in their marginal productivity.

_____ 18. All other things being equal, a more pleasant job will pay a lower wage than a less pleasant job.

_____ 19. If accumulating human capital at a central location creates external benefits, then wage differentials may not be eliminated in the long run.

_____ 20. When two groups are paid different wages, the differential must be a result of discrimination.

MULTIPLE CHOICE QUESTIONS

_____ 21. Leisure consists of all activities other than
   A. consumption.
   B. sleep.
   C. household production.
   D. labor.

_____ 22. At the worker's optimum, the wage rate equals the marginal value of
   A. leisure.
   B. labor.
   C. consumption.
   D. income.

_____ 23. Suppose that the wage rate exceeds a worker's marginal value of leisure. Then the worker
   A. should choose to work fewer hours.
   B. earns the maximum rent for his human capital.
   C. is being exploited by the employer.
   D. will be better off with increased work effort.

_____ 24. A decrease in a worker's nonlabor income causes
   A. an increase in the amount of labor he supplies.
   B. a decrease in the wage rate.
   C. an increase in his work effort only if the substitution effect outweighs the income effect.
   D. an increase in his marginal value of leisure.

_____ 25. Which of the following situations will result in an increase in the laborer's work effort?
   A. An increase in his nonlabor income.
   B. A higher wage rate, assuming the substitution effect dominates the labor income effect.
   C. An increase in his marginal value of leisure.
   D. A permanent technological improvement that raises labor's marginal product.

_____ 26. If the wage rate falls, then the substitution effect causes an individual's work effort to
   A. fall.
   B. rise.
   C. remain unchanged.
   D. react unpredictably.

_____ 27. Workers' incomes rise when the wage rate increases, so they tend to increase leisure and reduce work effort. This phenomenon is known as
   A. compensating differential.
   B. the income effect.
   C. the substitution effect.
   D. intertemporal substitution.

_____ 28. All other things being equal, an additional payment is needed to compensate workers for unpleasant aspects of their job. This additional payment is known as
   A. rent on human capital.
   B. nonlabor income.
   C. compensating differential.
   D. surplus value.

_____ 29. Which of the following statements about the labor supply curve is *false?*
  A. The substitution effect always helps to make the labor supply curve upward sloping.
  B. The individual's labor supply curve is upward sloping only if the substitution and income effects are in the same direction.
  C. An individual's labor supply curve may become backward bending at high wage rates.
  D. Income effects are negligible at low wage rates.

_____ 30. Labor supply may increase when wages are temporarily high, because workers will engage in
  A. human capital investment.
  B. unionizing.
  C. negotiations for compensating differentials.
  D. intertemporal substitution.

_____ 31. Suppose workers own capital and a technological improvement permanently raises the marginal product of labor throughout the economy. Which of the following may *not* occur?
  A. The demand for labor will rise.
  B. The supply of labor will fall.
  C. The equilibrium quantity of labor will fall.
  D. The equilibrium wage rate will rise.

_____ 32. Suppose workers own capital and a technological improvement raises the marginal product of labor throughout the economy, but workers believe that this improvement is only temporary. How must the analysis of this situation be changed to take into account intertemporal substitution?
  A. Intertemporal substitution will lower labor's marginal product, so the increase in the demand for labor will be lessened.
  B. Intertemporal substitution will reinforce the substitution effect, so the possibility of a backward-bending labor supply curve is eliminated.
  C. Intertemporal substitution will make the shifts in the labor supply and demand curves even larger, so the resulting increase in the wage rate will be magnified.
  D. Intertemporal substitution will increase the supply of labor, offsetting and perhaps overcoming the income effect of the technological improvement.

_____ 33. Workers are paid rent for the specialized skills and talents resulting from earlier investments in their lives, and this rent is included in the workers' wages. In this situation, different workers are paid different wages because
  A. they have different amounts of human capital.
  B. they have differing access to capital.
  C. they receive different compensating differentials.
  D. discrimination is occurring in the labor market.

_____ 34. Wages may include compensating differentials because
   A.   workers embody differing amounts of human capital.
   B.   a market-oriented policy is needed to compensate for past and present
        discrimination.
   C.   some jobs are inherently more risky or unpleasant than other jobs.
   D.   otherwise workers' intertemporal substitution will cause fluctuations in labor
        supply.

_____ 35. Suppose employers are indifferent between hiring whites and hiring blacks, but they
        discriminate against blacks because their white employees have a distaste for
        associating with blacks. A theory of discrimination based on this premise would
        predict
   A.   substantial wage differentials between whites and blacks.
   B.   a heavily segregated work force.
   C.   less access to capital for black workers than for white workers.
   D.   more pleasant occupations for white workers than for black workers.

REVIEW QUESTIONS

36. Describe the substitution and income effects caused by a decrease in a worker's wage rate.

37. Consider an increase in workers' productivity. Why might such a change lead to reduced labor supply? Why might such a change lead to increased labor supply?

38. Why can an individual's labor supply curve be backward bending?

39.   What is meant by intertemporal substitution? When will workers tend to engage in intertemporal substitution?

40.   Briefly discuss three reasons why different workers are paid different wage rates.

41.   Why is it difficult to find a theory of discrimination that is consistent with sustained wage differentials? What other problems do economists face when they try to determine if discrimination is responsible for wage differentials?

PROBLEMS

42.   Consider a worker who has no nonlabor income and can earn a wage of $10 per hour. The worker's budget line is shown in the diagram on the right, where consumption is measured in dollars for convenience. Suppose that the government imposes a 50% tax on labor income, but it simultaneously gives all workers a $20 tax rebate. This type of tax scheme is known as a negative income tax (NIT).

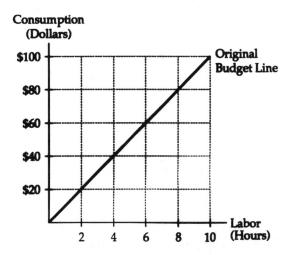

i.   On the above diagram, draw the worker's budget line after the NIT is imposed. When would the NIT make the worker better off? When would it make the worker worse off?

ii.   Consider a worker who earned $20 before the NIT was imposed. How does the NIT affect the amount of labor supplied by this worker? Explain, using substitution and income effects.

iii.   Consider a worker who earned $60 before the NIT was imposed. How does the NIT affect the amount of labor supplied by the worker? Explain, using substitution and income effects.

43. Suppose there are three occupations: carpenters, electricians, and secretaries. The labor
     demand curve for each occupation is linear, with a vertical intercept at $12 per hour and a
     horizontal intercept at 600 laborers. The labor force consists of 300 men and 300 women,
     whose labor supplies are perfectly inelastic. Because of discrimination in training and
     hiring, men can only be employed as carpenters and electricians, and women can only be
     employed as secretaries. This situation is illustrated in the diagrams below.

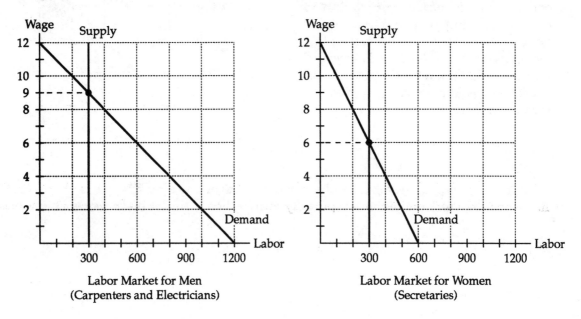

Labor Market for Men	Labor Market for Women
(Carpenters and Electricians)	(Secretaries)

i.   What wages are paid to men and women when discrimination occurs? What is causing
     the wage differential?

ii. **Suppose legal protections against discrimination are implemented, allowing men and
     women to work in any of the three occupations. Assuming the three jobs require
     similar skills and are equally desirable, what will happen in the labor market in the
     long run? What will be the wage rates for the three occupations? Illustrate this
     situation on the above graphs.**

iii. Calculate the social gains created by the labor market before and after discrimination.
     What effect does the elimination of discrimination have on the market's efficiency?

44.   Consider the market for labor. How would each of the following events affect the wage rate and employment?

i.   A stock market crash cuts workers' interest and dividends in half.

ii.   Poor weather conditions temporarily reduce the productivity of agricultural workers.

iii.   Foreign investors build new factories across the nation.

45. Suppose the typical worker in a unionized labor force is paid $6 per hour and works 40 hours per week. For each of the following events, will the typical worker want to work more or fewer hours, or is the effect ambiguous? Use substitution and income effects to justify your responses.

    i.   The union negotiates a wage increase of $1.50 per hour.

    ii.   The union passes an annual dues increase of $120 per member.

    iii.   The union fails to negotiate a wage increase, but it does negotiate an overtime pay rate of $9 per hour for any hours worked in excess of 40 hours per week.

SOLUTIONS

Completion Exercises

1. consumption
2. leisure
3. nonlabor income
4. marginal value of leisure
5. backward bending

6. substitution effect
7. income effect
8. intertemporal substitution
9. human capital
10. compensating differential

True-False Exercises

11. FALSE. When the wage rate falls, the substitution effect causes the worker to supply <u>fewer</u> hours of labor.
12. TRUE.
13. FALSE. The income effect may outweigh the substitution effect when wages are relatively <u>high</u>.
14. FALSE. An individual's labor supply curve <u>may either slope upwards or bend backward</u>.
15. FALSE. An increase in nonlabor incomes leads to <u>an increase</u> in the wage rate.
16. FALSE. When workers own capital, an increase in their marginal productivity <u>leads to an increase</u> in their nonlabor income.
17. FALSE. Workers engage in intertemporal substitution when faced with a <u>temporary</u> increase in their marginal productivity.
18. TRUE.
19. TRUE.
20. FALSE. When two groups <u>with the same marginal productivity</u> are paid different wages, the differential must be a result of discrimination.

Multiple Choice Questions

21. D. This statement is simply the definition of leisure.
22. A. The wage rate is the worker's opportunity cost of additional leisure.
23. D. If the marginal value of leisure is smaller than the wage rate, then the last hour of leisure has a lower value than the wage rate, so the worker should continue to supply additional labor.

24.   A. A worker demands less leisure when he has less nonlabor income, so he supplies more labor.

25.   B. The individual's labor supply curve is upward sloping as long as the substitution effect is larger than the opposing income effect.

26.   A. The price of leisure falls, so the individual chooses to have more leisure hours and fewer labor hours.

27.   B. The labor income effect tends to reduce the quantity of labor supplied when the wage rate rises.

28.   C. Compensating differentials pay workers to undertake jobs that are particularly risky or unpleasant.

29.   B. If leisure is a normal good, the income effect is always in opposition to the substitution effect. The individual's labor supply curve is upward sloping if the substitution effect is the larger.

30.   D. Workers will shift work schedules and vacation times to work more when wages are temporarily high.

31.   C. The higher productivity increases the demand for labor, which places upward pressure on the equilibrium quantity of labor. The income effect will reduce the supply of labor, which places downward pressure on the equilibrium quantity of labor. Therefore, the equilibrium quantity of labor may rise or fall.

32.   D. Workers will use intertemporal substitution to increase their current labor supply and take advantage of the temporarily high wages.

33.   A. Human capital refers to the workers' productive skills.

34.   C. Compensating differentials are used to compensate workers for particularly unpleasant or risky occupations.

35.   B. In economic models of discrimination, profit-maximizing behavior frequently leads to the prediction that some firms hire only whites and some firms hire only blacks. However, profit-maximizing behavior also eliminates any wage differentials between whites and blacks.

Review Questions

36.   A decrease in the wage rate has two effects on the worker's decision to supply labor. First, the price of consuming leisure has fallen, so the worker chooses to have more leisure and

less consumption. This substitution effect causes a fall in the amount of labor supplied by the worker. Second, the lower wage reduces the worker's real income, so he chooses to have less leisure and less consumption. This income effect causes a rise in the amount of labor supplied by the worker.

37. When workers become more productive, the value of capital rises and the owners of capital experience an increase in nonlabor income. If workers themselves own capital, then workers' nonlabor income rises. The resulting income effect causes labor supply to fall. On the other hand, if the productivity increase is temporary, workers may engage in intertemporal substitution and increase their labor supply to benefit from temporarily high wages.

38. The individual's supply of labor contains a substitution effect that works with the law of demand and an income effect that works against the law of demand. The income effect will be small for relatively low wage rates, so the labor supply curve will be upward sloping at these wages. However, the income effect is likely to be large for relatively high wage rates, so the individual's labor supply curve may begin to bend backwards.

39. Intertemporal substitution refers to laborers' adjusting their work hours to take advantage of the periods when wages are highest. Whenever wages are expected to be higher in one period than in another, laborers will engage in intertemporal substitution. In particular, if workers believe that a market change is temporary and not permanent, intertemporal substitution will cause shifts in the labor supply curve.

40. First, workers may receive different rents for their skills because of differences in their human capital. Second, workers may have different access to capital, and this can cause wage differentials if the positive externalities created by human capital accumulation prevent some mobility of capital. Third, compensating differentials may be necessary to compensate workers for especially risky or unpleasant aspects of their occupations.

41. If discrimination causes one group to have lower wages, profit-maximizing behavior would cause firms to seek out those employees. Consequently, that group's wages would be bid up, and the wage differential would be eliminated. Finding an acceptable theory is one problem economists face in measuring the degree of discrimination in the labor market. Economists also have statistical problems in isolating the various factors relevant to the labor decision. Voluntary choices by workers can cause wage differences, and this phenomenon may explain some of the wage differences thought to be caused by

discrimination. Another problem is that the effects of past discrimination are hard to separate from the effects of present discrimination.

Problems

42. i.   The new budget line has a slope of $5 per hour and a vertical intercept equal to the tax rebate of $20 as shown in the diagram on the right. If the worker earned $40 or less before the NIT is imposed, then the worker is made better off because his initial optimum is on or below his new budget line. If the worker earned more than $40 before the NIT is imposed, and if the substitution effect of the wage change is not too large, then his new optimum is below his original budget line, and so he is worse off.

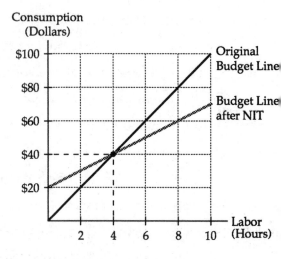

ii.   The NIT causes this worker to reduce his work effort. The lower after-tax wage reduces the price of leisure, so the substitution effect causes the worker to reduce the quantity of labor he supplies. The tax rebate makes the worker wealthier, so the resulting income effect also causes him to reduce the quantity of labor he supplies.

iii. A worker who earned $60 before the NIT was imposed may either increase or decrease his work effort because the substitution and income effects are in opposite directions. The substitution effect is identical to that for the poorer worker; the lower price of leisure causes the worker to reduce the amount of labor he supplies. However, the tax rebate is too small to overcome the income effect of the lower wage. The worker is less wealthy after the NIT, so the resulting income effect causes him to increase the amount of labor he supplies.

43. i.   Men are paid a wage of $9 per hour, while women are paid only $6 per hour. The source of the wage differential is the artificial segmentation of the labor market. In

effect women are being crowded into a single industry, and the relatively low demand and relatively high supply cause women to be paid a lower wage than men.

ii. If the jobs are equally desirable, the wages must be equalized in the long run. The supply of carpenters and electricians will rise, and the supply of secretaries will fall, until there are 200 workers in each industry. The men's wage will fall and the women's wage will rise, until both equal $8 per hour. This situation is illustrated in the graphs below.

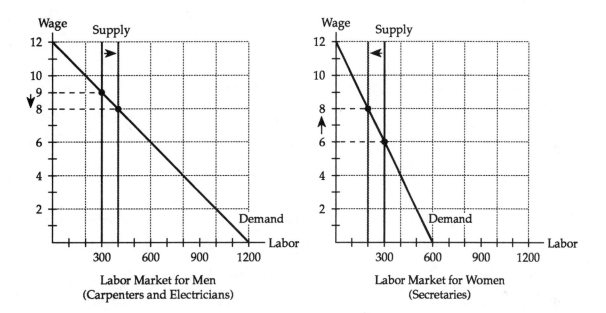

Labor Market for Men
(Carpenters and Electricians)

Labor Market for Women
(Secretaries)

iii. Since the labor supplies are perfectly inelastic, social gain is the area beneath the demand curve out to the number of workers. When discrimination is in force, the men's market creates $3,150 of social gain (a rectangle with area $2,700 and a triangle of $450), the women's market creates $2,700 of social gain (a rectangle with area $1,800 and a triangle of $900), for a total of $5,850 of social gain. When discrimination is eliminated, the market for carpenters and electricians creates $4,000 of social gain (a rectangle with area $3,200 and a triangle of $800), the market for secretaries creates $2,000 of social gain (a rectangle with area $1,600 and a triangle of $400), for a total of $6,000 of social gain. Ending discrimination increased social gain and thus improved efficiency by eliminating the artificial segmentation of the labor market.

44. i. The interest and dividends are nonlabor income. Workers increase their supply of labor when their nonlabor income falls, so the wage rate falls and total employment rises. The amount of labor supplied by any given individual may either rise or fall.

ii.   The fall in workers' productivity leads to lower labor demand and hence a lower wage. The wage reduction is only temporary, so workers will engage in intertemporal substitution. Workers will decrease their labor supply in the present and plan to increase their labor supply sometime in the future when wages are higher. The wage rate, total employment, and individual work effort all decline.

iii. Factories and labor are complements in production, so the additional capital causes an increase in labor's marginal product. The demand for labor rises. The nonlabor income created by the factories is earned by foreigners, not domestic workers. Labor supply does not shift because there is no change in workers' nonlabor income. The wage rate, total employment, and individual work effort all increase.

45. i.   The wage increase creates both substitution and income effects. The substitution effect causes the worker to provide more labor and consume less leisure, while the income effect causes the worker to provide less labor and consume more leisure. The effect on employment is ambiguous.

ii.   The size of the dues increase does not depend on a worker's labor income, so the dues increase is equivalent to a loss of nonlabor income. There is no change in the wage rate, so there is no substitution effect. The income effect leads to more labor and less consumption. The typical worker chooses to work more hours per week.

iii. For more than 40 hours per week of work, the typical worker's new budget line lies above the old budget line. For 40 or fewer hours per week of work, the new and old budget lines coincide. The worker's new budget line has a kink and becomes steeper right at the initial optimum. Thus, the worker's new optimum must lie above, to the right, and on a higher indifference curve than the initial optimum. The typical worker chooses to work more hours per week and have some overtime. The substitution effect leads to greater work effort while the income effect leads to lesser work effort, but the substitution effect must dominate in this case.

CHAPTER 17

ALLOCATING GOODS OVER TIME

This chapter concludes a three-chapter unit on the markets for factors of production. The market for capital and the determination of the interest rate are the focus for the chapter. The first half of the chapter introduces the necessary concepts, and the second half shows how to use supply and demand curves and the representative-agent model to analyze changes in the interest rate.

KEY TERMS

- Lender
- Borrower
- Bond
- Present value
- Face value
- Discount
- Maturity date

- Coupon bond
- Perpetuity
- Nominal interest rate
- Real interest rate
- Default risk
- Risk premium
- Dividends

- Exhaustible resource
- Endowment
- Representative agent
- Ricardian Equivalence Theorem
- Marginal product of capital (MP_K)

KEY IDEAS

- **Section 17.1.** The real interest rate (denoted by r) establishes relative prices between present and future goods. In particular, the relative price of current consumption in terms of future consumption is $1 + r$. The present value of future consumption is obtained by using the discount factor $\frac{1}{(1+r)}$. The present value of a perpetuity is $\frac{1}{r}$ times the annual payment. When bonds are denominated in dollars, the sum of the real interest rate and the inflation rate, which is called the nominal interest rate, must be used to calculate present values.

- **Section 17.2.** The value of either a productive asset or a financial asset equals the present value of the stream of dividends it produces. This result implies that the price of an exhaustible resource grows at the rate of interest if the marginal cost of extraction is negligible.

◆   **Section 17.3.** Indifference curves showing the consumer's tastes between current and future consumption can be used to derive his demand for current consumption. Changes in the equilibrium interest rate may be analyzed using either the supply and demand curves for current consumption or the representative-agent model.

◆   **Section 17.4.** An economy's resources may be used to produce either consumption goods or capital goods. In equilibrium, the marginal product of capital equals the real interest rate, so the demand curve for capital coincides with the marginal product of capital curve. Any resources not demanded for capital are available for current consumption. Therefore, an upward-sloping supply curve for current consumption may be derived from the marginal product of capital curve.

COMPLETION EXERCISES

1.   A borrower's promise of future payment is called a _____.

2.   The price of a bond equals the _____ of its promised delivery.

3.   The difference between a bond's price and its face value is called the

    _____.

4.   When a bond promises payment in dollars, its present value must be calculated using the

    _____.

5.   The additional interest that a lender receives as compensation for the risk that the borrower may default is called a _____.

6.   Because every barrel of oil consumed today implies that one less barrel of oil will be available in the future, oil is said to be an _____.

7.   The value of a productive asset is equal to the present value of the stream of _____ that is produces.

8.   A firm's demand curve for capital coincides with its _____ curve.

9.   The representative agent is neither a net lender nor a net borrower, so the representative agent's optimum must coincide with his _____ point.

10.   In many circumstances, government borrowing has no effect on the interest rate—this result is known as the _____.

TRUE-FALSE EXERCISES

_____   11.   In order to lend, one must be willing to sell a bond.

_____   12.   Interest rates and bond prices are directly related.

_____   13.   Real and nominal interest rates are equal when default risk is zero.

_____   14.   The value of an asset equals the present value of the stream of dividends it produces.

_____   15.   When customers are aware of differences in quality, firm are more likely to engage in planned obsolescence.

_____   16.   The price of an exhaustible resource grows at exactly the rate of interest as long as the marginal extraction costs are large.

_____   17.   An expected decrease in the availability of future goods leads to a rise in the interest rate.

_____   18.   Ricardian equivalence shows that, under many circumstances, government spending is a matter of indifference.

_____   19.   Profit-maximizing firms will invest in additional capital as long as the marginal product of capital exceeds the discount rate.

_____   20.   The representative agent's optimum coincides with his endowment point.

MULTIPLE CHOICE QUESTIONS

_____ 21. A bond with a $60,000 face value sells at a $10,000 discount one year prior to its maturity. The nominal interest rate paid by the bond is
A. 6 percent.
B. 8.33 percent.
C. 16.67 percent.
D. 20 percent.

_____ 22. Which of the following statements about bonds is *false?*
A.   The buyer of a bond is a borrower, and the seller of a bond is a lender.
B.   A bond sells at a discount, which is the difference between its face value and its price.
C.   The value of a bond rises when the interest rate falls.
D.   The discount of a bond denominated in dollars is calculated using the nominal interest rate.

_____ 23. What is the present value of a perpetuity paying $120 per year when the interest rate is 8%?
A. $960.
B. $1,111.
C. $1,296.
D. $1,500.

_____ 24. Suppose you have $10,000 deposited in an IRA account that pays a nominal interest rate of 10%. You expect inflation to remain at 4% or less. What real interest rate are you planning to earn on this IRA account?
A. 10%.
B. At least 6%.
C. At least 4%.
D. At least 2.5%.

_____ 25. The market rate of interest is 20%. A producer can make a quality improvement in his product that will increase its value to consumers by $36 per year for a three-year period. Should the producer make the quality improvement?
A.   No, because it will substantially lower his sales.
B.   Yes, as long as it costs less than $36.
C.   Yes, as long as it costs less than $91.
D.   Yes, as long as it costs less than $180.

_____ 26. Suppose the government spends $3,000 per person this year. The market for borrowing and lending is competitive, and the market interest rate is 10%. Which of the following plans to finance the government's spending is best for consumers?
A.   A tax of $3,000 per person this year.
B.   A tax of $3,300 per person next year.
C.   An annual tax of $300 per person forever.
D.   All of the above plans have the same effect on consumers.

◆◆◆ Questions 27 and 28 refer to the diagram on the right, which shows a consumer's choice between current and future consumption.

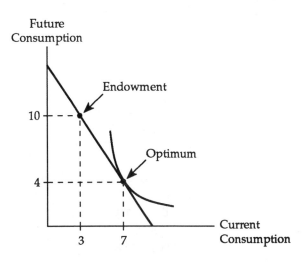

_____ 27. The consumer can lend and borrow at the interest rate of
A. 0.5 percent.
B. 1.5 percent.
C. 50 percent.
D. 150 percent.

_____ 28. The consumer shown in the diagram is
A. a net borrower.
B. a net lender.
C. the representative agent.
D. a net demander of bonds.

_____ 29. The market rate of interest is 5%. The government imposes a tax of $30 per acre on farmland. The supply of farmland is fixed, and the market for farmland is competitive. The year after the tax is imposed, Dr. White sells an acre of land on which he grew tobacco. How is the economic burden of the tax divided between Dr. White and the new landowner?
A. The tax costs Dr. White $600, and it costs the new landowner nothing.
B. Dr. White pays $30 in taxes, and the new landowner pays $30 annually for as long as he owns the land.
C. The entire burden of the tax falls on the new landowner, because Dr. White increases the price of his land by $30 to compensate him for the tax.
D. The price of Dr. White's land falls so that the burden of the tax is equally divided between him and the new landowner.

_____ 30. The market rate of interest is 15%. The price of coal is determined competitively, and the marginal cost of extracting coal from the mines is assumed to be zero. Owners of coal mines, after taking their current plans to mine coal into account, expect the price of coal to be $50 per ton this year and $55 per ton next year. If the owners want to maximize their profits, how should they adjust their plans to mine coal?
A. Owners should do more mining this year and less mining next year.
B. Owners should do less mining this year and more mining next year.
C. The owners should continue their plans to mine coal without any changes.
D. Changes in the owners' plans are irrelevant, because their profits will be the same no matter when they mine the coal.

_____ 31. Which of the following may *not* cause an increase in the interest rate?
A. A decrease in consumers' current wealth that does not affect their future wealth.
B. An increase in consumers' future wealth that is independent of the productivity of capital.
C. An increase in the future productivity of capital.
D. A permanent increase in productivity that is effective immediately.

_____ 32. The Ricardian Equivalence Theorem states that
   A.   government spending financed by debt and government spending financed by taxation have the same effect on the interest rate.
   B.   the representative-agent model and the supply and demand for current consumption must arrive at identical conclusions regarding any change in the interest rate.
   C.   a burden of an annual tax on land falls completely on the person who owns the land when the tax is imposed.
   D.   a rise in the price of bonds is equivalent to a fall in the interest rate.

_____ 33. When investment is possible, the supply of current consumption is determined by
   A.   the marginal value of current consumption.
   B.   the marginal product for capital.
   C.   people's endowments.
   D.   the present value of the dividends people earn from their assets.

_____ 34. Suppose the marginal product of capital is expressed as a percentage of output. If the interest rate is larger than the marginal product of capital, then
   A.   people's holdings of capital will fall until its marginal product equals the interest rate.
   B.   the demand for capital will increase.
   C.   increased investment in capital and a shortage of lenders will lower the interest rate and raise the marginal product of capital.
   D.   the representative agent's budget line is steeper than his indifference curve at his endowment point.

_____ 35. Suppose that the supply of current consumption is fixed by people's endowments and that investment in capital is impossible. Also suppose that a temporary improvement in productivity increases people's current endowments but does not affect their future endowments. Which of the following does *not* occur?
   A.   The representative agent's endowment point shifts to the right.
   B.   The representative agent's budget line becomes flatter.
   C.   The supply and demand curves for current consumption both shift to the right, with the shift in demand being the larger of the two.
   D.   The equilibrium interest rate falls.

REVIEW QUESTIONS

36. What are bonds and perpetuities? How are the prices of bonds and perpetuities calculated?

37. How are productive assets and financial assets similar? How are they different?

38. Why does the competitive price of an exhaustible resource grow at the rate of interest when marginal extraction costs are zero? How is the analysis modified when extraction costs are present?

39.   What does the Ricardian Equivalence Theorem state? What can prevent the Ricardian Equivalence Theorem from being true for the economy?

40.   When is the supply curve for current consumption vertical? When is it upward sloping?

41.   What factors can decrease the demand for current consumption? What factors can decrease the supply for current consumption? In each case, how is the equilibrium interest rate affected?

PROBLEMS

42. i.   Use substitution and income effects to explain why a borrower's demand curve for current consumption must be downward sloping.

ii.   Use substitution and income effects to show that a lender's demand curve for current consumption may not be downward sloping. Is the law of demand more likely to be violated at high or low interest rates in this case? Explain.

iii. Use the representative-agent model to show that the market demand curve for the entire economy's current consumption must be upward sloping.

43. This problem explores the tax advantages of Individual Retirement Accounts (IRAs).

    i.   Suppose you have invested $X in an account that will earn an interest rate of r. The government taxes the interest you earn at the rate t. What is the after-tax rate of interest that you are earning?

    ii.   Suppose you have $X of extra income this year. You decide to use this extra income for retirement purposes by making an investment for n years which will earn the rate of interest r. However, your extra income and your interest income are both taxed at the rate t. Find a formula showing how much you will be able to withdraw after n years.

    iii.   Now suppose that the government sets up an IRA program. Under certain conditions, the income you place in the IRA and the interest income earned are not taxed. However, you will have to pay a tax at the rate t when you withdraw your IRA funds. Find a formula showing how much you would be able to withdraw after n years if the investment described in part ii is placed in an IRA.

    iv.   Suppose you have $2,000 in extra income to invest for 20 years at an interest rate of 10%. Also suppose that you are in a 30% tax bracket. Use the formulas you developed in parts ii and iii to calculate the difference between making a non-IRA and an IRA investment. What tax advantage does the IRA offer that accounts for this difference?

44. Determine how each of the following situations would affect the demand for current consumption, the supply of current consumption, and the interest rate.

    i. Scientists announce that a new superconductor, which will cut the energy consumption of machinery in half, will be available next year.

    ii. A deadly plague sweeps the nation and kills 10% of the population.

    iii. Pests and insects breed in record numbers due to unusual weather conditions, damaging this year's crops but not affecting future crops.

45.   Consider the representative-agent model for determining the interest rate. Apples are
assumed to be the only good in the world. The supply of current consumption is fixed by
people's endowments, and investment in capital is impossible. Consumers' preferences for
current and future consumption are assumed to be homothetic (i.e., along any ray from the
origin, the indifference curves all have the same slope).

i.   Suppose a blight attacks apple
orchards, reducing current and
future endowments by equal
percentages. Complete the
diagram on the right to show
how this situation affects the
representative agent. (The
agent's initial optimum is
labeled A; label the agent's new
optimum B.) What happens to
the demand and supply of
current consumption, and what
happens to the equilibrium rate
of interest?

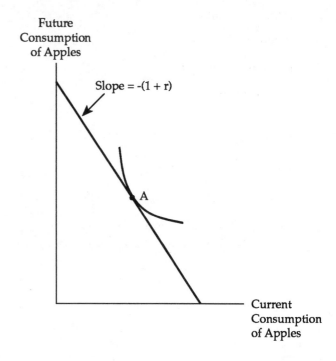

ii.   Suppose instead that the
orchards are expected to
partially recover from the blight
in the future, so that the blight
reduces current endowments by
a greater percentage than future
endowments. Repeat part i for
this situation.

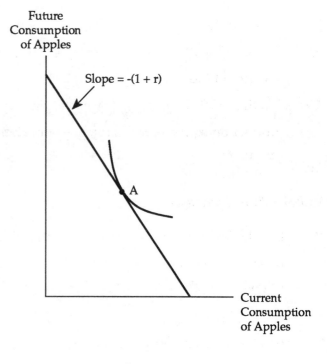

SOLUTIONS

Completion Exercises

1. bond
2. present value
3. discount
4. nominal interest rate
5. risk premium

6. exhaustible resource
7. dividends
8. marginal product of capital
9. endowment
10. Ricardian Equivalence Theorem

True-False Exercises

11. FALSE. In order to lend, one must be willing to <u>buy</u> a bond.

12. FALSE. Interest rates and bond prices are <u>inversely</u> related.

13. FALSE. Real and nominal interest rates are equal when <u>the inflation rate</u> is zero.

14. TRUE.

15. FALSE. When customers are aware of differences in quality, firm <u>have no incentive</u> to engage in planned obsolescence.

16. FALSE. The price of an exhaustible resource grows at exactly the rate of interest as long as the marginal extraction costs are <u>negligible</u>.

17. FALSE. An expected decrease in the availability of future goods leads to a <u>fall</u> in the interest rate.

18. FALSE. Ricardian equivalence shows that, under many circumstances, government <u>debt</u> is a matter of indifference.

19. FALSE. Profit-maximizing firms will invest in additional capital as long as the marginal product of capital exceeds the <u>interest</u> rate.

20. TRUE.

Multiple Choice Questions

21. D. The bond has a present value of $50,000, and this equals the discounted value of the bond's face value, which is $60,000 \cdot \frac{1}{(1+r)}$. Solving this equation for r yields
$$50,000 = 60,000 \cdot \tfrac{1}{(1+r)} \implies 1 + r = \tfrac{6}{5} = 1.20 \implies r = 0.20 \text{ or } 20\%.$$

22. A. The buyer of a bond is purchasing the promise of future goods, and the seller of the bond is receiving present goods in exchange. Therefore, the bond's seller is borrowing from the bond's buyer.

23.   D.   To obtain the present value of a perpetuity, multiply its annual payment by $1/r$. In this case, the perpetuity is worth $120 \cdot 1/0.08 = \$120 \cdot 12.5 = \$1,500$.

24.   B.   The nominal interest rate minus the inflation rate equals the real interest rate.

25.   C.   The producer can profit if the cost of the quality improvement is less than its value to consumers. The present value of the proposed improvement is $\$36 + \$36 \cdot 1/1.20 + \$36 \cdot 1/(1.20)^2$, which equals $\$36 + \$30 + \$25$ or $\$91$.

26.   D.   All three plans have the same present value, so the consumer's budget line is the same under all three plans.

27.   C.   The magnitude of the budget line's slope equals 1 plus the real interest rate. In this case, the slope of the budget line equals $1\frac{1}{2}$, so the interest rate is $\frac{1}{2} = 0.50$ or 50%.

28.   A.   The consumer chooses more current goods and fewer future goods than are contained in his endowment, so he is a net borrower.

29.   A.   The demand for farmland will shift down by the present value of the tax, which is $600 per acre. The supply of farmland is vertical, so the price of land falls precisely by $600 per acre and the entire burden of the tax falls on the present landowners.

30.   A.   The owners should mine coal so that its price grows at the rate of interest. Their current mining plans would cause the price of coal to grow at 10% annually, which is smaller than the current interest rate of 15%. Thus saving coal is not profitable, so they should reduce next year's mining of coal and increase this year's.

31.   D.   If there is a permanent increase in productivity that is effective immediately, then the representative agent's endowment point shifts to the northeast. Therefore, the representative agent's budget line may become steeper or flatter, so the equilibrium interest rate may rise or fall. If the representative agent's indifference curves are homothetic, then the equilibrium interest rate remains unchanged.

32.   A.   The Ricardian Equivalence Theorem states that, under certain conditions, taxation and government debt have the same effects on the supply and demand for current consumption.

33.   B.   Any current resources that are not demanded for capital are available for current consumption. Therefore, the supply curve for current consumption is determined by the demand curve for capital, which coincides with the marginal product of capital curve.

34. A. If the interest rate is larger than the marginal product of capital, then no one is willing to borrow to invest in capital. The amount of capital will fall and the marginal product of capital will rise as existing capital becomes worn out and discarded.

35. C. The interest rate must fall because the representative agent's budget line is flatter. Therefore, the increase in the supply of current consumption must be larger than the increase in the demand for current consumption.

Review Questions

36. A bond is a borrower's promise to deliver goods or make a monetary payment at some future date. A perpetuity is a coupon bond that promises to pay some fixed amount annually throughout the future. If a bond promises to make a single payment n years in the future, then the price of the bond is that payment times $1/(1+r)^n$, where r is the annual interest rate. The price of a perpetuity is its fixed annual payment times $1/r$. In both situations, the real interest rate should be used if the future payments are in the form of delivered goods, and the nominal interest rate should be used if the bond or perpetuity is denominated in dollars.

37. Both productive assets and financial assets pay dividends to their owners. The dividends paid by a productive asset are the future goods produced by the asset. On the other hand, the dividends paid by a financial asset can be either cash payments or shares in the ownership of new productive assets. In either case, the value of the asset is determined by the present value of the stream of dividends that it provides.

38. When an exhaustible resource is competitively priced, the future price of the resource must equal the opportunity cost of its production. Assume that the marginal cost of extracting the resource is zero. If the owner of an exhaustible resource chooses to sell one unit in the future, then he sacrifices both the opportunity to sell that unit today and the opportunity to earn interest on the revenue from that sale. Therefore, the future price of the resource must equal 1 + r times the current price of the resource, where r is the interest rate.

   If the marginal extraction cost is not zero, and if the owner chooses to sell the resource in the future instead of the present, then he earns interest from postponing the cost that he incurs from extracting the resource. The opportunity cost of future production is thus reduced by the rate of interest times the marginal cost of extraction. Therefore, the future price of the resource equals 1 + r times the current price of the resource minus r times the marginal cost of extraction.

39.   According to the Ricardian Equivalence Theorem, the method of financing government spending will not affect the interest rate. Taxation and government debt cause the same shifts in the supply and demand curves for current consumption, and therefore they have the same effects on the interest rate. The Ricardian Equivalence Theorem will not hold if either misperceptions or default risks are significant. When misperceptions occur, people do not realize that government debt must be paid for by future taxes, so they do not reduce their demand for current consumption by as much as if they were immediately taxed. When default risks are significant, people must pay higher interest rates to borrow money than does the government. Therefore, people will be wealthier and their demand for current consumption will be higher if the government borrows instead of using taxes.

40.   If current goods cannot be converted into future goods either by storage or by capital investment, then the supply curve for current consumption is vertical. In this case, the supply is completely determined by consumers' endowments. The supply curve for current consumption is upward sloping when storage or capital investment is possible. In the latter situation, the supply curve is derived from the marginal product of capital.

41.   If consumers' present or future wealth falls, then their demand for current consumption will decrease. Lower demand for current consumption will decrease the equilibrium interest rate. If consumers' current endowments decrease or if the marginal product of capital rises, then the supply curve for current consumption will shift to the left. A technological improvement is the most likely cause of an increase in the marginal product of capital. A reduced supply of current consumption will increase the equilibrium interest rate.

Problems

42.   i.   Suppose the interest rate rises. The relative price of current consumption increases, so the substitution effect causes the consumer to demand less current consumption and more future consumption. If the consumer is a borrower, then the higher interest rate makes him worse off. Therefore, the income effect causes the consumer to reduce both his current and future consumption. The substitution and income effects both support the law of demand.

ii. Suppose the interest rate rises. The substitution effect is the same as described in part i. If the consumer is a lender, however, the higher interest rate makes him better off. The resulting income effect causes a lender to demand more current and future consumption. Therefore, the substitution and income effects move in opposite directions, and the law of demand holds only if the substitution effect outweighs the income effect. The income effect will be small for low interest rates and will be larger at high interest rates, so the law of demand is most likely to be violated at high interest rates.

iii. The representative agent cannot be a net borrower or a net lender. The representative agent always chooses to consume his endowment point, so he experiences no income effect if the interest rate changes. Put another way, every dollar borrowed in the economy is also a dollar lent, so the economy-wide income effects must sum to zero. Therefore, only substitution effects are relevant to the market demand for current consumption, and so the economy's demand curve for current consumption must be downward sloping.

43. i. You earn rX in interest. The government collects the fraction t of this amount, which equals trX. You get to keep $rX - $trX = $(1 - t)rX$ in interest income. Therefore, the after-tax interest rate is $(1 - t)$ times r.

ii. The government takes tX of your X in extra income. You are left with $X - $tX = $(1 - t)X$ to invest. Your interest income is taxed, so you earn an interest rate of $(1 - t) \cdot r$. This investment compounds for n years, so you will withdraw $(1 - t)X \cdot [1 + (1 - t) \cdot r]^n$.

iii. When you invest in the IRA, you invest the full X at the interest rate r compounded for n years. Therefore, you will withdraw $X \cdot (1 + r)^n$. The government takes the fraction t of this amount, so you are left with $(1 - t)X \cdot (1 + r)^n$.

iv. Without the IRA, your $2,000 earns $(1 - t)X \cdot [1 + (1 - t) \cdot r]^n = \$1,400 \cdot (1.07)^{20} = \$1,400 \cdot 3.870 = \$5,418$. With the IRA, your $2,000 earns substantially more because of the tax-free interest: $(1 - t)X \cdot (1 + r)^n = \$1,400 \cdot (1.10)^{20} = \$1,400 \cdot 6.727 = \$9,418$. The IRA offers the advantage of tax-free interest. With the IRA you earn the interest rate r; without the IRA you only earn the interest rate $(1 - t) \cdot r$.

44. i. The new superconductor raises the marginal value of capital, thus raising the demand for capital and lowering the supply of current consumption. The increased future

wealth anticipated from the new superconductor increases the demand for current consumption. Both forces cause the interest rate to rise.

ii. The plague reduces the population, which leads to a decline in the demand for current consumption. As long as labor and capital are complements in production, the smaller labor force reduces the demand for capital and raises the supply of current consumption. Both forces cause the interest rate to fall.

iii. The damage to this year's crops lowers the supply of current consumption. The reduction in wealth lowers the demand for current consumption, but this fall in demand will be smaller than the fall in supply (because the reduction in wealth will also lower the demand for future consumption). Consequently, the interest rate will rise.

45. i. Since current and future endowments fall by the same percentage, the initial endowment point A and the new endowment point B must lie on the same ray from the origin. Since preferences are homothetic, the indifference curves have the same slopes at points A and B, thus the equilibrium interest rate remains unchanged. This situation is shown in the diagram below.

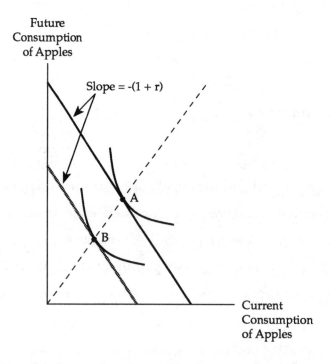

In this situation, the demand and supply of current consumption both fall because of the reduced endowments. However, they fall by the same amount (i.e., the demand

and supply curves shift to the left by the same amount), leaving the equilibrium interest rate unchanged.

ii. Current endowments fall by a greater percentage than future endowments, so point B must lie above the ray from the origin containing point A. When preferences are homothetic, the indifference curves will have steeper slopes above a ray from the origin than along the ray itself. Thus, the indifference curve at the new endowment point B must be steeper than at the initial endowment point A, which implies that the equilibrium interest rate rises. As shown in the diagram below, the new interest rate r′ must be greater than the initial interest rate r.

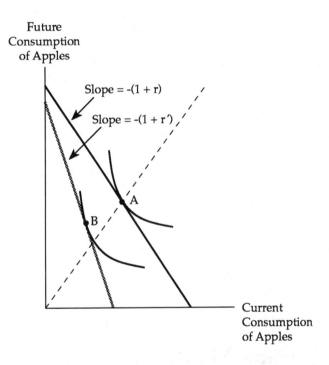

As in part i, the demand and supply of current consumption both fall because of the reduced endowments. However, since the future endowments are not as severely affected by the blight as the current endowment, the demand for current consumption falls by less than the supply of current consumption. Thus, the equilibrium interest rate rises in this situation.

CHAPTER 18

RISK AND UNCERTAINTY

The models studied in previous chapters are based on the assumption that economic agents have a great deal of information which is known with certainty. However, the future is always unknown, and individuals and firms must deal with the risk and uncertainty they face. This chapter surveys several of the models and ideas that have been developed to explain economic behavior under risk and uncertainty.

KEY TERMS

- State of the world
- Ex ante
- Ex post
- Expected value
- Law of large numbers
- Riskiness
- Risk-free
- Fair odds
- Diversify
- Risk-neutral
- Risk-averse

- Risk-preferring
- Moral hazard
- Adverse selection
- Uninsurable risk
- Futures contract
- Futures market
- Spot market
- Spot price
- Speculator
- Returns
- Expected return

- Standard deviation
- Investors
- Portfolios
- Efficient set
- Efficient portfolio
- Capital asset pricing model
- Market line
- Market portfolio
- Rational expectations

KEY IDEAS

- **Section 18.1.** Indifference curves showing a person's ex ante preferences between two different states of the world are used to analyze consumer choice under uncertainty. A person is risk-neutral if his preferences are based solely on the expected value of a basket of outcomes. A person is risk-averse when he chooses the least risky basket among those with the same expected value. A risk-averse person will accept a sufficiently small bet at favorable odds, but he will decline a large bet at those same odds.

◆ **Section 18.2.** Insurance companies are prevented from offering customers fair odds for a variety of reasons. The moral hazard problem arises because people behave more recklessly when they are insured, so insurance companies must adjust the odds accordingly. The adverse selection problem occurs because fair odds are different for different people, but the insurance company has no way of determining who has what odds. Finally, some risks, called uninsurable risks, cannot be diversified by the insurance company.

◆ **Section 18.3.** Futures markets allow a person to insure against the possibility of an unfavorably high or low future price for a product. Speculators attempt to earn money in the futures market by outguessing the market. Speculators increase social gain when they are successful, but they lower social gain if their predictions about the market are incorrect.

◆ **Section 18.4.** Investors purchase portfolios of financial assets to try to increase their wealth. The expected value of a portfolio is equal to the average of its individual stocks' expected returns, and the standard deviation of a portfolio is no greater than the average of its individual stocks' standard deviations. A risk-averse investor always holds a portfolio combining a risk-free asset and a market portfolio. A portfolio which is representative of all risky assets found in the economy is guaranteed to be a market portfolio.

◆ **Section 18.5.** Rational expectations exist when economic agents have no reason to change their expectations. Economic predictions based on past experience may prove to be incorrect, because changes in circumstances can alter people's rational expectations, eliminating the basis for that past experience.

COMPLETION EXERCISES

1. Preferences between baskets of outcomes before the state of the world is known are called _____ preferences.

2. The law of large numbers states that if a bet is repeated many times, then the average outcome equals the _____ of the bet.

3. When offered two baskets with the same expected value, a _____ person prefers the basket with the lesser amount of risk.

4. A risk-neutral person is indifferent about a bet offered at _____.

5. Insurance companies limit the purchases of policies designed for people who are good risks, because _____ prevents them from knowing whether a person is a good risk or a poor risk.

6. If a large number of people are all adversely affected by the same state of the world, then that state creates an _____ because an insurance company cannot diversify its risk.

7. An agreement to deliver a specified amount of a commodity at some future date for a prearranged price is called a _____.

8. A person who tries to outguess the market and profit from buying and selling in the spot and futures markets is called a _____.

9. A rational investor always holds a portfolio that combines the risk-free asset with the _____ in some proportion.

10. People are said to have _____ when their expectations do not create systematic, correctable errors.

TRUE-FALSE EXERCISES

_____ 11. The indifference curves representing a risk-averse individual's ex ante preferences are downward-sloping straight lines.

_____ 12. A risk-averse individual accepts a bet at favorable odds only if it is sufficiently large.

_____ 13. If fire insurance were a competitive industry with no operating costs, then insurance companies could offer fair odds to customers.

_____ 14. For an event to be insurable, an insurance company must be able to diversify its risks.

_____ 15. A risk-averse farmer, when faced with an uncertain future price, will choose to sell a futures contract that offers fair odds.

_____ 16. A speculator who believes next month's demand for wheat will be higher than others expect will sell futures contracts for wheat.

_____ 17. A portfolio's expected return equals the average of the expected returns of its individual stocks.

_____ 18. A portfolio's standard deviation equals the average of the standard deviations of its individual stocks.

_____ 19. When people have rational expectations, their predictions turn out to be correct at least half of the time.

_____ 20. An econometric equation that accurately reflects past experience can be invalidated by behavioral changes.

MULTIPLE CHOICE QUESTIONS

_____ 21. Which of the following statements about an individual's preferences under uncertainty is *false?*
A. The individual's preferences are ex ante preferences.
B. The preferences depend on the probabilities associated with the states of the world.
C. At risk-free baskets, the magnitude of the slope of the indifference curves equals the ratio of the probabilities associated with the states of the world.
D. The indifference curves, like those in the standard consumer-choice model, are convex.

_____ 22. When an individual is offered fair odds, all baskets on his budget line
A. have the same level of riskiness.
B. have the same expected value.
C. are equally desirable.
D. offer the same level of diversification.

_____ 23. Suppose an individual is offered a gamble at fair odds. If the individual is indifferent about how much he bets, then he
A. is risk-averse.
B. is risk-preferring.
C. is risk-neutral.
D. may be either risk-averse or risk-neutral.

_____ 24. When a risk-averse individual is offered a gamble at fair odds,
   A. he chooses the basket with the least risk.
   B. he bets everything on one or the other outcome.
   C. he accepts the gamble if the bet is sufficiently small.
   D. he is indifferent as to the amount he bets.

_____ 25. Suppose an individual is given the opportunity to place a bet at favorable odds. How will he respond if he is risk-averse?
   A. He will accept the bet.
   B. He will decline the bet.
   C. He will accept the bet if it is sufficiently small, but he will decline the bet if it is too large.
   D. He will accept the bet if it is sufficiently large, but he will be indifferent about the bet if it is too small.

_____ 26. The moral hazard problem arises because
   A. some states of the world adversely affect large numbers of individuals.
   B. insurance companies are unable to distinguish people who are good risks from those who are poor risks.
   C. some people want to purchase insurance at favorable odds, causing losses for the insurance companies.
   D. people with insurance tend to take more risks than people without insurance.

_____ 27. You cannot purchase fair-odds insurance against an uninsurable risk like nuclear war, because the insurance company cannot
   A. fully monitor your behavior.
   B. affect the likelihood of the event.
   C. diversify the risk.
   D. profit from policies issued to risk-preferring customers.

_____ 28. People who wear seat beats are less likely to have serious injuries in auto accidents than people who don't, but an insurance company has no way of determining which policy holders actually wear seat belts. The insurance company cannot offer unlimited insurance at fair odds for seat-belt wearers because of
   A. risk-preferring behavior.   C. uninsurable risk.
   B. adverse selection.   D. moral hazard.

_____ 29. Suppose that a stock currently sells for $200. The stock returns either –$60 or $100 with equal probability. The expected return of the stock is
   A. 10%.   C. 30%.
   B. 20%.   D. 40%.

_____ 30. Suppose that a stock currently sells for $200. The stock returns either –$60 or $100 with equal probability. The standard deviation of the stock is
   A. 10%.   C. 30%.
   B. 20%.   D. 40%.

_____ 31. Consider a portfolio for which there is no other portfolio with both a lower standard deviation and a higher expected return. This portfolio must
   A. lie on the market line.   C. be an efficient portfolio.
   B. be the market portfolio.   D. be a risk-free asset.

_____ 32. Suppose a risk-free asset and a variety of risky assets are available. A risk-averse investor will choose to hold
   A. a portfolio from the efficient set.
   B. only the risk-free asset.
   C. the market portfolio.
   D. a portfolio which combines the risk-free asset and the market portfolio.

_____ 33. Suppose speculators believe that the demand for a commodity will be lower in the future than what suppliers in the market currently expect. Which of the following will *not* occur?
   A. Speculators will purchase futures contracts.
   B. The future spot price expected by suppliers will be bid down.
   C. Suppliers will react to the speculators' actions by increasing current supplies and reducing future supplies.
   D. The speculators will increase social gain if they are correct in their expectations.

◆◆◆ Questions 34 and 35 refer to the following tables, which show the demand and supply for a particular market. Demand is uncertain, with D_1 and D_2 each occurring 50% of the time. Suppliers must base their decisions on the expected price and must sell all goods they bring to the market at the going market price.

Demand D_1		Demand D_2		Supply	
Quantity	Price	Quantity	Price	Quantity	Price
5 units	$6 per unit	25 units	$6 per unit	10 units	$1 per unit
10	5	30	5	15	2
15	4	35	4	20	3
20	3	40	3	25	4
25	2	45	2	30	5
30	1	50	1	35	6

_____ 34. Suppose suppliers are expecting a price of $5 per unit. How will suppliers revise their expectations about the market price?
   A. Suppliers will revise their price expectations downward.
   B. Suppliers will revise their price expectations upward.
   C. Suppliers will not revise their price expectations, because the expectation that the price is $5 per unit is rational.
   D. Suppliers will not revise their price expectations, because their expectations are correct 50% of the time.

_____ 35. If suppliers have rational expectations, how many units of their good will they bring to the market?
   A. 20 units.   C. 30 units.
   B. 25 units.   D. 35 units.

REVIEW QUESTIONS

36. What is meant by risk-neutral behavior? Why are corporations more likely than individuals to exhibit risk-neutral behavior?

37. How do risk-neutral and risk-averse individuals respond when offered the opportunity to place a bet at fair odds? How do they respond if the bet is at favorable odds?

38. Briefly describe three reasons why an insurance company may not offer customers fair odds despite the fact that it is highly diversified.

39.   How can speculation in futures markets improve economic welfare?

40.   What portfolio will a risk-averse investor choose to hold when a risk-free asset and many risky assets are available?

41.   What are rational expectations? How will suppliers with rational expectations behave when facing uncertain demand?

PROBLEMS

42.   Suppose two professional tennis players are about to play in an exhibition match. The winner of the match receives $100,000, and the loser receives $40,000. Before the match, one player offers the other the opportunity to "split the pot." The players share the prize money when they split the pot, with each receiving ½ · ($100,000 + $40,000) or $70,000 regardless of the outcome of their match.

i.   Suppose the tennis player is risk-averse and believes that he has a 50–50 chance of winning the match. Will he agree to split the pot? On the axes to the right, design a diagram that illustrates this situation.

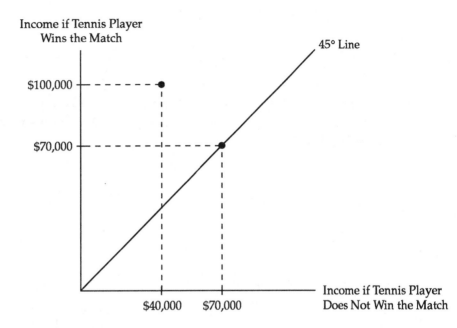

ii.   On the axes to the right, design a diagram that shows a risk-averse player will choose not to split the pot when he believes that he has a sufficiently large chance of winning the match.

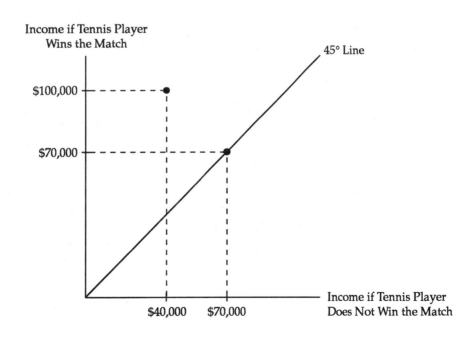

43.   i.   Suppose a $1 state lottery ticket offers a 1 in 10,000 chance of winning $5,000. What is the expected value of the lottery ticket? Is the state offering fair, favorable, or unfavorable odds in its lottery?

       ii.   Suppose a risk-averse person has the opportunity to purchase the lottery ticket described in part i. If the person chooses not to purchase the ticket, then his income is the same whether or not the ticket is a winner. If he chooses to purchase the ticket, then his basket will lie above the 45° line as shown below. Will a risk-averse person purchase the lottery ticket? Why or why not? Use the axes below to provide a sketch justifying your answer.

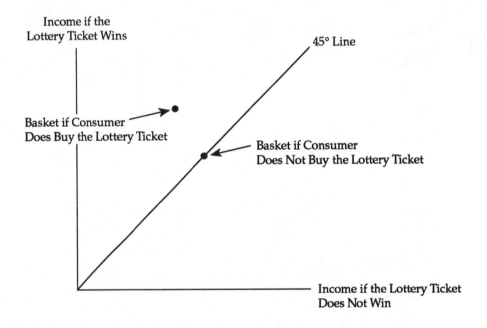

       iii. The analysis in part ii suggests that risk-averse individuals never purchase lottery tickets. However, lotteries are very popular. Why might a risk-averse individual choose to purchase a lottery ticket?

44. Consider a risk-averse investor who is purchasing a risk-free asset and the market portfolio. Assume that as the investor's income rises, he prefers to have a higher expected return and a lower standard deviation. Suppose that the return of the risk-free asset increases as shown in the diagram below.

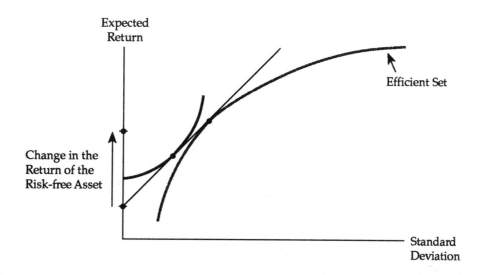

i. Complete the above diagram to show how the market portfolio and the investor's asset holdings are affected. Will the standard deviation of the market portfolio rise or fall? Will the expected return of the market portfolio rise or fall?

ii. Will the standard deviation of the investor's asset holdings rise or fall, or is the change uncertain? Explain, using substitution and income effects.

iii. Will the expected return of the investor's asset holdings rise or fall, or is the change uncertain? Explain, using substitution and income effects.

45. Let U denote the economy's unemployment rate, π denote the actual inflation rate, and π^e denote people's expected inflation rate. Suppose the true relationship among these variables is given by the equation $U = 0.04 - 0.5(\pi - \pi^e)$.

　　　　For the past 10 years, the government has allowed the money supply to grow at a constant 3% annual rate. People have rational expectations and they recognize that, on average, the economy's inflation rate equals the growth rate in the money supply.

　　i.　An econometrician believes that the relationship between the inflation and unemployment rates is given by the equation $U = A - B\pi$. The econometrician uses data from the past 10 years to estimate this equation. What values will the econometrician find for A and B?

　　ii.　For the past 10 years, the unemployment rate has averaged 4%. Policymakers want to lower the unemployment rate to 3%. If the econometrician's equation is used to formulate policy, what will policymakers do to the money supply?

　　iii.　If people are aware of the policy change, what will happen to the inflation and unemployment rates? Will the econometrician's equation still be valid? Why or why not?

SOLUTIONS

Completion Exercises

1. ex ante
2. expected value
3. risk-averse
4. fair odds
5. adverse selection

6. uninsurable risk
7. futures contract
8. speculator
9. market portfolio
10. rational expectations

True-False Exercises

11. FALSE. The indifference curves representing a risk-averse individual's ex ante preferences are downward-sloping and convex.

12. FALSE. A risk-averse individual accepts a bet at favorable odds only if it is sufficiently small.

13. FALSE. If fire insurance were a competitive industry with no operating costs, then insurance companies must offer unfair odds to customers to account for moral hazard, adverse selection, and uninsurable risks.

14. TRUE.

15. TRUE.

16. FALSE. A speculator who believes next month's demand for wheat will be higher than others expect will purchase futures contracts for wheat.

17. TRUE.

18. FALSE. A portfolio's standard deviation is less than or equal to the average of the standard deviations of its individual stocks.

19. FALSE. When people have rational expectations, their predictions do not lead to systematic, correctable errors.

20. TRUE.

Multiple Choice Questions

21. D. Only risk-averse individuals have convex indifference curves. The indifference curves are linear if the individual is risk-neutral and are concave if he is risk-preferring.

22. B. When fair odds are offered, the budget line coincides with an iso-expected value line.

23.   C. When the odds are fair, all points on the budget line have the same expected value but different levels of riskiness. If the individual is indifferent among these points, then he must be indifferent about risk. Therefore, he must be risk-neutral.

24.   A. When the odds are fair, all points on the budget line have the same expected value but different levels of riskiness. Of these baskets, a risk-averse individual prefers the one with the least risk.

25.   C. When the odds are favorable, a small movement along the budget line will move the risk-averse individual to a higher indifference curve, and so he is willing to accept a small bet. However, a bet that is too large is also too risky and would put the risk-averse person on a lower indifference curve.

26.   D. Moral hazard occurs when the act of being insured causes the individual to change his behavior, altering the probabilities associated with the states of the world.

27.   C. An uninsurable risk cannot be diversified because a large number of people are adversely affected in the same state of the world.

28.   B. Adverse selection occurs when some people are good risks and some are poor risks, but the two groups cannot be distinguished.

29.   A. The expected return of the stock is $\frac{1}{2} \cdot -60 + \frac{1}{2} \cdot 100 = -30 + 50 = 20$ dollars, which is 10% of the price of the stock.

30.   D. The stock's outcome is $20 \pm \$80$, and so the spread is $80, which is 40% of the stock's price.

31.   C. If an investor owns a portfolio that lies on the efficient set, then he cannot improve both the expected return and the standard deviation he receives.

32.   D. When a risk-free asset is available, the investor's choice lies on the market line. Points on the market line are obtained by combining the risk-free asset with the market portfolio.

33.   A. Speculators will sell futures contracts, because they believe that the future spot price will be lower than expected. They are planning to purchase the commodity at a low price in the future and resell it at the higher price they have "locked in" with the futures contract.

34.   A. Suppliers will bring 30 units to the market when they expect the price of their commodity to be $5 per unit. They will receive a price of $1 per unit when demand is D_1 and a price of $5 per unit when demand is D_2, so on average they receive $3 per unit. The average price is lower than the suppliers' expected price, so they will revise their expectations downward.

35.   B. When the suppliers' expected price is $4 per unit, the quantity supplied is 25 units, which is also equal to the average quantity demanded.

Review Questions

36.   Risk-neutral behavior occurs when an agent is indifferent between two baskets with the same expected outcome regardless of their riskiness. Corporations are more likely than individuals to exhibit risk-neutral behavior for three reasons. First, corporations participate in a large number of risky ventures, so they are better able to diversify their risk than are individuals. Second, corporations, unlike individuals, do not face a budget constraint, and they can often borrow sufficient funds to keep operating if they lose substantial assets in a risky venture. Third, corporate stockholders diversify their risk by owning shares in many different corporations. Consequently, stockholders are only interested in maximizing their expected returns, so they want their corporations to exhibit risk-neutral behavior.

37.   A risk-neutral individual is indifferent regarding a bet at fair odds, while a risk-averse individual places his bet so that his outcome is the same no matter what state of the world occurs. A risk-neutral individual bets everything when offered favorable odds, while a risk-averse individual places a bet at favorable odds only if it is sufficiently small.

38.   Insurance companies cannot offer fair odds because of the problems of moral hazard, adverse selection, and uninsurable risks. Moral hazard occurs because people who are insured tend to take more risks than people who are uninsured. The very act of obtaining insurance changes the odds, and the insurance company must offer odds accordingly. Adverse selection occurs when the insurance company cannot distinguish people who are good risks from those who are poor risks. It must limit the amount of insurance available at the most favorable odds to discourage poor risks from purchasing these policies. Uninsurable risks occur because some states of the world adversely affect large numbers of people, so the insurance company cannot offer fair odds because it cannot diversify its risk.

39.   Speculators buy and sell futures contracts based on their beliefs about future demand, and these actions will bid up or down the price of futures contracts. Suppliers' expectations about the future spot price are affected by the speculators' actions, and they readjust their supplies accordingly. When speculators' expectations are correct, their behavior alerts suppliers to changes in the marginal value of the commodity, and the resulting adjustments in supply increase social gain.

40.   A rational, risk-averse investor chooses to hold some combination of the risk-free asset and the market portfolio (i.e., the portfolio where the market line is tangent to the efficient set). These combinations all lie on the market line and offer the investor the highest expected return for any given standard deviation. A market portfolio can be constructed by combining all the risky assets in the economy in proportion to their existing quantities.

41.   Rational expectations occur when the expectations of market participants eventually lead to a situation where those expectations are, on average, correct. When demand fluctuates from day to day, rational expectations cause suppliers to adjust their quantities until the corresponding price from the supply curve equals the average price that they receive. This equilibrium occurs where the supply curve crosses the average demand curve.

Problems

42.   i.   The risk-averse tennis player will choose the option with the least amount of riskiness when faced with options that offer the same expected value. Therefore, he accepts the offer to split the pot, as shown in the diagram below.

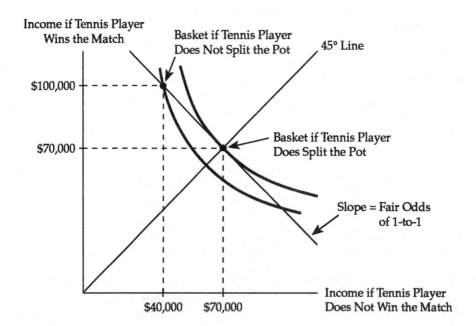

ii.   If the tennis player believes that he has a better than 50–50 chance of winning the match, then the offer to split the pot is at unfavorable odds. The tennis player would prefer to bear the risk of the final match instead of accepting the unfavorable odds if he believes that his odds of winning are sufficiently large. This situation is illustrated in the diagram below. (In fact, since the indifference curve is flatter than the 1-to-1 odds line when the player does not split the pot, this diagram shows a risk-averse player who believes the odds are enough in his favor that he is willing to accept a sufficiently small side wager at 1-to-1 odds that he will win the match.)

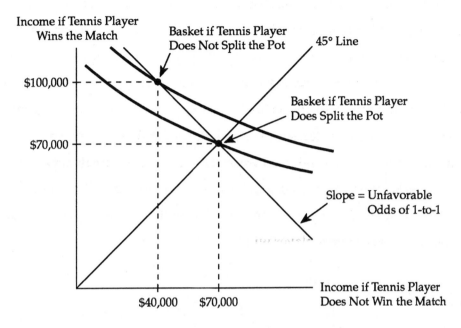

43. i.   The lottery ticket pays $0 in 9,999 out of 10,000 cases, and it pays $5,000 in 1 out of every 10,000 cases. A ticket's expected value is thus $0 · $^{9,999}/_{10,000}$ + $5,000 · $^{1}/_{10,000}$ = $0 + $0.50 = $0.50. A $1 lottery ticket has an expected value of only 50¢, so the state is offering unfavorable odds.

     ii.   This situation is illustrated below. (The diagram is not drawn to scale—the cost of the

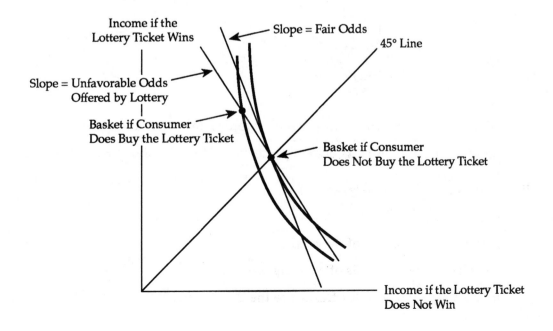

lottery ticket is exaggerated and the potential lottery prize money is reduced for clarity.) If a risk-averse person does not purchase a lottery ticket, then he is in a risk-free situation. If the lottery offered fair odds, he would not purchase a lottery ticket since risk-averse agents choose the risk-free situation. Thus, a risk-averse person certainly would not purchase a lottery ticket when the odds are unfavorable.

iii.   One possibility is that people incorrectly perceive their odds of winning the lottery and believe that it offers a small bet at favorable odds. A more plausible explanation is that lotteries are often sold in the form of games, such as choosing lotto numbers or rubbing off game pieces. The enjoyment that a risk-averse person receives from playing the game may be enough compensation for placing a small bet at unfavorable odds.

44.   i.   The market portfolio moves to the right on the efficient set because the market line is flatter. Therefore, the market portfolio has both a higher expected return and a higher standard deviation.

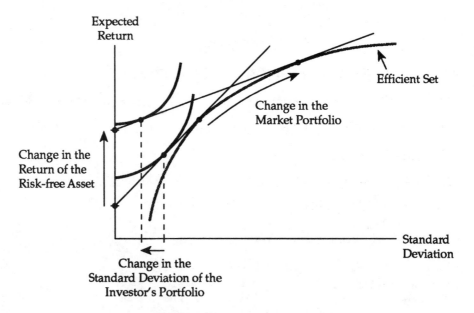

ii.   When the risk-free asset offers a higher return, taking on the additional risk of the market portfolio offers a relatively smaller addition to the portfolio's expected return. The resulting substitution effect causes the investor to want a lower standard deviation. The increase in the risk-free asset's return also increases the investor's real income. The resulting income effect causes the investor to also choose a lower standard deviation. Both the substitution and the income effects cause the risk-averse investor to lower the standard deviation of his holding.

iii. When the market line becomes flatter, the investor must pay a higher "price" (i.e., a greater standard deviation) for his portfolio's expected return. The resulting substitution effect causes the investor to want a lower expected return. On the other hand, the income effect causes the investor to choose a higher expected return. The change in the investor's expected return is uncertain, because the substitution and income effects are in opposition.

45. i. People's expected inflation rate π^e is 3% or 0.03 during the time period that the econometrician is considering. Thus, the econometrician's data will show U = 0.04 – $0.5(\pi - 0.03) = 0.04 - 0.5\pi + 0.015 = 0.055 - 0.5\pi$. The econometrician will find that A = 0.055 and B = 0.5.

ii. The econometrician's equation suggests that every 1 percentage point added to the inflation rate will reduce the unemployment rate by 0.5 percentage points. In an attempt to achieve their goal of 3% unemployment, the policymakers will increase the growth rate in the money supply from 3% to 5%. The average inflation rate will then increase to 5%, and according to the econometrician's equation, the unemployment rate will fall to 3% ($0.055 - 0.5 \cdot 0.05 = 0.055 - 0.025 = 0.03$).

iii. If people are aware of the policy change, their expected inflation rate rises from 3% to 5%. Since the average inflation rate has also risen to 5%, the true equation shows that unemployment, on average, will remain at 4% ($0.04 - 0.5 \cdot (0.05 - 0.05) = 0.04 - 0 = 0.04$). The econometrician's equation is no longer valid because the policy change caused people to rationally revise their expectations.

CHAPTER 19

WHAT IS ECONOMICS?

This chapter concludes our survey of microeconomic theory by reexamining the types of problems studied in economics and the methods used to address them.

KEY TERMS

- Optimization
- Equimarginality
- Equilibrium condition

- Nash equilibrium
- Walrasian equilibrium
- Exogenous variable

- Economic dynamics
- Rationality assumption
- Robustness

KEY IDEAS

- **Section 19.1.** Economists, like other social scientists, attempt to explain and predict human behavior. The distinguishing feature of economic analysis is its emphasis on rational decision making in the face of scarcity. Economic analysis generally begins with an explicit set of assumptions about individuals' desires and the nature of the constraints that they face. The second step in economic analysis uses the principle of equimarginality to determine the solution to the economic problem. Finally, economic analysis requires the choice of an appropriate equilibrium condition and an analysis of the resulting equilibria.

- **Section 19.2.** Economists, like all other scientists, make simplifying assumptions to make the problems they analyze tractable. Economic models start with the simplifying assumption of rational behavior. In reality, people are often rational enough so that there are no unexploited profit opportunities; economic behavior in this situation closely resembles that in the imaginary world of economic models where people are fully rational. Consequently, the rationality assumption simplifies economic models but leaves them robust.

◆ **Section 19.3.** Economic explanations attempt to explain phenomena on the basis of rational behavior. When faced with behavior which on the surface appears totally foolish, an economist searches for the constraints and incentives which show that the behavior is perfectly rational. If the resulting explanation has testable implications, it is all the more desirable.

◆ **Section 19.4.** Traditionally, economists restricted their study to the production, exchange, and consumption of marketable commodities. In the past 30 years, economists have shown that their ideas can be successfully applied to a much wider variety of problems. The economic approach has been used to study love and marriage, the decision to have children, criminal behavior, legal institutions, and even medieval agriculture. Economic ideas appear to apply to all humans—past and present—and even to animals.

CONCLUDING REMARKS

We hope that our survey of microeconomic theory has sharpened your economic intuition and given you a better understanding of the basic tools used in the discipline. Reflect on the economic models we have introduced throughout the text, and notice the basic steps of formulation, optimization, and equilibrium in these models. Reconsider the many examples in the text, and notice the roles of incentives and rational behavior in the explanations offered for the phenomena. Finally, search out your own economic problems and try to offer your own economic explanations; the final problem set of the textbook gives some suggestions. Even though economics preaches some very simple ideas, it is difficult to become a good economist. Practice and experience are the best teachers.

THE USE OF KNOWLEDGE IN SOCIETY*

F. A. HAYEK

I

What is the problem we wish to solve when we try to construct a rational economic order?

On certain familiar assumptions the answer is simple enough. *If* we possess all the relevant information, *if* we can start out from a given system of preferences and *if* we command complete knowledge of available means, the problem which remains is purely one of logic. That is, the answer to the question of what is the best use of the available means is implicit in our assumptions. The conditions which the solution of this optimum problem must satisfy have been fully worked out and can be stated best in mathematical form: put at their briefest, they are that the marginal rates of substitution between any two commodities or factors must be the same in all their different uses.

This, however, is emphatically *not* the economic problem which society faces. And the economic calculus which we have developed to solve this logical problem, though an important step toward the solution of the economic problem of society, does not yet provide an answer to it. The reason for this is that the "data" from which the economic calculus starts are never for the whole society "given" to a single mind which could work out the implications, and can never be so given.

The peculiar character of the problem of a rational economic order is determined precisely by the fact that the knowledge of the circumstances of which we must make use never exists in concentrated or integrated form, but solely as the dispersed bits of incomplete and frequently contradictory knowledge which all the separate individuals possess. The economic problem of society is thus not merely a problem of how to allocate "given" resources—if "given" is taken to mean given to a single mind which deliberately solves the problem set by these "data." It is rather a problem of how to secure the best use of resources known to any of the members of society, for ends whose relative importance only these individuals know. Or, to put it briefly, it is a problem of the utilization of knowledge not given to anyone in its totality.

This character of the fundamental problem has, I am afraid, been rather obscured than illuminated by many of the recent refinements of economic theory, particularly by many of the uses made of mathematics. Though the problem with which I want primarily to deal in this paper is the problem of a rational economic organization, I shall in its course be led again and again to point to its close connections with

---

*Reprinted by permission of the American Economic Association from *American Economic Review*, September 1945.

certain methodological questions. Many of the points I wish to make are indeed conclusions toward which diverse paths of reasoning have unexpectedly converged. But as I now see these problems, this is no accident. It seems to me that many of the current disputes with regard to both economic theory and economic policy have their common origin in a misconception about the nature of the economic problem of society. This misconception in turn is due to an erroneous transfer to social phenomena of the habits of thought we have developed in dealing with the phenomena of nature.

II

In ordinary language we describe by the word "planning" the complex of interrelated decisions about the allocation of our available resources. All economic activity is in this sense planning; and in any society in which many people collaborate, this planning, whoever does it, will in some measure have to be based on knowledge which, in the first instance, is not given to the planner but to somebody else, which somehow will have to be conveyed to the planner. The various ways in which the knowledge on which people base their plans is communicated to them is the crucial problem for any theory explaining the economic process. And the problem of what is the best way of utilizing knowledge initially dispersed among all the people is at least one of the main problems of economic policy—or of designing an efficient economic system.

The answer to this question is closely connected with that other question which arises here, that of *who* is to do the planning. It is about this question that all the dispute about "economic planning" centers. This is not a dispute about whether planning is to be done or not. It is a dispute as to whether planning is to be done centrally, by one authority for the whole economic system, or is to be divided among many individuals. Planning in the specific sense in which the term is used in contemporary controversy necessarily means central planning—direction of the whole economic system according to one unified plan. Competition, on the other hand, means decentralized planning by many separate persons. The half-way house between the two, about which many people talk but which few like when they see it, is the delegation

of planning to organized industries, or, in other words, monopoly.

Which of these systems is likely to be more efficient depends mainly on the question under which of them we can expect that fuller use will be made of the existing knowledge. And this, in turn, depends on whether we are more likely to succeed in putting at the disposal of a single central authority all the knowledge which ought to be used but which is initially dispersed among many different individuals, or in conveying to the individuals such additional knowledge as they need in order to enable them to fit their plans in with those of others.

III

It will at once be evident that on this point the position will be different with respect to different kinds of knowledge; and the answer to our question will therefore largely turn on the relative importance of the different kinds of knowledge; those more likely to be at the disposal of particular individuals and those which we should with greater confidence expect to find in the possession of an authority made up of suitably chosen experts. If it is today so widely assumed that the latter will be in a better position, this is because one kind of knowledge, namely, scientific knowledge, occupies how so prominent a place in public imagination that we tend to forget that it is not the only kind that is relevant. It may be admitted that, so far as scientific knowledge is concerned, a body of suitably chosen experts may be in the best position to command all the best knowledge available—though this is of course merely shifting the difficulty to the problem of selecting the experts. What I wish to point out is that, even assuming that this problem can be readily solved, it is only a small part of the wider problem.

Today it is almost heresy to suggest that scientific knowledge is not the sum of all knowledge. But a little reflection will show that there is beyond question a body of very important but unorganized knowledge which cannot possibly be called scientific in the sense of knowledge of general rules: the knowledge of the particular circumstances of time and place. It is with respect to this that practically every individual has some advantage over all others in that he possesses unique information of which beneficial use might be made, but of which use can be made only if the decisions depending on it are left to him or are made with his active cooperation. We need to remember only how much we have to learn in any occupation after we have completed our theoretical training, how big a part of our working life we spend learning particular jobs, and how valuable an asset in all walks of life is knowledge of people, of local conditions, and special circumstances. To know of and put to use a machine not fully employed, or somebody's skill which could be better utilized, or to be aware of a surplus stock which can be drawn upon during an interruption of supplies, is socially quite as useful as the knowledge of better alternative techniques. And the shipper who earns his living from using otherwise empty or half-filled journeys of tramp-steamers, or the estate agent whose whole knowledge is almost exclusively one of temporary opportunities, or the *arbitrageur* who gains from local differences of commodity prices, are all performing eminently useful functions based on special knowledge of circumstances of the fleeting moment not known to others.

It is a curious fact that this sort of knowledge should today be generally regarded with a kind of contempt, and that anyone who by such knowledge gains an advantage over somebody better equipped with theoretical or technical knowledge is thought to have acted almost disreputably. To gain an advantage from better knowledge of facilities of communication or transport is sometimes regarded as almost dishonest, although it is quite as important that society make use of the best opportunities in this respect as in using the latest scientific discoveries. This prejudice has in a considerable measure affected the attitude toward commerce in general compared with that toward production. Even economists who regard themselves as definitely above the crude materialist fallacies of the past constantly commit the same mistake where activities directed toward the acquisition of such practical knowledge are concerned—apparently because in their scheme of things all such knowledge is supposed to be "given." The common idea now seems to be that all such knowledge should as a matter of course be readily at the command of everybody, and the reproach of irrationality leveled against the existing economic order is frequently based on the fact that it is not so available. This view disregards the fact that the method by which

such knowledge can be made as widely available as possible is precisely the problem to which we have to find an answer.

IV

If it is fashionable today to minimize the importance of the knowledge of the particular circumstances of time and place, this is closely connected with the smaller importance which is now attached to change as such. Indeed, there are few points on which the assumptions made (usually only implicitly) by the "planners" differ from those of their opponents as much as with regard to the significance and frequency of changes which will make substantial alterations of production plans necessary. Of course, if detailed economic plans could be laid down for fairly long periods in advance and then closely adhered to, so that no further economic decisions of importance would be required, the task of drawing up a comprehensive plan governing all economic activity would appear much less formidable.

It is, perhaps, worth stressing that economic problems arise always and only in consequence of change. So long as things continue as before, or at least as they were expected to, there arise no new problems requiring a decision, no need to form a new plan. The belief that changes, or at least day-to-day adjustments, have become less important in modern times implies the contention that economic problems also have become less important. This belief in the decreasing importance of change is, for that reason, usually held by the same people who argue that the importance of economic considerations has been driven into the background by the growing importance of technological knowledge.

Is it true that, with the elaborate apparatus of modern production, economic decisions are required only at long intervals, as when a new factory is to be erected or a new process to be introduced? Is it true that, once a plant has been built, the rest is all more or less mechanical, determined by the character of the plant, and leaving little to be changed in adapting to the ever-changing circumstances of the moment?

The fairly widespread belief in the affirmative is not, so far as I can ascertain, borne out by the practical experience of the business man. In a competitive industry at any rate—and such an industry alone can serve as a test—the task of keeping cost from rising requires a constant struggle, absorbing a great part of the energy of the manager. How easy it is for an inefficient manager to dissipate the differentials on which profitability rests, and that it is possible, with the same technical facilities, to produce with a great variety of costs, are among the commonplaces of business experience which do not seem to be equally familiar in the study of the economist. The very strength of the desire, constantly voiced by producers and engineers, to be able to proceed untrammeled by considerations of money costs, is eloquent testimony to the extent to which these factors enter into their daily work.

One reason why economists are increasingly apt to forget about the constant small changes which make up the whole economic picture is probably their growing preoccupation with statistical aggregates, which show a very much greater stability than the movements of the detail. The comparative stability of the aggregates cannot, however, be accounted for—as the statisticians seem occasionally to be inclined to do—by the "law of large numbers" or the mutual compensation of random changes. The number of elements with which we have to deal is not large enough for such accidental forces to produce stability. The continuous flow of goods and services is maintained by constant deliberate adjustments, by new dispositions made every day in the light of circumstances not known the day before, by B stepping in at once when A fails to deliver. Even the large and highly mechanized plant keeps going largely because of an environment upon which it can draw for all sorts of unexpected needs; tiles for its roof, stationery for its forms, and all the thousand and one kinds of equipment in which it cannot be self-contained and which the plans for the operation of the plant require to be readily available in the market.

This is, perhaps, also the point where I should briefly mention the fact that the sort of knowledge with which I have been concerned is knowledge of the kind which by its nature cannot enter into statistics and therefore cannot be conveyed to any central authority in statistical form. The statistics which such a central authority would have to use would have to be arrived at precisely by abstracting from minor differences between the things, by lumping together, as resources of one kind, items which differ as regards location, quality, and other particulars, in a way which may be very significant for the

specific decision. It follows from this that central planning based on statistical information by its nature cannot take direct account of these circumstances of time and place, and that the central planner will have to find some way or other in which the decisions depending on them can be left to the "man on the spot."

V

If we can agree that the economic problem of society is mainly one of rapid adaptation to changes in the particular circumstances of time and place, it would seem to follow that the ultimate decisions must be left to the people who are familiar with these circumstances, who know directly of the relevant changes and of the resources immediately available to meet them. We cannot expect that this problem will be solved by first communicating all this knowledge to a central board which, after integrating *all* knowledge, issues its orders. We must solve it by some form of decentralization. But this answers only part of our problem. We need decentralization because only thus can we ensure that the knowledge of the particular circumstances of time and place will be promptly used. But the "man on the spot" cannot decide solely on the basis of his limited but intimate knowledge of the facts of his immediate surroundings. There still remains the problem of communicating to him such further information as he needs to fit his decisions into the whole pattern of changes of the larger economic system. How much knowledge does he need to do so successfully? Which of the events which happen beyond the horizon of his immediate knowledge are of relevance to his immediate decision, and how much of them need he know?

There is hardly anything that happens anywhere in the world that *might* not have an effect on the decision he ought to make. But he need not know of these events as such, nor of *all* their effects. It does not matter for him *why* at the particular moment more screws of one size than of another are wanted, *why* paper bags are more readily available than canvas bags, or *why* skilled labor, or particular machine tools, have for the moment become more difficult to acquire. All that is significant for him is *how much more or less* difficult to procure they have become compared with other things with which he is also concerned, or how much more or less urgently wanted are the alternative things he produces or uses. It is always a question of the relative importance of the particular things with which he is concerned, and the causes which alter their relative importance are of no interest to him beyond the effect on those concrete things of his own environment.

It is in this connection that what I have called the economic calculus proper helps us, at least by analogy, to see how this problem can be solved, and in fact is being solved, by the price system. Even the single controlling mind, in possession of all the data for some small, self-contained economic system, would not—every time some small adjustment in the allocation of resources had to be made—go explicitly through all the relations between ends and means which might possibly be affected. It is indeed the great contribution of the pure logic of choice that it has demonstrated conclusively that even such a single mind could solve this kind of problem only by constructing and constantly using rates of equivalence (or "values," or "marginal rates of substitution"), i.e., by attaching to each kind of scarce resource a numerical index which cannot be derived from any property possessed by that particular thing, but which reflects, or in which is condensed, its significance in view of the whole means-end structure. In any small change he will have to consider only these quantitative indices (or "values") in which all the relevant information is concentrated; and by adjusting the quantities one by one, he can appropriately rearrange his dispositions without having to solve the whole puzzle ab initio, or without needing at any stage to survey it at once in all its ramifications.

Fundamentally, in a system where the knowledge of the relevant facts is dispersed among many people, prices can act to coordinate the separate actions of different people in the same way as subjective values help the individual to coordinate the parts of his plan. It is worth contemplating for a moment a very simple and commonplace instance of the action of the price system to see what precisely it accomplishes. Assume that somewhere in the world a new opportunity for the use of some raw material, say tin, has arisen, or that one of the sources of supply of tin has been eliminated. It does not matter for our purpose—and it is very significant that it does not matter—which of these two causes has made tin more scarce. All that the users of tin need to know is that some of the tin they used to consume is now more profitably employed elsewhere, and that in consequence they must economize tin. There is no need for the great majority of them even to know where the more urgent need has arisen, or in favor of what other needs they ought to husband the supply. If only some of them know directly of the new demand, and switch resources over to it, and if the people who are aware of the new gap thus created in turn fill it from still other sources, the effect will rapidly spread throughout the whole economic system and influence not only all the uses of tin, but also those of its substitutes and the substitutes of these substitutes, the supply of all the things made of tin, and their substitutes, and so on; and all this without the great majority of those instrumental in bringing about these substitutions knowing anything at all about the original cause of these changes. The whole acts as one market, not because any of its members survey the whole field, but because their limited individual fields of vision sufficiently overlap so that through many intermediaries the relevant information is communicated to all. The mere fact that there is one price for any commodity—or rather that local prices are connected in a manner determined by the cost of transport, etc.—brings about the solution which (it is just conceptually possible) might have been arrived at by one single mind possessing all the information which is in fact dispersed among all the people involved in the process.

VI

We must look at the price system as such a mechanism for communicating information if we want to understand its real function—a function which, of course, it fulfills less perfectly as prices grow more rigid. (Even when quoted prices have become quite rigid, however, the forces which would operate through changes in price still operate to a considerable extent through changes in the other terms of the contract.) The most significant fact about this system is the economy of knowledge with which it operates, or how little the individual participants need to know in order to be able to take the right action. In abbreviated form, by a kind of symbol, only the most essential information is passed on, and passed on only to those concerned. It is more than a metaphor to describe the price system as a kind of machinery for registering change, or a system of telecommunications which enables individual producers to watch merely the movement of a few pointers, as an engineer might watch the hands of a few dials, in order to adjust their activities to changes of which they may never know more than is reflected in the price movement.

Of course, these adjustments are probably never "perfect" in the sense in which the economist conceives of them in his equilibrium analysis. But I fear that our theoretical habits of approaching the problem with the assumption of more or less perfect knowledge on the part of almost everyone has made us somewhat blind to the true function of the price mechanism and led us to apply rather misleading standards in judging its efficiency. The marvel is that in a case like that of a scarcity of one raw material, without an order being issued, without more than perhaps a handful of people knowing the cause, tens of thousands of people whose identity could not be ascertained by months of investigation, are made to use the material or its products more sparingly; *i.e.*, they move in the right direction. This is enough of a marvel even if, in a constantly changing world, not all will hit it off so perfectly that their profit rates will always be maintained at the same constant or "normal" level.

I have deliberately used the word "marvel" to shock the reader out of the complacency with which we often take the working of this mechanism for granted. I am convinced that if it were the result of deliberate human design, and if the people guided by the price changes understood that their decisions have significance far beyond their immediate aim, this mechanism would have been acclaimed as one of the greatest triumphs of the human mind. Its misfortune is the double one that is not the product of human design and that the people guided by it usually do not know why they are made to do what they do. But those who clamor for "conscious direction" — and who cannot believe that anything which has evolved without design (and even without our understanding it) should solve problems which we should not be able to solve consciously — should remember this: The problem is precisely how to extend the span of our utilization of resources beyond the span of the control of any one mind; and, therefore, how to dispense with the need of conscious control and how to provide inducements which will make the

individuals do the desirable things without anyone having to tell them what to do.

The problem which we meet here is by no means peculiar to economics but arises in connection with nearly all truly social phenomena, with language and most of our cultural inheritance, and constitutes really the central theoretical problem of all social science. As Alfred Whitehead has said in another connection, "It is a profoundly erroneous truism, repeated by all copy-books and by eminent people when they are making speeches, that we should cultivate the habit of thinking what we are doing. The precise opposite is the case. Civilization advances by extending the number of important operations which we can perform without thinking about them." This is of profound significance in the social field. We make constant use of formulas, symbols, and rules whose meaning we do not understand and through the use of which we avail ourselves of the assistance of knowledge which individually we do not possess. We have developed these practices and institutions by building upon habits and institution which have proved successful in their own sphere and which have in turn become the foundation of the civilization we have built up.

The price system is just one of those formations which man has learned to use (though he is still very far from having learned to make the best use of it) after he had stumbled upon it without understanding it. Through it not only a division of labor but also a coordinated utilization of resources based on an equally divided knowledge has become possible. The people who like to deride any suggestion that this may be so usually distort the argument by insinuating that it asserts that by some miracle just that sort of system has spontaneously grown up which is best suited to modern civilization. It is the other way round: man has been able to develop that division of labor on which our civilization is based because he happened to stumble upon a method which made it possible. Had he not done so he might still have developed some other, altogether different, type of civilization, something like the "state" of the termite ants, or some other, altogether unimaginable type. All that we can say is that nobody has yet succeeded in designing an alternative system in which certain features of the existing one can be preserved which are dear even to those who most violently assail it — such as particularly the extent to which the individual can choose his pursuits and consequently freely use his own knowledge and skill.

VII

It is in many ways fortunate that the dispute about the indispensability of the price system for any rational calculation in a complex society is now no longer conducted entirely between camps holding different political views. The thesis that without the price system we could not preserve a society based on such extensive division of labor as ours was greeted with a howl of derision when it was first advanced by von Mises twenty-five years ago. Today the difficulties which some still find in accepting it are no longer mainly political, and this makes for an atmosphere much more conducive to reasonable discussion. When we find Leon Trotsky arguing that "economic accounting is unthinkable without market relations"; when Professor Oscar Lange promises Professor von Mises a statue in the marble halls of the future Central Planning Board; when Professor Abba P. Lerner rediscovers Adam Smith and emphasizes that the essential utility of the price system consists in inducing the individual, while seeking his own interest, to do what is in the general interest, the differences can indeed no longer be ascribed to political prejudice. The remaining dissent seems clearly to be due to purely intellectual, and more particularly methodological, differences.

A recent statement by Professor Joseph Schumpeter in his *Capitalism, Socialism and Democracy* provides a clear illustration of one of the methodological differences which I have in mind. Its author is preeminent among those economists who approach economic phenomena in the light of a certain branch of positivism. To him these phenomena accordingly appear as objectively given quantities of commodities impinging directly upon each other, almost, it would seem, without any intervention of human minds. Only against this background can I account for the following (to me startling) pronouncement. Professor Schumpeter argues that the possibility of a rational calculation in the absence of markets for the factors of production follows for the theorist "from the elementary proposition that consumers in evaluating ('demanding') consumers' goods *ipso facto* also

evaluate the means of production which enter into the production of these goods."[1]

Taken literally, this statement is simply untrue. The consumers do nothing of the kind. What Professor Schumpeter's *"ipso facto"* presumably means is that the valuation of the factors of production is implied in, or follows necessarily from, the valuation of consumers' goods. But this, too, is not correct. Implication is a logical relationship which can be meaningfully asserted only of propositions simultaneously present to one and the same mind. It is evident, however, that the values of the factors of production do not depend solely on the valuation of the consumers' goods but also on the conditions of supply of the various factors of production. Only to a mind to which all these facts were simultaneously known would the answer necessarily follow from the facts given to it. The practical problem, however, arises precisely because these facts are never so given to a single mind, and because, in consequence, it is necessary that in the solution of the problem knowledge should be used that is dispersed among many people.

The problem is thus in no way solved if we can show that all the facts, *if* they were known to a single mind (as we hypothetically assume them to be given to the observing economist), would uniquely determine the solution; instead we must show how a solution is produced by the interactions of people each of whom possesses only partial knowledge. To assume all the

[1] J. Schumpeter, *Capitalism, Socialism, and Democracy* (New York, Harper, 1942), p. 175. Professor Schumpeter is, I believe, also the original author of the myth that Pareto and Barone have "solved" the problem of socialist calculation. What they, and many others, did was merely to state the conditions which a rational allocation of resources would have to satisfy, and to point out that these were essentially the same as the conditions of equilibrium of a competitive market. This is something altogether different from showing how the allocation of resources satisfying these conditions can be found in practice. Pareto himself (from whom Barone has taken practically everything he has to say), far from claiming to have solved the practical problem, in fact explicitly denies that it can be solved without the help of the market. See his *Manuel d'économie pure* (2nd ed., 1927), pp. 233-234. The relevant passage is quoted in an English translation at the beginning of my article on "Socialist Calculation: The Competitive 'Solution,'" in *Economica*, New Series, Vol. VIII, No. 26 (May, 1940), p. 125.

knowledge to be given to a single mind in the same manner in which we assume it to be given to us as the explaining economists is to assume the problem away and to disregard everything that is important and significant in the real world.

That an economist of Professor Schumpeter's standing should thus have fallen into a trap which the ambiguity of the term "datum" sets to the unwary can hardly be explained as a simple error. It suggests rather that there is something fundamentally wrong with an approach which habitually disregards an essential part of the phenomena with which we have to deal: the unavoidable imperfection of man's knowledge and the consequent need for a process by which knowledge is constantly communicated and acquired. Any approach, such as that of much of mathematical economics with its simultaneous equations, which in effect starts from the assumption that people's *knowledge* corresponds with the objective *facts* of the situation, systematically leaves out what is our main task to explain. I am far from denying that in our system equilibrium analysis has a useful function to perform. But when it comes to the point where it misleads some of our leading thinkers into believing that the situation which it describes has direct relevance to the solution of practical problems, it is time that we remember that it does not deal with the social process at all and that it is no more than a useful preliminary to the study of the main problem.

THE PROBLEM OF SOCIAL COST*

RONALD COASE[1]

I. The Problem to Be Examined

This paper is concerned with those actions of business firms which have harmful effects on others. The standard example is that of a factory the smoke from which has harmful effects on those occupying neighbouring properties. The economic analysis of such a situation has usually proceeded in terms of a divergence between the private and social product of the factory, in which economists have largely followed the treatment of Pigou in *The Economics of Welfare*. The conclusions to which this kind of analysis seems to have led most economists are that it would be desirable to make the owner of the factory liable for the damage caused to those injured by the smoke, or alternatively, to place a tax on the factory owner varying with the amount of smoke produced and equivalent in money terms to the damage it would cause, or finally, to exclude the factory from residential districts (and presumably from other areas in which the emission of smoke would have harmful effects on others). It is my contention that the suggested courses of action are inappropriate, in that they lead to results which are not necessarily, or even usually, desirable.

II. The Reciprocal Nature of the Problem

The traditional approach has tended to obscure the nature of the choice that has to be made. The question is commonly thought of as one in which A inflicts harm on B and what has to be decided is: how should we restrain A? But this is wrong. We are dealing with a problem of a reciprocal nature. To avoid the harm to B would inflict harm on A. The real question that has to be decided is: should A be allowed to harm B or should B be allowed to harm A? The problem is to avoid the more serious harm. I instanced in

*Reprinted by permission of The University of Chicago Press from the *Journal of Law and Economics* by R. H. Coase.

[1]This article, although concerned with a technical problem of economic analysis, arose out of the study of the Political Economy of Broadcasting which I am now conducting. The argument of the present article was implicit in a previous article dealing with the problem of allocating radio and television frequencies ("The Federal Communications Commission," 2 *J. Law & Econ.* [1959]) but comments which I have received seemed to suggest that it would be desirable to deal with the question in a more explicit way and without reference to the original problem for the solution of which the analysis was developed.

my previous article[1] the case of a confectioner the noise and vibrations from whose machinery disturbed a doctor in his work. To avoid harming the doctor would inflict harm on the confectioner. The problem posed by this case was essentially whether it was worth while, as a result of restricting the methods of production which could be used by the confectioner, to secure more doctoring at the cost of a reduced supply of confectionery products. Another example is afforded by the problem of straying cattle which destroy crops on neighbouring land. If it is inevitable that some cattle will stray, an increase in the supply of meat can only be obtained at the expense of a decrease in the supply of crops. The nature of the choice is clear: meat or crops. What answer should be given is, of course, not clear unless we know the value of what is obtained as well as the value of what is sacrificed to obtain it. To give another example, Professor George J. Stigler instances the contamination of a stream.[2] If we assume that the harmful effect of the pollution is that it kills the fish, the question to be decided is: is the value of the fish lost greater or less than the value of the product which the contamination of the stream makes possible. It goes almost without saying that this problem has to be looked at in total *and* at the margin.

III. The Pricing System with Liability for Damage

I propose to start my analysis by examining a case in which most economists would presumably agree that the problem would be solved in a completely satisfactory manner: when the damaging business has to pay for all damage caused *and* the pricing system works smoothly (strictly this means that the operation of a pricing system is without cost).

A good example of the problem under discussion is afforded by the case of straying cattle which destroy crops growing on neighbouring land. Let us suppose that a farmer and cattle-raiser are operating on neighbouring properties. Let us further suppose that, without any fencing between the properties, an increase

in the size of the cattle-raiser's herd increases the total damage to the farmer's crops. What happens to the marginal damage as the size of the herd increases is another matter. This depends on whether the cattle tend to follow one another or to roam side by side, on whether they tend to be more or less restless as the size of the herd increases and on other similar factors. For my immediate purpose, it is immaterial what assumption is made about marginal damage as the size of the herd increases.

To simplify the argument, I propose to use an arithmetical example. I shall assume that the annual cost of fencing the farmer's property is $9 and that the price of the crop is $1 per ton. Also, I assume that the relation between the number of cattle in the herd and the annual crop loss is as follows:

Number in herd (steers)	Annual crop loss (tons)	Crop loss per additional steer (tons)
1	1	1
2	3	2
3	6	3
4	10	4

Given that the cattle-raiser is liable for the damage caused, the additional annual cost imposed on the cattle-raiser if he increased his herd from, say, 2 to 3 steers is $3 and in deciding on the size of the herd, he will take this into account along with his other costs. That is, he will not increase the size of the herd unless the value of the additional meat produced (assuming that the cattle-raiser slaughters the cattle) is greater than the additional costs that this will entail, including the value of the additional crops destroyed. Of course, if, by the employment of dogs, herdsmen, aeroplanes, mobile radio and other means, the amount of damage can be reduced, these means will be adopted when their cost is less than the value of the crop which they prevent being lost. Given that the annual cost of fencing is $9, the cattle-raiser who wished to have a herd with 4 steers or more would pay for fencing to be erected and maintained, assuming that other means of attaining the same end would not do so more cheaply. When the fence is erected, the marginal cost due to the liability for damage becomes zero, except to the extent that an increase in the size of the herd necessitates a stronger and therefore more expensive fence

[1]Coase, "The Federal Communications Commission," 2 *J. Law & Econ.* 26-27 (1959).

[2]G. J. Stigler, *The Theory of Price*, 105 (1952).

because more steers are liable to lean against it at the same time. But, of course, it may be cheaper for the cattle-raiser not to fence and to pay for the damaged crops, as in my arithmetical example, with 3 or fewer steers.

It might be thought that the fact that the cattle-raiser would pay for all crops damaged would lead the farmer to increase his planting if a cattle-raiser came to occupy the neighbouring property. But this is not so. If the crop was previously sold in conditions of perfect competition, marginal cost was equal to price for the amount of planting undertaken and any expansion would have reduced the profits of the farmer. In the new situation, the existence of crop damage would mean that the farmer would sell less on the open market but his receipts for a given production would remain the same, since the cattle-raiser would pay the market price for any crop damaged. Of course, if cattle-raising commonly involved the destruction of crops, the coming into existence of a cattle-raising industry might raise the price of the crops involved and farmers would then extend their planting. But I wish to confine my attention to the individual farmer.

I have said that the occupation of a neighbouring property by a cattle-raiser would not cause the amount of production, or perhaps more exactly the amount of planting, by the farmer to increase. In fact, if the cattle-raising has any effect, it will be to decrease the amount of planting. The reason for this is that, for any given tract of land, if the value of the crop damaged is so great that the receipts from the sale of the undamaged crop are less than the total costs of cultivating that tract of land, it will be profitable for the farmer and the cattle-raiser to make a bargain whereby that tract of land is left uncultivated. This can be made clear by means of an arithmetical example. Assume initially that the value of the crop obtained from cultivating a given tract of land is $12 and that the cost incurred in cultivating this tract of land is $10, the net gain from cultivating the land being $2. I assume for purposes of simplicity that the farmer owns the land. Now assume that the cattle-raiser starts operations on the neighbouring property and that the value of the crops damaged is $1. In this case $11 is obtained by the farmer from sale on the market and $1 is obtained from the cattle-raiser for damage suffered and the net gain remains $2. Now suppose that the cattle-raiser finds it profitable to increase the size of his herd, even though the amount of damage rises to $3;

which means that the value of the additional meat production is greater than the additional costs, including the additional $2 payment for damage. But the total payment for damage is now $3. The net gain to the farmer from cultivating the land is still $2. The cattle-raiser would be better off if the farmer would agree not to cultivate his land for any payment less than $3. The farmer would be agreeable to not cultivating the land for any payment greater than $2. There is clearly room for a mutually satisfactory bargain which would lead to the abandonment of cultivation.[1] But the same argument applies not only to the whole tract cultivated by the farmer but also to any subdivision of it. Suppose, for example, that the cattle have a well-defined route, say, to a brook or to a shady area. In these circumstances, the amount of damage to the crop along the route may well be great and if so, it could be that the farmer and the cattle-raiser would find it profitable to make a bargain whereby the farmer would agree not to cultivate this strip of land.

But this raises a further possibility. Suppose that there is such a well-defined route. Suppose further that the value of the crop that would be obtained by cultivating this strip of land is $10 but that the cost of cultivation is $11. In the absence of the cattle-raiser, the land would not be cultivated. However, given the presence of the cattle-raiser, it could well be that if the strip was cultivated, the whole crop would be destroyed by

---

[1]The argument in the text has proceeded on the assumption that the alternative to cultivation of the crop is abandonment of cultivation altogether. But this need not be so. There may be crops which are less liable to damage by cattle but which would not be as profitable as the crop grown in the absence of damage. Thus, if the cultivation of a new crop would yield a return to the farmer of $1 instead of $2, and the size of the herd which would cause $3 damage with the old crop would cause $1 damage with the new crop, it would be profitable to the cattle-raiser to pay any sum less than $2 to induce the farmer to change his crop (since this would reduce damage liability from $3 to $1) and it would be profitable for the farmer to do so if the amount received was more than $1 (the reduction in his return caused by switching crops). In fact, there would be room for a mutually satisfactory bargain in all cases in which a change of crop would reduce the amount of damage by more than it reduces the value of the crop (excluding damage)—in all cases, that is, in which a change in the crop cultivated would lead to an increase in the value of production.

the cattle. In which case, the cattle-raiser would be forced to pay $10 to the farmer. It is true that the farmer would lose $1. But the cattle-raiser would lose $10. Clearly, this is a situation which is not likely to last indefinitely since neither party would want this to happen. The aim of the farmer would be to induce the cattle-raiser to make a payment in return for an agreement to leave this land uncultivated. The farmer would not be able to obtain a payment greater than the cost of fencing off this piece of land nor so high as to lead the cattle-raiser to abandon the use of the neighbouring property. What payment would in fact be made would depend on the shrewdness of the farmer and the cattle-raiser as bargainers. But as the payment would not be so high as to cause the cattle-raiser to abandon this location and as it would not vary with the size of the herd, such an agreement would not affect the allocation of resources, but would merely alter the distribution of income and wealth as between the cattle-raiser and the farmer.

I think it is clear that if the cattle-raiser is liable for damage caused and the pricing system works smoothly, the reduction in the value of production elsewhere will be taken into account in computing the additional cost involved in increasing the size of the herd. This cost will be weighed against the value of the additional meat production and, given perfect competition in the cattle industry, the allocation of resources in cattle-raising will be optimal. What needs to be emphasized is that the fall in the value of production elsewhere which would be taken into account in the costs of the cattle-raiser may well be less than the damage which the cattle would cause to the crops in the ordinary course of events. This is because it is possible, as a result of market transactions, to discontinue cultivation of the land. This is desirable in all cases in which the damage that the cattle would cause, and for which the cattle-raiser would be willing to pay, exceeds the amount which the farmer would pay for the use of the land. In conditions of perfect competition, the amount which the farmer would pay for the use of the land is equal to the difference between the value of the total production when the factors are employed on this land and the value of the additional product yielded in their next best use (which would be what the farmer would have to pay for the factors). If damage exceeds the amount the farmer would pay for the use of the land, the value of the additional product of the factors employed

elsewhere would exceed the value of the total product in this use after damage is taken into account. It follows that it would be desirable to abandon cultivation of the land and to release the factors employed for production elsewhere. A procedure which merely provided for payment for damage to the crop caused by the cattle but which did not allow for the possibility of cultivation being discontinued would result in too small an employment of factors of production in cattle-raising and too large an employment of factors in cultivation of the crop. But given the possibility of market transactions, a situation in which damage to crops exceeded the rent of the land would not endure. Whether the cattle-raiser pays the farmer to leave the land uncultivated or himself rents the land by paying the land-owner an amount slightly greater than the farmer would pay (if the farmer was himself renting the land), the final result would be the same and would maximise the value of production. Even when the farmer is induced to plant crops which it would not be profitable to cultivate for sale on the market, this will be a purely short-term phenomenon and may be expected to lead to an agreement under which the planting will cease. The cattle-raiser will remain in that location and the marginal cost of meat production will be the same as before, thus having no long-run effect on the allocation of resources.

IV.   The Pricing System with No Liability for Damage

I now turn to the case in which, although the pricing system is assumed to work smoothly (that is, costlessly), the damaging business is not liable for any of the damage which it causes. This business does not have to make a payment to those damaged by its actions. I propose to show that the allocation of resources will be the same in this case as it was when the damaging business was liable for damage caused. As I showed in the previous case that the allocation of resources was optimal, it will not be necessary to repeat this part of the argument.

I return to the case of the farmer and the cattle-raiser. The farmer would suffer increased damage to his crop as the size of the herd increased. Suppose that the size of the cattle-raiser's herd is 3 steers (and that this is the size of the herd that would be maintained if crop damage was not taken into account). Then the farmer would be willing to pay up to $3 if the cattle-raiser would reduce his herd to 2 steers, up to $5 if the herd were reduced to 1 steer and would pay up to $6 if cattle-raising was abandoned. The cattle-raiser would therefore receive $3 from the farmer if he kept 2 steers instead of 3. This $3 foregone is therefore part of the cost incurred in keeping the third steer. Whether the $3 is a payment which the cattle-raiser has to make if he adds the third steer to his herd (which it would be if the cattle-raiser was liable to the farmer for damage caused to the crop) or whether it is a sum of money which he would have received if he did not keep a third steer (which it would be if the cattle-raiser was not liable to the farmer for damage caused to the crop) does not affect the final result. In both cases $3 is part of the cost of adding a third steer, to be included along with the other costs. If the increase in the value of production in cattle-raising through increasing the size of the herd from 2 to 3 is greater than the additional costs that have to be incurred (including the $3 damage to crops), the size of the herd will be increased. Otherwise, it will not. The size of the herd will be the same whether the cattle-raiser is liable for damage caused to the crop or not.

It may be argued that the assumed starting point—a herd of 3 steers—was arbitrary. And this is true. But the farmer would not wish to pay to avoid crop damage which the cattle-raiser would not be able to cause. For example, the maximum annual payment which the farmer could be induced to pay could not exceed $9, the annual cost of fencing. And the farmer would only be willing to pay this sum if it did not reduce his earnings to a level that would cause him to abandon cultivation of this particular tract of land. Furthermore, the farmer would only be willing to pay this amount if he believed that, in the absence of any payment by him, the size of the herd maintained by the cattle-raiser would be 4 or more steers. Let us assume that this is the case. Then the farmer would be willing to pay up to $3 if the cattle-raiser would reduce his herd to 3 steers, up to $6 if the herd were reduced to 2 steers, up to $8 if one steer only were kept and up to $9 if cattle-raising were abandoned. It will be noticed that the change in the starting point has not altered the amount which would accrue to the cattle-raiser if he reduced the size of his herd by any given amount. It is still true that the cattle-raiser could receive an additional $3 from

the farmer if he agreed to reduce his herd from 3 steers to 2 and that the $3 represents the value of the crop that would be destroyed by adding the third steer to the herd. Although a different belief on the part of the farmer (whether justified or not) about the size of the herd that the cattle-raiser would maintain in the absence of payments from him may affect the total payment he can be induced to pay, it is not true that this different belief would have any effect on the size of the herd that the cattle-raiser will actually keep. This will be the same as it would be if the cattle-raiser had to pay for damage caused by his cattle, since a receipt foregone of a given amount is the equivalent of a payment of the same amount.

It might be thought that it would pay the cattle-raiser to increase his herd about the size that he would wish to maintain once a bargain had been made, in order to induce the farmer to make a larger total payment. And this may be true. It is similar in nature to the action of the farmer (when the cattle-raiser was liable for damage) in cultivating land on which, as a result of an agreement with the cattle-raiser, planting would subsequently be abandoned (including land which would not be cultivated at all in the absence of cattle-raising). But such manoeuvres are preliminaries to an agreement and do not affect the long-run equilibrium position, which is the same whether or not the cattle-raiser is held responsible for the crop damage brought about by his cattle.

It is necessary to know whether the damaging business is liable or not for damage caused since without the establishment of this initial delimitation of rights there can be no market transactions to transfer and recombine them. But the ultimate result (which maximises the value of production) is independent of the legal position if the pricing system is assumed to work without cost.

V. The Problem Illustrated Anew

The harmful effects of the activities of a business can assume a wide variety of forms. An early English case concerned a building which, by obstructing currents of air, hindered the operation of a windmill.[1] A recent case in Florida

---

[1] See Gale on *Easements* 237-39 (13th ed. M. Bowles 1959).

concerned a building which cast a shadow on the cabana, swimming pool and sunbathing areas of a neighbouring hotel.[1] The problem of straying cattle and the damaging of crops which was the subject of detailed examination in the two preceding sections, although it may have appeared to be rather a special case, is in fact but one example of a problem which arises in many different guises. To clarify the nature of my argument and to demonstrate its general applicability, I propose to illustrate it anew by reference to four actual cases.

Let us first reconsider the case of *Sturges v. Bridgman*[2] which I used as an illustration of the general problem in my article on "The Federal Communications Commission." In this case, a confectioner (in Wigmore Street) used two mortars and pestles in connection with his business (one had been in operation in the same position for more than 60 years and the other for more than 26 years). A doctor then came to occupy neighbouring premises (in Wimpole Street). The confectioner's machinery caused the doctor no harm until, eight years after he had first occupied the premises, he built a consulting room at the end of his garden right against the confectioner's kitchen. It was then found that the noise and vibration caused by the confectioner's machinery made it difficult for the doctor to use his new consulting room. "In particular ... the noise prevented him from examining his patients by auscultation[3] for diseases of the chest. He also found it impossible to engage with effect in any occupation which required thought and attention." The doctor therefore brought a legal action to force the confectioner to stop using his machinery. The courts had little difficulty in granting the doctor the injunction he sought. "Individual cases of hardship may occur in the strict carrying out of the principle upon which we found our judgment, but the negation of the principle would lead even more to individual hardship, and would at the same time produce a

prejudicial effect upon the development of land for residential purposes."

The court's decision established that the doctor had the right to prevent the confectioner from using his machinery. But, of course, it would have been possible to modify the arrangements envisaged in the legal ruling by means of a bargain between the parties. The doctor would have been willing to waive his right and allow the machinery to continue in operation if the confectioner would have paid him a sum of money which was greater than the loss of income which he would suffer from having to move to a more costly or less convenient location or from having to curtail his activities at this location or, as was suggested as a possibility, from having to build a separate wall which would deaden the noise and vibration. The confectioner would have been willing to do this if the amount he would have to pay the doctor was less than the fall in income he would suffer if he had to change his mode of operation at this location, abandon his operation or move his confectionery business to some other location. The solution of the problem depends essentially on whether the continued use of the machinery adds more to the confectioner's income than it subtracts from the doctor's.[4] But now consider the situation if the confectioner had won the case. The confectioner would then have had the right to continue operating his noise and vibration-generating machinery without having to pay anything to the doctor. The boot would have been on the other foot: the doctor would have had to pay the confectioner to induce him to stop using the machinery. If the doctor's income would have fallen more through continuance of the use of this machinery than it added to the income of the confectioner, there would clearly be room for a bargain whereby the doctor paid the confectioner to stop using the machinery. That is to say, the circumstances in which it would not pay the confectioner to continue to use the machinery and to compensate the doctor for the losses that this would bring (if the doctor had the right to prevent the confectioner's using his machinery) would be those in which it would be in the interest of the doctor to make a payment to the confectioner which would induce him to discontinue the use of the machinery (if the

[1]See *Fontainebleu Hotel Corp. v. Forty-Five Twenty-Five, Inc.*, 114 So. 2d 357 (1959).

[2]11 Ch. D. 852 (1879).

[3]Auscultation is the act of listening by ear or stethoscope in order to judge by sound the condition of the body.

[4]Note that what is taken into account is the change in income after allowing for alterations in methods of production, location, character of product, etc.

confectioner had the right to operate the machinery). The basic conditions are exactly the same in this case as they were in the example of the cattle which destroyed crops. With costless market transactions, the decision of the courts concerning liability for damage would be without effect on the allocation of resources. It was of course the view of the judges that they were affecting the working of the economic system—and in a desirable direction. Any other decision would have had "a prejudicial effect upon the development of land for residential purposes," an argument which was elaborated by examining the example of a forge operating on a barren moor, which was later developed for residual purposes. The judges' view that they were settling how the land was to be used would be true only in the case in which the costs of carrying out the necessary market transactions exceeded the gain which might be achieved by any rearrangement of rights. And it would be desirable to preserve the areas (Wimpole Street or the moor) for residential or professional use (by giving non-industrial users the right to stop the noise, vibration, smoke, etc., by injunction) only if the value of the additional residential facilities obtained was greater than the value of cakes or iron lost. But of this the judges seem to have been unaware.

Another example of the same problem is furnished by the case of Cooke v. Forbes.[1] One process in the weaving of cocoa-nut fibre matting was to immerse it in bleaching liquids after which it was hung out to dry. Fumes from a manufacturer of sulphate of ammonia had the effect of turning the matting from a bright to a dull and blackish color. The reason for this was that the bleaching liquid contained chloride of tin, which, when affected by sulphuretted hydrogen, is turned to a darker colour. An injunction was sought to stop the manufacturer from emitting the fumes. The lawyers for the defendant argued that if the plaintiff "were not to use … a particular bleaching liquid, their fibre would not be affected; that their process is unusual, not according to the custom of the trade, and even damaging to their own fabrics." The judge commented: "… it appears to me quite plain that a person has a right to carry on upon his own property a manufacturing process in which he uses chloride of tin, or any sort of

metallic dye, and that his neighbour is not at liberty to pour in gas which will interfere with his manufacture. If it can be traced to the neighbour, then, I apprehend, clearly he will have a right to come here and ask for relief." But in view of the fact that the damage was accidental and occasional, that careful precautions were taken and that there was no exceptional risk, an injunction was refused, leaving the plaintiff to bring an action for damages if he wished. What the subsequent developments were I do not know. But it is clear that the situation is essentially the same as that found in Sturges v. Bridgman, except that the cocoa-nut fibre matting manufacturer could not secure an injunction but would have to seek damages from the sulphate of ammonia manufacturer. The economic analysis of the situation is exactly the same as with the cattle which destroyed crops. To avoid the damage, the sulphate of ammonia manufacturer could increase his precautions or move to another location. Either course would presumably increase his costs. Alternatively he could pay for the damage. This he would do if the payments for damage were less than the additional costs that would have to be incurred to avoid the damage. The payments for damage would then become part of the cost of production of sulphate of ammonia. Of course, if, as was suggested in the legal proceedings, the amount of damage could be eliminated by changing the bleaching agent (which would presumably increase the costs of the matting manufacturer) and if the additional cost was less than the damage that would otherwise occur, it should be possible for the two manufacturers to make a mutually satisfactory bargain whereby the new bleaching agent was used. Had the court decided against the matting manufacturer, as a consequence of which he would have had to suffer the damage without compensation, the allocation of resources would not have been affected. It would pay the matting manufacturer to change his bleaching agent if the additional cost involved was less than the reduction in damage. And since the matting manufacturer would be willing to pay the sulphate of ammonia manufacturer an amount up to his loss of income (the increase in costs or the damage suffered) if he would cease his activities, this loss of income would remain a cost of production for the manufacturer of sulphate of ammonia. This case is indeed analytically exactly the same as the cattle example.

[1] L. R. 5 Eq. 166 (1867-1868).

Bryant v. Lefever[1] raised the problem of the smoke nuisance in a novel form. The plaintiff and the defendants were occupiers of adjoining houses, which were of about the same height.

> Before 1876 the plaintiff was able to light a fire in any room of his house without the chimneys smoking; the two houses had remained in the same condition some thirty or forty years. In 1876 the defendants took down their house, and began to rebuild it. They carried up a wall by the side of the plaintiff's chimneys much beyond its original height, and stacked timber on the roof of their house, and thereby caused the plaintiff's chimneys to smoke whenever he lighted fires.

The reason, of course, why the chimneys smoked was that the erection of the wall and the stacking of the timber prevented the free circulation of air. In a trial before a jury, the plaintiff was awarded damages of £40. The case then went to the Court of Appeals where the judgment was reversed. Bramwell, L.J., argued:

> ... it is said, and the jury have found, that the defendants have done that which caused a nuisance to the plaintiff's house. We think there is no evidence of this. No doubt there is a nuisance, but it is not of the defendant's causing. They have done nothing in causing the nuisance. Their house and their timber are harmless enough. It is the plaintiff who causes the nuisance by lighting a coal fire in a place the chimney of which is placed so near the defendants' wall, that the smoke does not escape, but comes into the house. Let the plaintiff cease to light his fire, let him move his chimney, let him carry it higher, and there would be no nuisance. Who then, causes it? It would be very clear that the plaintiff did, if he had built his house or chimney after the defendants had put up the timber on theirs, and it is really the same though he did so before the timber was there. But (what is in truth the same answer), if the defendants cause the nuisance, they have a right to do so. If the plaintiff has not the right to the passage of air, except subject to the defendants' right to build or put timber on their house, then his right is subject to their right, and though a

[1]4 C.P.D. 172 (1878-1879).

nuisance follows from the exercise of their right, they are not liable.

And Cotton, L.J., said:

> Here it is found that the erection of the defendants' wall has sensibly and materially interfered with the comfort of human existence in the plaintiff's house, and it is said this is a nuisance for which the defendants are liable. Ordinarily this is so, but the defendants have done so, not by sending on to the plaintiff's property any smoke or noxious vapour, but by interrupting the egress of smoke from the plaintiff's house in a way to which ... the plaintiff has no legal right. The plaintiff creates the smoke, which interferes with his comfort. Unless he has ... a right to get rid of this in a particular way which has been interfered with by the defendants, he cannot sue the defendants, because the smoke made by himself, for which he has not provided any effectual means of escape, causes him annoyance. It is as if a man tried to get rid of liquid filth arising on his own land by a drain into his neighbour's land. Until a right had been acquired by user, the neighbour might stop the drain without incurring liability by so doing. No doubt great inconvenience would be caused to the owner of the property on which the liquid filth arises. But the act of his neighbour would be a lawful act, and he would not be liable for the consequences attributable to the fact that the man had accumulated filth without providing any effectual means of getting rid of it.

I do not propose to show that any subsequent modification of the situation, as a result of bargains between the parties (conditioned by the cost of stacking the timber elsewhere, the cost of extending the chimney higher, etc.), would have exactly the same result whatever decision the courts had come to since this point has already been adequately dealt with in the discussion of the cattle example and the two previous cases. What I shall discuss is the argument of the judges in the Court of Appeals that the smoke nuisance was not caused by the man who erected the wall but by the man who lit the fires. The novelty of the situation is that the smoke nuisance was suffered by the man who lit the fires and not by some third person. The question is not a trivial one since it lies at the heart of the problem under discussion. Who caused the smoke nuisance? The answer seems fairly clear. The smoke nuisance was caused both by the man who built the wall *and* by the man who lit the fires. Given the fires, there would have been no smoke nuisance without the wall; given the wall, there would have been no smoke nuisance without the fires. Eliminate the wall *or* the fires and the smoke nuisance would disappear. On the marginal principle it is clear that *both* were responsible and *both* should be forced to include the loss of amenity due to the smoke as a cost in deciding whether to continue the activity which gives rise to the smoke. And given the possibility of market transactions, this is what would in fact happen. Although the wall-builder was not liable legally for the nuisance, as the man with the smoking chimneys would presumably be willing to pay a sum equal to the monetary worth to him of eliminating the smoke, this sum would therefore become for the wall-builder a cost of continuing to have the high wall with the timber stacked on the roof.

The judges' contention that it was the man who lit the fires who alone caused the smoke nuisance is true only if we assume that the wall is the given factor. This is what the judges did by deciding that the man who erected the higher wall had a legal right to do so. The case would have been even more interesting if the smoke from the chimneys had injured the timber. Then it would have been the wall-builder who suffered the damage. The case would then have closely paralleled *Sturges v. Bridgman* and there can be little doubt that the man who lit the fires would have been liable for the ensuing damage to the timber, in spite of the fact that no damage had occurred until the high wall was built by the man who owned the timber.

Judges have to decide on legal liability but this should not confuse economists about the nature of the economic problem involved. In the case of the cattle and the crops, it is true that there would be no crop damage without the cattle. It is equally true that there would be no crop damage without the crops. The doctor's work would not have been disturbed if the confectioner had not worked his machinery; but the machinery would have disturbed no one if the doctor had not set up his consulting room in that particular place. The matting was blackened by the fumes from the sulphate of ammonia manufacturer; but no damage would have occurred if the matting manufacturer had not chosen to hang out his matting in a particular

place and to use a particular bleaching agent. If we are to discuss the problem in terms of causation, both parties cause the damage. If we are to attain an optimum allocation of resources, it is therefore desirable that both parties should take the harmful effect (the nuisance) into account in deciding on their course of action. It is one of the beauties of a smoothly operating pricing system that, as has already been explained, the fall in the value of production due to the harmful effect would be a cost for both parties.

Bass v. Gregory[1] will serve as an excellent final illustration of the problem. The plaintiffs were the owners and tenant of a public house called the Jolly Anglers. The defendant was the owner of some cottages and a yard adjoining the Jolly Anglers. Under the public house was a cellar excavated in the rock. From the cellar, a hole or shaft had been cut into an old well situated in the defendant's yard. The well therefore became the ventilating shaft for the cellar. The cellar "had been used for a particular purpose in the process of brewing, which, without ventilation, could not be carried on." The cause of the action was that the defendant removed a grating from the mouth of the well, "so as to stop or prevent the free passage of air from [the] cellar upwards through the well...." What caused the defendant to take this step is not clear from the report of the case. Perhaps "the air ... impregnated by the brewing operations" which "passed up the well and out into the open air" was offensive to him. At any rate, he preferred to have the well in his yard stopped up. The court had first to determine whether the owners of the public house could have a legal right to a current of air. If they were to have such a right, this case would have to be distinguished from *Bryant v. Lefever* (already considered). This, however, presented no difficulty. In this case, the current of air was confined to "a strictly defined channel." In the case of *Bryant v. Lefever*, what was involved was "the general current of air common to all mankind." The judge therefore held that the owners of the public house could have the right to a current of air whereas the owner of the private house in *Bryant v. Lefever* could not. An economist might be tempted to add "but the air moved all the same." However, all that had been decided at this stage of the argument was that there could be a legal right, not that the owners

---

[1]25 Q.B.D. 481 (1890).

of the public house possessed it. But evidence showed that the shaft from the cellar to the well had existed for over forty years and that the use of the well as a ventilating shaft must have been known to the owners of the yard since the air, when it emerged, smelt of the brewing operations. The judge therefore held that the public house had such a right by the "doctrine of lost grant." This doctrine states "that if a legal right is proved to have existed and been exercised for a number of years the law ought to presume that it had a legal origin."[1] So the owner of the cottages and yard had to unstop the well and endure the smell.

The reasoning employed by the courts in determining legal rights will often seem strange to an economist because many of the factors on which the decision turns are, to an economist, irrelevant. Because of this, situations which are, from an economic point of view, identical will be treated quite differently by the courts. The economic problem in all cases of harmful effects is how to maximise the value of production. In the case of *Bass v. Gregory* fresh air was drawn in through the well which facilitated the production of beer but foul air was expelled through the well which made life in the adjoining houses less pleasant. The economic problem was to decide which to choose: a lower cost of beer and worsened amenities in adjoining houses or a higher cost of beer and improved amenities. In deciding this question, the "doctrine of lost grant" is about as relevant as the colour of the

judge's eyes. But it has to be remembered that the immediate question faced by the courts is *not* what shall be done by whom *but* who has the legal right to do what. It is always possible to modify by transactions on the market the initial legal delimitation of rights. And, of course, if such market transactions are costless, such a rearrangement of rights will always take place if it would lead to an increase in the value of production.

VI.   The Cost of Market Transactions Taken into Account

The argument has proceeded up to this point on the assumption (explicit in Sections III and IV and tacit in Section V) that there were no costs involved in carrying out market transactions. This is, of course, a very unrealistic assumption. In order to carry out a market transaction it is necessary to discover who it is that one wishes to deal with, to inform people that one wishes to deal and on what terms, to conduct negotiations leading up to a bargain, to draw up the contract, to undertake the inspection needed to make sure that the terms of the contract are being observed, and so on. These operations are often extremely costly, sufficiently costly at any rate to prevent many transactions that would be carried out in a world in which the pricing system worked without cost.

In earlier sections, when dealing with the problem of the rearrangement of legal rights through the market, it was argued that such a rearrangement would be made through the market whenever this would lead to an increase in the value of production. But this assumed costless market transactions. Once the costs of carrying out market transactions are taken into account it is clear that such a rearrangement of rights will only be undertaken when the increase in the value of the production consequent upon the rearrangement is greater than the costs which would be involved in bringing it about. When it is less, the granting of an injunction (or the knowledge that it would be granted) or the liability to pay damages may result in an activity being discontinued (or may prevent its being started) which would be undertaken if market transactions were costless. In these conditions the initial delimitation of legal rights does have an effect on the efficiency with which the economic

---

[1] It may be asked why a lost grant could not also be presumed in the case of the confectioner who had operated one mortar for more than 60 years. The answer is that until the doctor built the consulting room at the end of his garden there was no nuisance. So the nuisance had not continued for many years. It is true that the confectioner in his affidavit referred to "an invalid lady who occupied the house upon one occasion, about thirty years before" who "requested him if possible to discontinue the use of the mortars before eight o'clock in the morning" and that there was some evidence that the garden wall had been subjected to vibration. But the court had little difficulty in disposing of this line of argument: "... this vibration, even if it existed at all, was so slight, and the complaint, if it can be called a complaint, of the invalid lady ... was of so trifling a character, that ... the Defendant's acts would not have given rise to any proceeding either at law or in equity" (11 Ch. D. 863). That is, the confectioner had not committed a nuisance until the doctor built his consulting room.

system operates. One arrangement of rights may bring about a greater value of production than any other. But unless this is the arrangement of rights established by the legal system, the costs of reaching the same result by altering and combining rights through the market may be so great that this optimal arrangement of rights, and the greater value of production which it would bring, may never be achieved. The part played by economic considerations in the process of delimiting legal rights will be discussed in the next section. I will take the initial delimitation of rights and the costs of carrying out market transactions as given.

It is clear that an alternative form of economic organisation which could achieve the same result at less cost than would be incurred by using the market would enable the value of production to be raised. As I explained many years ago, the firm represents such an alternative to organising production through market transactions.[1] Within the firm individual bargains between the various cooperating factors of production are eliminated and for a market transaction is substituted an administrative decision. The rearrangement of production then takes place without the need for bargains between the owners of the factors of production. A landowner who has control of a large tract of land may devote his land to various uses taking into account the effect that the interrelations of the various activities will have on the net return of the land, thus rendering unnecessary bargains between those undertaking the various activities. Owners of a large building or of several adjoining properties in a given area may act in much the same way. In effect, using our earlier terminology, the firm would acquire the legal rights of all the parties and the rearrangement of activities would not follow on a rearrangement of rights by contract, but as a result of an administrative decision as to how the rights should be used.

It does not, of course, follow that the administrative costs of organising a transaction through a firm are inevitably less than the costs of the market transactions which are superseded. But where contracts are peculiarly difficult to draw up and an attempt to describe what the parties have agreed to do or not to do (e.g. the amount and kind of a smell or noise that they

may make or will not make) would necessitate a lengthy and highly involved document and, where, as is probable, a long-term contract would be desirable;[2] it would be hardly surprising if the emergence of a firm or the extension of the activities of an existing firm was not the solution adopted on many occasions to deal with the problem of harmful effects. This solution would be adopted whenever the administrative costs of the firm were less than the costs of the market transactions that it supersedes and the gains which would result from the rearrangement of activities greater than the firm's costs of organising them. I do not need to examine in great detail the character of this solution since I have explained what is involved in my earlier article.

But the firm is not the only possible answer to this problem. The administrative costs of organising transactions within the firm may also be high, and particularly so when many diverse activities are brought within the control of a single organisation. In the standard case of a smoke nuisance, which may affect a vast number of people engaged in a wide variety of activities, the administrative costs might well be so high as to make any attempt to deal with the problem within the confines of a single firm impossible. An alternative solution is direct government regulation. Instead of instituting a legal system of rights which can be modified by transactions on the market, the government may impose regulations which state what people must or must not do and which have to be obeyed. Thus, the government (by statute or perhaps more likely through an administrative agency) may, to deal with the problem of smoke nuisance, decree that certain methods of production should or should not be used (e.g., that smoke preventing devices should be installed or that coal or oil should not be burned) or may confine certain types of business to certain districts (zoning regulations).

The government is, in a sense, a superfirm (but of a very special kind) since it is able to influence the use of factors of production by administrative decision. But the ordinary firm is subject to checks in its operations because of the competition of other firms, which might administer the same activities at lower cost and also because there is always the alternative of market transactions as against organisation

---

[1]See Coase, "The Nature of the Firm," 4 *Economica*, New Series, 386 (1937). Reprinted in *Readings in Price Theory*, 331 (1952).

[2]For reasons explained in my earlier article, see *Readings in Price Theory*, n. 14 at 337.

within the firm if the administrative costs become too great. The government is able, if it wishes, to avoid the market altogether, which a firm can never do. The firm has to make market agreements with the owners of the factors of production that it uses. Just as the government can conscript or seize property, so it can decree that factors of production should only be used in such-and-such a way. Such authoritarian methods save a lot of trouble (for those doing the organising). Furthermore, the government has at its disposal the police and the other law enforcement agencies to make sure that its regulations are carried out.

It is clear that the government has powers which might enable it to get some things done at a lower cost than could a private organisation (or at any rate one without special governmental powers). But the governmental administrative machine is not itself costless. It can, in fact, on occasion be extremely costly. Furthermore, there is no reason to suppose that the restrictive and zoning regulations, made by a fallible administration subject to political pressures and operating without any competitive check, will necessarily always be those which increase the efficiency with which the economic system operates. Furthermore, such general regulations which must apply to a wide variety of cases will be enforced in some cases in which they are clearly inappropriate. From these considerations it follows that direct governmental regulation will not necessarily give better results than leaving the problem to be solved by the market or the firm. But equally there is no reason why, on occasion, such governmental administrative regulation should not lead to an improvement in economic efficiency. This would seem particularly likely when, as is normally the case with the smoke nuisance, a large number of people are involved and in which therefore the costs of handling the problem through the market or the firm may be high.

There is, of course, a further alternative, which is to do nothing about the problem at all. And given that the costs involved in solving the problem by regulations issued by the governmental administrative machine will often be heavy (particularly if the costs are interpreted to include all the consequences which follow from the Government engaging in this kind of activity), it will no doubt be commonly the case that the gain which would come from regulating the actions which give rise to the harmful effects

will be less than the costs involved Government regulation.

The discussion of the problem of harmf effects in this section (when the costs of mark transactions are taken into account) is extreme inadequate. But at least it has made clear that t problem is one of choosing the appropriate soc arrangement for dealing with the harmful effect All solutions have costs and there is no reason suppose that government regulation is called f simply because the problem is not well handle by the market or the firm. Satisfactory views policy can only come from a patient study how, in practice, the market, firms an governments can handle the problem of harmf effects. Economists need to study the work of t broker in bringing parties together, t effectiveness of restrictive covenants, t problems of the large-scale real-esta development company, the operation Government zoning and other regulati activities. It is my belief that economists, a policy-makers generally, have tended to ove estimate the advantages which come fro governmental regulation. But this belief, even justified, does not do more than suggest th government regulation should be curtailed. does not tell us where the boundary line shou be drawn. This, it seems to me, has to come fro a detailed investigation of the actual results handling the problem in different ways. But would be unfortunate if this investigation we undertaken with the aid of a faulty econom analysis. The aim of this article is to indicate wh the economic approach to the problem should b

VII. The Legal Delimitation of Rights ar the Economic Problem

The discussion in Section V not only served illustrate the argument but also afforded glimpse at the legal approach to the problem harmful effects. The cases considered were English but a similar selection of American cas could easily be made and the character of t reasoning would have been the same. Of cour if market transactions were costless, all th matters (questions of equity apart) is that t rights of the various parties should be we defined and the results of legal actions easy forecast. But as we have seen, the situation quite different when market transactions are costly as to make it difficult to change the arrangement of rights established by the law. In such cases, the courts directly influence economic activity. It would therefore seem desirable that the courts should understand the economic consequences of their decisions and should, insofar as this is possible without creating too much uncertainty about the legal position itself, take these consequences into account when making their decisions. Even when it is possible to change the legal delimitation of rights through market transactions, it is obviously desirable to reduce the need for such transactions and thus reduce the employment of resources in carrying them out.

A thorough examination of the presuppositions of the courts in trying such cases would be of great interest but I have not been able to attempt it. Nevertheless it is clear from cursory study that the courts have often recognized the economic implications of their decisions and are aware (as many economists are not) of the reciprocal nature of the problem. Furthermore, from time to time, they take these economic implications into account, along with other factors, in arriving at their decisions. The American writers on this subject refer to the question in a more explicit fashion than do the British. Thus, to quote Prosser on Torts, a person may

make use of his own property or ... conduct his own affairs at the expense of some harm to his neighbors. He may operate a factory whose noise and smoke cause some discomfort to others, so long as he keeps within reasonable bounds. It is only when his conduct is unreasonable, *in the light of its utility and the harm which results* [italics added], that it becomes a nuisance.... As it was said in an ancient case in regard to candle-making in a town, "Le utility del chose excusera le noisomeness del stink."

The world must have factories, smelters, oil refineries, noisy machinery and blasting, even at the expense of some inconvenience to those in the vicinity and the plaintiff may be required to accept some not unreasonable discomfort for the general good.[1]

---

[1]See W. L. Prosser, *The Law of Torts* 398-99, 412 (2d ed. 1955). The quotation about the ancient case concerning candle-making is taken from Sir James Fitzjames Stephen, *A General View of the Criminal Law of England* 106 (1890). Sir James Stephen gives no

The standard British writers do not state as explicitly as this that a comparison between the utility and harm produced is an element in deciding whether a harmful effect should be considered a nuisance. But similar views, if less strongly expressed, are to be found.[2] The doctrine that the harmful effect must be substantial before the court will act is, no doubt, in part a reflection of the fact that there will almost always be some gain to offset the harm. And in the reports of individual cases, it is clear that the judges have had in mind what would be lost as well as what would be gained in deciding whether to grant an injunction or award damages. Thus, in refusing to prevent the destruction of a prospect by a new building, the judge stated:

I know no general rule of common law, which ... says, that building so as to stop another's prospect is a nuisance. Was that the case, there could be no great towns; and I must grant injunctions to all the new buildings in this town....[3]

In *Webb v. Bird*[4] it was decided that it was not a nuisance to build a schoolhouse so near a windmill as to obstruct currents of air and hinder the working of the mill. An early case seems to

---

reference. He perhaps had in mind *Rex v. Ronkett*, included in Seavey, Keeton and Thurston, *Cases on Torts* 604 (1950). A similar view to that expressed by Prosser is to be found in F. V. Harper and F. James, *The Law of Torts* 67-74 (1956); *Restatement, Torts* §§ 826, 827 and 828.

[2]See Winfield on *Torts* 541-48 (6th ed. T. E. Lewis 1954); Salmond on the *Law of Torts* 181-90 (12th ed. R.F.V. Heuston 1957); H. Street, *The Law of Torts* 221-29 (1959).

[3]*Attorney General v. Doughty*, 2 Ves. Sen. 453, 28 Eng. Rep. 290 (Ch. 1752). Compare in this connection the statement of an American judge, quoted in Prosser, *op. cit. supra* n. 16 at 413 n. 54: "Without smoke, Pittsburgh would have remained a very pretty village," Musmanno, J., in *Versailles Borough v. McKeesport Coal & Coke Co.*, 1935, 83 Pitts. Leg. J. 379, 385.

[4]10 C.B. (N.S.) 268, 142 Eng. Rep. 445 (1861); 13 C.B. (N.S.) 841, 143 Eng. Rep. 332 (1863).

have been decided in an opposite direction. Gale commented:

> In old maps of London a row of windmills appears on the heights to the north of London. Probably in the time of King James it was thought an alarming circumstance, as affecting the supply of food to the city, that anyone should build so near them as to take the wind out from their sails.[1]

In one of the cases discussed in Section V, *Sturges v. Bridgman*, it seems clear that the judges were thinking of the economic consequences of alternative decisions. To the argument that if the principle that they seemed to be following:

> were carried out to its logical consequences, it would result in the most serious practical inconveniences, for a man might go — say into the midst of the tanneries of *Bermondsey*, or into any other locality devoted to any particular trade or manufacture of a noisy or unsavoury character, and by building a private residence upon a vacant piece of land put a stop to such trade or manufacture altogether,

the judges answered that

> whether anything is a nuisance or not is a question to be determined, not merely by an abstract consideration of the thing itself, but in reference to its circumstances; What would be a nuisance in *Belgrave Square* would not necessarily be so in *Bermondsey*; and where a locality is devoted to a particular trade or manufacture carried on by the traders or manufacturers in a particular and established manner not constituting a public nuisance, Judges and juries would be justified in finding, and may be trusted to find, that the trade or manufacture so carried on in that locality is not a private or actionable wrong.[2]

That the character of the neighbourhood is relevant in deciding whether something is, or is not, a nuisance, is definitely established.

> He who dislikes the noise of traffic must not set up his abode in the heart of a great city. He who loves peace and quiet must not live in a locality devoted to the business of making boilers or steamships.[3]

What has emerged has been described as "planning and zoning by the judiciary."[4] Of course there are sometimes considerable difficulties in applying the criteria.[5]

An interesting example of the problem is found in *Adams v. Ursell*[6] in which a fried fish shop in a predominantly working-class district was set up near houses of a "much better character." England without fish-and-chips is a contradiction in terms and the case was clearly one of high importance. The judge commented:

> It was urged that an injunction would cause great hardship to the defendant and to the poor people who get food at his shop. The answer to that is that it does not follow that the defendant cannot carry on his business in another more suitable place somewhere in the neighbourhood. It by no means follows that because a fried fish shop is a nuisance in one place it is a nuisance in another.

In fact, the injunction which restrained Mr. Ursell from running his shop did not even extend to the whole street. So he was presumably able to move to other premises near houses of "a much worse character," the inhabitants of which would no doubt consider the availability of fish-and-chips to outweigh the pervading odour and "fog or mist" so graphically described by the plaintiff. Had there been no other "more suitable place in the neighbourhood," the case would have been more difficult and the decision might have been different. What would "the poor people" have

---

[1]See Gale on *Easements* 238, n. 6 (13th ed. M. Bowles 1959).

[2]11 Ch.D. 865 (1879).

[3]Salmond on the *Law of Torts* 182 (12th ed. R.F.V. Heuston 1957).

[4]C. M. Haar, *Land-Use Planning, A Casebook on the Use, Misuse, and Re-use of Urban Land* 95 (1959).

[5]See, for example, *Rushmer v. Polsue and Alfieri, Ltd.* [1906] 1 Ch. 234, which deals with the case of a house in a quiet situation in a noisy district.

[6][1913] 1 Ch. 269.

had for food? No English judge would have said: "Let them eat cake."

The courts do not always refer very clearly to the economic problem posed by the cases brought before them but it seems probable that in the interpretation of words and phrases like "reasonable" or "common or ordinary use" there is some recognition, perhaps largely unconscious and certainly not very explicit, of the economic aspects of the questions at issue. A good example of this would seem to be the judgment in the Court of Appeals in *Andreae v. Selfridge and Company Ltd.*[1] In this case, a hotel (in Wigmore Street) was situated on part of an island site. The remainder of the site was acquired by Selfridges which demolished the existing buildings in order to erect another in their place. The hotel suffered a loss of custom in consequence of the noise and dust caused by the demolition. The owner of the hotel brought an action against Selfridges for damages. In the lower court, the hotel was awarded £4,500 damages. The case was then taken on appeal.

The judge who had found for the hotel proprietor in the lower court said:

I cannot regard what the defendants did on the site of the first operation as having been commonly done in the ordinary use and occupation of land or houses. It is neither usual nor common, in this country, for people to excavate a site to a depth of 60 feet and then to erect upon that site a steel framework and fasten the steel frames together with rivets.... Nor is it, I think, a common or ordinary use of land, in this country, to act as the defendants did when they were dealing with the site of their second operation—namely, to demolish all the houses that they had to demolish, five or six of them I think, if not more, and to use for the purpose of demolishing them pneumatic hammers.

Sir Wilfred Greene, M.R., speaking for the Court of Appeals, first noted

that when one is dealing with temporary operations, such as demolition and re-building, everybody has to put up with a certain amount of discomfort, because operations of that kind cannot be carried on at all without a certain amount of noise and a certain amount of dust.

Therefore, the rule with regard to interference must be read subject to this qualification....

He then referred to the previous judgment:

With great respect to the learned judge, I take the view that he has not approached this matter from the correct angle. It seems to me that it is not possible to say ... that the type of demolition, excavation and construction in which the defendant company was engaged in the course of these operations was of such an abnormal and unusual nature as to prevent the qualification to which I have referred coming into operation. It seems to me that, when the rule speaks of the common or ordinary use of land, it does not mean that the methods of using land and building on it are in some way to be stabilised for ever. As time goes on new inventions or new methods enable land to be more profitably used, either by digging down into the earth or by mounting up into the skies. Whether, from other points of view, that is a matter which is desirable for humanity is neither here nor there; but it is part of the normal use of land, to make use upon your land, in the matter of construction, of what particular type and what particular depth of foundations and particular height of building may be reasonable, in the circumstances, and in view of the developments of the day.... Guests at hotels are very easily upset. People coming to this hotel, who were accustomed to a quiet outlook at the back, coming back and finding demolition and building going on, may very well have taken the view that the particular merit of this hotel no longer existed. That would be a misfortune for the plaintiff; but assuming that there was nothing wrong in the defendant company's works, assuming the defendant company was carrying on the demolition and its building, productive of noise though it might be, with all reasonable skill, and taking all reasonable precautions not to cause annoyance to its neighbors, then the plaintiff might lose all her clients in the hotel because they have lost the amenities of an open and quiet place behind, but she would have no cause of complaint.... [But those] who say that their interference with the comfort of their neighbors is justified because their operations are normal and usual and conducted with proper care and skill are under a specific duty ... to use that reasonable and proper care and skill. It is not a correct attitude

---

[1][1938] 1 Ch. 1.

to take to say: 'We will go on and do what we like until somebody complains!' ... Their duty is to take proper precautions and to see that the nuisance is reduced to a minimum. It is no answer for them to say: 'But this would mean that we should have to do the work more slowly than we would like to do it, or it would involve putting us to some extra expense.' All these questions are matters of common sense and degree, and quite clearly it would be unreasonable to expect people to conduct their work so slowly or so expensively, for the purpose of preventing a transient inconvenience, that the cost and trouble would be prohibitive.... In this case, the defendant company's attitude seems to have been to go on until somebody complained, and further, that its desire to hurry its work and conduct it according to its own ideas and its own convenience was to prevail if there was a real conflict between it and the comfort of its neighbors. That ... is not carrying out the obligation of using reasonable care and skill.... The effect comes to this ... the plaintiff suffered an actionable nuisance; ... she is entitled, not to a nominal sum, but to a substantial sum, based upon those principles ... but in arriving at the sum ... I have discounted any loss of custom ... which might be due to the general loss of amenities owing to what was going on at the back....

The upshot was that the damages awarded were reduced from £4,500 to £1,000.

The discussion in this section has, up· to this point, been concerned with court decisions arising out of the common law relating to nuisance. Delimitation of rights in this area also comes about because of statutory enactments. Most economists would appear to assume that the aim of governmental action in this field is to extend the scope of the law of nuisance by designating as nuisances activities which would not be recognized as such by the common law. And there can be no doubt that some statutes, for example, the Public Health Acts, have had this effect. But not all Governmental enactments are of this kind. The effect of much of the legislation in this area is to protect businesses from the claims of those they have harmed by their actions. There is a long list of legalized nuisances.

The position has been summarized in Halsbury's *Laws of England* as follows:

Where the legislature directs that a thing shall in all events be done or authorises certain works at a particular place for a specific purpose or grants powers with the intention that they shall be exercised, although leaving some discretion as to the mode of exercise, no action will lie at common law for nuisance or damage which is the inevitable result of carrying out the statutory powers so conferred. This is so whether the act causing the damage is authorised for public purposes or private profit. Acts done under powers granted by persons to whom Parliament has delegated authority to grant such powers, for example, under provisional orders of the Board of Trade, are regarded as having been done under statutory authority. In the absence of negligence it seems that a body exercising statutory powers will not be liable to an action merely because it might, by acting in a different way, have minimised an injury.

Instances are next given of freedom from liability for acts authorised:

An action has been held not to be against a body exercising its statutory powers without negligence in respect of the flooding of land by water escaping from watercourses, from water pipes, from drains, or from a canal; the escape of fumes from sewers; the escape of sewage; the subsidence of a road over a sewer; vibration or noise caused by a railway; fires caused by authorised acts; the pollution of a stream where statutory requirements to use the best known method of purifying before discharging the effluent have been satisfied; interference with a telephone or telegraph system by an electric tramway; the insertion of poles for tramways in the subsoil; annoyance caused by things reasonably necessary for the excavation of authorised works; accidental damage caused by the placing of a grating in a roadway; the escape of tar acid; or interference with the access of a frontager by a street shelter or safety railings on the edge of a pavement.[1]

The legal position in the United States would seem to be essentially the same as in England, except that the power of the legislatures to

---

[1]See 30 Halsbury, *Laws of England* 690-91 (3d ed. 1960), Article on Public Authorities and Public Officers.

authorise what would otherwise be nuisances under the common law, at least without giving compensation to the person harmed, is somewhat more limited, as it is subject to constitutional restrictions.[1] Nonetheless, the power is there and cases more or less identical with the English cases can be found. The question has arisen in an acute form in connection with airports and the operation of aeroplanes. The case of *Delta Air Corporation v. Kersey, Kersey v. City of Atlanta*[2] is a good example. Mr. Kersey bought land and built a house on it. Some years later the City of Atlanta constructed an airport on land immediately adjoining that of Mr. Kersey. It was explained that his property was "a quiet, peaceful and proper location for a home before the airport was built, but dust, noises and low flying of airplanes caused by the operation of the airport have rendered his property unsuitable as a home," a state of affairs which was described in the report of the case with a wealth of distressing detail. The judge first referred to an earlier case, *Thrasher v. City of Atlanta*[3] in which it was noted that the City of Atlanta had been expressly authorised to operate an airport.

> By this franchise aviation was recognised as a lawful business and also as an enterprise affected with a public interest ... all persons using [the airport] in the manner contemplated by law are within the protection and immunity of the franchise granted by the municipality. An airport is not a nuisance per se, although it might become such from the manner of its construction or operation.

Since aviation was a lawful business affected with a public interest and the construction of the airport was authorised by statute, the judge next referred to *Georgia Railroad and Banking Co. v. Maddox*[4] in which it was said:

Where a railroad terminal yard is located and its construction authorized, under statutory powers, if it be constructed and operated in a proper manner, it cannot be adjudged a nuisance. Accordingly, injuries and inconveniences to persons residing near such a yard, from noises of locomotives, rumbling of cars, vibrations produced thereby, and smoke, cinders, soot and the like, which result from the ordinary and necessary, therefore proper, use and operation of such a yard, are not nuisances, but are the necessary concomitants of the franchise granted.

In view of this, the judge decided that the noise and dust complained of by Mr. Kersey "may be deemed to be incidental to the proper operation of an airport, and as such they cannot be said to constitute a nuisance." But the complaint against low flying was different:

> ... can it be said that flights ... at such a low height [25 to 50 feet above Mr. Kersey's house] as to be imminently dangerous to ... life and health ... are a necessary concomitant of an airport? We do not think this question can be answered in the affirmative. No reason appears why the city could not obtain lands of an area [sufficiently large] ... as not to require such low flights.... For the sake of public convenience adjoining-property owners must suffer such inconvenience from noise and dust as result from the usual and proper operation of an airport, but their private rights are entitled to preference in the eyes of the law where the inconvenience is not one demanded by a properly constructed and operated airport.

Of course this assumed that the City of Atlanta could prevent the low flying and continue to operate the airport. The judge therefore added:

From all that appears, the conditions causing the low flying may be remedied; but if on the trial it should appear that it is indispensable to the public interest that the airport should continue to be operated in its present condition, it may be said that the petitioner should be denied injunctive relief.

---

[1] See Prosser, *op. cit. supra* n. 16 at 421; Harper and James, *op. cit. supra* n. 16 at 86-87.

[2] Supreme Court of Georgia 193 Ga. 862, 20 S.E. 2d 245 (1942).

[3] 178 Ga. 514, 173 S.E. 817 (1934).

[4] 116 Ga. 64, 42 S.E. 315 (1902).

In the course of another aviation case, *Smith v. New England Aircraft Co.*,[1] the court surveyed the law in the United States regarding the legalizing of nuisances and it is apparent that, in the broad, it is very similar to that found in England:

> It is the proper function of the legislative department of government in the exercise of the police power to consider the problems and risks that arise from the use of new inventions and endeavor to adjust private rights and harmonize conflicting interests by comprehensive statutes for the public welfare.... There are ... analogies where the invasion of the airspace over underlying land by noise, smoke, vibration, dust and disagreeable odors, having been authorized by the legislative department of government and not being in effect a condemnation of the property although in some measure depreciating its market value, must be borne by the landowner without compensation or remedy. Legislative sanction makes that lawful which otherwise might be a nuisance. Examples of this are damages to adjacent land arising from smoke, vibration and noise in the operation of a railroad ...; the noise of ringing factory bells ...; the abatement of nuisances ...; the erection of steam engines and furnaces ...; unpleasant odors connected with sewers, oil refining and storage of naphtha....

Most economists seem to be unaware of all this. When they are prevented from sleeping at night by the roar of jet planes overhead (publicly authorised and perhaps publicly operated), are unable to think (or rest) in the day because of the noise and vibration from passing trains (publicly authorised and perhaps publicly operated), find it difficult to breathe because of the odour from a local sewage farm (publicly authorised and perhaps publicly operated) and are unable to escape because their driveways are blocked by a road obstruction (without any doubt, publicly devised), their nerves frayed and mental balance disturbed, they proceed to declaim about the disadvantages of private enterprise and the need for Government regulation.

While most economists seem to be under a misapprehension concerning the character of the situation with which they are dealing, it is also the case that the activities which they would like

to see stopped or curtailed may well be socially justified. It is all a question of weighing up the gains that would accrue from eliminating these harmful effects against the gains that accrue from allowing them to continue. Of course, it is likely that an extension of Government economic activity will often lead to this protection against action for nuisance being pushed further than is desirable. For one thing, the Government is likely to look with a benevolent eye on enterprises which it is itself promoting. For another, it is possible to describe the committing of a nuisance by public enterprise in a much more pleasant way than when the same thing is done by private enterprise. In the words of Lord Justice Sir Alfred Denning:

> ... the significance of the social revolution of today is that, whereas in the past the balance was much too heavily in favor of the rights of property and freedom of contract, Parliament has repeatedly intervened so as to give the public good its proper place.[2]

There can be little doubt that the Welfare State is likely to bring an extension of that immunity from liability for damage, which economists have been in the habit of condemning (although they have tended to assume that this immunity was a sign of too little Government intervention in the economic system). For example, in Britain, the powers of local authorities are regarded as being either absolute or conditional. In the first category, the local authority has no discretion in exercising the power conferred on it. "The absolute power may be said to cover all the necessary consequences of its direct operation even if such consequences amount to nuisance." On the other hand, a conditional power may only be exercised in such a way that the consequences do not constitute a nuisance.

> It is the intention of the legislature which determines whether a power is absolute or conditional.... [As] there is the possibility that the social policy of the legislature may change from time to time, a power which in one era would be construed as being conditional, might in another era be interpreted as being absolute in order to further the policy of the Welfare State.

[1]270 Mass. 511, 523, 170 N.E. 385, 390 (1930).

[2]See Sir Alfred Denning, *Freedom Under the Law* 71 (1949).

This point is one which should be borne in mind when considering some of the older cases upon this aspect of the law of nuisance.[1]

It would seem desirable to summarize the burden of this long section. The problem which we face in dealing with actions which have harmful effects is not simply one of restraining those responsible for them. What has to be decided is whether the gain from preventing the harm is greater than the loss which would be suffered elsewhere as a result of stopping the action which produces the harm. In a world in which there are costs of rearranging the rights established by the legal system, the courts, in cases relating to nuisance, are, in effect, making a decision on the economic problem and determining how resources are to be employed. It was argued that the courts are conscious of this and that they often make, although not always in a very explicit fashion, a comparison between what would be gained and what lost by preventing actions which have harmful effects. But the delimitation of rights is also the result of statutory enactments. Here we also find evidence of an appreciation of the reciprocal nature of the problem. While statutory enactments add to the list of nuisances, action is also taken to legalize what would otherwise be nuisances under the common law. The kind of situation which economists are prone to consider as requiring corrective Government action is, in fact, often the result of Government action. Such action is not necessarily unwise. But there is a real danger that extensive Government intervention in the economic system may lead to the protection of those responsible for harmful effects being carried too far.

VIII. Pigou's Treatment in "The Economics of Welfare"

The fountainhead for the modern economic analysis of the problem discussed in this article is Pigou's *Economics of Welfare* and, in particular, that section of Part II which deals with divergences between social and private net products which come about because

one person, A, in the course of rendering some service, for which payment is made, to a second person B, incidentally also renders services or disservices to other persons (not producers of like services), of such a sort that payment cannot be exacted from the benefited parties or compensation enforced on behalf of the injured parties.[2]

Pigou tells us that his aim in Part II of *The Economics of Welfare* is

to ascertain how far the free play of self-interest, acting under the existing legal system, tends to distribute the country's resources in the way most favorable to the production of a large national dividend, and how far it is feasible for State action to improve upon 'natural' tendencies.[3]

To judge from the first part of this statement, Pigou's purpose is to discover whether any improvements could be made in the existing arrangements which determine the use of resources. Since Pigou's conclusion is that improvements could be made, one might have expected him to continue by saying that he proposed to set out the changes required to bring them about. Instead, Pigou adds a phrase which contrasts "natural" tendencies with State action, which seems in some sense to equate the present arrangements with "natural" tendencies and to imply that what is required to bring about these improvements is State action (if feasible). That this is more or less Pigou's position is evident from Chapter 1 of Part II.[4] Pigou starts by referring to "optimistic followers of the classical

[1] M. B. Cairns, *The Law of Tort in Local Government* 28-32 (1954).

[2] A. C. Pigou, *The Economics of Welfare* 183 (4th ed. 1932). My references will all be to the fourth edition but the argument and examples examined in this article remained substantially unchanged from the first edition in 1920 to the fourth in 1932. A large part (but not all) of this analysis had appeared previously in *Wealth and Welfare* (1912).

[3] *Id.* at xii.

[4] *Id.* at 127-30.

economists"[1] who have argued that the value of production would be maximised if the Government refrained from any interference in the economic system and the economic arrangements were those which come about "naturally." Pigou goes on to say that if self-interest does promote economic welfare, it is because human institutions have been devised to make it so. (This part of Pigou's argument, which he develops with the aid of a quotation from Cannan, seems to me to be essentially correct.) Pigou concludes:

> But even in the most advanced States there are failures and imperfections.... there are many obstacles that prevent a community's resources from being distributed ... in the most efficient way. The study of these constitutes our present problem.... its purpose is essentially practical. It seeks to bring into clearer light some of the ways in which it now is, or eventually may become, feasible for governments to control the play of economic forces in such ways as to promote the economic welfare, and through that, the total welfare, of their citizens as a whole.[2]

Pigou's underlying thought would appear to be: Some have argued that no State action is needed. But the system has performed as well as it has because of State action. Nonetheless, there are still imperfections. What additional State action is required?

If this is a correct summary of Pigou's position, its inadequacy can be demonstrated by examining the first example he gives of a divergence between private and social products.

> It might happen ... that costs are thrown upon people not directly concerned, through, say, uncompensated damage done to surrounding woods by sparks from railway engines. All such effects must be included—some of them will be positive, others negative elements—in reckoning up the social net product of the marginal

increment of any volume of resources turned into any use or place.[3]

The example used by Pigou refers to a real situation. In Britain, a railway does not normally have to compensate those who suffer damage by fire caused by sparks from an engine. Taken in conjunction with what he says in Chapter 9 of Part II, I take Pigou's policy recommendations to be, first, that there should be State action to correct this "natural" situation and, second, that the railways should be forced to compensate those whose woods are burnt. If this is a correct interpretation of Pigou's position, I would argue that the first recommendation is based on a misapprehension of the facts and that the second is not necessarily desirable.

Let us consider the legal position. Under the heading "Sparks from engines," we find the following in Halsbury's *Laws of England*:

> If railway undertakers use steam engines on their railway without express statutory authority to do so, they are liable, irrespective of any negligence on their part, for fires caused by sparks from engines. Railway undertakers are, however, generally given statutory authority to use steam engines on their railway; accordingly, if an engine is constructed with the precautions which science suggests against fire and is used without negligence, they are not responsible at common law for any damage which may be done by sparks.... In the construction of an engine the undertaker is bound to use all the discoveries which science has put within its reach in order to avoid doing harm, provided they are such as it is reasonable to require the company to adopt, having proper regard to the likelihood of the damage and to the cost and convenience of the remedy; but it is not negligence on the part of an undertaker if it refuses to use an apparatus the efficiency of which is open to bona fide doubt.

To this general rule, there is a statutory exception arising from the Railway (Fires) Act, 1905, as amended in 1923. This concerns agricultural land or agricultural crops.

> In such a case the fact that the engine was used under statutory powers does not affect the liability of the company in an action for the

---

[1]In *Wealth and Welfare*, Pigou attributes the "optimism" to Adam Smith himself and not to his followers. He there refers to the "highly optimistic theory of Adam Smith that the national dividend, in given circumstances of demand and supply, tends 'naturally' to a maximum" (p. 104).

[2]Pigou, *op. cit. supra* n. 35 at 129-30.

---

[3]*Id.* at 134.

damage…. These provisions, however, only apply where the claim for damage … does not exceed £200, [£100 in the 1905 Act] and where written notice of the occurrence of the fire and the intention to claim has been sent to the company within seven days of the occurrence of the damage and particulars of the damage in writing showing the amount of the claim in money not exceeding £200 have been sent to the company within twenty-one days.

Agricultural land does not include moorland or buildings and agricultural crops do not include those led away or stacked.[1] I have not made a close study of the parliamentary history of this statutory exception, but to judge from debates in the House of Commons in 1922 and 1923, this exception was probably designed to help the smallholder.[2]

Let us return to Pigou's example of uncompensated damage to surrounding woods caused by sparks from railway engines. This is presumably intended to show how it is possible "for State action to improve on 'natural' tendencies." If we treat Pigou's example as referring to the position before 1905, or as being an arbitrary example (in that he might just as well have written "surrounding buildings" instead of "surrounding woods"), then it is clear that the reason why compensation was not paid must have been that the railway had statutory authority to run steam engines (which relieved it of liability for fires caused by sparks). That this was the legal position was established in 1860, in a case, oddly enough, which concerned the burning of surrounding woods by a railway,[3] and the law on this point has not been changed (apart from the one exception) by a century of railway legislation, including nationalisation. If we treat Pigou's example of "uncompensated damage done to surrounding woods by sparks from railway engines" literally, and assume that it refers to the period after 1905, then it is clear

---

[1]See 31 Halsbury, *Laws of England* 474-75 (3d ed. 1960), Article on Railways and Canals, from which this summary of the legal position, and all quotations, are taken.

[2]See 152 H.C. Deb. 2622-63 (1922); 161 H.C. Deb. 2935-55 (1923).

[3]*Vaughan v. Taff Vale Railway Co.*, 3 H. and N. 743 (Ex. 1858) and 5 H. and N. 679 (Ex. 1860).

---

that the reason why compensation was not paid must have been that the damage was more than £100 (in the first edition of *The Economics of Welfare*) or more than £200 (in later editions) or that the owner of the wood failed to notify the railway in writing within seven days of the fire or did not send particulars of the damage, in writing, within twenty-one days. In the real world, Pigou's example could only exist as a result of a deliberate choice of the legislature. It is not, of course, easy to imagine the construction of a railway in a state of nature. The nearest one can get to this is presumably a railway which uses steam engines "without express statutory authority." However, in this case the railway would be obliged to compensate those whose woods it burnt down. That is to say, compensation would be paid in the absence of Government action. The only circumstances in which compensation would not be paid would be those in which there had been Government action. It is strange that Pigou, who clearly thought it desirable that compensation should be paid, should have chosen this particular example to demonstrate how it is possible "for State action to improve on 'natural' tendencies."

Pigou seems to have had a faulty view of the facts of the situation. But it also seems likely that he was mistaken in his economic analysis. It is not necessarily desirable that the railway should be required to compensate those who suffer damage by fires caused by railway engines. I need not show here that, if the railway could make a bargain with everyone having property adjoining the railway line and there were no costs involved in making such bargains, it would not matter whether the railway was liable for damage caused by fires or not. This question has been treated at length in earlier sections. The problem is whether it would be desirable to make the railway liable in conditions in which it is too expensive for such bargains to be made. Pigou clearly thought it was desirable to force the railway to pay compensation and it is easy to see the kind of argument that would have led him to this conclusion. Suppose a railway is considering whether to run an additional train or to increase the speed of an existing train or to install spark-preventing devices on its engines. If the railway were not liable for fire damage, then, when making these decisions, it would not take into account as a cost the increase in damage resulting from the additional train or the faster train or the failure to install spark-preventing devices. This is the source of the divergence between private and social net products. It results in the railway performing acts which will lower the value of total production—and which it would not do if it were liable for the damage. This can be shown by means of an arithmetical example.

Consider a railway, which is *not* liable for damage by fires caused by sparks from its engines, which runs two trains per day on a certain line. Suppose that running one train per day would enable the railway to perform services worth $150 per annum and running two trains a day would enable the railway to perform services worth $250 per annum. Suppose further that the cost of running one train is $50 per annum and two trains $110 per annum. Assuming perfect competition, the cost equals the fall in the value of production elsewhere due to the employment of additional factors of production by the railway. Clearly the railway would find it profitable to run two trains per day. But suppose that running one train per day would destroy by fire crops worth (on an average over the year) $60 and two trains a day would result in the destruction of crops worth $120. In these circumstances running one train per day would raise the value of total production but the running of a second train would reduce the value of total production. The second train would enable additional railway services worth $100 per annum to be performed. But the fall in the value of production elsewhere would be $100 per annum; $50 as a result of the employment of additional factors of production and $60 as a result of the destruction of crops. Since it would be better if the second train were not run and since it would not run if the railway were liable for damage caused to crops, the conclusion that the railway should be made liable for the damage seems irresistible. Undoubtedly it is this kind of reasoning which underlies the Pigovian position.

The conclusion that it would be better if the second train did not run is correct. The conclusion that it is desirable that the railway should be made liable for the damage it causes is wrong. Let us change our assumption concerning the rule of liability. Suppose that the railway is liable for damage from fires caused by sparks from the engine. A farmer on lands adjoining the railway is then in the position that, if his crop is destroyed by fires caused by the railway, he will receive the market price from the railway; but if his crop is not damaged, he will receive the market price by sale. It therefore becomes a

matter of indifference to him whether his crop is damaged by fire or not. The position is very different when the railway is *not* liable. Any crop destruction through railway-caused fires would then reduce the receipts of the farmer. He would therefore take out of cultivation any land for which the damage is likely to be greater than the net return of the land (for reasons explained at length in Section III). A change from a regime in which the railway is *not* liable for damage to one in which it *is* liable is likely therefore to lead to an increase in the amount of cultivation on lands adjoining the railway. It will also, of course, lead to an increase in the amount of crop destruction due to railway-caused fires.

Let us return to our arithmetical example. Assume that, with the changed rule of liability, there is a doubling in the amount of crop destruction due to railway-caused fires. With one train per day, crops worth $120 would be destroyed each year and two trains per day would lead to the destruction of crops worth $240. We saw previously that it would not be profitable to run the second train if the railway had to pay $60 per annum as compensation for damage. With damage at $120 per annum the loss from running the second train would be $60 greater. But now let us consider the first train. The value of the transport services furnished by the first train is $150. The cost of running the train is $50. The amount that the railway would have to pay out as compensation for damage is $120. It follows that it would not be profitable to run any trains. With the figures in our example we reach the following result: if the railway is not liable for fire-damage, two trains per day would be run; if the railway is liable for fire-damage, it would cease operations altogether. Does this mean that it is better that there should be no railway? This question can be resolved by considering what would happen to the value of total production if it were decided to exempt the railway from liability for fire-damage, thus bringing it into operation (with two trains per day).

The operation of the railway would enable transport services worth $250 to be performed. It would also mean the employment of factors of production which would reduce the value of production elsewhere by $100. Furthermore it would mean the destruction of crops worth $120. The coming of the railway will also have led to the abandonment of cultivation of some land. Since we know that, had this land been cultivated, the value of the crops destroyed by fire would have been $120, and since it is unlikely that the total crop on this land would have been destroyed, it seems reasonable to suppose that the value of the crop yield on this land would have been higher than this. Assume it would have been $160. But the abandonment of cultivation would have released factors of production for employment elsewhere. All we know is that the amount by which the value of production elsewhere will increase will be less than $160. Suppose that it is $150. Then the gain from operating the railway would be $250 (the value of the transport services) minus $100 (the cost of the factors of production) minus $120 (the value of crops destroyed by fire) minus $160 (the fall in the value of crop production due to the abandonment of cultivation) plus $150 (the value of production elsewhere of the released factors of production). Overall, operating the railway will increase the value of total production by $20. With these figures it is clear that it is better that the railway should not be liable for the damage it causes, thus enabling it to operate profitably. Of course, by altering the figures, it could be shown that there are other cases in which it would be desirable that the railway should be liable for the damage it causes. It is enough for my purpose to show that, from an economic point of view, a situation in which there is "uncompensated damage done to surrounding woods by sparks from railway engines" is not necessarily undesirable. Whether it is desirable or not depends on the particular circumstances.

How is it that the Pigovian analysis seems to give the wrong answer? The reason is that Pigou does not seem to have noticed that his analysis is dealing with an entirely different question. The analysis as such is correct. But it is quite illegitimate for Pigou to draw the particular conclusion he does. The question at issue is not whether it is desirable to run an additional train or a faster train or to install smoke-preventing devices; the question at issue is whether it is desirable to have a system in which the railway has to compensate those who suffer damage from the fires which it causes or one in which the railway does not have to compensate them. When an economist is comparing alternative social arrangements, the proper procedure is to compare the total social product yielded by these different arrangements. The comparison of private and social products is neither here nor there. A simple example will demonstrate this. Imagine a town in which there are traffic lights.

A motorist approaches an intersection and stops because the light is red. There are no cars approaching the intersection on the other street. If the motorist ignored the red signal, no accident would occur and the total product would increase because the motorist would arrive earlier at his destination. Why does he not do this? The reason is that if he ignored the light he would be fined. The private product from crossing the street is less than the social product. Should we conclude from this that the total product would be greater if there were no fines for failing to obey traffic signals? The Pigovian analysis shows us that it is possible to conceive of better worlds than the one in which we live. But the problem is to devise practical arrangements which will correct defects in one part of the system without causing more serious harm in other parts.

I have examined in considerable detail one example of a divergence between private and social products and I do not propose to make any further examination of Pigou's analytical system. But the main discussion of the problem considered in this article is to be found in that part of Chapter 9 in Part II which deals with Pigou's second class of divergence and it is of interest to see how Pigou develops his argument. Pigou's own description of this second class of divergence was quoted at the beginning of this section. Pigou distinguishes between the case in which a person renders services for which he receives no payment and the case in which a person renders disservices and compensation is not given to the injured parties. Our main attention has, of course, centred on this second case. It is therefore rather astonishing to find, as was pointed out to me by Professor Francesco Forte, that the problem of the smoking chimney—the "stock instance"[1] or "classroom example"[2] of the second case—is used by Pigou as an example of the first case (services rendered without payment) and is never mentioned, at any rate explicitly, in connection with the second case.[3] Pigou points out that factory owners who

[1]Sir Dennis Robertson, I *Lectures on Economic Principles* 162 (1957).

[2]E. J. Mishan, "The Meaning of Efficiency in Economics," 189, *The Banker's Magazine* 482 (June 1960).

[3]Pigou, *op. cit. supra* n. 35 at 184.

devote resources to preventing their chimneys from smoking render services for which they receive no payment. The implication, in the light of Pigou's discussion later in the chapter, is that a factory owner with a smoking chimney should be given a bounty to induce him to install smoke-preventing devices. Most modern economists would suggest that the owner of the factory with the smokey chimney should be taxed. It seems a pity that economists (apart from Professor Forte) do not seem to have noticed this feature of Pigou's treatment since a realisation that the problem could be tackled in either of these two ways would probably have led to an explicit recognition of its reciprocal nature.

In discussing the second case (disservices without compensation to those damaged), Pigou says that they are rendered "when the owner of a site in a residential quarter of a city builds a factory there and so destroys a great part of the amenities of neighbouring sites; or, in a less degree, when he uses his site in such a way as to spoil the lighting of the house opposite; or when he invests resources in erecting buildings in a crowded centre, which by contracting the air-space and the playing room of the neighbourhood, tend to injure the health and efficiency of the families living there."[1] Pigou is, of course, quite right to describe such actions as "uncharged disservices." But he is wrong when he describes these actions as "anti-social."[2] They may or may not be. It is necessary to weight the harm against the good that will result. Nothing could be more "anti-social" than to oppose any action which causes any harm to anyone.

The example with which Pigou opens his discussion of "uncharged disservices" is not, as I have indicated, the case of the smokey chimney but the case of the overrunning rabbits: "... incidental uncharged disservices are rendered to third parties when the game-preserving activities of one occupier involve the overrunning of a neighboring occupier's land by rabbits.... " This example is of extraordinary interest, not so much because the economic analysis of the case is essentially any different from that of the other

examples, but because of the peculiarities of the legal position and the light it throws on the part which economics can play in what is apparently the purely legal question of the delimitation of rights.

The problem of legal liability for the actions of rabbits is part of the general subject of liability for animals.[3] I will, although with reluctance, confine my discussion to rabbits. The early cases relating to rabbits concerned the relations between the lord of the manor and commoners, since, from the thirteenth century on, it became usual for the lord of the manor to stock the commons with conies (rabbits), both for the sake of the meat and the fur. But in 1597, in *Boulston's* case, an action was brought by one landowner against a neighbouring landowner, alleging that the defendant had made coney-burrows and that the conies had increased and had destroyed the plaintiff's corn. The action failed for the reason that

> ... so soon as the coneys come on his neighbor's land he may kill them, for they are ferae naturae, and he who makes the coney-boroughs has no property in them, and he shall not be punished for the damage which the coneys do in which he has no property, and which the other may lawfully kill.[4]

---

[1]*Id.* at 185-86.

[2]*Id.* at 186 n. 1. For similar unqualified statements see Pigou's lecture "Some Aspects of the Housing Problem" in B. S. Rowntree and A. C. Pigou, "Lectures on Housing," in 18 *Manchester Univ. Lectures* (1914).

[3]See G. L. Williams, *Liability for Animals—An Account of the Development and Present Law of Tortious Liability for Animals. Distress Damage Feasant and the Duty to Fence, in Great Britain, Northern Ireland and the Common Law Dominions* (1939). Part Four, "The Action of Nuisance, in Relation to Liability for Animals," 236-62, is especially relevant to our discussion. The problem of liability for rabbits is discussed in this part, 238-47. I do not know how far the common law in the United States regarding liability for animals has diverged from that in Britain. In some Western States of the United States, the English common law regarding the duty to fence has not been followed, in part because "the considerable amount of open, uncleared land made it a matter of public policy to allow cattle to run at large" (Williams, *op. cit. supra* 227). This affords a good example of how a different set of circumstances may make it economically desirable to change the legal rule regarding the delimitation of rights.

[4]5 Coke (Vol. 3) 104 b. 77 Eng. Rep., 216, 217.

As *Boulston's* case has been treated as binding—Bray, J., in 1919, said that he was not aware that *Boulston's* case has ever been overruled or questioned[1]—Pigou's rabbit example undoubtedly represented the legal position at the time *The Economics of Welfare* was written.[2] And in this case, it is not far from the truth to say that the state of affairs which Pigou describes came about because of an absence of Government action (at any rate in the form of statutory enactments) and was the result of "natural" tendencies.

Nonetheless, *Boulston's* case is something of a legal curiosity and Professor Williams makes no secret of his distaste for this decision:

> The conception of liability in nuisance as being based upon ownership is the result, apparently, of a confusion with the action of cattle-trespass, and runs counter to both the principle and to the medieval authorities on the escape of water, smoke, and filth.... The prerequisite of any satisfactory treatment of the subject is the final abandonment of the pernicious doctrine in *Boulston's* case.... Once *Boulston's* case disappears, the way will be clear for a rational restatement of the whole subject, on lines that will harmonize with the principles prevailing in the rest of the law of nuisance.[3]

The judges in *Boulston's* case were, of course, aware that their view of the matter depended on distinguishing this case from one involving nuisance:

> This cause is not like to the cases put, on the other side, of erecting a lime-kiln, dyehouse, or the like; for there the annoyance is by the act of the parties who make them; but it is not so here, for the conies of themselves went into the plaintiff's land, and he might take them when

they came upon his land, and make profit of them.[4]

Professor Williams comments:

> Once more the atavistic idea is emerging that the animals are guilty and not the landowner. It is not, of course, a satisfactory principle to introduce into a modern law of nuisance. If A. erects a house or plants a tree so that the rain runs or drips from it onto B.'s land, this is A.'s act for which he is liable; but if A. introduces rabbits into his land so that they escape from it into B.'s, this is the act of the rabbits for which A. is not liable—such is the specious distinction resulting from *Boulston's* case.[5]

It has to be admitted that the decision in *Boulston's* case seems a little odd. A man may be liable for damage caused by smoke or unpleasant smells, without it being necessary to determine whether he owns the smoke or the smell. And the rule in *Boulston's* case has not always been followed in cases dealing with other animals. For example, in *Bland v. Yates*,[6] it was decided that an injunction could be granted to prevent someone from keeping an *unusual and excessive* collection of manure in which flies bred and which infested a neighbour's house. The question of who owned the flies was not raised. An economist would not wish to object because legal reasoning sometimes appears a little odd. But there is a sound economic reason for supporting Professor Williams' view that the problem of liability for animals (and particularly rabbits) should be brought within the ordinary law of nuisance. The reason is not that the man who harbours rabbits is solely responsible for the damage; the man whose crops are eaten is equally responsible. And given that the costs of market transactions make a rearrangement of rights impossible, unless we know the particular circumstances, we cannot say whether it is desirable or not to make the man who harbours rabbits responsible for the damage committed by the rabbits on neighbouring properties. The

---

[1]See *Stearn v. Prentice Bros. Ltd.* (1919), 1 K.B., 395, 397.

[2]I have not looked into recent cases. The legal position has also been modified by statutory enactments.

[3]Williams, *op. cit. supra* n. 49 at 242, 258.

[4]*Boulston v. Hardy*, Cro. Eliz., 547, 548, 77 Eng. Rep. 216.

[5]Williams, *op. cit. supra* n. 49 at 243.

[6]58 Sol.J. 612 (1913-1914).

objection to the rule in *Boulston's* case is that, under it, the harbourer of rabbits can *never* be liable. It fixes the rule of liability at one pole: and this is as undesirable, from an economic point of view, as fixing the rule at the other pole and making the harbourer of rabbits always liable. But, as we saw in Section VII, the law of nuisance, as it is in fact handled by the courts, is flexible and allows for a comparison of the utility of an act with the harm it produces. As Professor Williams says: "The whole law of nuisance is an attempt to reconcile and compromise between conflicting interests...."[1] To bring the problem of rabbits within the ordinary law of nuisance would not mean *inevitably* making the harbourer of rabbits liable for damage committed by the rabbits. This is not to say that the sole task of the courts in such cases is to make a comparison between the harm and the utility of an act. Nor is it to be expected that the courts will always decide correctly after making such a comparison. But unless the courts act very foolishly, the ordinary law of nuisance would seem likely to give economically more satisfactory results than adopting a rigid rule. Pigou's case of the overrunning rabbits affords an excellent example of how problems of law and economics are interrelated, even though the correct policy to follow would seem to be different from that envisioned by Pigou.

Pigou allows one exception to his conclusion that there is a divergence between private and social products in the rabbit example. He adds: "... unless ... the two occupiers stand in the relation of landlord and tenant, so that compensation is given in an adjustment of the rent."[2] This qualification is rather surprising since Pigou's first class of divergence is largely concerned with the difficulties of drawing up satisfactory contracts between landlords and tenants. In fact, all the recent cases on the problem of rabbits cited by Professor Williams involved disputes between landlords and tenants concerning sporting rights.[3] Pigou seems to make a distinction between the case in which no contract is possible (the second class) and that in which the contract is unsatisfactory (the first class). Thus he says that the second class of

divergences between private and social net product

cannot, like divergences due to tenancy laws, be mitigated by a modification of the contractual relation between any two contracting parties, because the divergence arises out of a service or disservice rendered to persons other than the contracting parties.[4]

But the reason why some activities are not the subject of contracts is exactly the same as the reason why some contracts are commonly unsatisfactory—it would cost too much to put the matter right. Indeed, the two cases are really the same since the contracts are unsatisfactory because they do not cover certain activities. The exact bearing of the discussion of the first class of divergence on Pigou's main argument is difficult to discover. He shows that in some circumstances contractual relations between landlord and tenant may result in a divergence between private and social products.[5] But he also goes on to show that Government-enforced compensation schemes and rent-controls will also produce divergences.[6] Furthermore, he shows that, when the Government is in a similar position to a private landlord, e.g. when granting a franchise to a public utility, exactly the same difficulties arise as when private individuals are involved.[7] The discussion is interesting but I have been unable to discover what general conclusions about economic policy, if any, Pigou expects us to draw from it.

Indeed, Pigou's treatment of the problems considered in this article is extremely elusive and the discussion of his views raises almost insuperable difficulties of interpretation. Consequently it is impossible to be sure that one has understood what Pigou really meant. Nevertheless, it is difficult to resist the conclusion, extraordinary though this may be in an economist of Pigou's stature, that the main source of this obscurity is that Pigou had not thought his position through.

---

[1]Williams, *op. cit. supra* n. 49 at 259.

[2]Pigou, *op. cit. supra* n. 35 at 185.

[3]Williams, *op. cit. supra* n. 49 at 244–47.

[4]Pigou, *op. cit. supra* n. 35 at 192.

[5]*Id.* 174–75.

[6]*Id.* 177–83.

[7]*Id.* 175–77.

IX.   The Pigovian Tradition

It is strange that a doctrine as faulty as that developed by Pigou should have been so influential, although part of its success has probably been due to the lack of clarity in the exposition. Not being clear, it was never clearly wrong. Curiously enough, this obscurity in the source has not prevented the emergence of a fairly well-defined oral tradition. What economists think they learn from Pigou, and what they tell their students, which I term the Pigovian tradition, is reasonably clear. I propose to show the inadequacy of this Pigovian tradition by demonstrating that both the analysis and the policy conclusions which it supports are incorrect.

I do not propose to justify my view as to the prevailing opinion by copious references to the literature. I do this partly because the treatment in the literature is usually so fragmentary, often involving little more than a reference to Pigou plus some explanatory comment, that detailed examination would be inappropriate. But the main reason for this lack of reference is that the doctrine, although based on Pigou, must have been largely the product of an oral tradition. Certainly economists with whom I have discussed these problems have shown a unanimity of opinion which is quite remarkable considering the meagre treatment accorded this subject in the literature. No doubt there are some economists who do not share the usual view but they must represent a small minority of the profession.

The approach to the problems under discussion is through an examination of the value of physical production. The private product is the value of the additional product resulting from a particular activity of a business. The social product equals the private product minus the fall in the value of production elsewhere for which no compensation is paid by the business. Thus, if 10 units of a factor (and no other factors) are used by a business to make a certain product with a value of $105; and the owner of this factor is not compensated for their use, which he is unable to prevent; and these 10 units of the factor would yield products in their best alternative use worth $100; then, the social product is $105 minus $100 or $5. If the business now pays for one unit of the factor and its price equals the value of its marginal product, then the social product rises to $15. If two units are paid for, the social product rises to $25 and so on until it reaches $105 when all units of the factor are paid for. It is not difficult to see why economists have so readily accepted this rather odd procedure. The analysis focuses on the individual business decision and since the use of certain resources is not allowed for in costs, receipts are reduced by the same amount. But of course, this means that the value of the social product has no social significance whatsoever. It seems to me preferable to use the opportunity cost concept and to approach these problems by comparing the value of the product yielded by factors in alternative uses or by alternative arrangements. The main advantage of a pricing system is that it leads to the employment of factors in places where the value of the product yielded is greatest and does so at less cost than alternative systems (I leave aside that a pricing system also eases the problem of the redistribution of income). But if through some God-given natural harmony factors flowed to the places where the value of the product yielded was greatest without any use of the pricing system and consequently there was no compensation, I would find it a source of surprise rather than a cause for dismay.

The definition of the social product is queer but this does not mean that the conclusions for policy drawn from the analysis are necessarily wrong. However, there are bound to be dangers in an approach which diverts attention from the basic issues and there can be little doubt that it has been responsible for some of the errors in current doctrine. The belief that it is desirable that the business which causes harmful effects should be forced to compensate those who suffer damage (which was exhaustively discussed in Section VIII in connection with Pigou's railway sparks example) is undoubtedly the result of not comparing the total product obtainable with alternative social arrangements.

The same fault is to be found in proposals for solving the problem of harmful effects by the use of taxes or bounties. Pigou lays considerable stress on this solution although he is, as usual, lacking in detail and qualified in his support.[1] Modern economists tend to think exclusively in terms of taxes and in a very precise way. The tax should be equal to the damage done and should therefore vary with the amount of the harmful effect. As it is not proposed that the proceeds of the tax should be paid to those suffering the

[1]Id. 192-4, 381 and *Public Finance* 94-100 (3d ed. 1947).

damage, this solution is not the same as that which would force a business to pay compensation to those damaged by its actions, although economists generally do not seem to have noticed this and tend to treat the two solutions as being identical.

Assume that a factory which emits smoke is set up in a district previously free from smoke pollution, causing damage valued at $100 per annum. Assume that the taxation solution is adopted and that the factory owner is taxed $100 per annum as long as the factory emits the smoke. Assume further that a smoke-preventing device costing $90 per annum to run is available. In these circumstances, the smoke-preventing device would be installed. Damage of $100 would have been avoided at an expenditure of $90 and the factory owner would be better off by $10 per annum. Yet the position achieved may not be optimal. Suppose that those who suffer the damage could avoid it by moving to other locations or by taking various precautions which would cost them, or be equivalent to a loss in income of, $40 per annum. Then there would be a gain in the value of production of $50 if the factory continued to emit its smoke and those now in the district moved elsewhere or made other adjustments to avoid the damage. If the factory owner is to be made to pay a tax equal to the damage caused, it would clearly be desirable to institute a double tax system and to make residents of the district pay an amount equal to the additional cost incurred by the factory owner (or the consumers of his products) in order to avoid the damage. In these conditions, people would not stay in the district or would take other measures to prevent the damage from occurring, when the costs of doing so were less than the costs that would be incurred by the producer to reduce the damage (the producer's object, of course, being not so much to reduce the damage as to reduce the tax payments). A tax system which was confined to a tax on the producer for damage caused would tend to lead to unduly high costs being incurred for the prevention of damage. Of course this could be avoided if it were possible to base the tax, not on the damage caused, but on the fall in the value of production (in its widest sense) resulting from the emission of smoke. But to do so would require a detailed knowledge of individual preferences and I am unable to imagine how the data needed for such a taxation system could be assembled. Indeed, the proposal to solve the smoke-pollution and

similar problems by the use of taxes bristles with difficulties: the problem of calculation, the difference between average and marginal damage, the interrelations between the damage suffered on different properties, etc. But it is unnecessary to examine these problems here. It is enough for my purpose to show that, even if the tax is exactly adjusted to equal the damage that would be done to neighbouring properties as a result of the emission of each additional puff of smoke, the tax would not necessarily bring about optimal conditions. An increase in the number of people living or of business operating in the vicinity of the smoke-emitting factory will increase the amount of harm produced by a given emission of smoke. The tax that would be imposed would therefore increase with an increase in the number of those in the vicinity. This will tend to lead to a decrease in the value of production of the factors employed by the factory, either because a reduction in production due to the tax will result in factors being used elsewhere in ways which are less valuable, or because factors will be diverted to produce means for reducing the amount of smoke emitted. But people deciding to establish themselves in the vicinity of the factory will not take into account this fall in the value of production which results from their presence. This failure to take into account costs imposed on others is comparable to the action of a factory owner in not taking into account the harm resulting from his emission of smoke. Without the tax, there may be too much smoke and too few people in the vicinity of the factory; but with the tax there may be too little smoke and too many people in the vicinity of the factory. There is no reason to suppose that one of these results is necessarily preferable.

I need not devote much space to discussing the similar error involved in the suggestion that smoke producing factories should, by means of zoning regulations, be removed from the districts in which the smoke causes harmful effects. When the change in the location of the factory results in a reduction in production, this obviously needs to be taken into account and weighed against the harm which would result from the factory remaining in that location. The aim of such regulation should not be to eliminate smoke pollution but rather to secure the optimum amount of smoke pollution, this being the amount which will maximise the value of production.

X.   A Change of Approach

It is my belief that the failure of economists to reach correct conclusions about the treatment of harmful effects cannot be ascribed simply to a few slips in analysis. It stems from basic defects in the current approach to problems of welfare economics. What is needed is a change of approach.

Analysis in terms of divergencies between private and social products concentrates attention on particular deficiencies in the system and tends to nourish the belief that any measure which will remove the deficiency is necessarily desirable. It diverts attention from those other changes in the system which are inevitably associated with the corrective measure, changes which may well produce more harm than the original deficiency. In the preceding sections of this article, we have seen many examples of this. But it is not necessary to approach the problem in this way. Economists who study problems of the firm habitually use an opportunity cost approach and compare the receipts obtained from a given combination of factors with alternative business arrangements. It would seem desirable to use a similar approach when dealing with questions of economic policy and to compare the total product yielded by alternative social arrangements. In this article, the analysis has been confined, as is usual in this part of economics, to comparisons of the value of production, as measured by the market. But it is, of course, desirable that the choice between different social arrangements for the solution of economic problems should be carried out in broader terms than this and that the total effect of these arrangements in all spheres of life should be taken into account. As Frank H. Knight has so often emphasized, problems of welfare economics must ultimately dissolve into a study of aesthetics and morale.

A second feature of the usual treatment of the problems discussed in this article is that the analysis proceeds in terms of a comparison between a state of laissez faire and some kind of ideal world. This approach inevitably leads to a looseness of thought since the nature of the alternatives being compared is never clear. In a state of laissez faire, is there a monetary, a legal or a political system and if so, what are they? In an ideal world, would there be a monetary, a legal or a political system and if so, what would they be? The answers to all these questions are shrouded in mystery and every man is free to draw whatever conclusions he likes. Actually very little analysis is required to show that an ideal world is better than a state of laissez faire, unless the definitions of a state of laissez faire and an ideal world happen to be the same. But the whole discussion is largely irrelevant for questions of economic policy since whatever we may have in mind as our ideal world, it is clear that we have not yet discovered how to get to it from where we are. A better approach would seem to be to start our analysis with a situation approximating that which actually exists, to examine the effects of a proposed policy change and to attempt to decide whether the new situation would be, in total, better or worse than the original one. In this way, conclusions for policy would have some relevance to the actual situation.

A final reason for the failure to develop a theory adequate to handle the problem of harmful effects stems from a faulty concept of a factor of production. This is usually thought of as a physical entity which the businessman acquires and uses (an acre of land, a ton of fertiliser) instead of as a right to perform certain (physical) actions. We may speak of a person owning land and using it as a factor of production but what the land-owner in fact possesses is the right to carry out a circumscribed list of actions. The rights of a land-owner are not unlimited. It is not even always possible for him to remove the land to another place, for instance, by quarrying it. And although it may be possible for him to exclude some people from using "his" land, this may not be true of others. For example, some people may have the right to cross the land. Furthermore, it may or may not be possible to erect certain types of buildings or to grow certain crops or to use particular drainage systems on the land. This does not come about simply because of Government regulation. It would be equally true under the common law. In fact it would be true under any system of law. A system in which the rights of individuals were unlimited would be one in which there were no rights to acquire.

If factors of production are thought of as rights, it becomes easier to understand that the right to do something which has a harmful effect (such as the creation of smoke, noise, smells, etc.) is also a factor of production. Just as we may use a piece of land in such a way as to prevent someone else from crossing it, or parking his car, or building his house upon it, so we may use it in such a way as to deny him a view or quiet or unpolluted air. The cost of exercising a right (of using a factor of production) is always the loss which is suffered elsewhere in consequence of the exercise of that right—the inability to cross land, to park a car, to build a house, to enjoy a view, to have peace and quiet or to breathe clean air.

It would clearly be desirable if the only actions performed were those in which what was gained was worth more than what was lost. But in choosing between social arrangements within the context of which individual decisions are made, we have to bear in mind that a change in the existing system which will lead to an improvement in some decisions may well lead to a worsening of others. Furthermore we have to take into account the costs involved in operating the various social arrangements (whether it be the working of a market or of a government department), as well as the costs involved in moving to a new system. In devising and choosing between social arrangements we should have regard for the total effect. This, above all, is the change in approach which I am advocating.

FASTGRAPH

On the following pages, selected diagrams from the textbook are reproduced. Remove these pages as needed, and use them in the classroom to assist you in notetaking. When your instructor uses an overhead transparency of an exhibit from the textbook, the corresponding page from FastGraph gives you a quick, easy-to-read copy of the same exhibit for taking notes, along with grid lines to help you reproduce other graphs from your instructor's lecture.

Exhibit 1–1. The Demand Curve

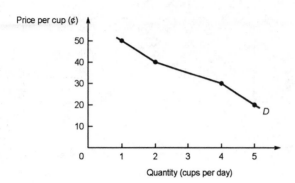

Exhibit 1–2. Shifting The Demand Curve

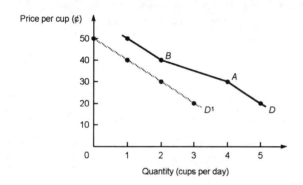

Exhibit 1–3. The Effect of a Sales Tax on Demand

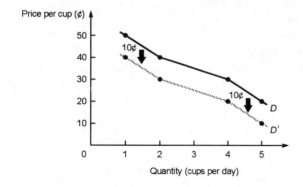

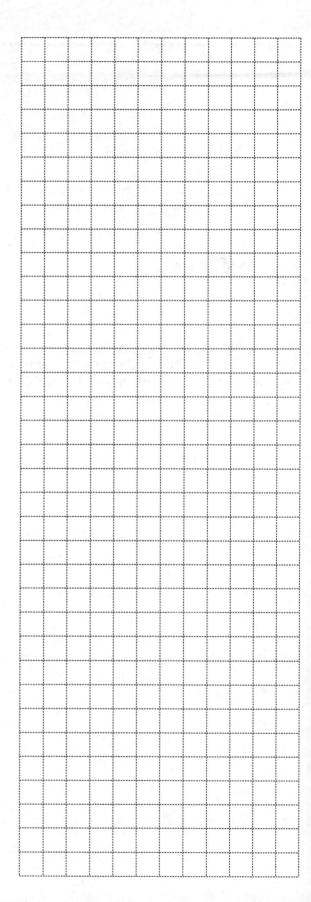

Exhibit 1–5. The Supply of Coffee

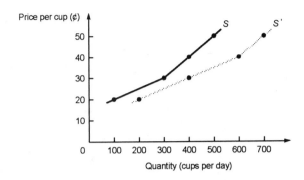

Exhibit 1–6. Effect of an Excise Tax

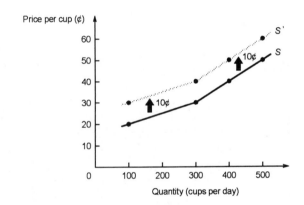

Exhibit 1–7. Equilibrium in the Market for Cement

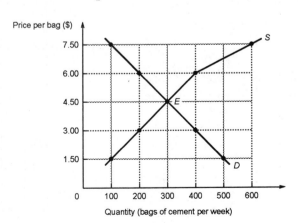

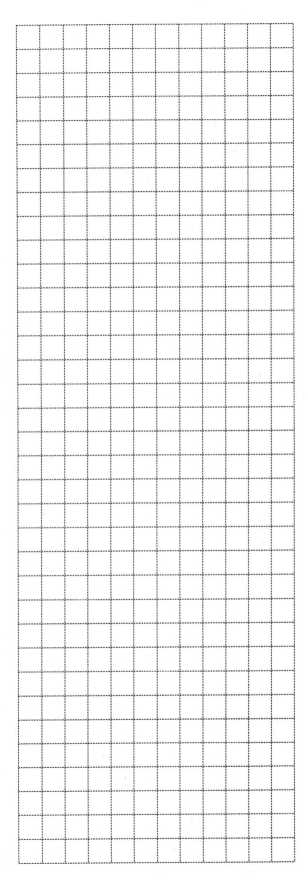

Exhibit 1–8. The Effects of Supply and Demand Shifts

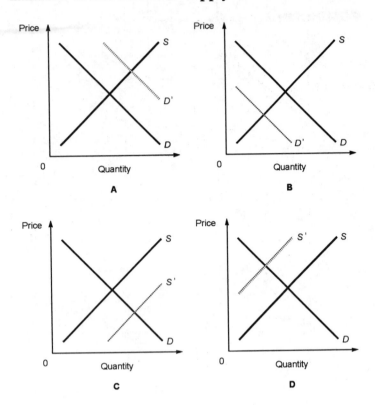

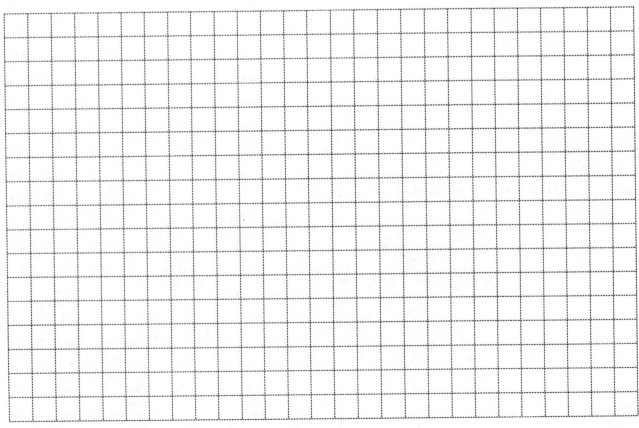

Exhibit 1–10. A Sales Tax versus an Excise Tax

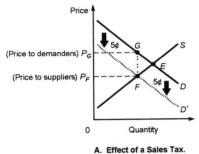

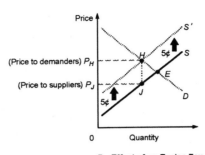

A. Effect of a Sales Tax.

B. Effect of an Excise Tax.

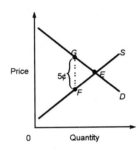

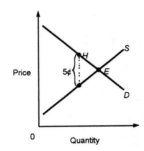

A′. A less cluttered version of Panel A.

B′. A less cluttered version of Panel B.

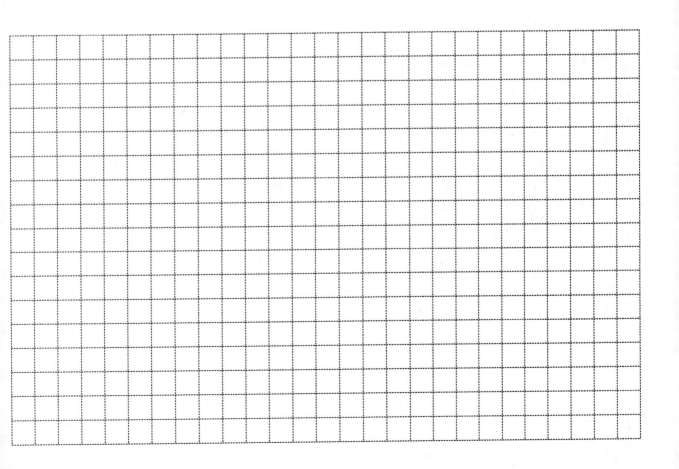

Exhibit 3–7. The Budget Line

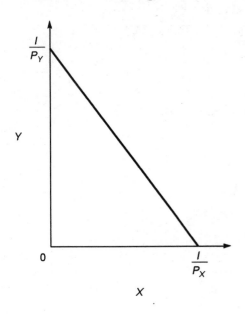

Exhibit 3–8. The Consumer Optimum

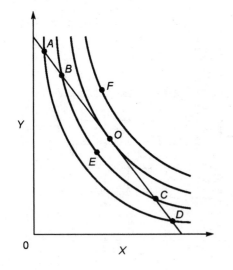

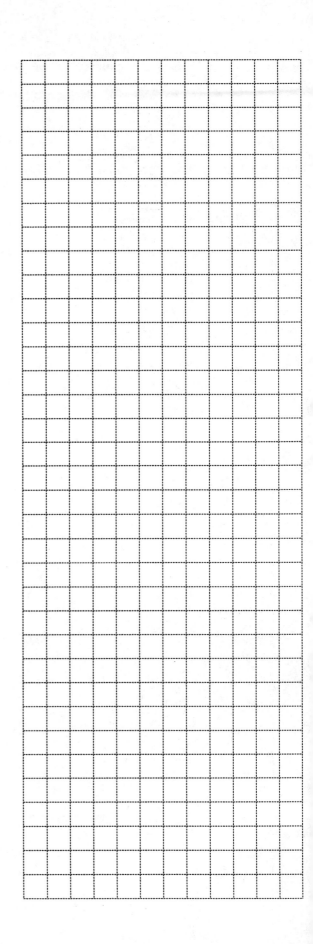

Exhibit 3–9. A Corner Solution

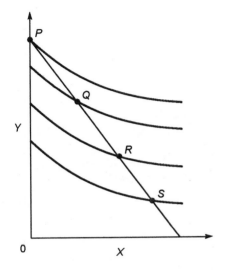

Exhibit 3–10. The Consumer's Choice with Nonconvex Indifference Curves

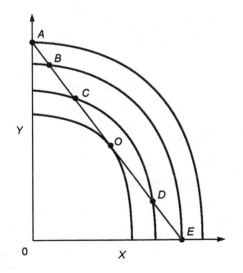

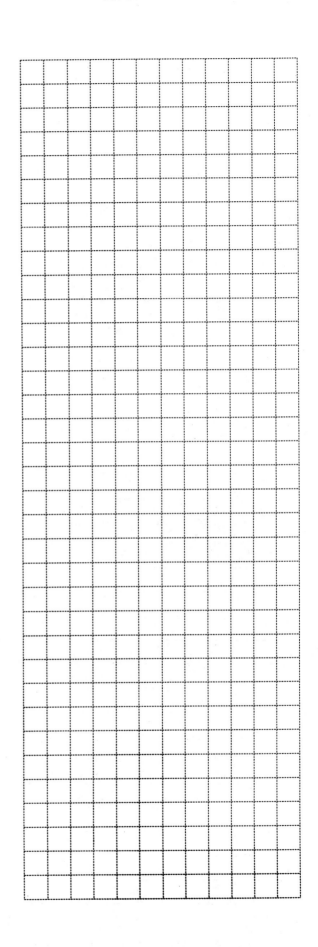

Exhibit 3–15. An Income Tax versus a Head Tax

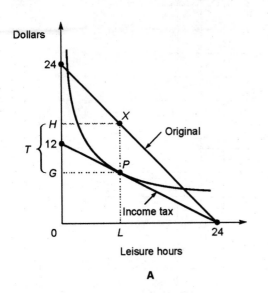

A

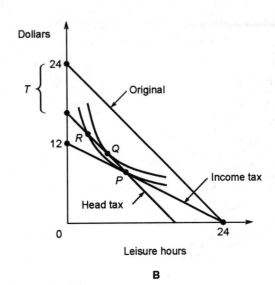

B

Exhibit 4–3. Normal versus Inferior Goods

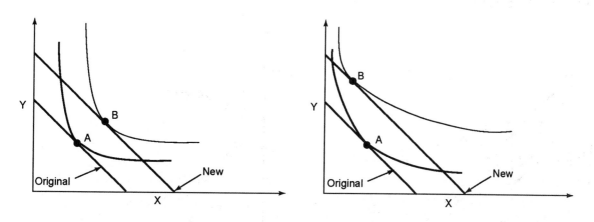

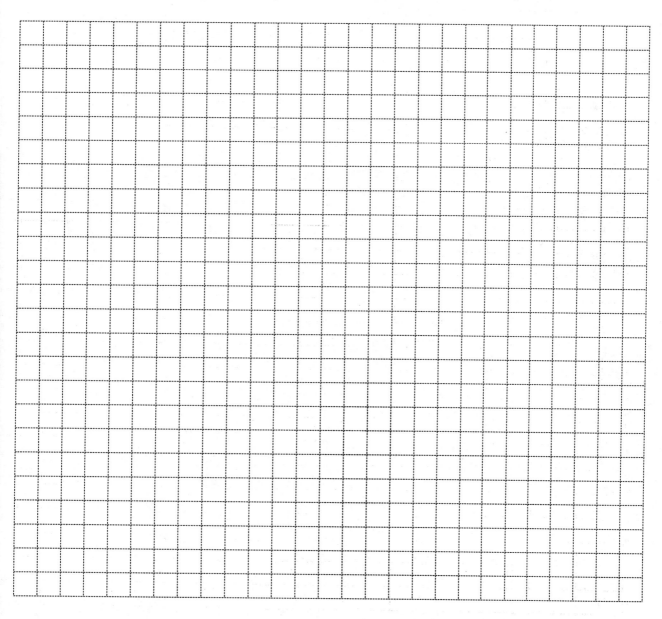

Exhibit 4–4. Deriving an Engel Curve

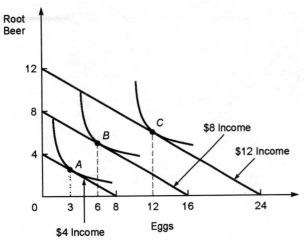

A. Beth's indifference curve

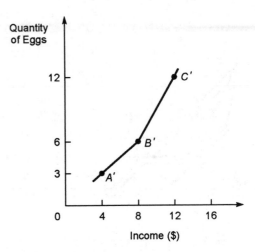

B. Beth's Engel curve

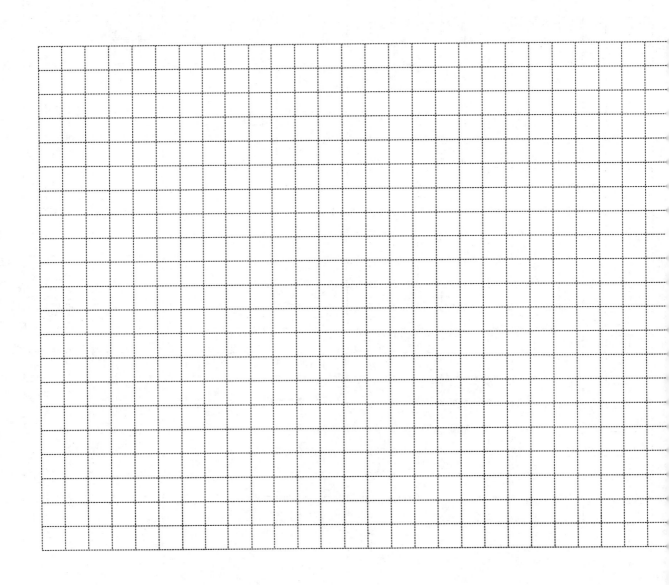

Exhibit 4–7. Non-Giffen versus Giffen Goods

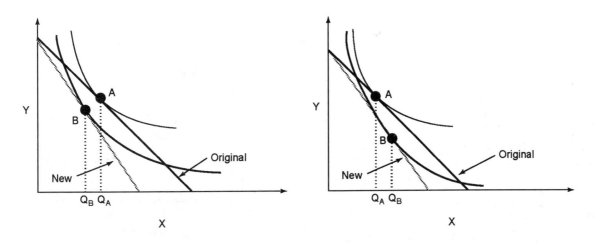

Exhibit 4-8. Deriving a Demand Curve

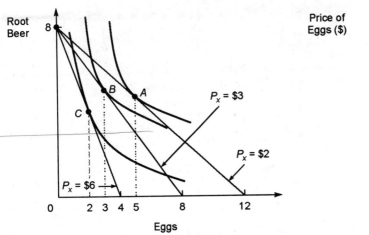

A: Beth's influence curves

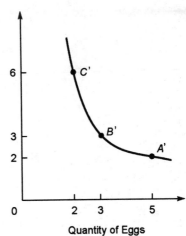

B: Beth's demand curve

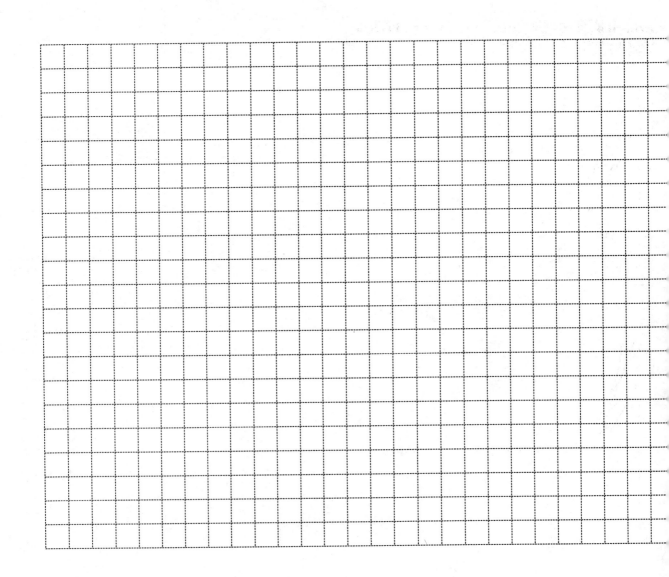

Exhibit 4–10. Substitution and Income Effects for a Normal Good

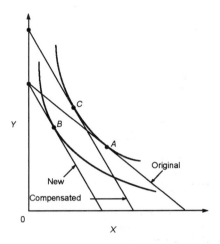

Exhibit 4–11. Substitution and Income Effects for Inferior and Giffen Goods

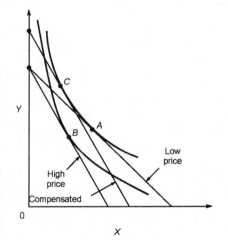

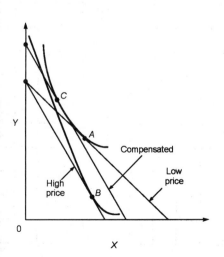

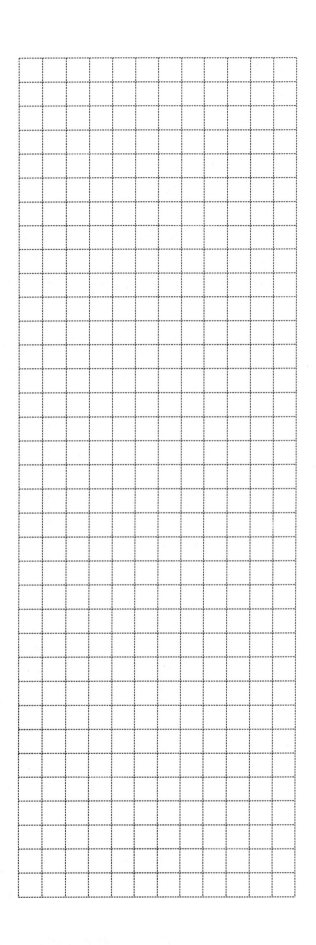

Exhibit 4–12. Compensated versus Ordinary Demand Curves

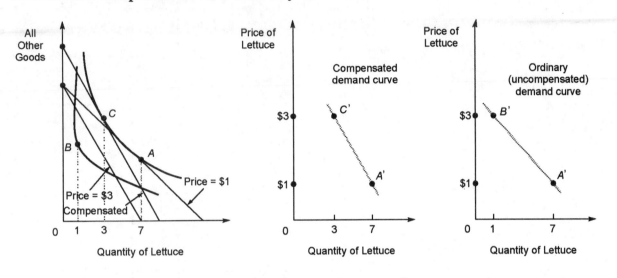

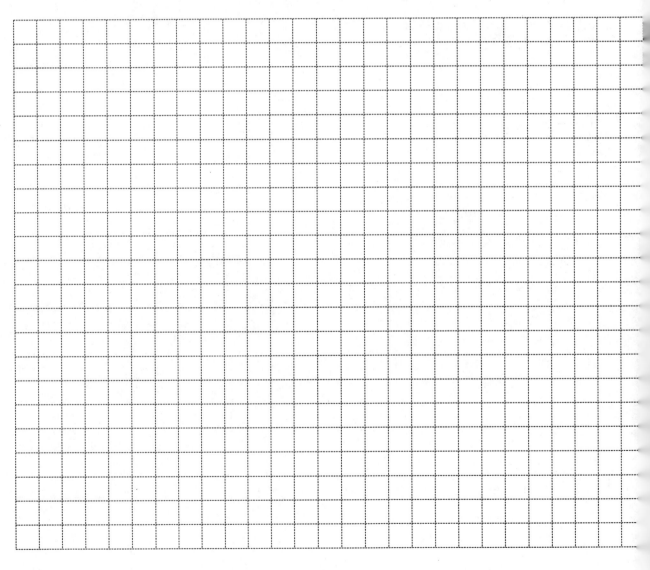

Exhibit 5–5. Maximizing Profits at the Tailor Dress Company

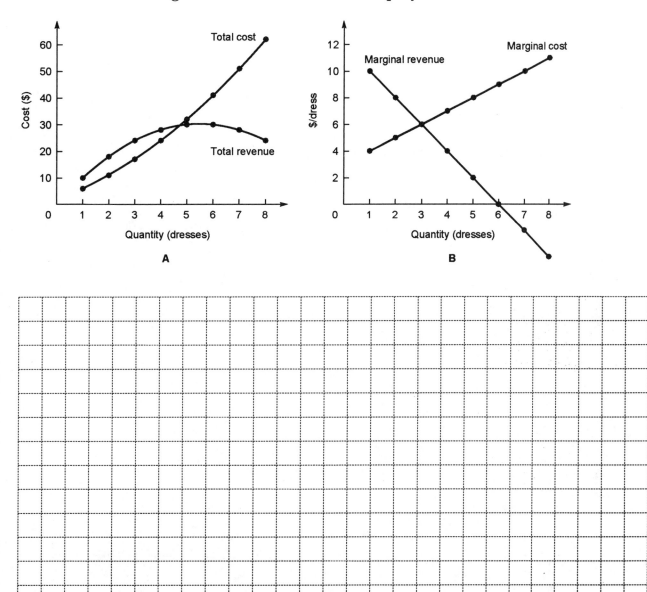

A

B

Exhibit 5–6. The Effect of a Rent Increase

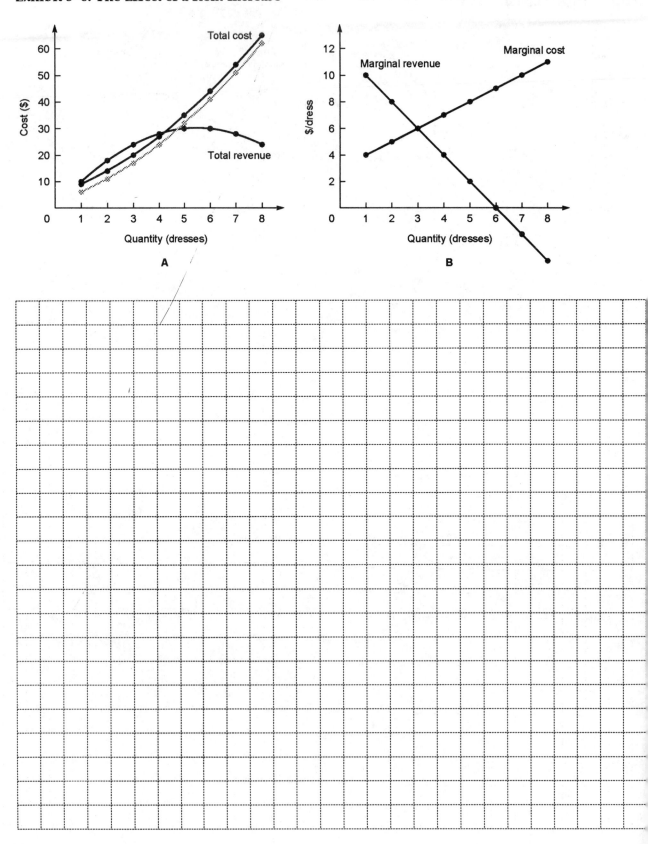

A

B

Exhibit 5–7. An Increase in the Price of Fabric

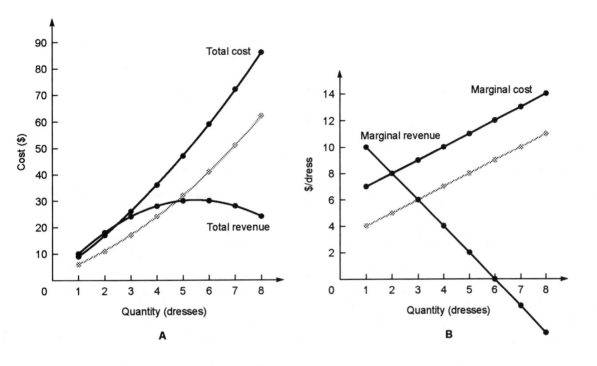

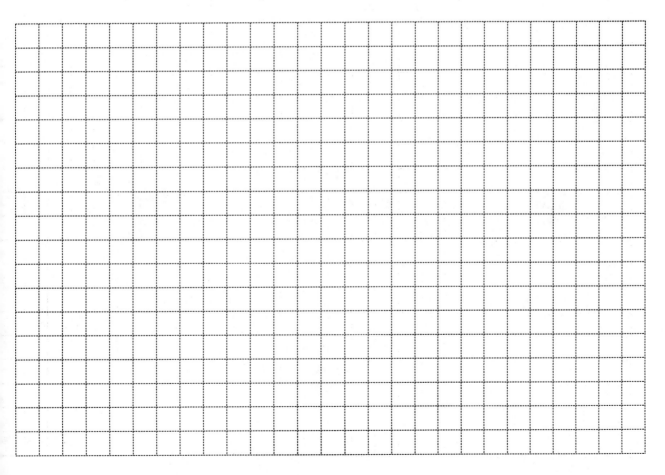

Exhibit 6–2. First and Second Stages of Production

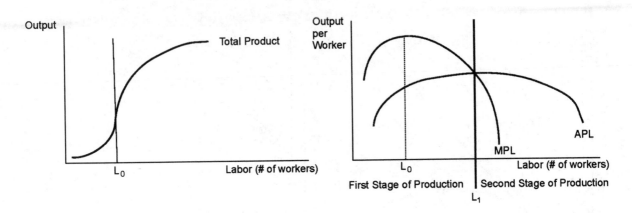

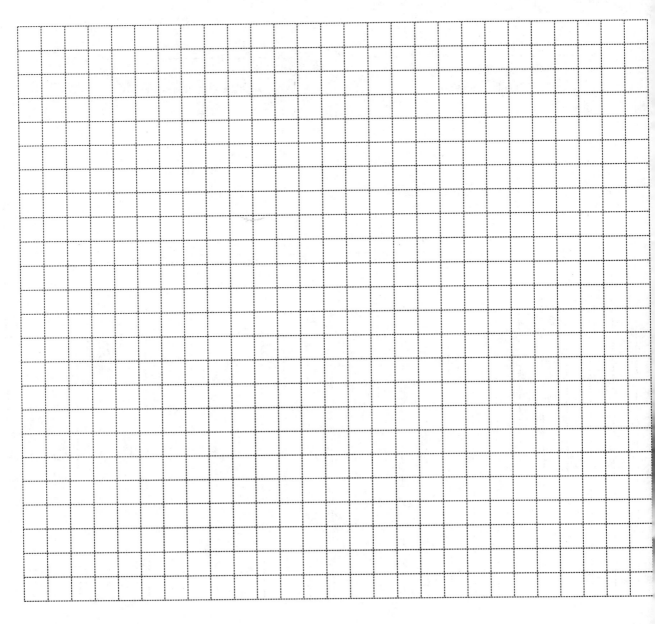

Exhibit 6–5. Product Curves and Cost Curves

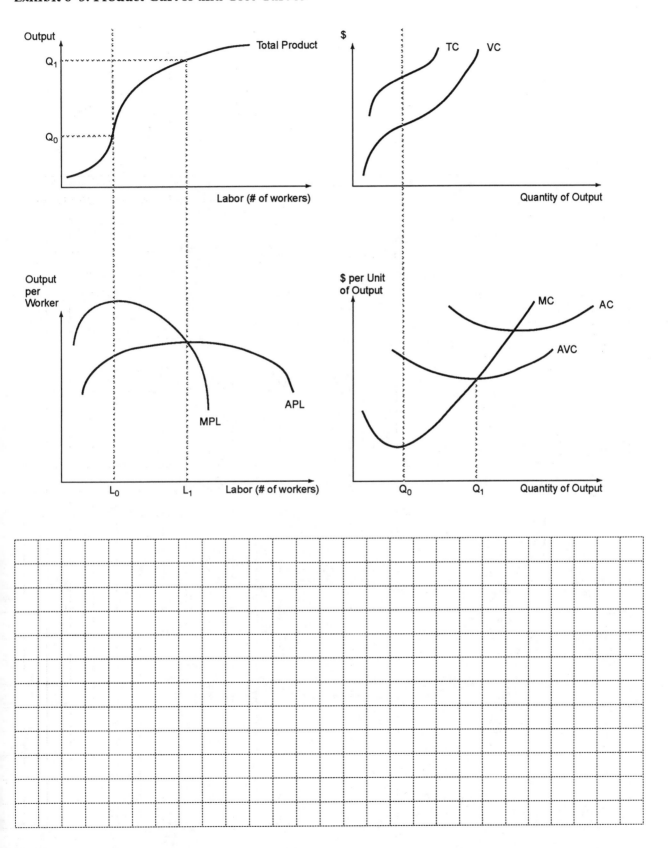

Exhibit 6–8. The Production Function

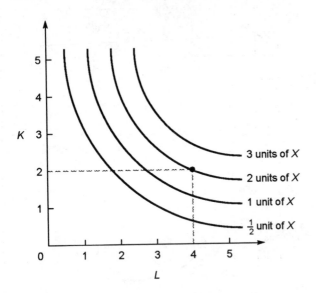

Exhibit 6–9. Cost Minimization

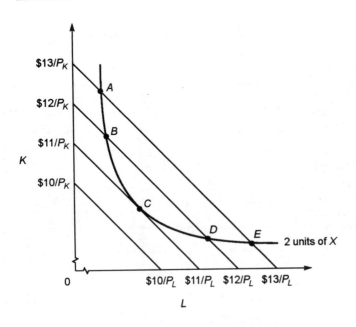

Exhibit 6–10. Maximizing Output for a Given Expenditure

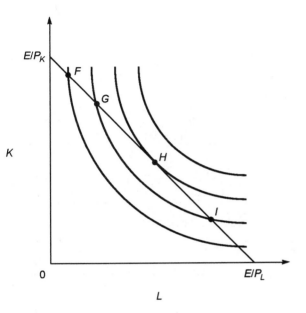

Exhibit 6–11. Deriving Long-Run Total Cost

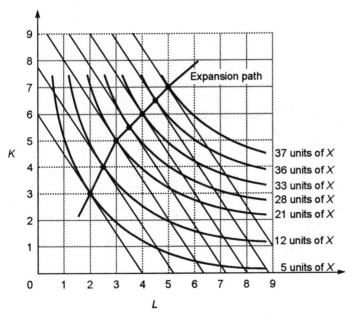

Exhibit 6–12. Long-Run Total, Marginal, and Average Costs

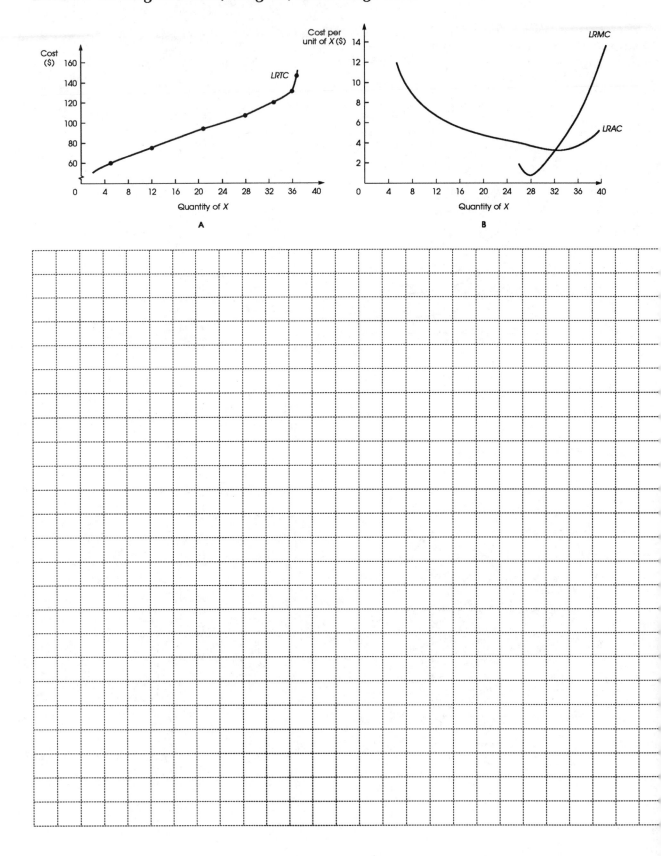

Exhibit 6–14. Many Short-Run Total Cost Curves

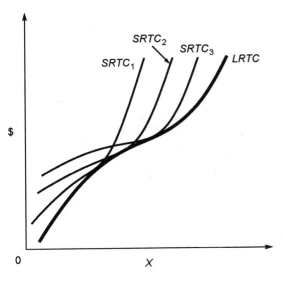

Exhibit 6–15. Many Short-Run Average Cost Curves

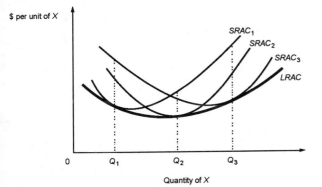

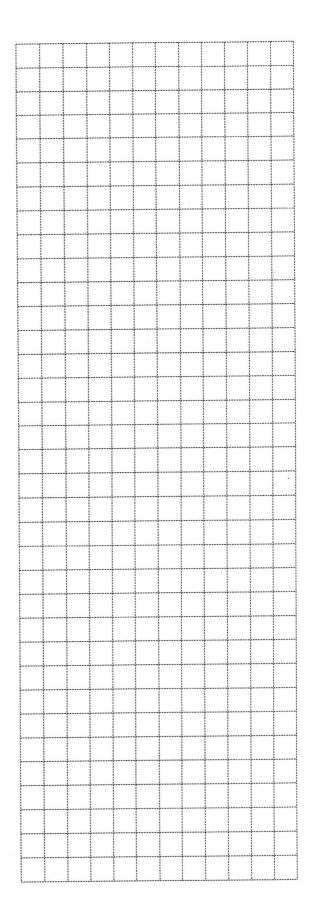

Exhibit 7–1. The Demand Curve for Wheat

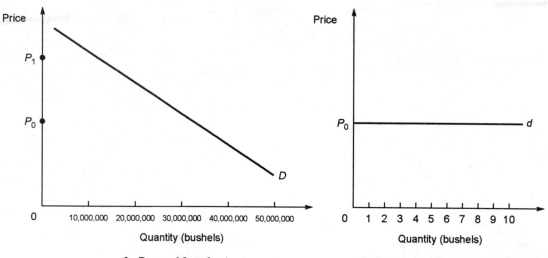

A. Demand for wheat

B. Demand for Farmer Adams's wheat

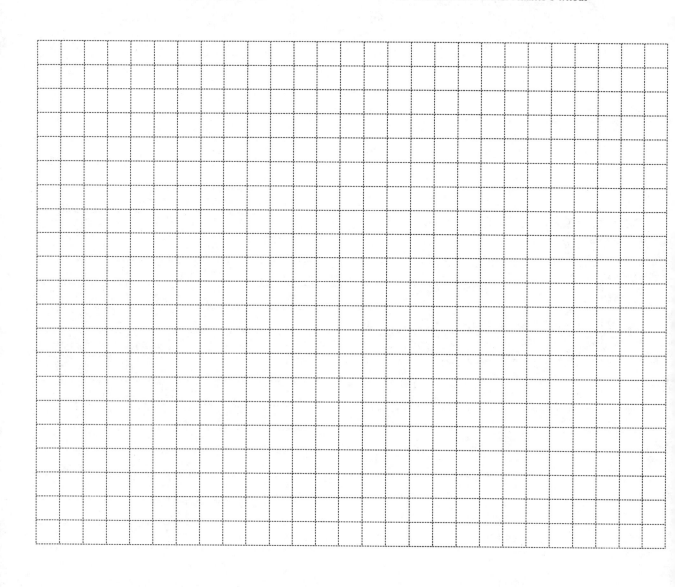

Exhibit 7–2. Total and Marginal Revenue at the Competitive Firm

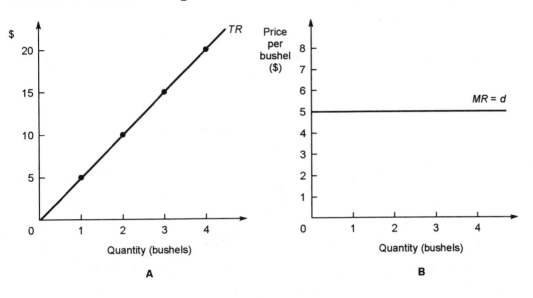

A

B

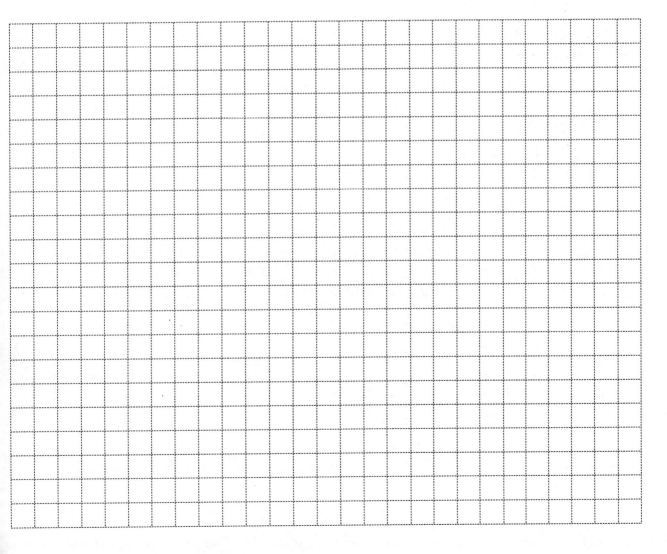

Exhibit 7–3. The Optimum of the Competitive Firm

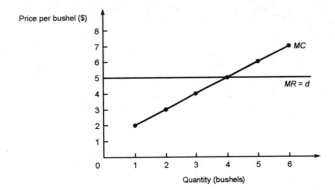

Exhibit 7–8. The Competitive Firm's Short-Run Supply Curve

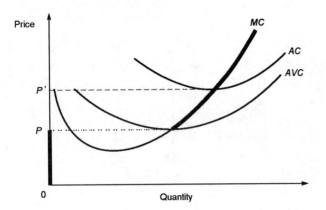

Exhibit 7–9. The Industry Supply Curve

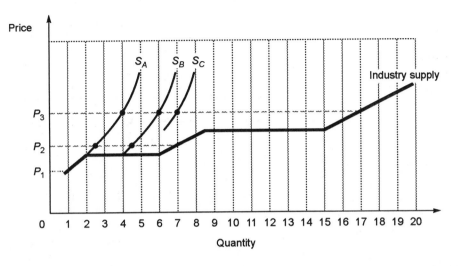

Exhibit 7–10. The Factor-Price Effect

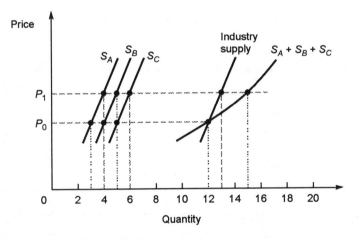

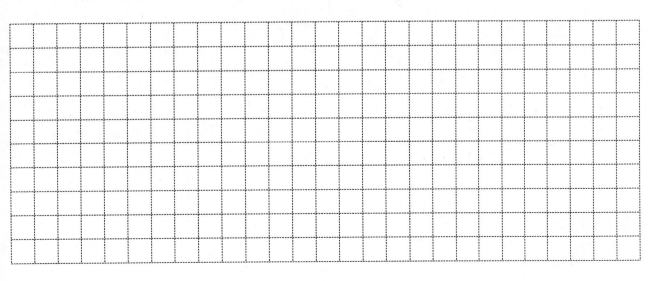

Exhibit 7–12. A Rise in Marginal Costs

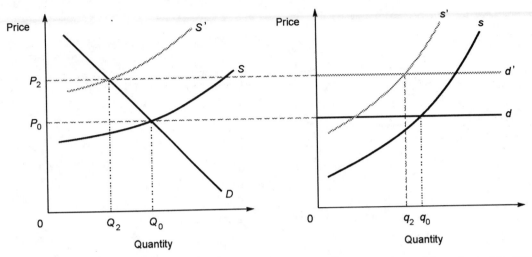

A. Supply and demand for output of the industry   B. Supply and demand for output of the firm

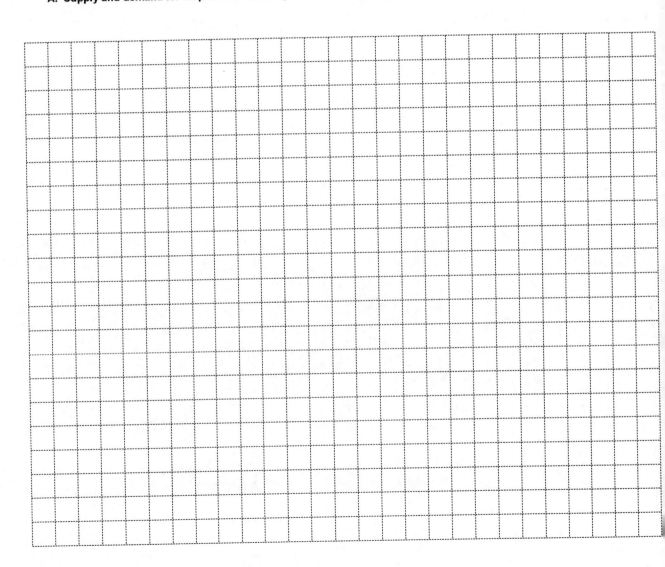

Exhibit 7–13. A Change in Demand

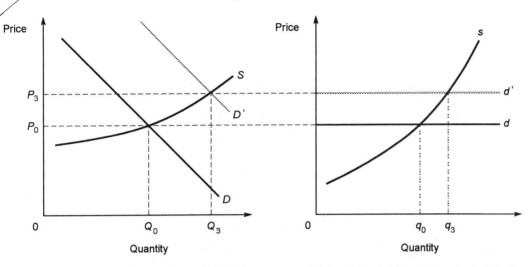

A. Supply and demand for output of the industry   B. Supply and demand for output of the firm

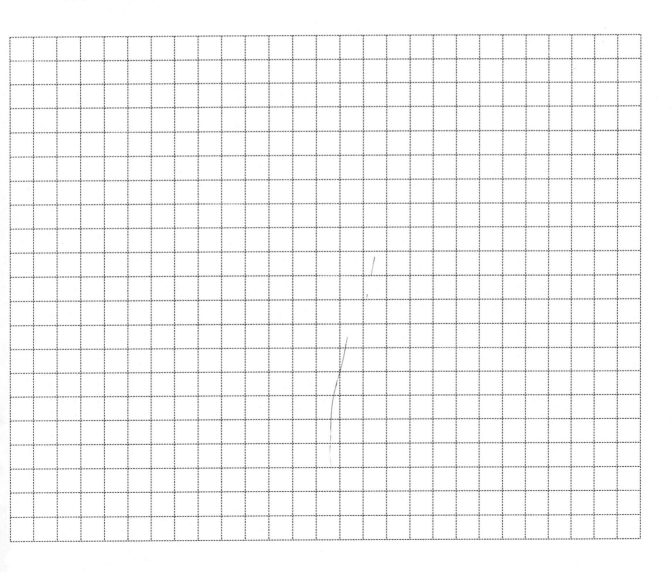

Exhibit 7–19. A Rise in Fixed Costs for a Constant-Cost Industry

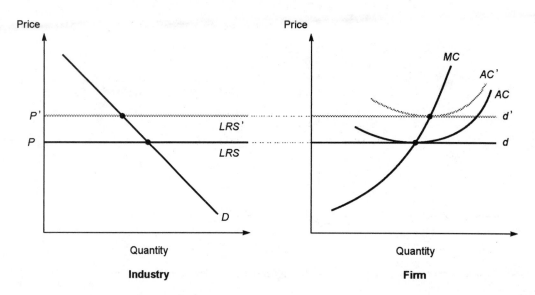

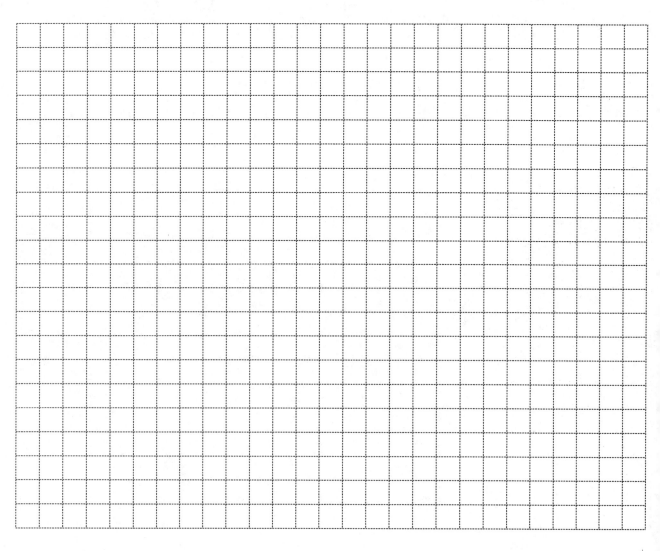

Exhibit 7–20. A Rise in Variable Costs for a Constant-Cost Industry

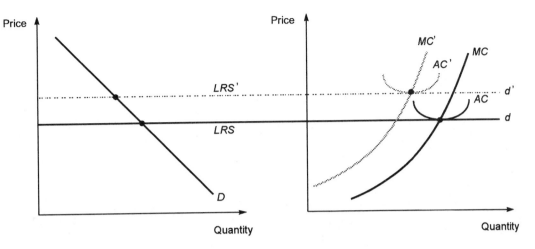

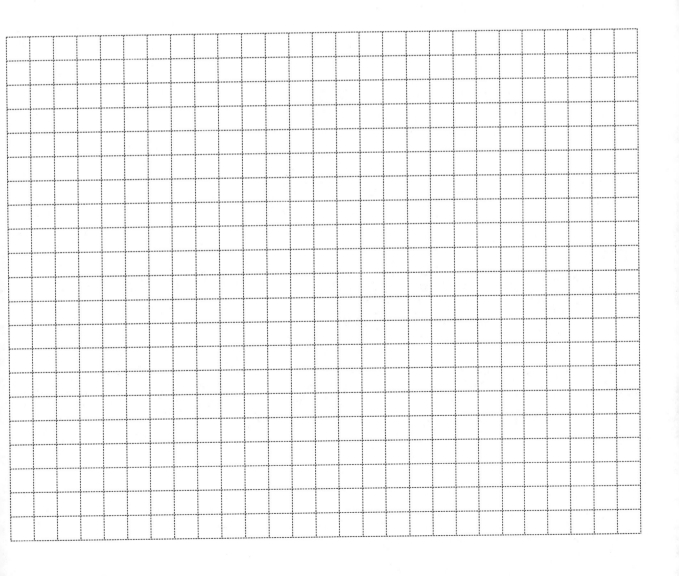

Exhibit 7–21. An Increase in Demand for a Constant-Cost Industry

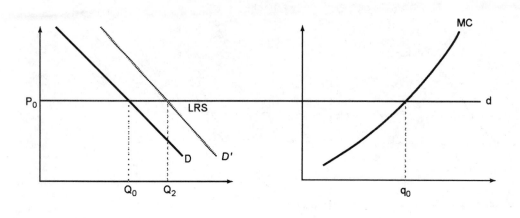

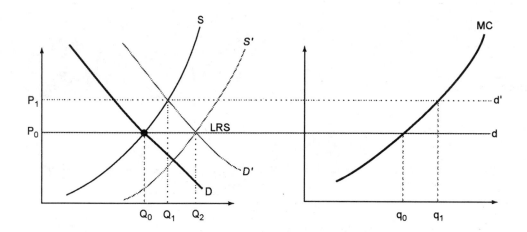

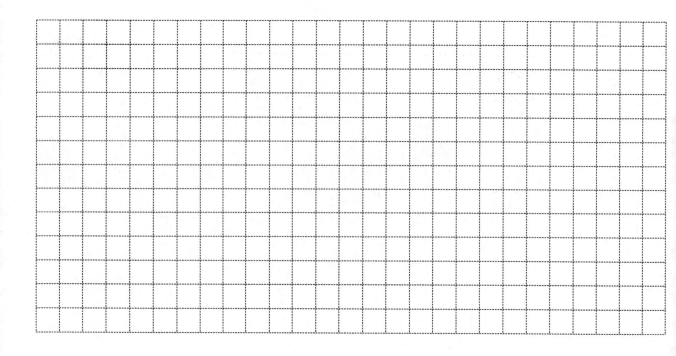

Exhibit 7–24. An Increase in Costs in an Increasing-Cost Industry

A. An increase in fixed costs

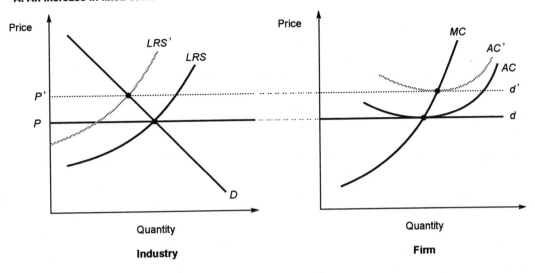

Industry   Firm

B. An increase in variable costs

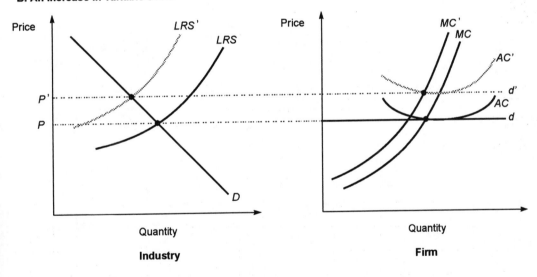

Industry   Firm

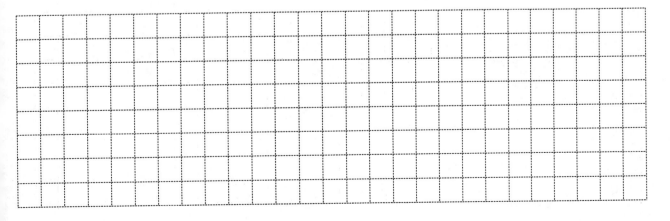

Exhibit 7–25. A Change in Demand

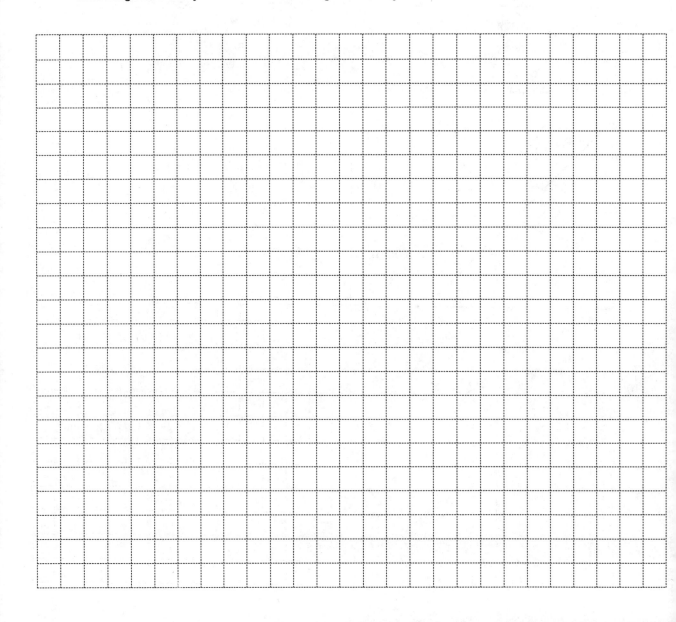

Increasing cost industry   Decreasing cost industry

Exhibit 8–2. Total Value

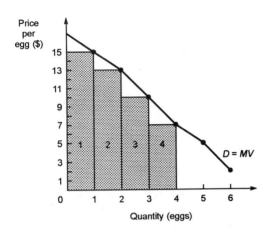

A

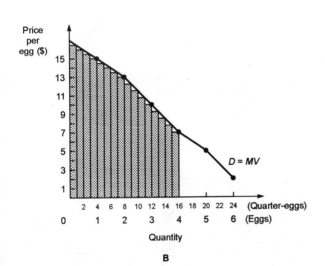

B

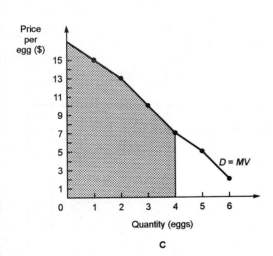

C

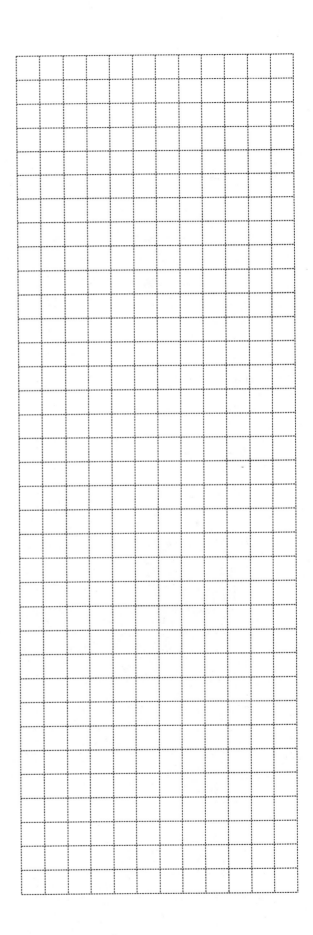

Exhibit 8–3. The Consumer's Surplus

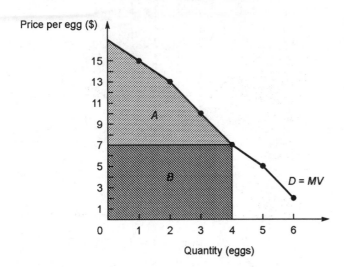

Exhibit 8–4. The Producer's Surplus

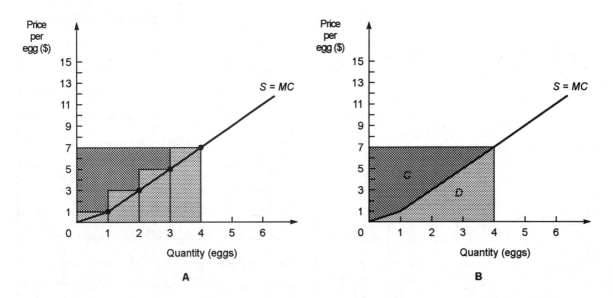

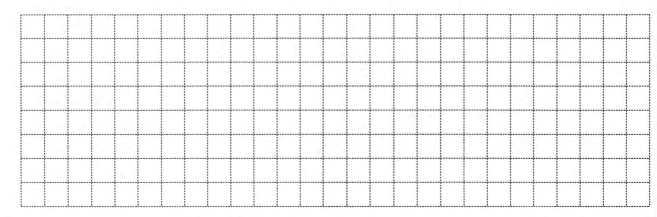

Exhibit 8–5. Welfare Gains

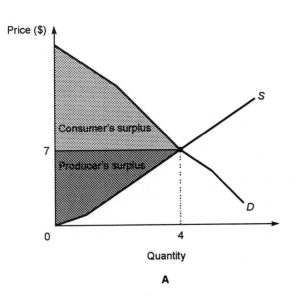

A

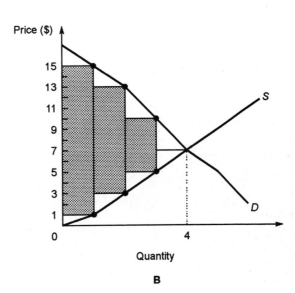

B

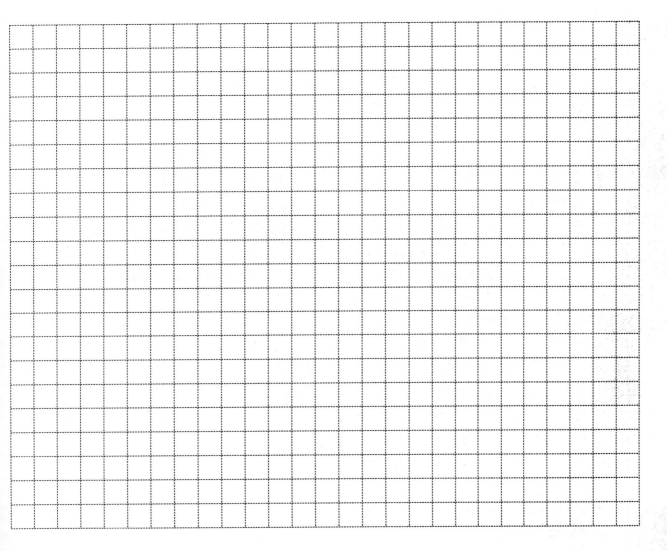

Exhibit 8–8. The Effect of a Sales Tax

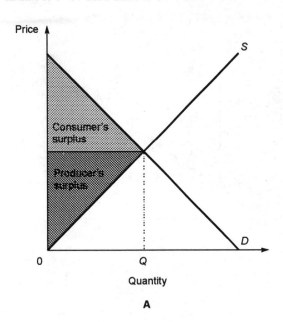

A

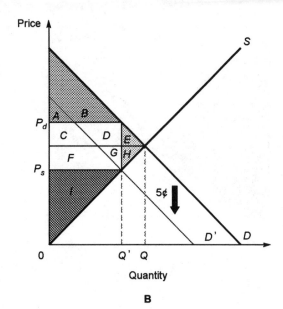

B

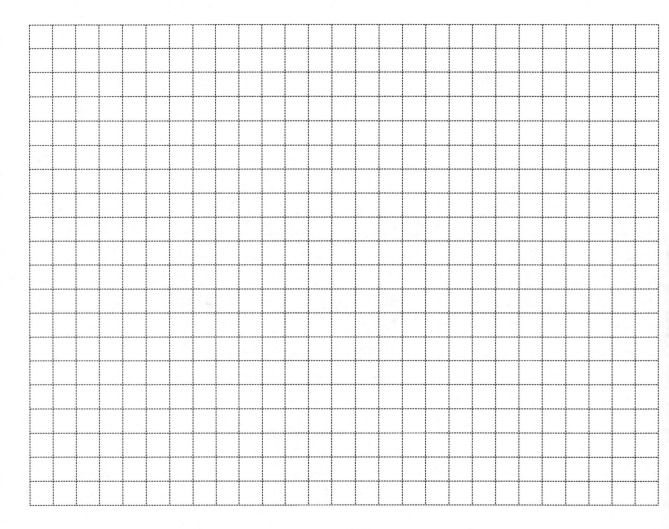

Exhibit 8–12. The Effects of a Subsidy

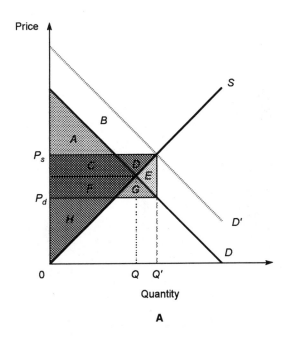

A

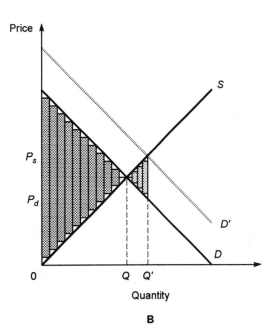

B

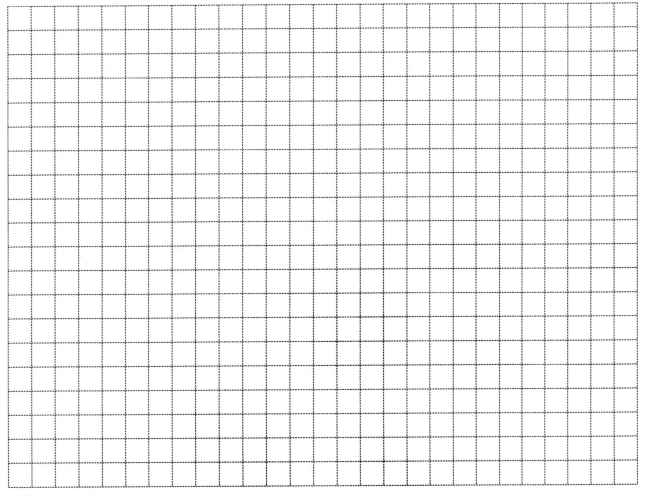

Exhibit 8–14. A Price Ceiling

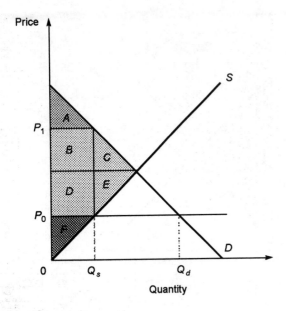

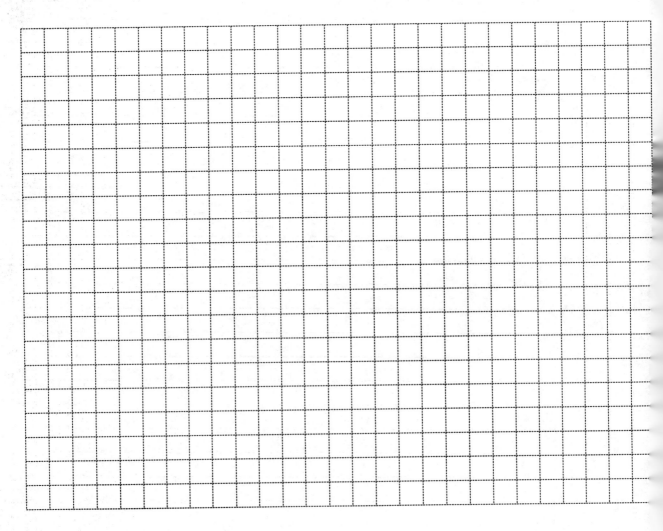

Exhibit 8–17. A Tariff When There Is a Domestic Industry

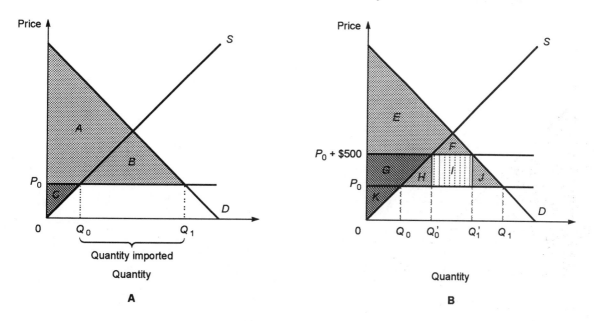

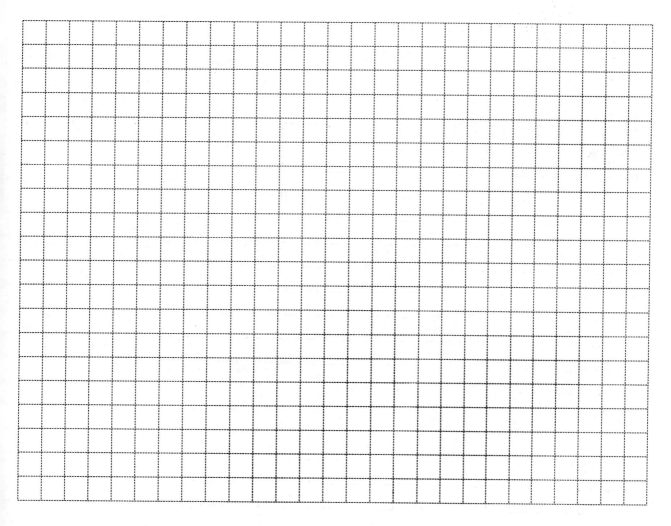

Exhibit 8–21. Trade in an Edgeworth Box Economy

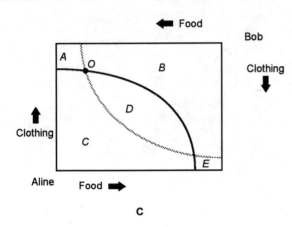

C

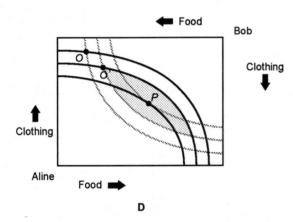

D

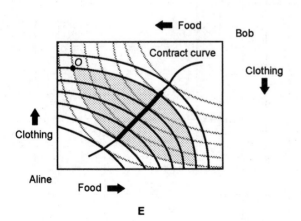

E

Exhibit 8–22. Competitive Equilibrium in an Edgeworth Box Economy

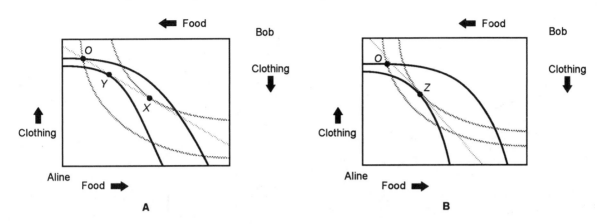

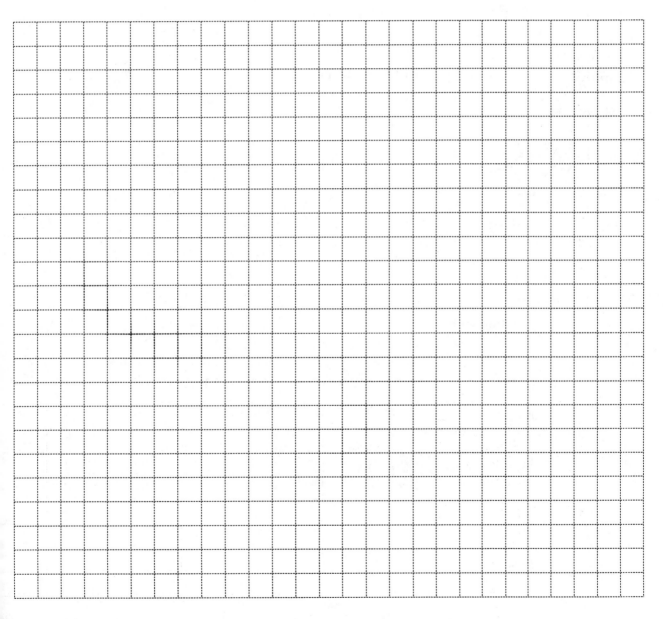

Exhibit 8–24. Production and Consumption with Foreign Trade

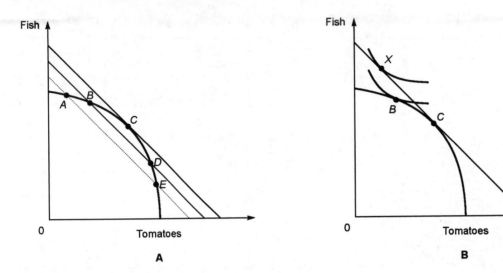

A

B

Exhibit 8–24. Autarkic versus World Relative Prices

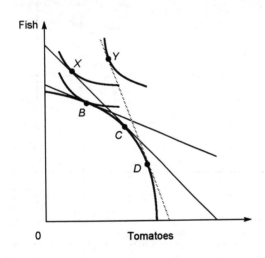

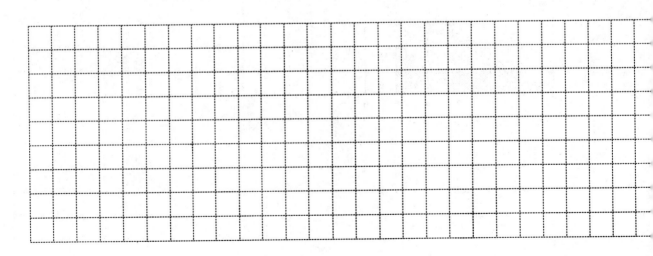

Exhibit 9–2. The Costs of Misallocation

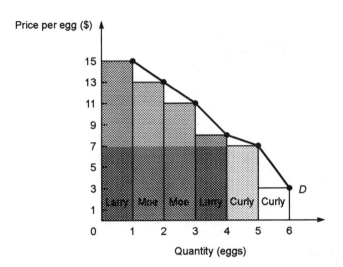

Exhibit 9–3. Planning versus Markets

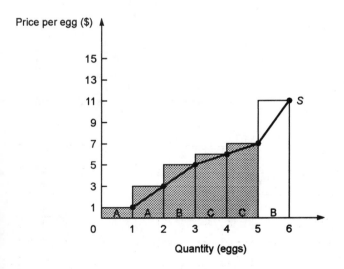

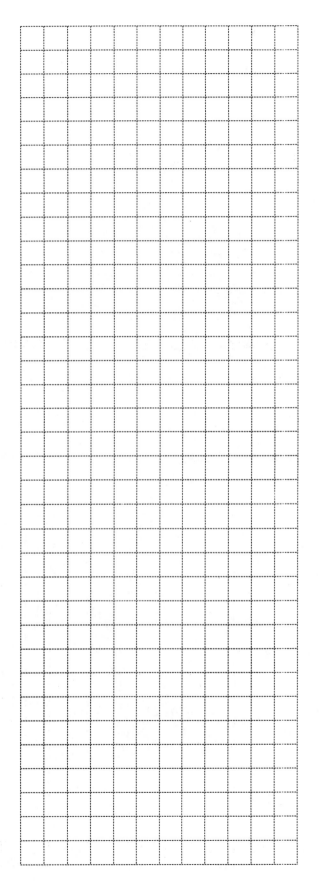

Exhibit 9–4. A Military Draft

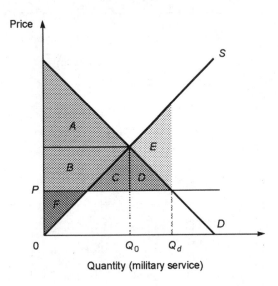

Quantity (military service)

Exhibit 9–6. Underestimating Deadweight Loss

Quantity (military service)

Exhibit 10–1. Monopoly Price and Output

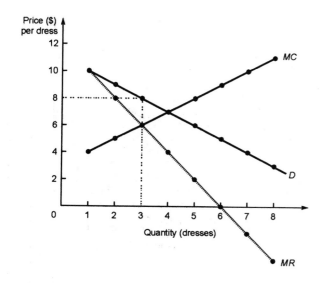

Exhibit 10–2. A Rise in Marginal Cost

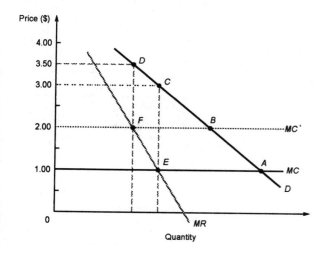

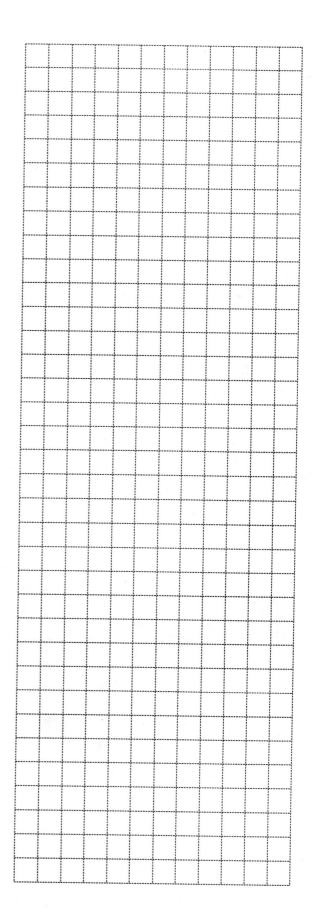

Exhibit 10–3. Monopoly versus Competition

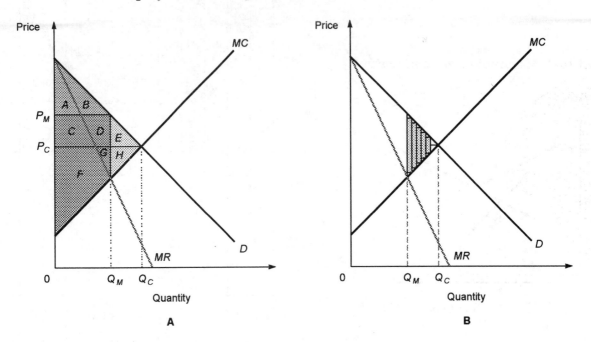

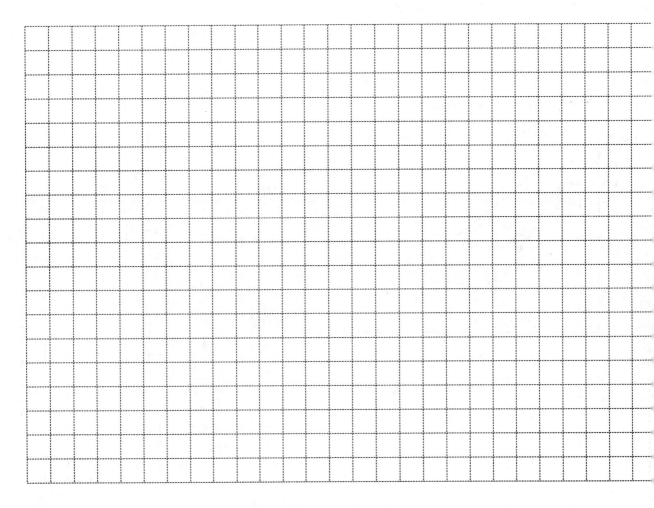

Exhibit 10–4. A Subsidized Monopolist

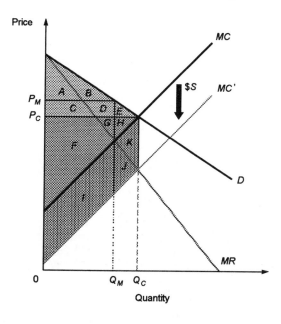

Exhibit 10–5. A Price Ceiling

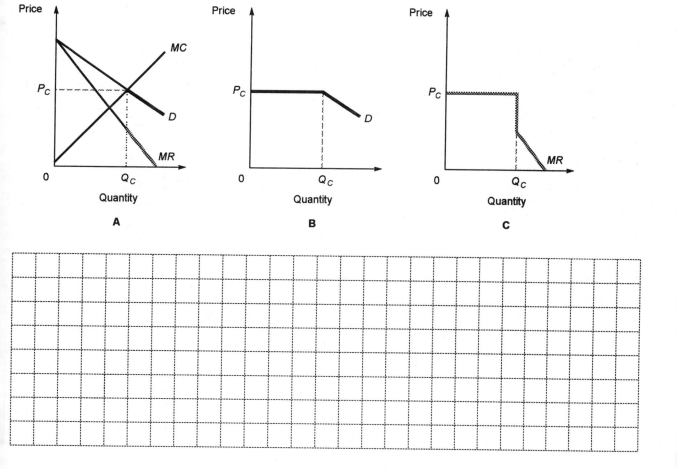

Exhibit 10–6. Zero Profits Regulation of Monopoly

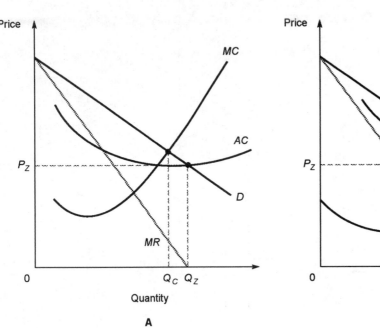
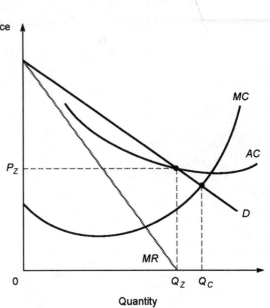

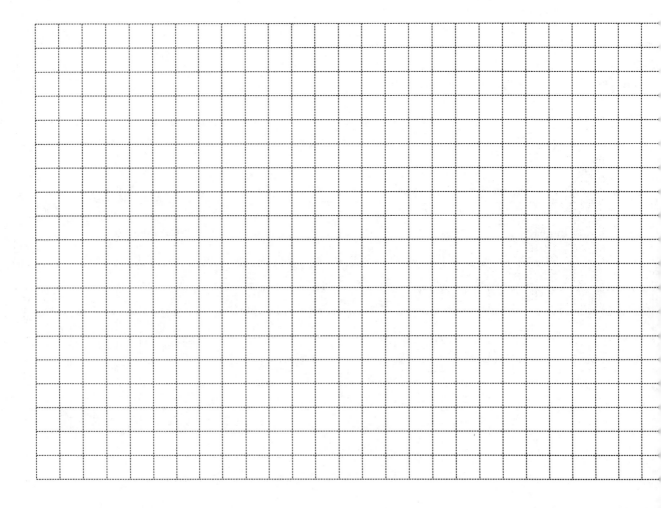

Exhibit 10-7. Natural Monopoly

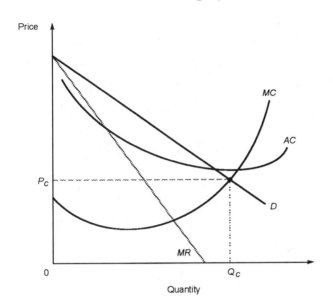

Exhibit 10-9. First-Degree Price Discrimination

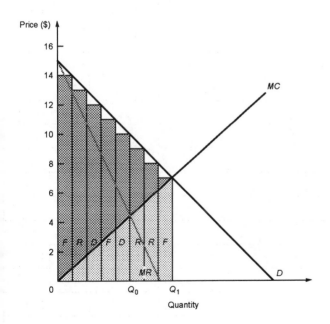

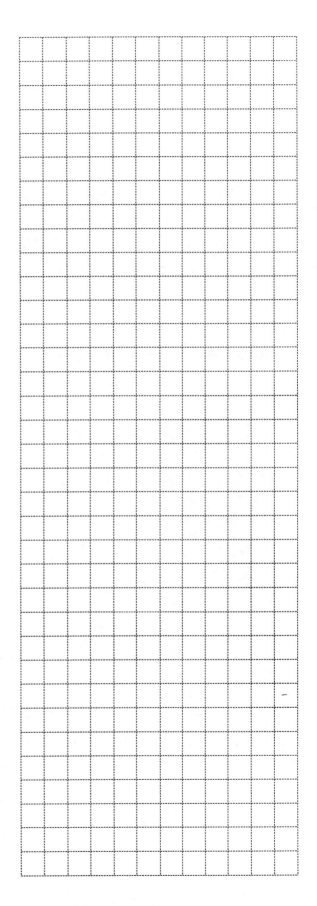

Exhibit 10–11. Third-Degree Price Discrimination by a Monopolist in Two Markets

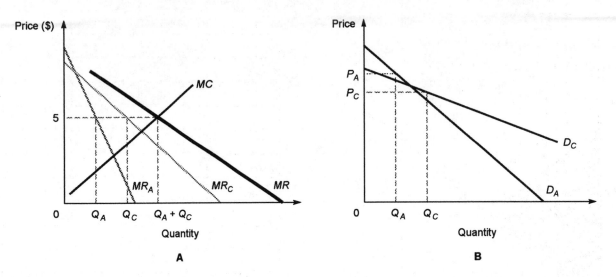

A

B

Exhibit 10–12. Pricing Strategy with a Two-Part Tariff

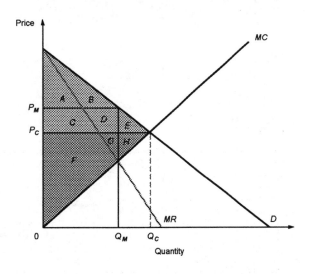

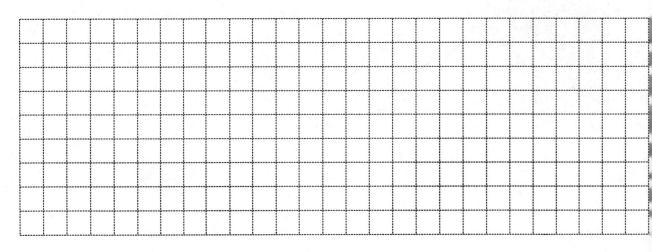

Exhibit 11–1. A Horizontal Merger

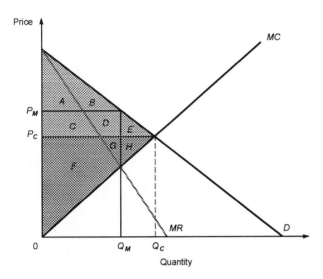

Exhibit 11–3. Vertical Integration

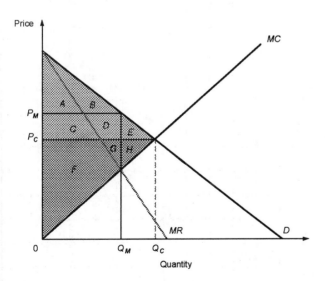

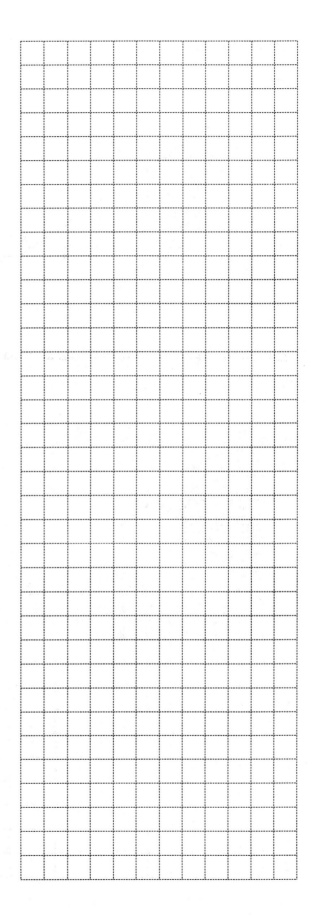

Exhibit 11–5. Resale Price Maintenance

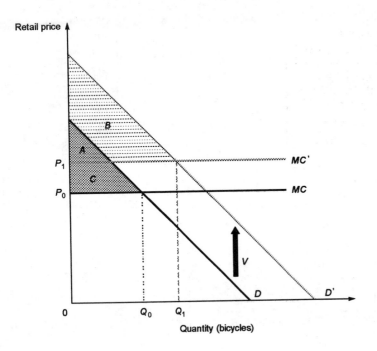

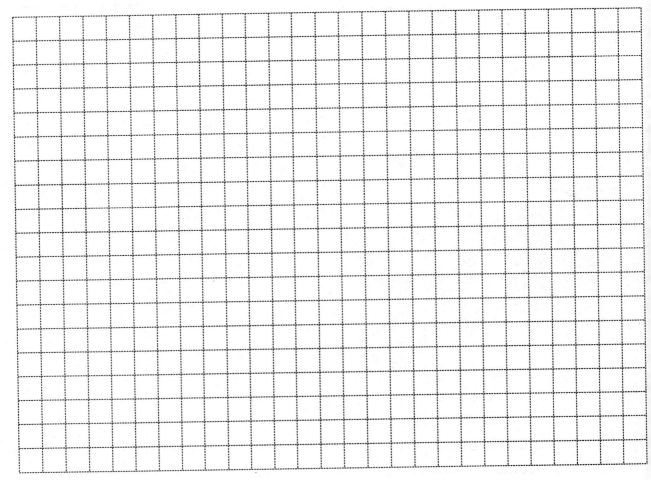

Exhibit 11–6. The Prisoner's Dilemma

		Action of Prisoner A	
		Confess	Not Confess
Action of Prisoner B	Confess	5 years each	A gets 10 years B gets 1 year
	Not Confess	A gets 1 year B gets 10 years	2 years each

Exhibit 11–7. The Breakdown of Cartels

		Action of Firm A	
		Cheat	Not Cheat
Action of Firm B	Cheat	$5 profit each	A gets $3 profit B gets $12 profit
	Not Cheat	A gets $12 profit B gets $3 profit	$10 profit each

Exhibit 11–8. A Contestable Market

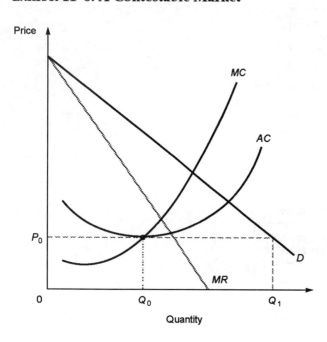

Exhibit 11–9. Natural Monopoly in a Contestable Market

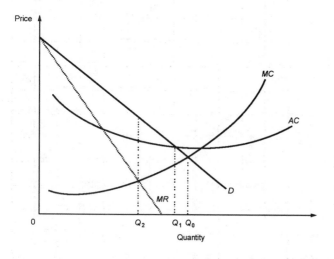

Exhibit 11-10. The Cournot Model of Oligopoly

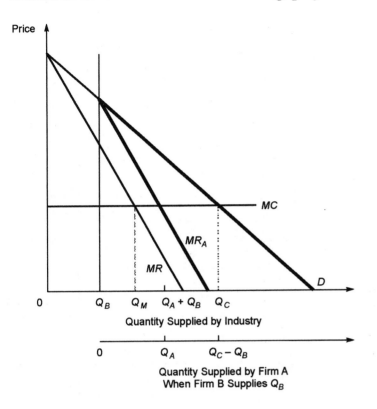

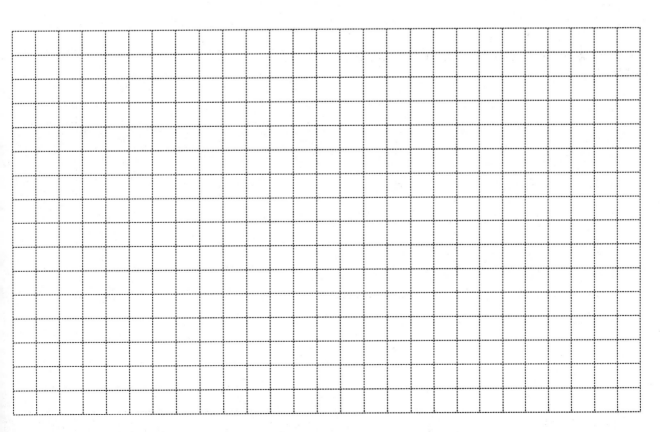

Exhibit 11–11. Monopolistic Competition

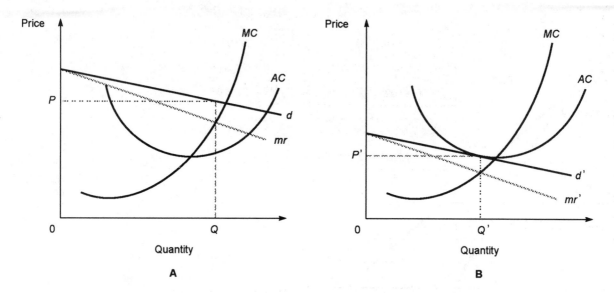

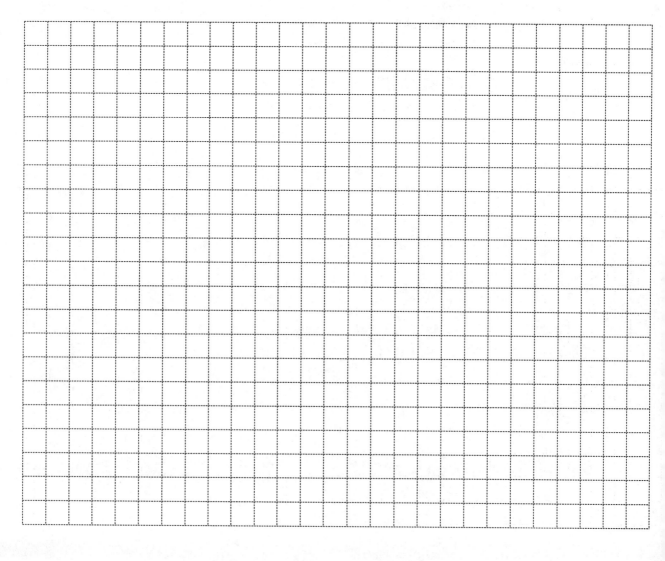

Exhibit 12-1. Pigs in a Box

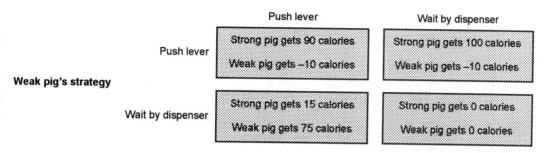

Strong pig's strategy

	Push lever	Wait by dispenser
Push lever	Strong pig gets 90 calories Weak pig gets −10 calories	Strong pig gets 100 calories Weak pig gets −10 calories
Wait by dispenser	Strong pig gets 15 calories Weak pig gets 75 calories	Strong pig gets 0 calories Weak pig gets 0 calories

Weak pig's strategy

Exhibit 12-2. The Prisoner's Dilemma

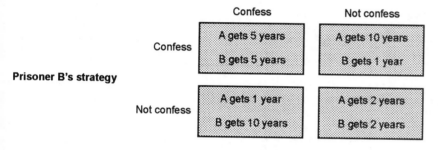

Prisoner A's strategy

	Confess	Not confess
Confess	A gets 5 years B gets 5 years	A gets 10 years B gets 1 year
Not confess	A gets 1 year B gets 10 years	A gets 2 years B gets 2 years

Prisoner B's strategy

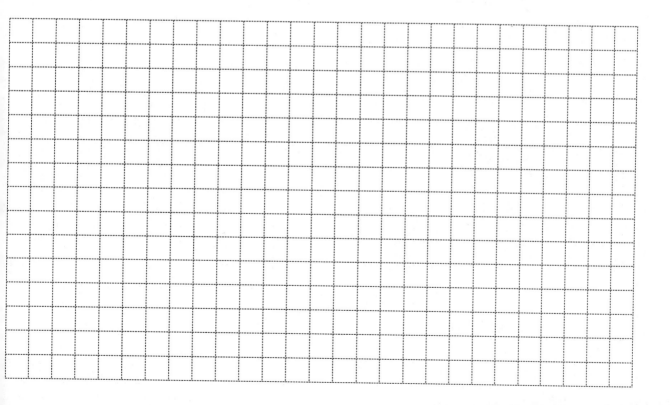

Exhibit 12–3. The Battle of the Sexes

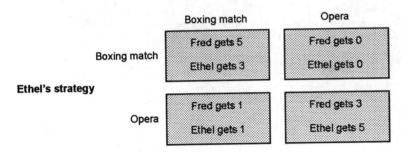

Fred's strategy

	Boxing match	Opera
Boxing match	Fred gets 5 / Ethel gets 3	Fred gets 0 / Ethel gets 0
Opera	Fred gets 1 / Ethel gets 1	Fred gets 3 / Ethel gets 5

Ethel's strategy

Exhibit 12–4. The Copycat Game

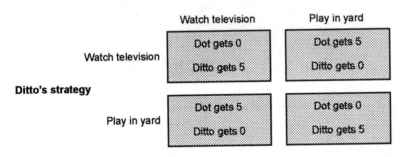

Dot's strategy

	Watch television	Play in yard
Watch television	Dot gets 0 / Ditto gets 5	Dot gets 5 / Ditto gets 0
Play in yard	Dot gets 5 / Ditto gets 0	Dot gets 0 / Ditto gets 5

Ditto's strategy

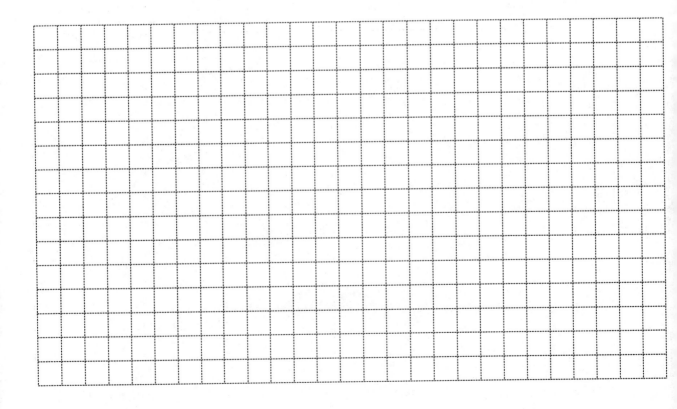

Exhibit 12–5. The Battle of the Sexes Revisited

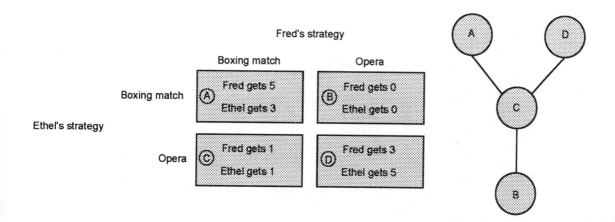

Exhibit 12–6. Pigs in a Box Revisited

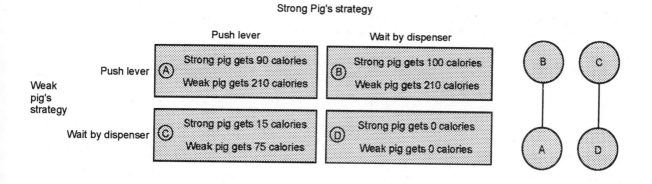

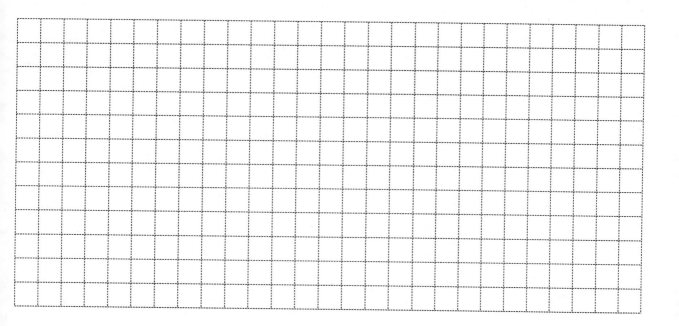

Exhibit 12–7. An Oligopoly Problem

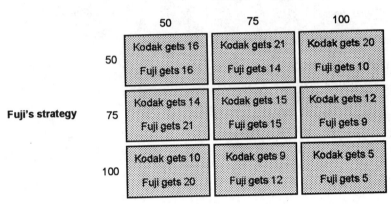

Kodak's strategy

	50	75	100
50	Kodak gets 16 Fuji gets 16	Kodak gets 21 Fuji gets 14	Kodak gets 20 Fuji gets 10
75	Kodak gets 14 Fuji gets 21	Kodak gets 15 Fuji gets 15	Kodak gets 12 Fuji gets 9
100	Kodak gets 10 Fuji gets 20	Kodak gets 9 Fuji gets 12	Kodak gets 5 Fuji gets 5

Fuji's strategy

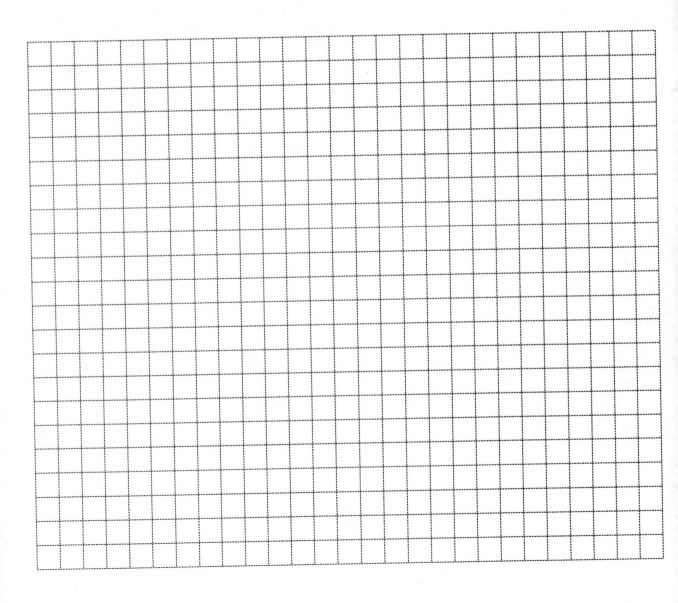

Exhibit 13–1. Private Costs versus Social Costs

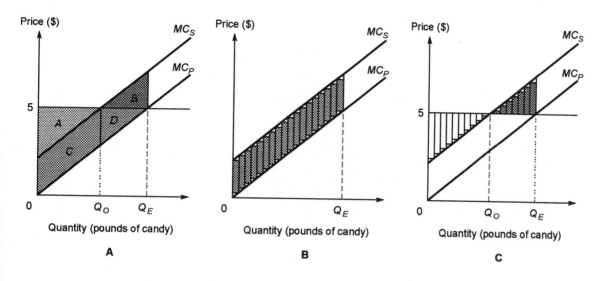

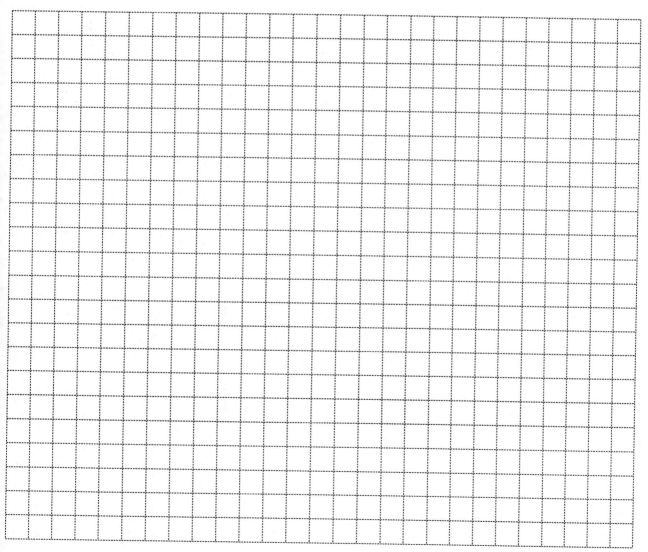

Exhibit 13–2. A Pigou Tax

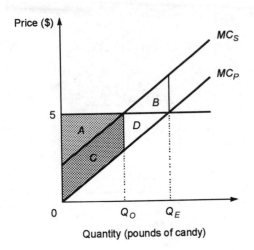

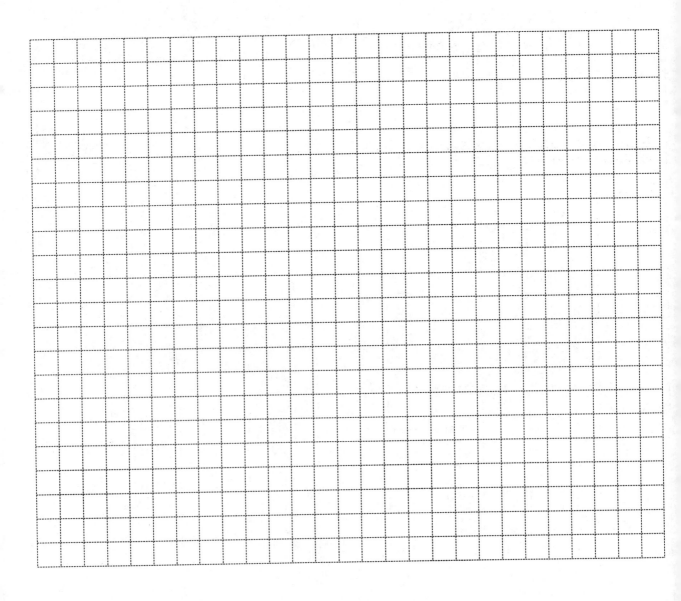

Exhibit 14–1. The Dissipation of Rents

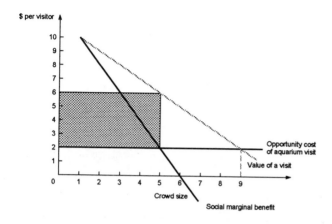

Exhibit 14–2. Gains from an Aquarium Whose Visitors Are Not Identical

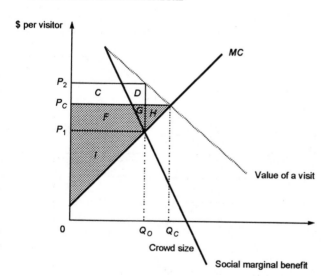

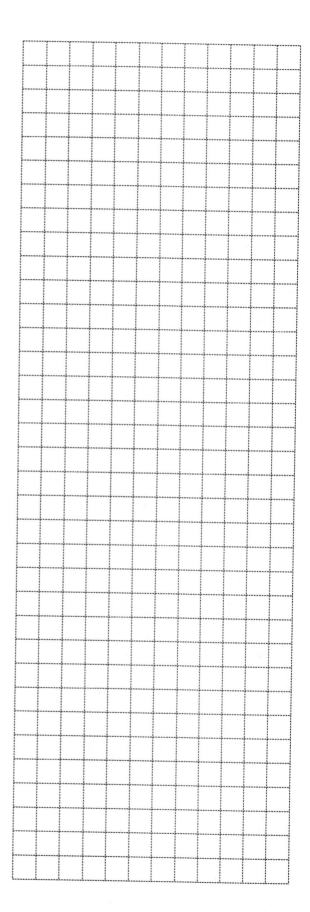

Exhibit 15–1. The Total, Marginal, and Marginal Revenue Products of Labor

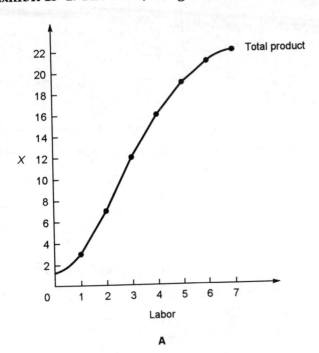

A

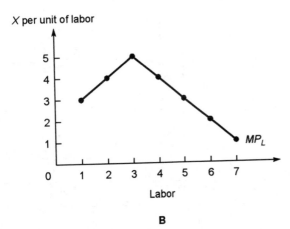

B

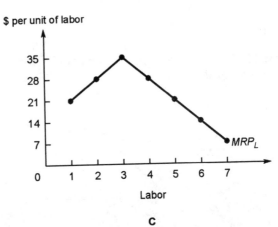

C

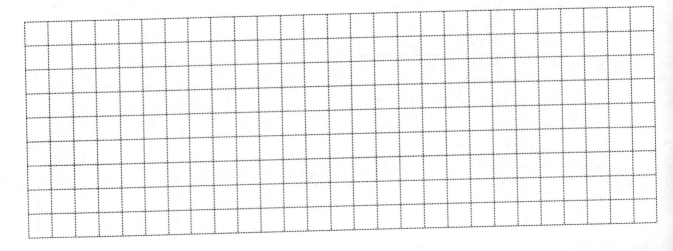

Exhibit 15-2. The Market for Labor and the Market for Output

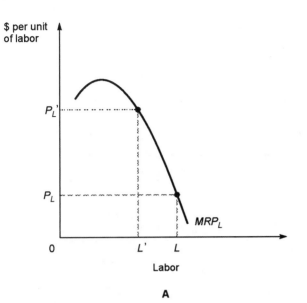

A

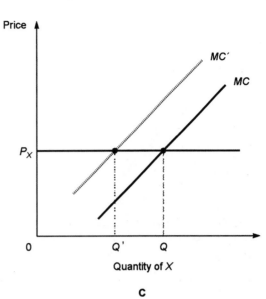

C

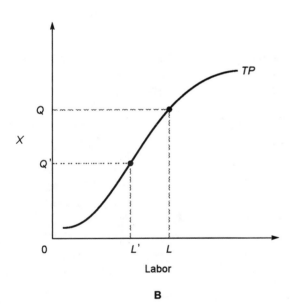

B

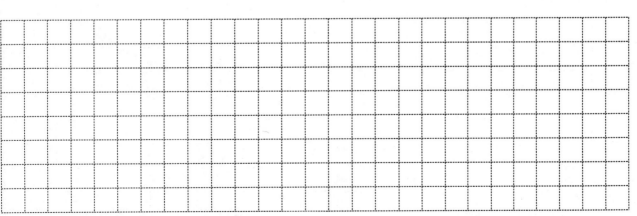

Exhibit 15–3. A Rise in the Price of Output

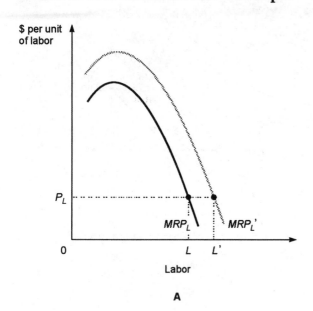

A

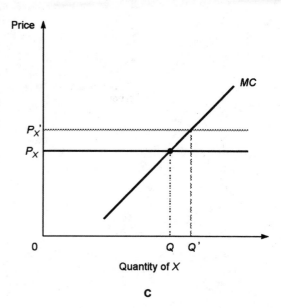

C

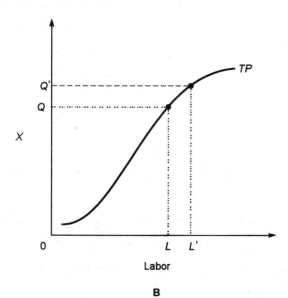

B

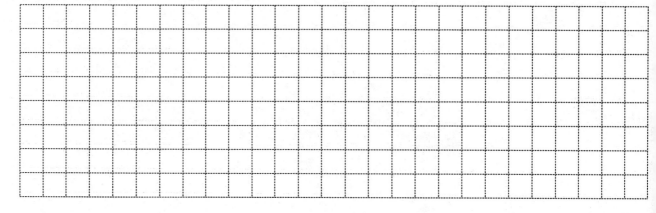

Exhibit 15–4. An Increase in Plant Size

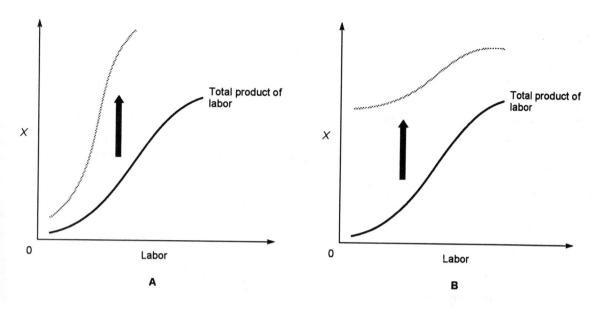

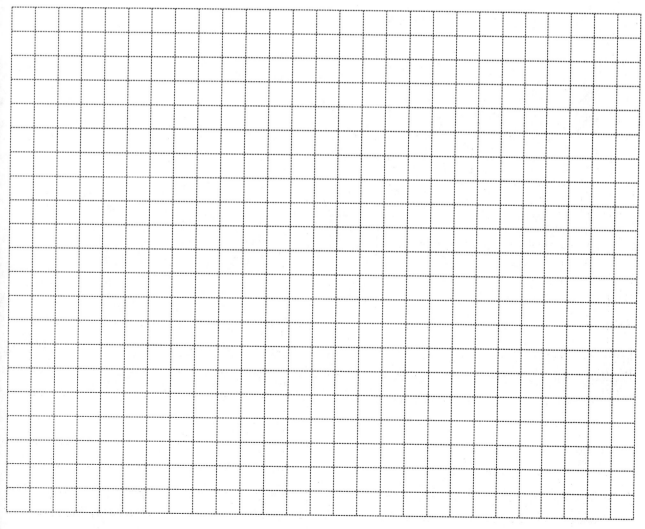

Exhibit 15–5. Constructing a Point on the Labor Demand Curve

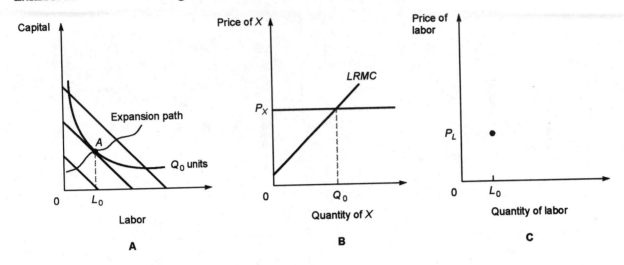

Exhibit 15–6. A Rise in the Wage Rate

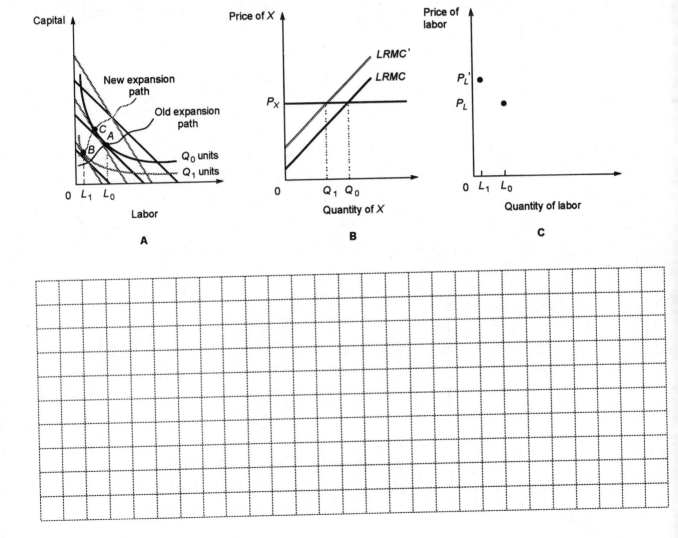

Exhibit 15-7. Two Possible Effects of a Rise in the Wage Rate

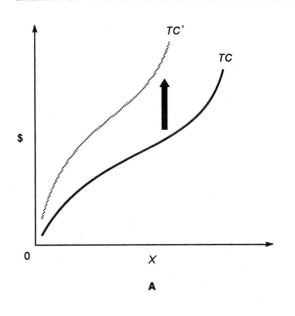

A

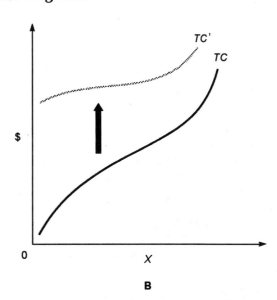

B

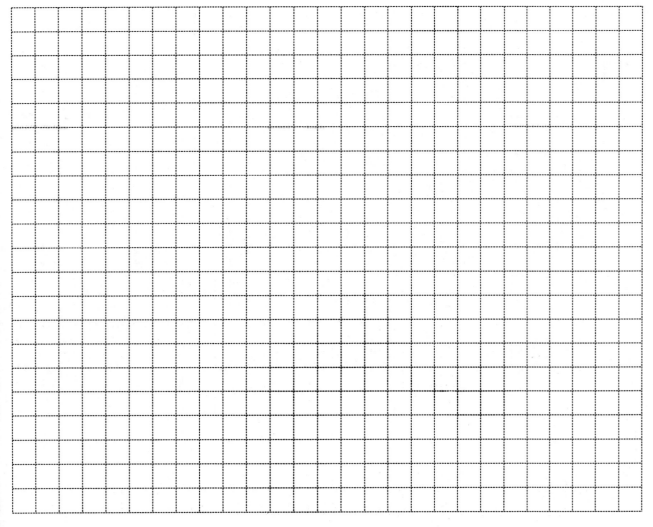

Exhibit 15–8. A Rise in the Wage of a Regressive Factor

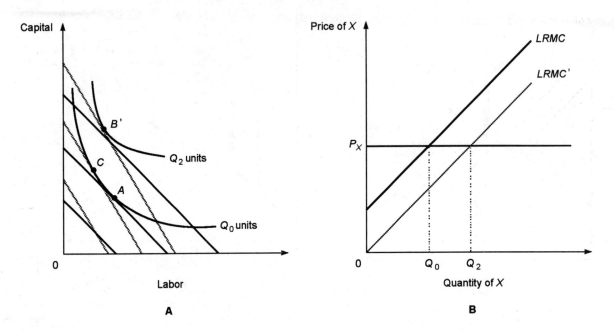

A

B

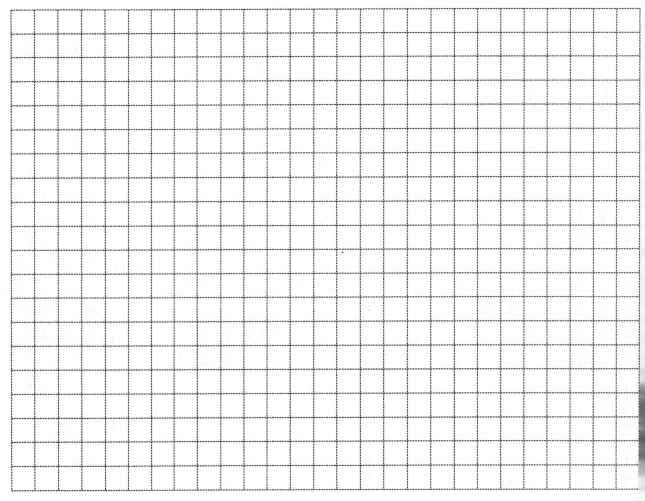

Exhibit 15–9. Labor Demand in the Short Run and the Long Run

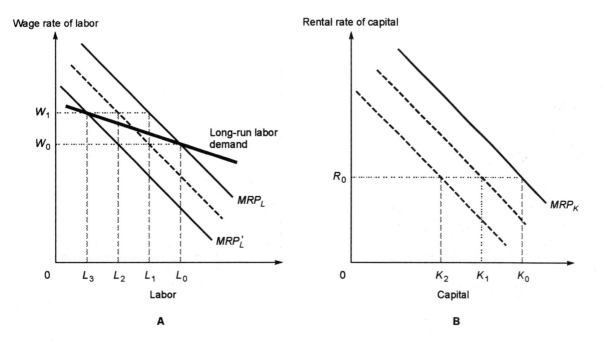

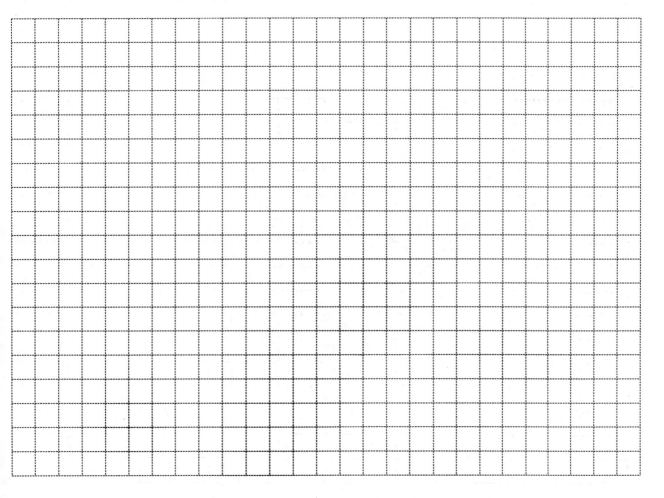

Exhibit 15–10. Monopsony

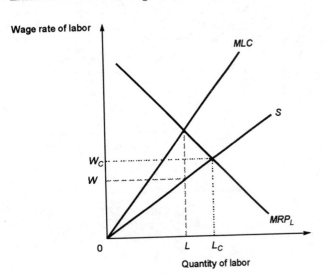

Exhibit 15–11. Labor's Share of Income

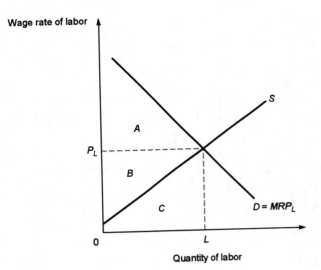

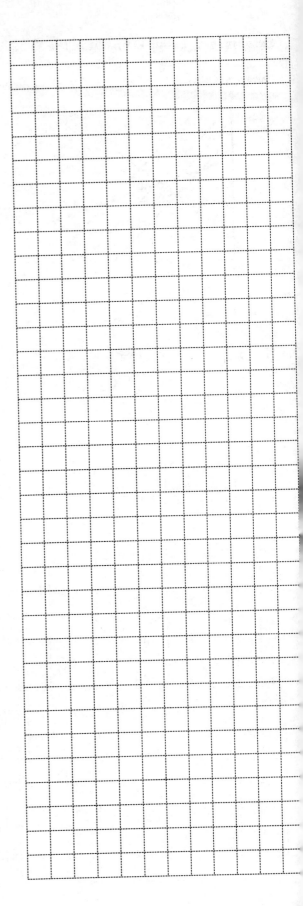

Exhibit 15–12. The Distribution of Rent

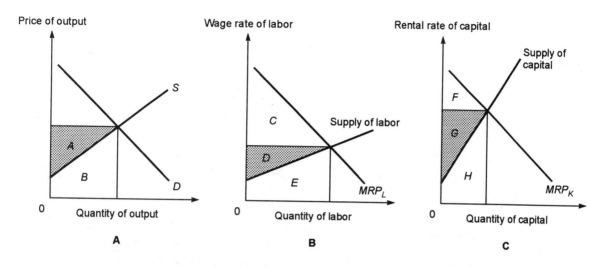

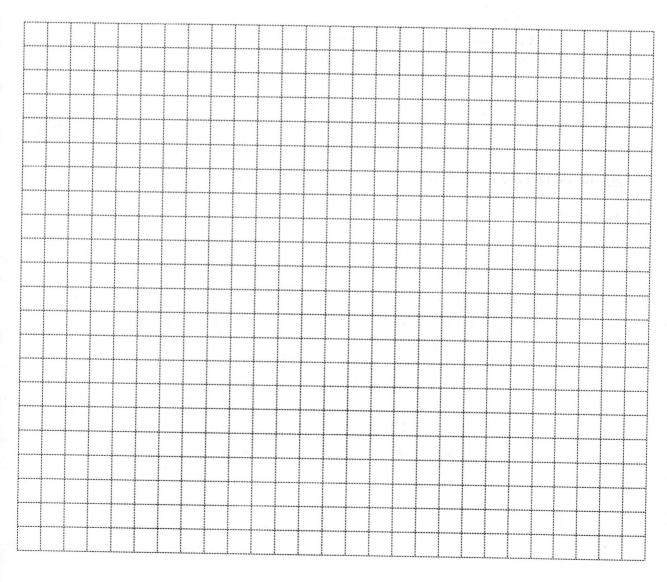

Exhibit 16–1. Consumption versus Leisure

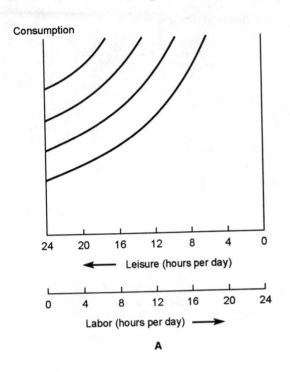

A

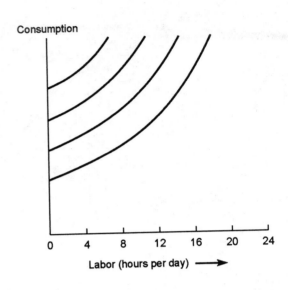

B

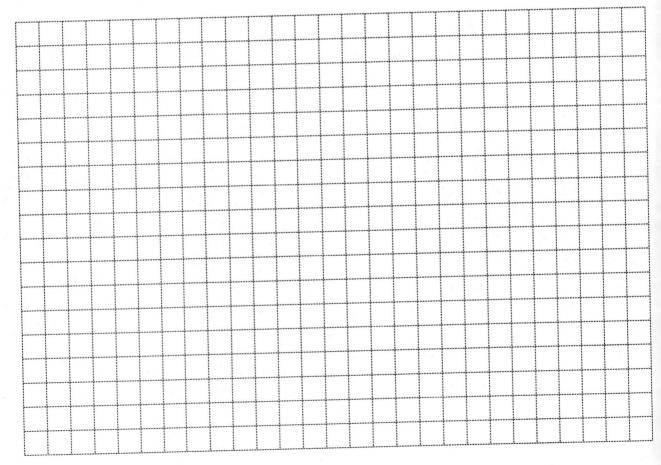

Exhibit 16–2. The Worker's Optimum

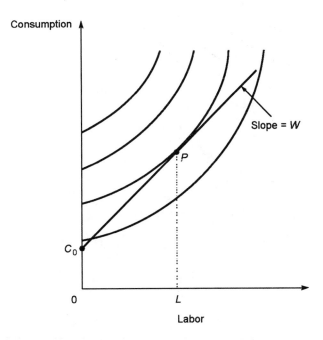

Exhibit 16–3. An Increase in Nonlabor Income

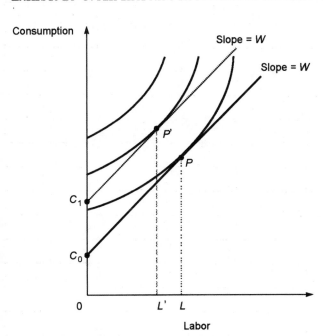

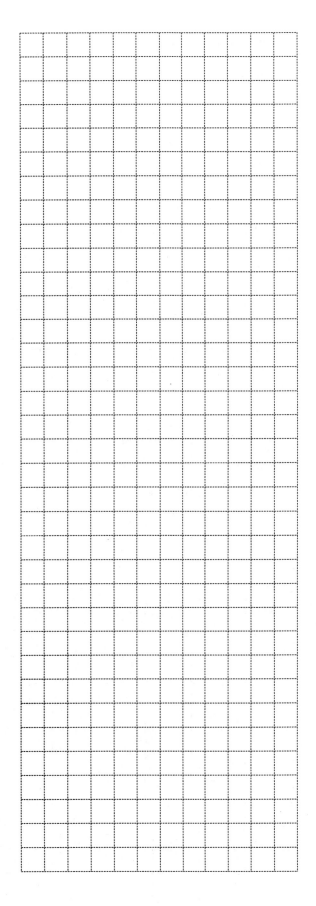

Exhibit 16–4. A Rise in the Wage Rate

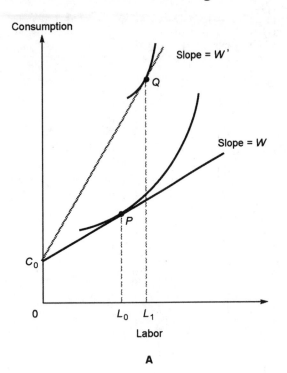

A

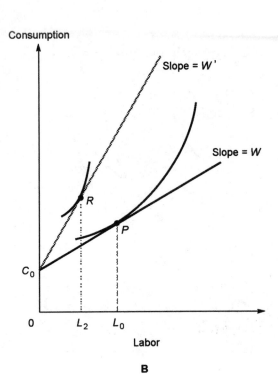

B

Exhibit 16–5. Income and Substitution Effects

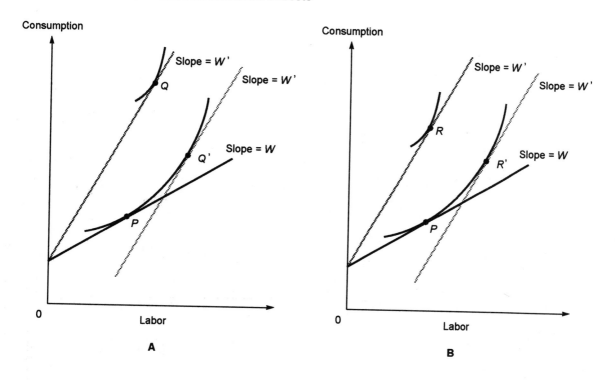

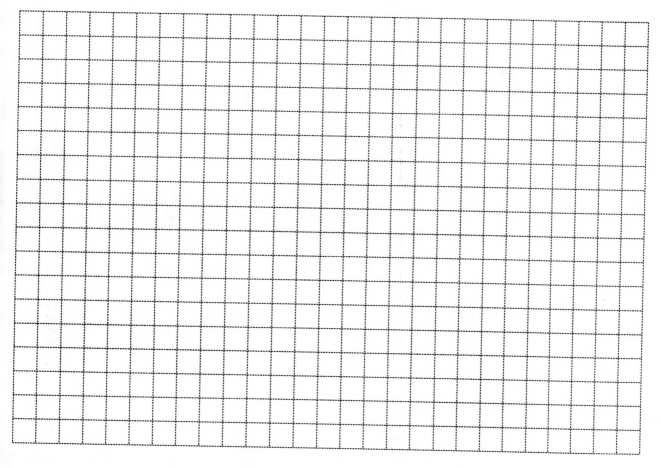

Exhibit 16–6. The Individual's Labor Supply Curve

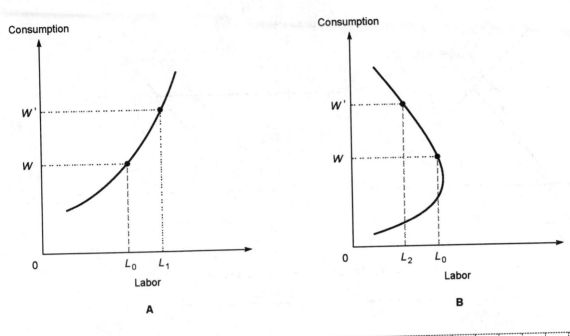

A

B

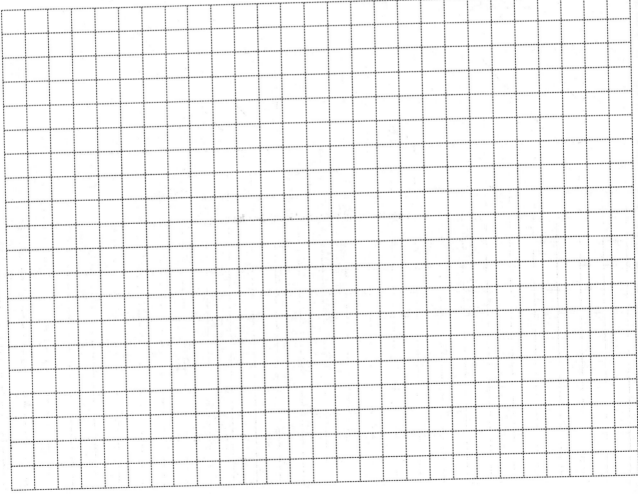

Exhibit 16–8. Increases in Nonlabor Income

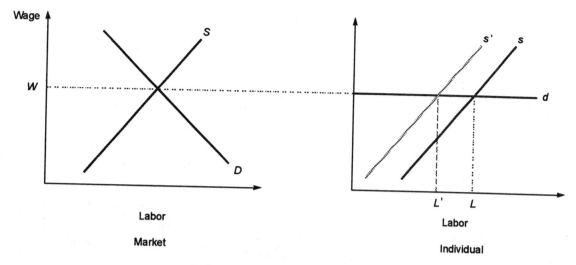

A. An Increase in One Worker's Nonlabor Income

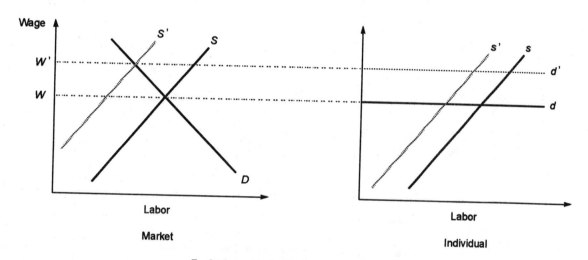

B. An Increase in All Workers' Nonlabor Income

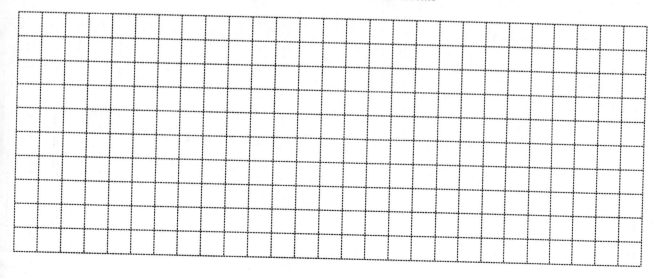

Exhibit 16–9. Increases in Marginal Productivity

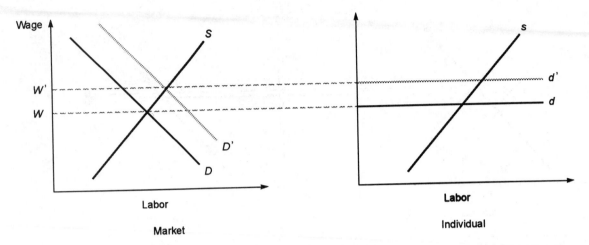

A. An Increase in Marginal Productivity

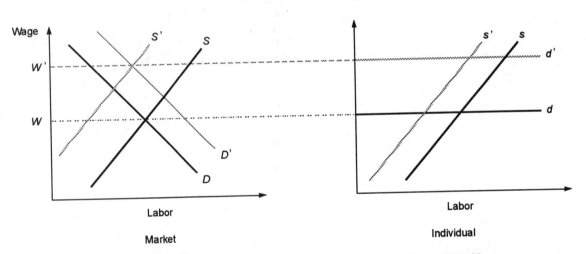

B. An Increase in Marginal Productivity That Increases Workers' Wealth

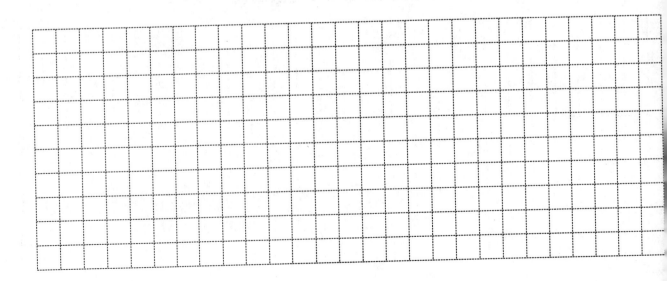

Exhibit 16–10. A Temporary Increase in Workers' Marginal Productivity

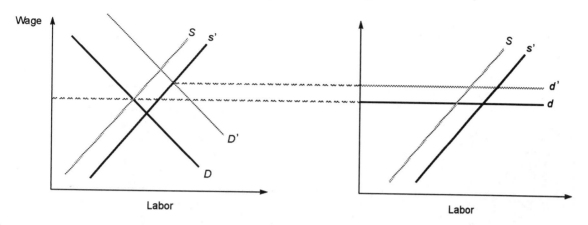

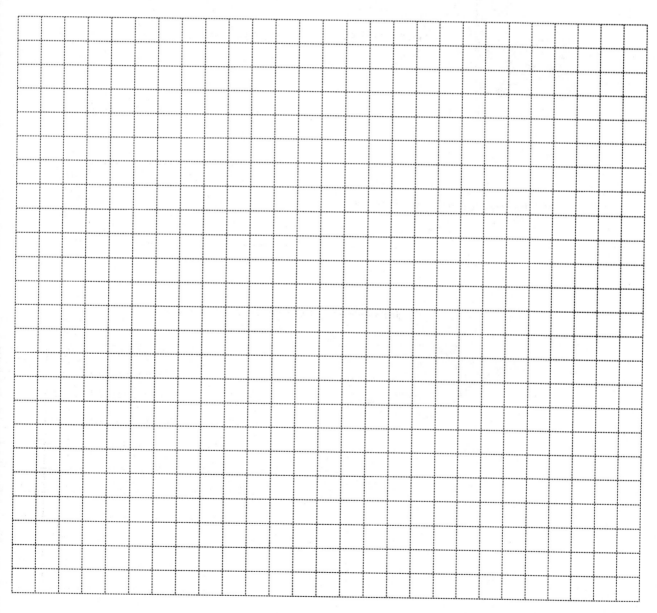

Exhibit 17-2. Old Taxes Are Fair Taxes

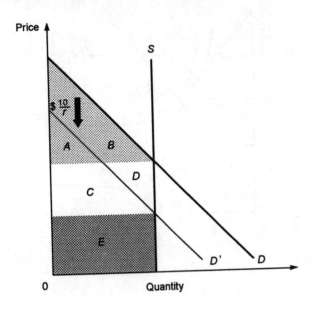

Exhibit 17-3. The Consumer's Preferences

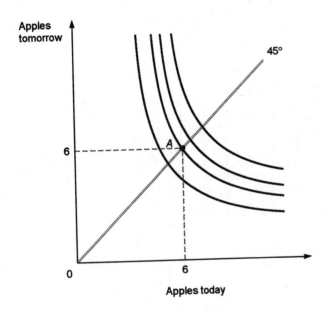

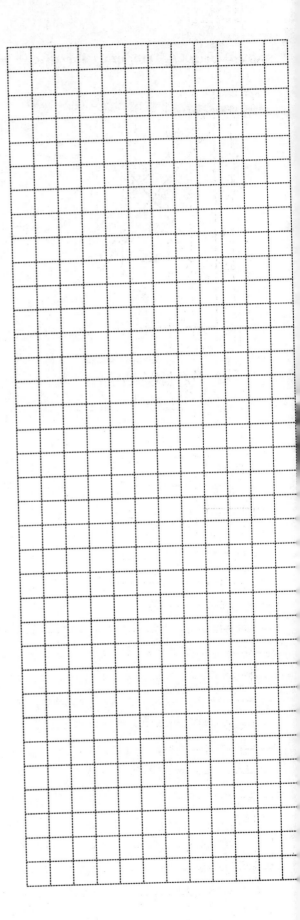

Exhibit 17–4. The Consumer's Choice

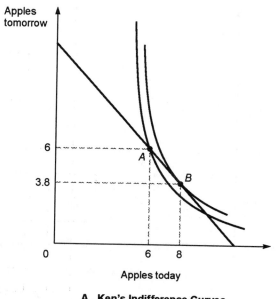

A. Ken's Indifference Curves

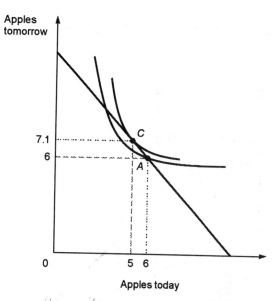

B. Barb's Indifference Curves

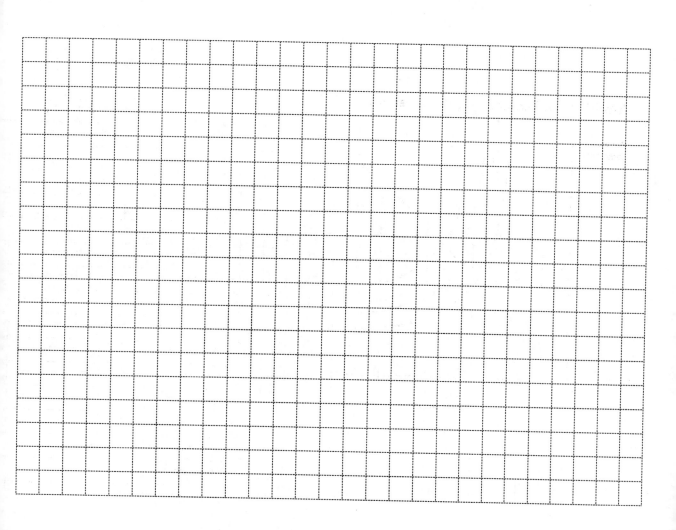

Exhibit 17-5. Ken's Demand for Current Consumption

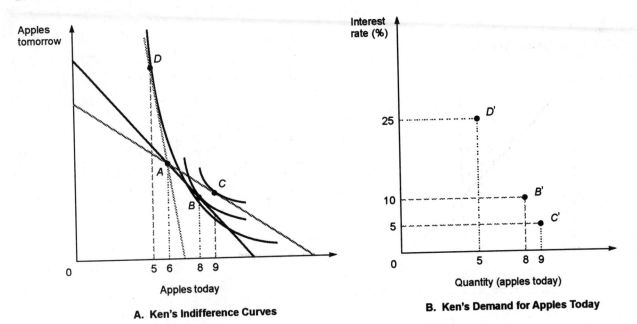

A. Ken's Indifference Curves

B. Ken's Demand for Apples Today

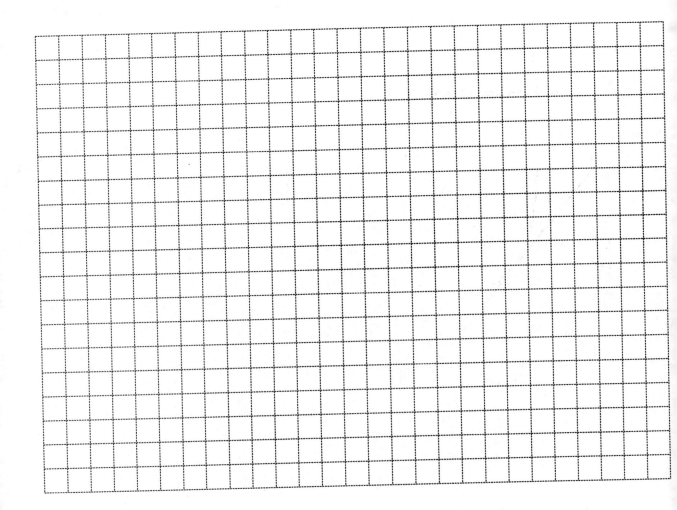

Exhibit 17–6. Equilibrium

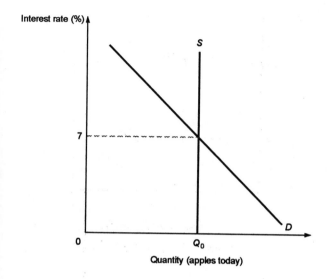

Exhibit 17–7. The Representative Agent

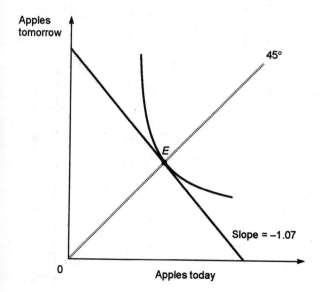

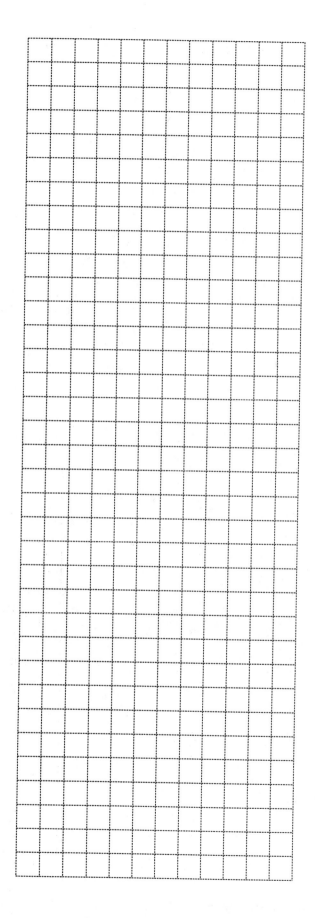

Exhibit 17–8. An Increase in the Future Apple Supply

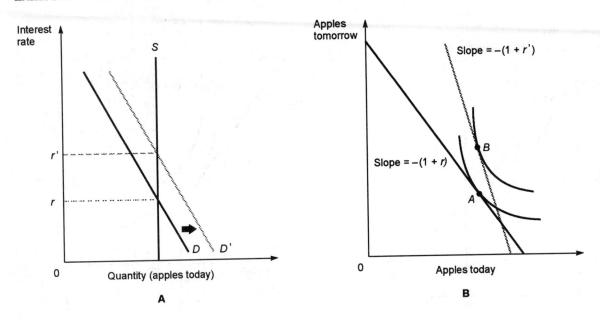

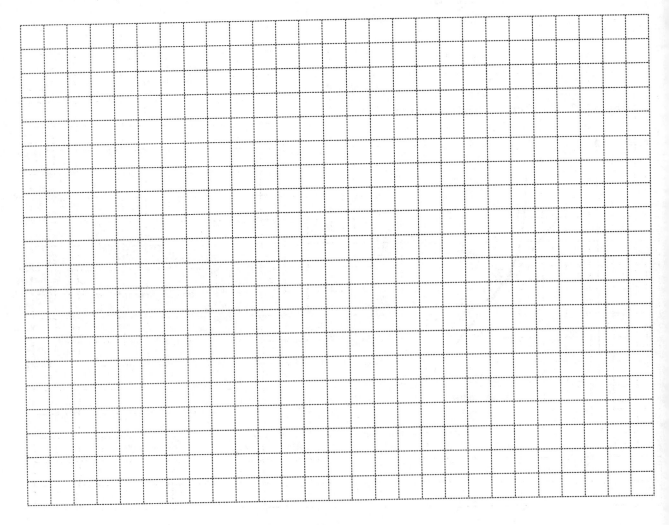

Exhibit 17–9. An Increase in the Current Apple Supply

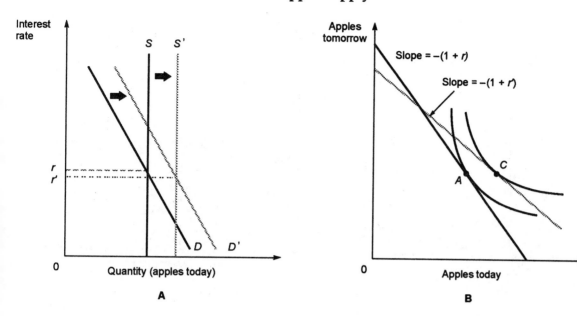

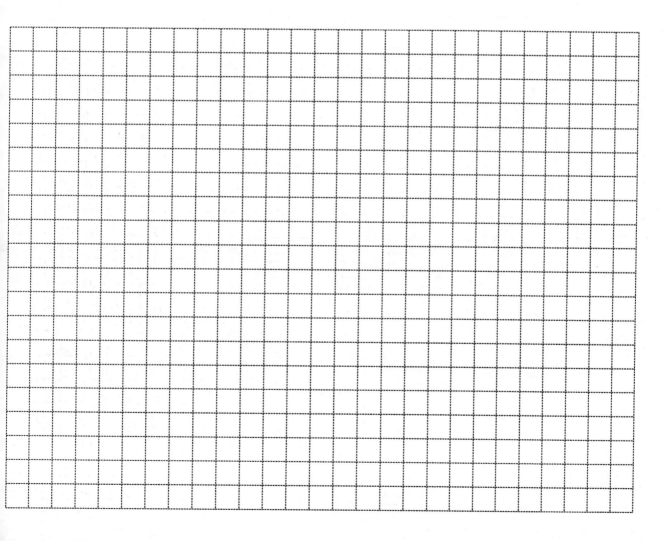

Exhibit 17–10. A Permanent Productivity Increase

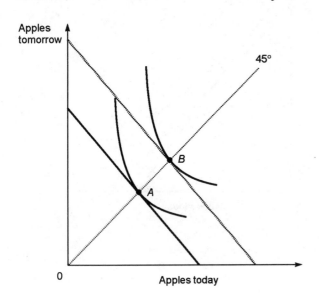

Exhibit 17–12. The Demand for Capital

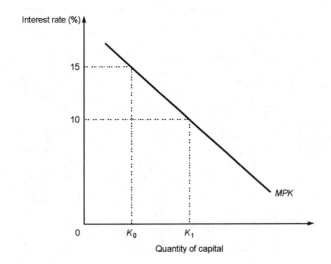

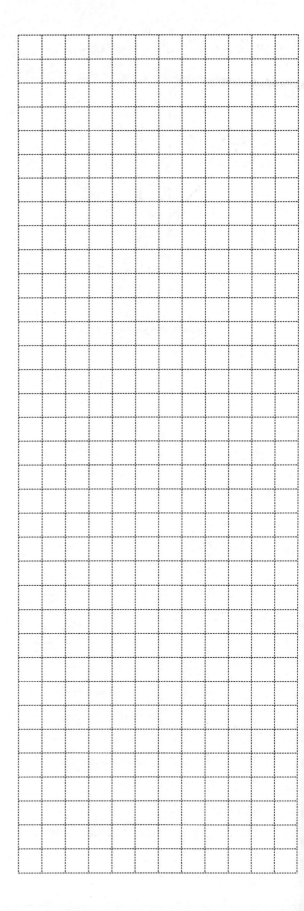

Exhibit 17–13. A Brighter Future

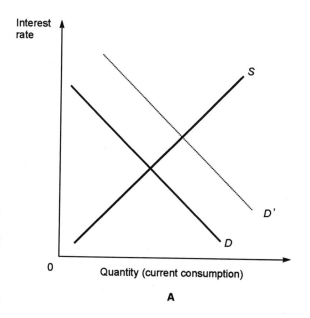

A

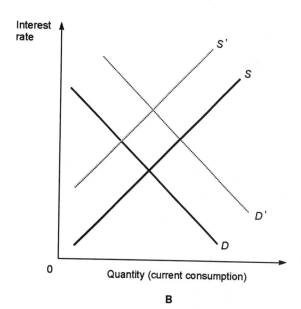

B

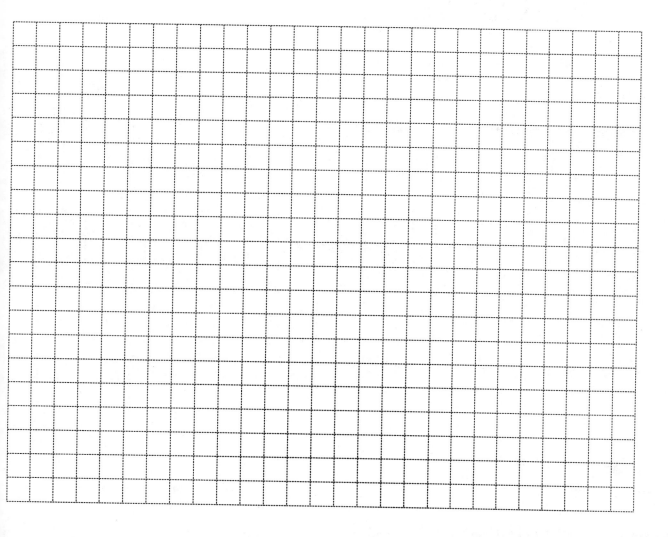

Exhibit 18–2. Baskets with the Same Expected Value

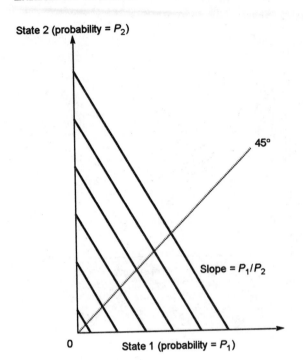

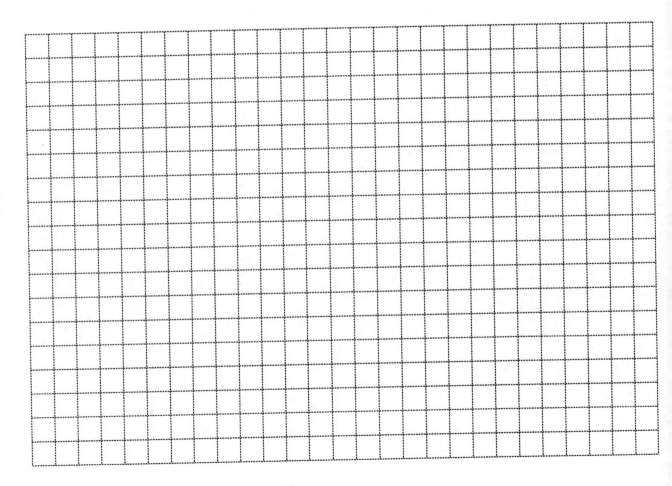

Exhibit 18–5. Risk Aversion

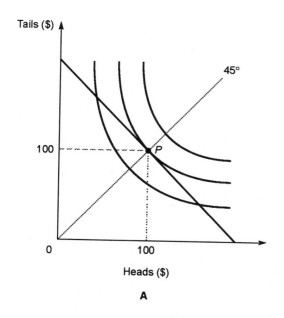

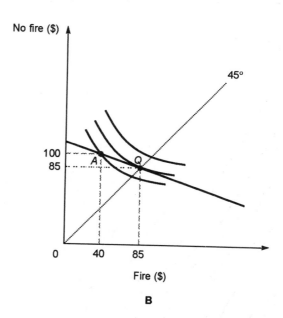

A

B

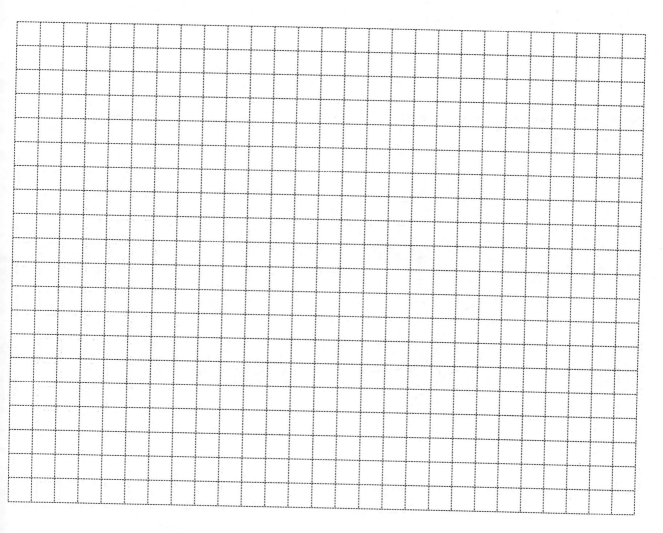

Exhibit 18–6. Risk Preference

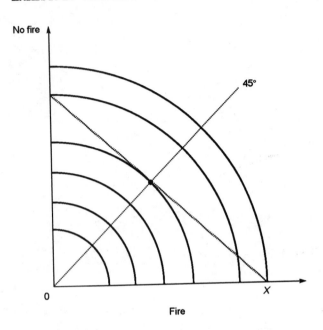

Exhibit 18–7. Risk Preference and Risk Aversion Combined

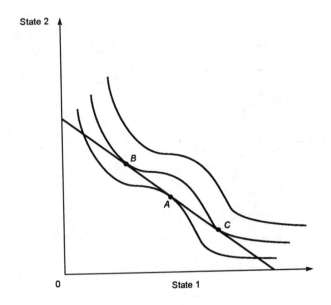

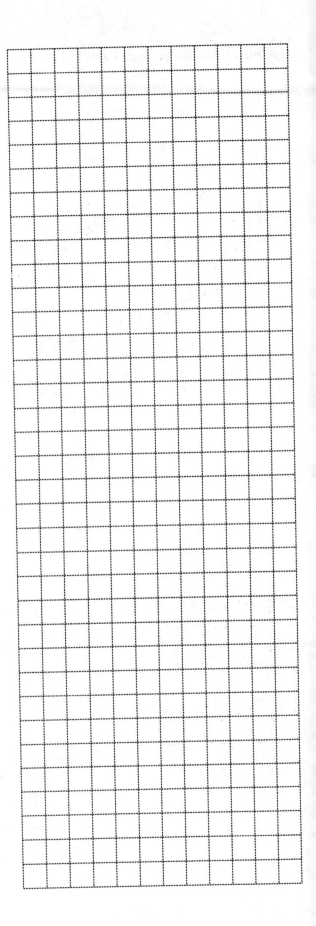

Exhibit 18–8. Gambling at Favorable Odds

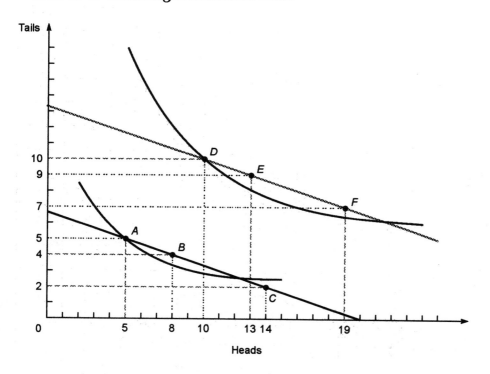

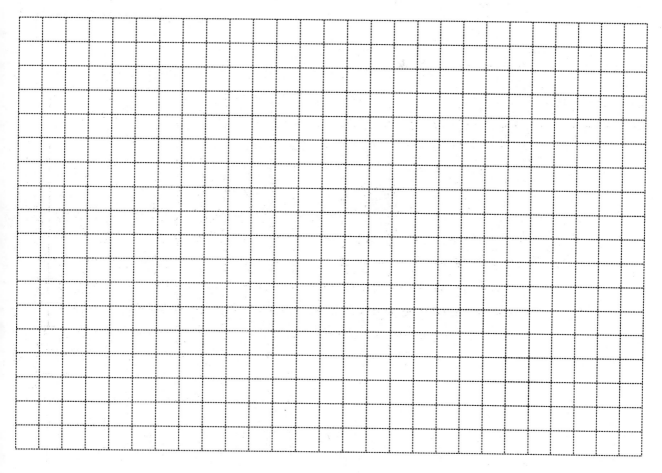

Exhibit 18–9. Adverse Selection

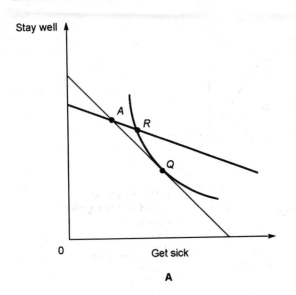

A

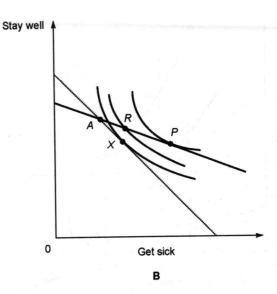

B

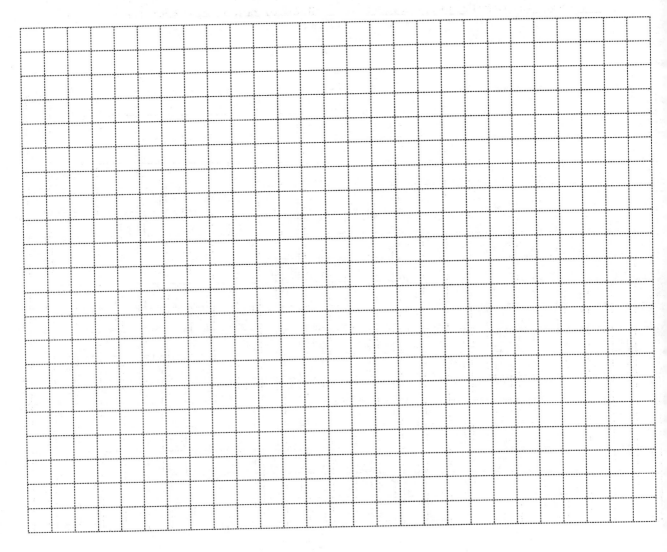

Exhibit 18–10. Speculation

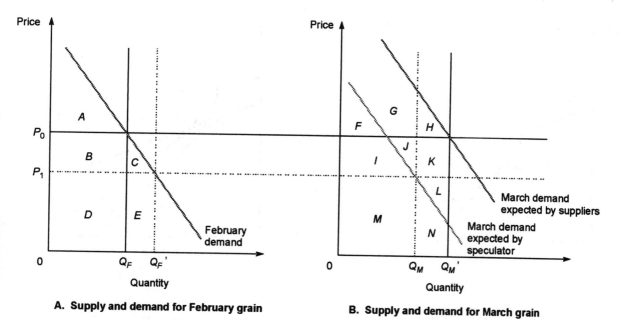

A. Supply and demand for February grain

B. Supply and demand for March grain

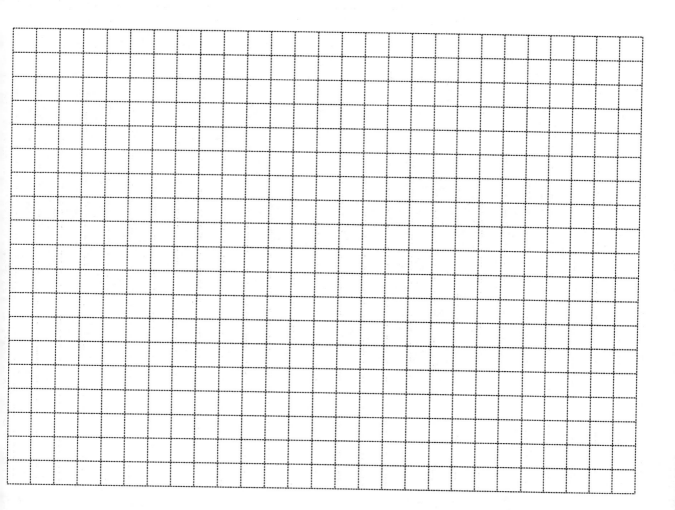

Exhibit 18–8. The Geometry of Portfolios

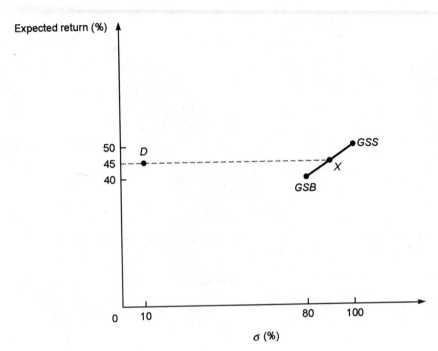

Exhibit 18–13. The Efficient Set

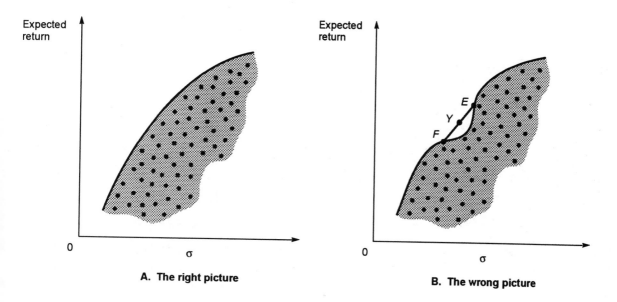

A. The right picture

B. The wrong picture

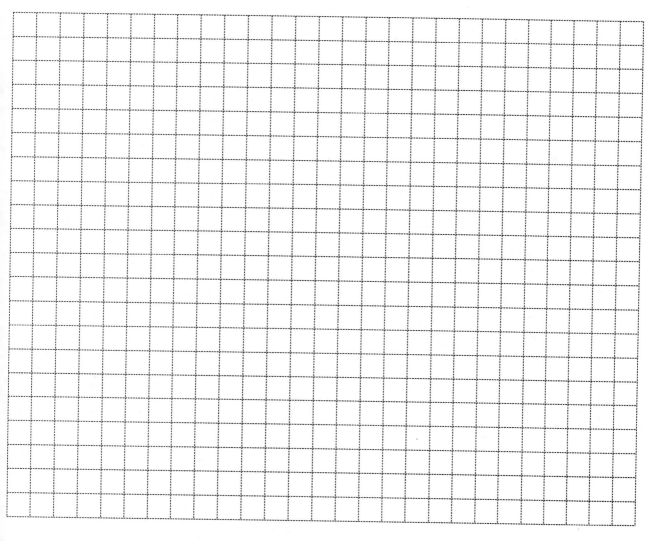

Exhibit 18–14. The Investor's Choice

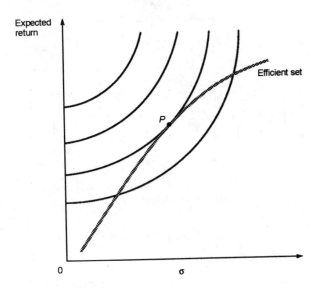

Exhibit 18–15. A Risk-Free Asset

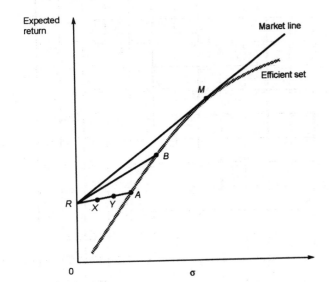

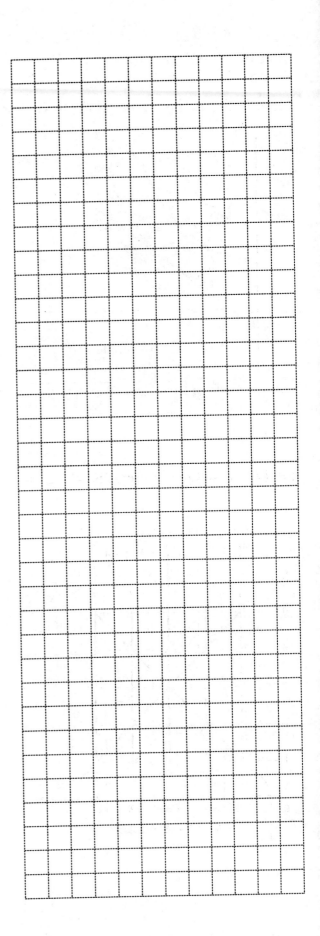

Exhibit 18–16. The Investor's Choice Revisited

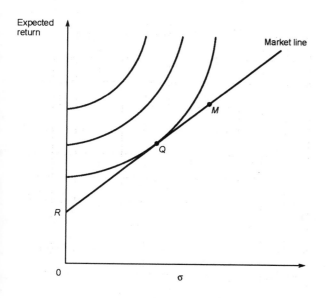

Exhibit 18–18. Rational Expectations

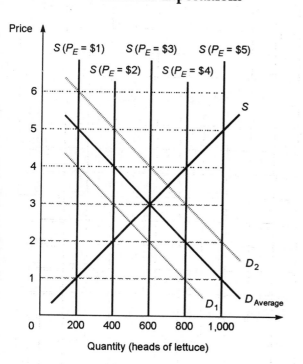

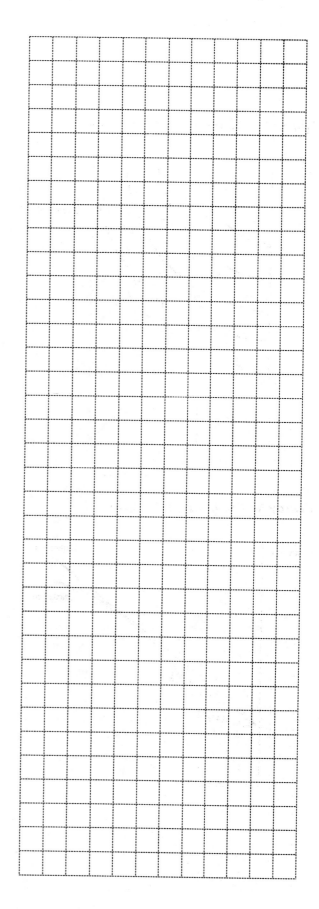

Exhibit 18–19. Lumberjacks' Income and the Price of Lettuce

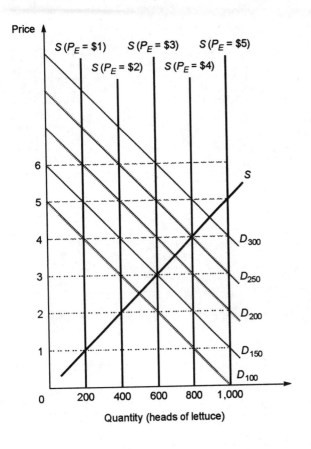

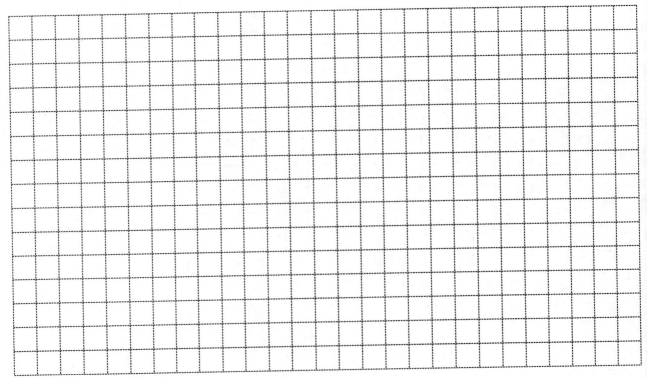

Exhibit 19–3. Rats as Rational Consumers

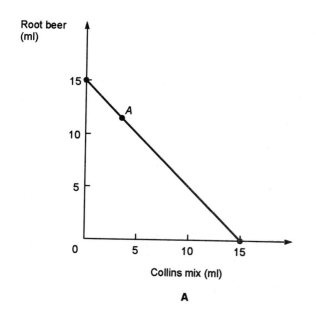

A

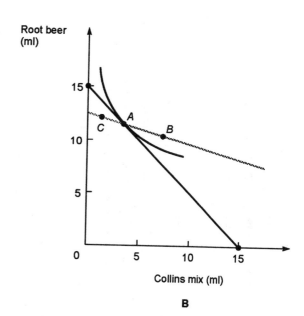

B

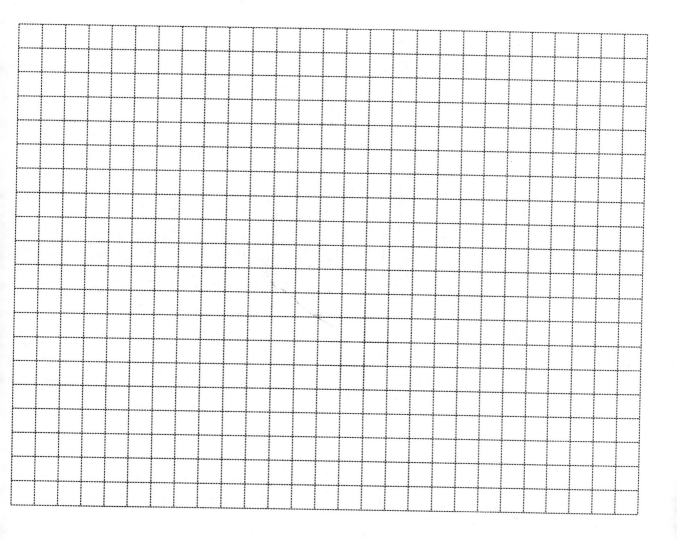

Exhibit 19–4. Pigeons and Labor Supply

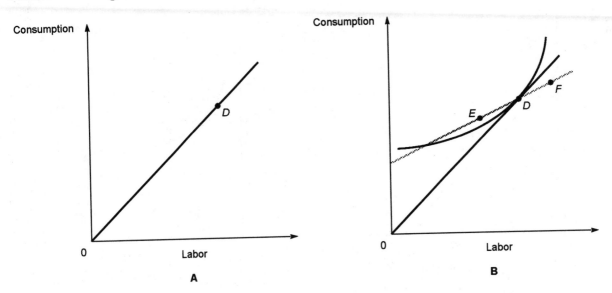

A

B

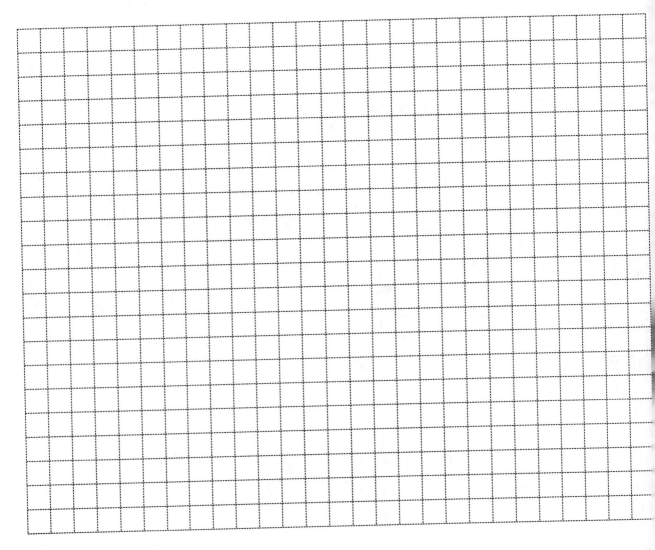